TRENDS IN CONTEMPORARY TRUST LAW

Trends in Contemporary Trust Law

General Editor
A. J. OAKLEY M. A., LL. B.
Of Lincoln's Inn, Barrister
Fellow of Trinity Hall, Cambridge

CLARENDON PRESS · OXFORD
1996

Oxford University Press, Great Clarendon Street, Oxford OX2 6DP
Oxford New York
Athens Auckland Bangkok Bogota Bombay
Buenos Aires Calcutta Cape Town Dar es Salaam
Delhi Florence Hong Kong Istanbul Karachi
Kuala Lumpur Madras Madrid Melbourne
Mexico City Nairobi Paris Singapore
Taipei Tokyo Toronto
and associated companies in
Berlin Ibadan

Oxford is a trade mark of Oxford University Press

Published in the United States by
Oxford University Press Inc., New York

British Library Cataloguing in Publication Data
Data available

Library of Congress Cataloging in Publication Data
Trends in contemporary trust law/A.J. Oakley.
p. cm.
Papers presented at the first International Conference on Trust Law held in Cambridge, United Kingdom, on Jan. 6–7, 1996, by the Faculty of Law, University of Cambridge.
Includes bibliographical references and index.
1. Trusts and trustees. I. Oakley, A. J. II. International Conference on Trust Law (1st: 1996: Cambridge, England)
K795.C66 1996
346.05′9—dc20
[342.659] 96-26406
ISBN 0-19-826286-8

1 3 5 7 9 10 8 6 4 2

Typeset by Best-set Typesetter Ltd., Hong Kong
Printed in Great Britain by
Biddles Ltd., Guildford and King's Lynn

Contents

Preface

The Papers published in this Volume are revised versions of the Papers which were originally presented at a Conference held in Cambridge on 6th and 7th January 1996 which I organised on behalf of the Faculty of Law at the University of Cambridge. Having in the last few years had the privilege of attending, either as a Delegate or as a Speaker, various International Conferences on Equity and Trust Law held in a number of different overseas venues such as Brisbane, Jerusalem and Victoria BC, it seemed to me to be about time that a Conference of this type was organised in the United Kingdom. The collaboration of the friends and colleagues from around the world who kindly agreed to chair sessions and to speak at the Conference, the financial and physical support of the Cambridge Faculty and financial support from The British Academy enabled the University of Cambridge to host what is thought to have been the first International Conference on Trust Law ever to have been held in the United Kingdom. It was attended by more than one hundred and forty delegates from twelve countries, equally divided between academics and practitioners.

The Papers were delivered in the same order as that in which they have now been published. Professor Gareth Jones QC, Downing Professor of the Laws of England in the University of Cambridge, opened the Conference and chaired the First Session, entitled 'The Changing Nature of Trust Doctrines', at which Paul Matthews spoke on 'The New Trust—Obligations Without Rights' and J. D. Davies spoke on 'Presumptions and Illegality'. The Hon. Justice W. M. C. Gummow, Judge of the High Court of Australia, chaired the Second Session, entitled 'The Changing Nature of Core Duties', at which Professor David Hayton spoke on 'The Irreducible Core Content of Trusteeship', Professor Donovan Waters QC spoke on 'The Protector: New Wine in Old Bottles?' and the Hon. Sir Robert Walker spoke on 'Some Trust Principles in the Pensions Context'. The Rt. Hon. Sir Peter Millett, Lord Justice of Appeal, chaired the Third Session, entitled 'Fiduciary Obligations and Liabilities', at which the Hon. Mr. Justice B. H. McPherson CBE spoke on 'Self-Dealing Trustees', R. P. Austin spoke on 'Moulding the Content of Fiduciary Duties', Professor Charles Rickett asked 'Where are we going with Equitable Compensation?' and the Hon. Justice P. D. Finn made 'A Comment' on the subject matter of the Session. Finally, the Rt. Hon. The Lord Nicholls of Birkenhead, Lord of Appeal in Ordinary, who subsequently also closed the Conference and very kindly agreed to write the Foreword to this

Volume, chaired the Fourth Session, entitled 'Ongoing Developments in Trust Law', at which I spoke on 'The Liberalising Nature of Remedies for Breach of Trust' and Sir William Goodhart QC spoke on 'Trust Law for the 21st Century'. Two further Papers, 'Taxing the Constructive Trustee' by John Glover and 'Equity's Reaction to Modern Domestic Relationships' by Anthony J. H. Morris QC, were offered to the Conference by their authors but unfortunately could not be fitted into the programme. However, they were nevertheless distributed to the Delegates and have therefore also been included in this Volume.

I am extremely grateful to the distinguished Chairmen and Speakers, who gave so generously of their time in order to ensure that the Conference was a success, and particularly to those of them who had to travel from Australasia and from Canada in the middle of the northern hemisphere winter in order to be able to do so. Although it is always invidious to single out individuals, I would like to express my particular thanks to Professor David Hayton, who encouraged me to organise the Conference and was a source of endless helpful advice, and to Professor Gareth Jones QC, who was an unfailing source of support within the Cambridge Faculty. I would also like to thank all those who attended the Conference for making the formal and informal discussion sessions so enjoyable for all the participants. Last but not least, I would like to thank The British Academy for their financial support and Oxford University Press both for agreeing to publish this Volume and for the rapidity and efficiency with which they have done so.

A. J. Oakley
Trinity Hall, Cambridge
24th April 1996

Foreword

by
The Rt. Hon. The Lord Nicholls of Birkenhead
Lord of Appeal in Ordinary

In January 1996 the Faculty of Law of the University of Cambridge was host to the first ever conference on trust law in the United Kingdom. It was a fitting that a two day conference should be devoted exclusively to this subject. The influence of equity is ever more pervasive, sometimes to the alarm of commercial lawyers. Always conscious of its historic origins and purpose, trust law retains its vigour. Its sound roots and its flexibility are its greatest strengths.

So the subject matter of trust law, and I include fiduciary obligations, ranges from the modern administration of formal trust and pension deeds to the use of trust concepts and remedies in response to all manner of sharp dealing and unacceptable behaviour. Indeed, given the contemporary importance of the subject, the only surprising feature of the conference was that it had no predecessor.

The papers delivered at the conference by distinguished speakers from several jurisdictions covered many aspects of this part of the law. The attendance of participants from more than ten countries testified to the importance of the subject throughout the common law world. The stimulating discussions which took place, formally and informally, are not capable of being reproduced. But it is eminently satisfactory that this publication will bring the papers themselves to a wider audience.

List of Contributors

R. P. AUSTIN was formerly Professor and Dean of the Faculty of Law at Sydney University. He is now a full time practitioner in the law firm of Minter Ellison in Sydney

J. D. DAVIES is a Fellow and Tutor in Law at St. Catherine's College, Oxford

HON JUSTICE P. D. FINN is a Judge of the Federal Court of Australia. Prior to joining the Court he was Professor of Law at the Australian National University in Canberra

JOHN GLOVER is a Senior Lectures in Law at Monash University in Victoria, Australia

SIR WILLIAM GOODHART QC is a distinguished member of the English Bar and the author of a number of practitioner's texts on equity. He is a member of the Vinelott Committee on Trust Law

PROFESSOR DAVID HAYTON is a Recorder, Professor of Law at King's College, London and the author of *Underhill*, the leading English practitioner's work on the Law of Trusts He is Secretary to the Vinelott Committee on Trust Law

PAUL MATTHEWS was at one time a Lecturer in Law at University College London, before becoming first a Partner and then a Consultant with Hopkins & Wood, Solicitors, London

MR JUSTICE B. H. MCPHERSON C. B. E. is a Judge of Appeal in Queensland and is one of Australia's best known Trust experts

ANTRONY J. H. MORRIS QC is a member of the Queensland Bar

A. J. OAKLEY is a Barrister, Fellow of Trinity Hall, and Lecturer in Law at the University of Cambridge. He is the author of *Constructive Trusts* and author of the most recent edition of *Parker and Mellows*: *The Modern Law of Trusts*

PROFESSOR CHARLES RICKETT is Professor of Law at the University of Auckland, and a well-known writer on all aspects of Trust Law

HON. SIR ROBERT WALKER is a Judge of the Chancery Division of the English High Court

PROFESSOR DONOVAN WATERS QC is both a well-known Canadian practitioner and Professor of Law at the University of Victoria, British Columbia. He is author of the principal Canadian text on Trust law

Table of Cases

Table of Statutes

Canada

Cook Islands

Cyprus

Jersey

Statutory Instruments

1

The New Trust: Obligations without Rights?

PAUL MATTHEWS

And if he did make a will, who knows who he would leave the farm to? He might leave it to Feckless, or even to Aimless, and that would mean a lot of legal trouble, for I doubt if two cows can inherit a farm.

Stella Gibbons, *Cold Comfort Farm*, Chapter 11.

INTRODUCTION

In the beginning, there were people. Trusts did not come into existence because animals, or trees in California, complained to the Chancellor that property given to trustees for their benefit was being mis-applied. They were called into existence because *people* complained, because *people* presented petitions, because *people* pleaded for justice before the Chancellor as the keeper of the King's conscience.[1] Animals and trees could not do that. Nor can they still, at any rate not in English law.[2]

The jurisprudence of the Court of Chancery built up the twin ideas of (i) the obligation of the *feoffee to uses*, or trustee, to hold the property for the benefit of the *cestui que use*, or beneficiary,[3] and (ii) the right of the beneficiary to obtain the use of the property.[4] These notions stood back to back: the trustees' obligation with regard to the property was co-relative to the beneficiary's right in it.[5] We may note in passing that the solidification over time of the beneficiary's personal right against the trustee into *an interest in the property*[6] had profound effects both here and elsewhere in the law. Had the right remained purely personal,[7] it might have developed into a law of obligations rather like the civil law of contract, i.e. voluntarily assumed obligations, without the need for a

[1] Holdsworth, *History of English Law* ('HEL'), i, 395–410; iv, 410–43; Baker, *Introduction to English Legal History* (3rd edn., 1990), 117, 121; *Re Astor's ST* [1952] Ch. 534, 541.

[2] Cf RSC Ord. 15, rr. 12–15 (representative actions) and Ord. 80 (persons under disability): both Orders deal with *persons* as parties to legal proceedings.

[3] HEL, n. 1 above, iv 430–1.

[4] *Ibid.* 437–43.

[5] *Re Astor's ST*, n. 1 above, 541.

[6] N. 1 above, 432–7; Maitland, 'Trust and Corporation', in *Selected Essays* (1936), Ch. IV.

[7] As in e.g. Scots law: see *Bell's Commentaries*, i, 36–7, Wilson and Duncan, *Trusts, Trustees and Executors* (2nd edn., 1995), paras. 1–42 to 1–51, and *Sharp* v. *Thompson* 1995 SLT 837, 850–1, 857; cf at 867–8.

doctrine of consideration.[8] This in turn might have assisted the development of purpose trusts. But it did not. And equity's *in rem*, property-based approach turned the enquiry about beneficiaries from 'who can enforce the trust obligation?' to 'who owns the trust property?' Thus it became an aspect of the rule now known as the rule in *Saunders* v. *Vautier*,[9] discussed later.

But stated in this original way, the concept of the trust could have nothing to do with carrying out purposes. We may speak of a rule 'against' purpose trusts. But the nature of the trust obligation did not admit of an obligation without a co-relative right. And rights were—and are—to be exercised, and property owned, by *people*, not by things.[10] As Bertrand Russell considered, once you start treating animals as rightholders, the next thing you know, it's Votes for Oysters.[11] So the rule against purpose trusts was axiomatic.[12] Contrary to what some commentators say,[13] it does not—could not—derive from the early nineteenth century case of *Morice* v. *Bishop of Durham*;[14] it had been in 'existence' for centuries before that case was decided.[15]

What about charity? Well, charity is different. It derived from the ecclesiastical jurisdiction,[16] not from that of the Chancery. Charity did not need to be performed through the medium of the trust. It was not so in English law at the outset, and even today it need not be. It could, for example, be carried out through a company.[17] And many legal systems have well developed laws of charity without recourse to, indeed without any knowledge of, trusts.[18] It is a historical accident that the Court of Chancery hijacked the charitable gift and squeezed it (with some difficulty) into the pre-existing framework of the trust.[19]

Although the rule against purpose trusts derived from a procedural

[8] Cf e.g. the doctrine of *cause* in French contract law: see Nicholas, *French Law of Contract* (2nd edn., 1992), 118–36.

[9] (1841) Cr. & Ph. 240.

[10] Hackney, *Understanding Equity & Trusts*, 70–1.

[11] *History of Western Philosophy* (2nd edn., 1961), 697–8.

[12] See also Gray (1902) 15 *Harv. LR* 509; Sweet (1917) 33 *LQR* 342, 361. Cf Smith (1930) 30 *Col. LR* 60.

[13] Including: Potter (1949) 13 *Conv. (NS)* 418, 419; Gravells (1977) 40 *MLR* 397, 413; Maudsley, *The Modern Law of Perpetuities* (1979), 168; Keane, *Equity and Trusts in Ireland*, para. 7.06; Gardner, *An Introduction to the Law of Trusts* (1990), 183–4; Ford and Lee, *Principles of the Law of Trusts* (2nd edn., 1990), para. 524; Hanbury and Martin, *Modern Equity* (14th edn., 1993), 357; Pettit, *Equity and the Law of Trusts* (7th edn., 1993), 50; Moffat, *Trusts Law* (2nd edn., 1994), 149; Parker and Mellows, *The Modern Law of Trusts* (6th edn., 1994), 112; Underhill and Hayton, *The Law of Trusts and Trustees* (15th edn., 1995), 91.

[14] (1804) 9 Ves. 399, affd. (1805) 10 Ves. 522.

[15] Cf Potter, n. 13 above, who says that it did not exist at all.

[16] See e.g. HEL, n. 1 above, i 625–30; Jones, *History of the Law of Charity*, Ch. 1.

[17] See the Charities Act 1993, s. 96.

[18] See e.g. Neuhoff and Pavel (eds.), *Trust and Foundations in Europe* (1971).

[19] *Ibid.*

point, there is no magic reason why it must be maintained in modern society. We can change the rules if we think it right. The law of charity itself shows that. Apart from charity, however, the judges have made almost no inroads on the no-purpose trust rule.[20] But the legislatures of some British colonies and Commonwealth States have made significant changes—even abolished it, as we shall see.[21] And the Hague Convention on the Law applicable to Trusts and on their Recognition[22] defines a trust so as to include one 'for a specified purpose'.[23] In legislative terms, Birnam Wood is coming to Dunsinane.

THE MODERN RULE

The modern rule in English law consists of a proposition, a number of genuine exceptions, and one or two quasi-exceptions. The proposition is simple, and was tersely put in *Re Wood*[24] by Harman J: '[a] gift on trust must have a *cestui que trust*.'[25] Because a beneficiary is able to enforce the trust obligation against the trustee, some commentators put the matter in terms instead of there being someone *who can enforce the trust*.[26] On this view of the rule, charity would not be an exception, because the Attorney General can enforce charitable trusts. We have seen that the *in rem* nature of the beneficiary's right renders this view anachronistic. And thus Harman J did not say '[a] gift on trust must have someone who can enforce it.' He said that there must be a *cestui que trust*, a person with a property right, a *beneficiary*.

It is true that in *Morice* v. *Bishop of Durham*[27] Sir William Grant MR said 'there must be somebody in whose favour the court can decree performance'. But[28] that case was not about beneficiaries: it was about certainty of objects. A testatrix attempted to give the residue of her personal estate for 'such objects of benevolence and liberality as the Bishop

[20] See below, text to nn. 38–71.

[21] See below, text to nn. 144–75.

[22] Negotiated in Oct. 1984 at the 15th Session of the Hague Conference on Private International Law, incorporated into English, Scottish, and Northern Irish law by the Recognition of Trusts Act 1987, and (as at the time of writing) ratified by the UK (including some colonies and dependencies), Italy, Australia, Canada (some provinces only), Malta, and the Netherlands.

[23] Art 2.

[24] [1949] Ch. 498, 501.

[25] See also *Bowman* v. *Secular Society* [1917] AC 406, 441; *Public Trustee* v. *Nolan* (1943) 43 SR (NSW) 169, 172; *Re Producers Defence Fund* [1954] VLR 246, 255; *Re Astor's ST*, n. 1 above, 540, 547. The rule in Scotland is in substance the same: see e.g. *M'Caig* v. *University of Glasgow*, 1907 SC 231; cf *M'Caig's Trustees* v. *United Free Church of Lismore*, 1915 SC 426, 432–3.

[26] e.g. Gravells, n. 13 above, 413; Crampin and Thomas in Glasson (ed.), *International Trust Laws*, B4–7; Gardner, n. 13 above, 183–91.

[27] N. 14 above, first instance, 405.

[28] *Pace* Millett (1985) 101 *LQR* 269, 281.

of Durham' should approve of. The next of kin claimed that this was not charitable, and hence void for uncertainty.[29] Both before Grant MR, and on appeal to Lord Eldon, the next of kin succeeded. Grant MR stated the principle to be: 'if there be a clear trust but for uncertain objects, the property, that is the subject of the trust, is undisposed of'[30] and, immediately before the statement 'there must be somebody' quoted above, he said, 'every other trust [than charity] must have a definite object'. Similarly, Lord Eldon said, '[i]t was the intention to create a trust the object being too indefinite, which has failed'.[31] In its context, Grant MR's dictum is quite consistent with this; the court must be able to *identify* the beneficiary. This is a question of certainty of objects,[32] not of enforcement of trust obligations.

So it is back to the basic rule: a trust requires a beneficiary. But, as I have already suggested, the other side of this rule is the idea that the beneficiary, being the owner in equity of the trust property, may require the legal owner to convey to him or at his direction. This is the well-known rule in *Saunders* v. *Vautier*.[33] (Again, it is a rule that existed long before the case that gave it its name.) And it applies however many persons the beneficial interest is divided among. If property is held on trust for A and B, or for A for life remainder to B, then A and B between them own the whole property and together they can call for it. Nor need the trust be a fixed trust. If property is held on trust for such of A, B, C, and D as the trustees shall select then A, B, C, and D between them own it. If it is held for such of A, B, and C as the trustee *may* select and in default on trust for D, then again A, B, C, and D between them own it.[34] All of this is important in understanding the beneficiary principle, and in particular in dealing with the so-called rule against inalienability, to which I shall return.[35]

EXCEPTIONS TO THE RULE

I said that there were some exceptions to the basic rule. Charity is the obvious one. We could pretend that 'society' as a whole is the benefi-

[29] Note the importance here of the Mortmain Act 1736. Had it been realty, they would have argued that it *was* charitable, so it would have failed by virtue of the Act: see Jones, n. 16 above, Ch. IX.

[30] N. 14 above, first instance, 405.

[31] N. 14 above, on appeal.

[32] This is not a new view: see e.g. Keeton, *Law of Trusts* (1st edn., 1934), 99.

[33] N. 9 above. But this rule does not apply in some American jurisdictions where the settlor's wishes 'are paramount to the wishes of the beneficiaries' and the latter cannot terminate the trust if this 'would run counter to the intention of the settlor': *Scott on Trusts*, para. 337.

[34] See [1984] *Conv.* 22, 23, for an expanded discussion of this.

[35] See below, text to nn. 86–106.

ciary,[36] but this is such a different kind of beneficiary from that in a private trust,[37] that in reality it is better seen as a simple exception, born of history rather than logic.

Other exceptions are more specific. They involve certain kinds of non-charitable purpose trusts,[38] variously described as 'occasions when Homer has nodded'[39] (i.e. wrong, but not to be put right), or as 'concessions to human weakness or sentiment'.[40] The usual list[41] is:

(1) trusts for the erection or maintenance of sepulchral monuments, graves, or tombs;
(2) trusts for the saying of masses, to the extent that they are not charitable;
(3) trusts for the maintenance of particular animals;
(4) trusts for the benefit of unincorporated associations;
(5) a miscellaneous group of trusts, of which the standard cases are
    (a) for the promotion of fox-hunting;
    (b) for the disposal of property of the testator for 'best spiritual advantage';
    (c) for the provision of a maintenance fund for an historic building.

The first class of case is not so much an anomaly in the law of trusts as a problem for English property law generally. For a testator to provide for funeral expenses diminishes the value of the interest taken by residuary legatees or next of kin, and benefits the person who would otherwise be obliged by law to make suitable arrangements for the disposal of the testator's remains.[42] Yet a specific provision by the testator for reasonable funeral expenses is valid,[43] even though it is not seen as a gift to the person with the disposal obligation. Nor is it a gift to or for the benefit of the undertaker or the stonemason or other persons employed in or about the funeral.[44] And *ex hypothesi* a grave or sepulchral monument cannot belong to the testator once the trust to erect or maintain it has

[36] e.g. Maitland, *Equity* (2nd edn., 1936), 51.

[37] e.g. 'society' cannot take the fund under the rule in *Saunders* v. *Vautier*.

[38] Note that, when Jersey drew up its trusts statute in 1984, *it left all these exceptions out*: Trusts (Jersey) Law 1984, Art. 10(2)(a)(iv).

[39] *Re Endacott* [1960] Ch. 232, 250.

[40] *Re Astor's ST*, n. 1 above, 547.

[41] Morris and Leach, *The Rule Against Perpetuities* (2nd edn.) 310; *Re Endacott*, n. 39 above, 246. In the US in the nineteenth century, there was a further category, namely trusts to emancipate slaves: see Gray, n. 12 above, 522–5.

[42] Ultimately the local authority: Public Health (Control of Diseases) Act 1984, s. 46.

[43] *Mellick* v. *President and Guardians of the Asylum* (1821) Jac. 180; *Trimmer* v. *Danby* (1856) 25 LJ Ch. 424.

[44] *Shaw* v. *Lawless* (1838) 5 Cl. & Fin. 129, 155–6; *Finden* v. *Stephens* (1846) 2 Ph. 142; *Foster* v. *Elsley* (1881) 19 Ch. D 518; *Gandy* v. *Gandy* (1885) 30 Ch. D 57; *M'Caig's Trustees* v. *United Free Church of Lismore*, n. 25 above, 434; *Haslemere Estates Ltd* v. *Baker* [1982] 3 All ER 525; cf *Gunning* v. *Buckfast Abbey Trustees*, *The Times*, 9 June 1994.

come into effect. Where the trust is *inter vivos* the grave or monument rarely belongs as a matter of law to the settlor. Thus it is nearly always a gift to improve or maintain *another person's property.* (If the trust involves church fabric,[45] or maintenance of *all* the graves in a churchyard,[46] it may indeed be charitable.) As we shall see later,[47] such gifts may be construed as gifts to the owner(s) of such property. But the owner (for example an ecclesiastical corporation or a local authority) is very unlikely to make such a claim. The courts have contented themselves with holding such trusts, if limited to the perpetuity period,[48] to be valid non-charitable purpose trusts without analysis.[49] The legislature has tried to avoid the problem by enabling local authorities to make long-term maintenance agreements with testators and relatives.[50] But of course people cannot be forced to do this. So there is a kind of stand-off between the law and the people, neither really grappling with the problem.[51]

The second group is easier. English trusts to say masses in public were formerly void as for superstitious uses.[52] Nowadays they will be charitable if the trust property is used to provide endowment for the priests concerned.[53] Otherwise such trusts may be valid as non-charitable purpose trusts.[54]

The third group concerns animals. Certain trusts for the benefit of animals generally will be charitable.[55] On the other hand, trusts for the maintenance or care of specific animals have been held valid as non-charitable purpose trusts.[56] But the problem of maintenance funds,

[45] *Hoare* v. *Osborne* (1866) LR 1 Eq. 585; *Re Rigley's Trust* (1867) 15 WR 190; *Re Hooper* [1932] 1 Ch. 38.

[46] *Re Vaughan* (1886) 33 Ch. D 187; *Re Manser* [1905] 1 Ch. 68; *Re Pardoe* [1906] 2 Ch. 184; *Re Eighmie* [1935] Ch. 524.

[47] See below, text to nn. 116–20.

[48] Cf *Pooley* v. *Royal Alexandra Hospital* (1932) 32 SR (NSW) 459; *Re Filshie* [1939] NZLR 91 (fund given for erecting and maintaining headstones held severed: valid as to erection; void for perpetuity as to maintenance).

[49] *Trimmer* v. *Danby* (1856) 25 LJ Ch. 424; *Mussett* v. *Bingle* [1876] WN 170; *Re Tyler* [1891] 3 Ch. 252, 258–9; *Pirbright* v. *Salwey* [1896] WN 86; *Re Hooper*, n. 45 above.

[50] Parish Councils and Burial Authorities (Miscellaneous Provisions) Act 1970, s. 1.

[51] Gray, n. 12 above, 530, thought this and charity were the only true exceptions to the beneficiary principle.

[52] *Re Fleetwood* (1880) 15 Ch. D 594, 609. The law was different in Ireland: see Gray, n. 12 above, 518–19; Sheridan (1953) 17 *Conv.* 46, 52.

[53] *Re Caus* [1934] Ch. 162; *Re Hetherington* [1990] Ch. 1.

[54] *Bourne* v. *Keane* [1919] AC 815, 874–5; *Re Gibbons* [1917] 1 Ir. R 448; *Re Khoo Cheng Teow* [1932] Straits Sett. LR 226. Cf *Leahy* v. *A.G. for NSW* [1959] AC 457.

[55] *Re Wedgwood* [1915] 1 Ch. 113; *Re Moss* [1949] 1 All ER 495; cf *Re Grove-Grady* [1929] 1 Ch. 557, [1931] WN 89.

[56] *Pettingall* v. *Pettingall* (1842) 11 LJ Ch. 176; *Mitford* v. *Reynolds* (1848) 16 Sim. 105; *Re Dean* (1889) 41 Ch. D 552; *Re Howard, The Times*, 30 Oct. 1908; *Re Haines, The Times*, 7 Nov. 1952; Matthews [1983] *LS Gaz.* 2451; cf *Re Kelly* [1932] IR 255, where the point was deliberately not taken on account of the very modest sums involved.

mentioned above in connection with monuments and graves, applies here too, and in an even more acute form. A testator's pet animal is his property. When he dies property in the animal passes under his will, in the residue if not specifically given. The owner cannot 'emancipate' the animal, as Romans might in classical times,[57] and as slave-owning Americans might in the nineteenth century.[58] The trust fund is therefore one for the improvement of the new owner's property. Can the new owner claim the new fund beneficially?[59] There is no authority. Yet.[60] The point has not been argued,[61] and, as we know, argued law is tough law. The converse is also true. To avoid this problem testators may make *contracts* with animal charities, or create *powers* to maintain them in their wills,[62] or confer interests in income *conditional* on the maintenance of the animal concerned.[63]

The fourth category is more doubtful. The idea that gifts to or trusts for unincorporated associations might form an exception to the 'no beneficiary' rule was derived from the view that there were no beneficiaries in such cases. But two developments have thrown doubt on that. First, a number of cases have demonstrated that, properly construed, all—or perhaps nearly all—such gifts or trusts *do* have beneficiaries.[64] So they are not an exception after all. Secondly, Goff J in *Re Denley*[65] appeared to modify the 'no beneficiary' rule to a degree at which most such trusts would not infringe it anyway (I shall return to *Re Denley* later). The whole subject of gifts to and trusts for unincorporated associations, and its

[57] See Buckland, *A Textbook of Roman Law* (3rd edn., 1963), 72–83; Thomas, *Textbook of Roman Law* (1976), 397–401.

[58] See in particular the cases of trusts to emancipate slaves discussed by Gray, n. 12 above, 522–5.

[59] See below, text to nn. 116–20, and cf *Re Bowes* [1896] 1 Ch. 507.

[60] Cf *Re Gassiot* (1901) 70 LJ Ch. 141 (gift of income to keep in repair painting given to X, defeasible on condition subsequent; held, gift of painting valid, but gift of income perpetuitous and void).

[61] Cf *Re Dean* (1889) 41 Ch. D 552, where the animals were bequeathed to the trustees themselves, together with a 50-year annuity for their upkeep. The trustees *did* argue that the annuity was a beneficial one to themselves, but not that it was one to benefit the trustees' property. The judge held that it was not given to the trustees beneficially, but that the 'trust' was valid, if unenforceable.

[62] Cf e.g. *Re Aberconway's ST* [1953] Ch. 647, 665, 669; *Re Sayer* [1957] Ch. 423; *Re Shaw* [1957] 1 All ER 745, 749; *Re Wootten* [1968] 2 All ER 618, 624.

[63] Cf *Re Chardon* [1928] Ch. 464; *Re Chambers' WT* [1950] Ch. 267.

[64] *Cocks* v. *Manners* (1871) LR 12 Eq. 574; *Re Clarke* [1901] 2 Ch. 110; *Re Drummond* [1914] 2 Ch. 90; *Re Smith* [1916] 1 Ch. 937; *Re Prevost* [1930] 2 Ch. 383; *Re Ogden* [1933] Ch. 678; *Re Turkington* [1937] 4 All ER 501; *Re Taylor* [1940] Ch. 481: *Re Price* [1943] Ch. 422; *Re Macaulay* [1943] Ch. 435; *Re Producers Defence Fund* [1954] VLR 246, 253; *Re Goode* [1960] VR 117; *Neville Estates Ltd* v. *Madden* [1962] Ch. 832; *Re Goodson* [1971] VR 801; *Re Recher's WT* [1972] Ch. 526; *Re Lipinski's WT* [1976] Ch. 235; *Re Bucks Constabulary Fund Trusts (No 2)* [1979] 1 WLR 936; *Public Trustees* v. *A.G.* [1985] ACLD 215; *News Group* v. *SOGAT* [1986] ICR 716; cf *Leahy* v. *A.G. for NSW*, n. 54 above; *Re Grant's WT* [1980] 1 WLR 360.

[65] [1969] 1 Ch. 373.

literature, is large,[66] and still growing,[67] so I shall not deal with it further now.

The last category is simply a small assembly—it does not merit the name 'collection'—of anomalous cases. They are:

(a) an English case upholding a gift to promote fox-hunting, on the bizarre ground that the person entitled in default could 'enforce' it by claiming the fund for itself if it was not applied for the primary purpose;[68]
(b) an Irish case upholding a gift of property to be disposed of to the testator's 'best spiritual advantage';[69] and
(c) a Scottish case involving a trust to provide a maintenance fund for a historic building;[70] this last case being acquiesced in by the parliamentary draftsman in relation to the whole of the United Kingdom.[71]

(Am I alone in finding humour in an Englishman hunting foxes, an Irishman saving his soul, and a Scotsman spending money to save tax?)

One final word on the exceptions other than charity. Where they apply, the 'trust' is in reality nothing more than a power.[72] The trustee cannot be *compelled* to perform the purpose, and if he does not there will be a gift over or a resulting trust.[73] But if he does perform it within its terms, he cannot be criticized. Hence these trusts are often called 'trusts of imperfect obligation'.[74] As we shall see,[75] some offshore jurisdictions, in enacting purpose-trust legislation, have sought directly to address this point. What is curious is that a purpose trust falling outside one of these exceptional cases will not be construed as a power in order to save it,[76] although, had it been *drafted* as a power, it might well have been valid.[77]

[66] e.g. Lloyd, *Law of Unincorporated Associations*; Ford, *Unincorporated Non-Profit Associations*; Warburton, *Unincorporated Associations*; Rickett (1980) 39 *CLJ* 88; Green (1980) 43 *MLR* 459; Green (1982) 45 *MLR* 564; Lee in Finn (ed.), *Essays in Equity* (1985); Warburton [1985] *Conv.* 318; Smart [1987] *Conv.* 415; Gardner [1992] *Conv.* 41; Underhill and Hayton, n. 13 above, 102–8.

[67] *Mea culpa*: [1995] *Conv.* 302.

[68] *Re Thompson* [1934] Ch. 342.

[69] *Re Gibbons* [1917] 1 Ir. R 448.

[70] *Glasgow Trades House* v. *IRC*, 1970 SC 101, 108, 113 (though the point seems to have been assumed).

[71] Inheritance Tax Act 1984, s. 77, Sch. 4, para. 3; but see para. 7, treating the Treasury as if it were a beneficiary of the trust, and also *Raikes* v. *Lygon* [1988] 1 All ER 884.

[72] See Hart (1937) 53 *LQR* 29, 33; Kiralfy (1950) 14 *Conv.* 374. Cf Potter (1949) 13 *Conv.* 418, 423.

[73] See e.g. *Re Thompson*, n. 68 above; *Re Gibbons*, n. 69 above, 453. Cf Ames (1892) 5 *Harv. LR* 389, 394–6.

[74] e.g. Hart (1899) 15 *LQR* 294; *Snell's Equity* (29th edn., 1990), 102; Hayton and Marshall, *Casebook and Commentary on Trusts* (9th edn.), 189.

[75] Below, text to nn. 164–5.

[76] *Re Shaw* [1957] 1 All ER 745, 749; *IRC* v. *Broadway Cottages Trust* [1955] Ch. 20, 36; *Re Endacott*, n. 39 above, 246; cf *Re Producers' Defence Fund* [1954] VLR 246, 255.

[77] See the cases in n. 62 above.

It seems a very formalistic objection that turns *some* purpose trusts into powers and enforces them, and avoids others altogether, *because* they were not drafted as powers.[78]

OTHER LIMITATIONS

But trusts do not fail only for want of a beneficiary. Even if they have one, or even if they are upheld under one of the exceptions just mentioned, there are other ways in which they may still fail. I must mention a few of these briefly, for they affect the discussion following (especially perpetuity).

Public Policy

Some purposes are criminal or otherwise undesirable, and would be struck down with or without beneficiaries. Thus a trust to pay the fines of convicted criminals[79] (who are plainly beneficiaries of the trust) will not be enforced. Nor will a trust positively to waste resources, e.g. by throwing the annual income into the sea,[80] or bricking up a house for twenty years.[81]

Delegation of Testamentary Power

It is sometimes said that testamentary non-charitable purpose trusts infringe the principle that the testator must make his own will, and must not leave it to others to make it for him.[82] But this objection does not mean that the testator cannot create valid powers of appointment, even in very general terms.[83] Yet that is what these 'trusts of imperfect obligation' amount to. So far as I know, no non-charitable purpose trust has ever been struck down for this reason.

Uncertainty and Unworkability

Much more significant in this context are uncertainty and unworkability. It was, after all, uncertainty that struck down the purpose trust in *Morice*

[78] Some Canadian jurisdictions have legislated to enable invalid purpose trusts to be construed as valid powers: Ontario Perpetuities Act, RSO 1990, c. P9, s. 16; Alberta Perpetuities Act, RSA 1980, c. P4, s. 20.

[79] *Thrupp* v. *Collett* (1858) 26 Beav. 125.

[80] *M'Caig* v. *University of Glasgow*, 1907 SC 231, 242.

[81] *Brown* v. *Burdett* (1882) 21 Ch. D 667. Though *quaere* whether, in a time of rapid capital appreciation and low income, this might not be a valid accumulation trust. The developer of Centre Point, a notorious 1960s central London office block (now listed!) was alleged to have made more money by keeping it empty than by letting it.

[82] *Leahy* v. *AG for NSW*, n. 54 above, 485; *Re Flavel's Trust* [1969] 2 All ER 232; cf *Houston* v. *Burns* [1918] AC 337, 342–3.

[83] *Re Beatty's WT* [1990] 3 All ER 844.

v. *Bishop of Durham*.[84] And even if there is sufficient certainty, the trust may be unworkable. Take a trust for the benefit of the inhabitants of West Yorkshire (about 2.5 million persons). Even if it is certain, it is unworkable, and fails.[85]

Inalienability/Perpetuity

However, probably the biggest cause of failure of non-charitable purpose trusts—especially those that fall into the exceptional categories already mentioned—is contravention of the rule against inalienability, or 'perpetual' trusts.[86] This rule has been overshadowed by the more famous rule against remoteness of vesting,[87] often simply known as 'the rule against perpetuities'. This is not least because a gift that transgresses one rule will nearly always transgress the other.[88] But they are different. Professor Hayton[89] expresses the rule in this way: '[p]ermitted non-charitable endowment purpose trusts [are] void unless from the outset they are certain to terminate by the end of the perpetuity period.' Thus he confines the rule to (a) *purpose* trusts, (b) which require the trust fund *to be preserved as an endowment*. But there is no reason in principle why the rule should be so confined. It is true that beneficiary trusts,[90] and trusts where capital as well as income can be disposed of, are less likely to fall foul of the rule, but if they transgress it the mischief is exactly the same.[91] As to the first point, there appears to be no clear authority before a dictum in *Re Wightwick's Will Trusts*.[92] As to the second, however, authority compels the view that the rule does not apply to cases where the donee concerned (often an unincorporated association) is able to

[84] N. 14 above.

[85] *R.* v. *District Auditor, ex p. West Yorkshire Metropolitan County Council* [1986] RVR 24.

[86] Maudsley, *The Modern Law of Perpetuities* (1979), 167, 170–8.

[87] Morris and Leach, *The Rule Against Perpetuities* (2nd edn., 1962); Maudsley, n. 86 above.

[88] e.g. *Re Flavel's WT* [1969] 2 All ER 232.

[89] Hayton and Marshall, *Cases and Commentary on the Law of Trusts* (9th edn.) 178.

[90] e.g. *Re Denley* [1969] 1 Ch. 373 (limited to the perpetuity period: valid).

[91] The mere fact that there *is* a power to spend capital does not mean it will be exercised, any more than the fact that the rule in *Saunders* v. *Vautier may* become applicable to the property means that it *must* do so.

[92] [1950] Ch. 260, 265. Similar views (confining the rule to purpose trusts) appear in Underhill and Hayton, n. 13 above, 166–7, 177–8. Hayton's view is also that of *Lewin on Trusts* (16th edn., 1984) by Mowbray, which itself may have been based on the dictum of Wynn-Parry J in *Re Wightwick's WT* [1950] Ch. 260, 265 (though neither the judge nor *Lewin* referred to certainty of *termination* within the perpetuity period). No similar statement appears in earlier editions of *Lewin*, nor in any edition of *Underhill* before the 13th (the first for which Professor Hayton was responsible). The cases cited in *Lewin* which precede *Wightwick* do not state the rule in terms restricting it to purpose trusts, but instead in general terms.

spend the capital.[93] Thus, for example, a gift to *erect* a tomb or gravestone will not be treated as perpetuitous, even though not expressly limited to the perpetuity period, whereas a gift for its *maintenance*, to be valid, must be so limited.[94]

On a different tack, it is difficult to see why the trust needs to be certain to *terminate* by the end of the period. Such a rule would be a rule against excessive *duration*, not against excessive *inalienability*. Although the former view is not without its adherents,[95] the weight of authority is in favour of the rule being against inalienability rather than duration.[96] The point is that the corpus of the trust fund (whatever its specific form from time to time) is in effect inalienable, because the rule in *Saunders* v. *Vautier* cannot be applied to it, i.e. the entire beneficial ownership cannot get together and demand that the trustee convey as they direct. The moment that the rule in *Saunders* v. *Vautier* can be applied to it, the corpus ceases to be inalienable. That the beneficial owners then choose to retain the fund in trust rather than demand it be paid over to them is—or should be—irrelevant.

For example, a fund held on trust for A for life, remainder to the longest serving of A's employees in service at his death for his or her life, remainder to the second longest serving such employee absolutely, is effectively inalienable during A's life. The fund ceases to be inalienable at A's death, because at that time the two employees' contingent interests vest and between them they are absolutely entitled to the fund. But if they choose to keep the trust in existence it does not thereby contravene the rule against inalienability. So a better formulation of the rule would be that a non-charitable trust is void unless from the outset it is certain that the rule in *Saunders* v. *Vautier* must be capable of being applied to it by the end of the perpetuity period.

What is the perpetuity period for this purpose? It is same as the common law perpetuity period for the rule against the remoteness of vesting, i.e. life or lives in being[97] plus twenty-one years.[98] The lives must be

[93] *Re Lipinski's WT*, n. 64 above, relying on *Re Macaulay* [1943] Ch. 435, 436, and *Re Price* [1943] Ch. 422. See also *Re Gibbons* [1917] 1 Ir. R 448, 452. But this may be a misinterpretation of the earlier cases (which predated the modern *Re Recher* [1972] Ch. 526 rule of construction of gifts to unincorporated associations), in which the courts lay stress on the fact that the associations concerned could spend capital and income *as they saw fit*: see *Re Cain* [1950] VLR 382, 391; *Re Westphal* [1972] NZLR 792. Cf *Leahy* v. *A.G. for NSW*, n. 54 above, 483; *Re Lawlor* [1934] VLR 22, 26–7, affd. [1934] CLR 1.

[94] *Re Filshie*, n. 48 above.

[95] Nathan, *Equity through the Cases* (1939), 165; Maudsley, *The Modern Law of Perpetuities* (1979), 167, 170; Underhill and Hayton.

[96] *Thellusson* v. *Woodford* (1805) 11 Ves. 112, 146; *Carne* v. *Long* (1860) 2 De G F & J 75, 80; *Re Chardon* [1928] Ch. 464, 467–8; *Re Wightwick's WT*, n. 92 above, 263–4; *Leahy* v. *A.G. for NSW*, n. 54 above, 482; Gray, n. 12 above; Sweet, n. 12 above, 342; Sheridan, n. 52 above.

[97] e.g. *Re Howard*, n. 56 above.

[98] *Re Khoo Cheng Teow*, n. 54 above; *Re Astor's ST*, n. 1 above.

human lives,[99] though in one case the court appears to have overlooked this point.[100] Where the settlor or testator has used expressions such as 'for so long as the law allows'[101] or 'so far as [the trustees] can legally do so',[102] the courts have benevolently construed this as a reference to twenty-one years. But the courts will not normally read such expressions in where they do not appear.[103] In one Irish case the court construed a gift of income without limit of time as an infinite number of annual gifts of income for one year, and held that the first twenty-one of these gifts were valid.[104]

Can the settlor or testator select an eighty-year perpetuity period for this purpose, pursuant to the (English) Perpetuities and Accumulations Act 1964, section 1? This rather parochial question has no clear answer. Morris and Leach[105] say that the answer is No. Maudsley[106] says the answer is Yes. It all depends on the true construction of section 15(4) of the Act. This provides:

> Nothing in this Act shall affect the operation of the rule of law rendering void for remoteness certain dispositions under which the property is limited to be applied for purposes other than the benefit of any person or class of persons in cases where the property may be so applied after the end of the perpetuity period.

We must remember first of all that the Act was primarily designed to reform the rules against remoteness of vesting. This subsection, by contrast, deals with a certain other 'rule of law', which it then goes on to describe. If the only rule with which the subsection is intended to deal is the precise one mentioned, the difficulty is that there is no such rule. But if (as we must suppose) the rule concerned is intended to be the rule against inalienability which we are discussing, then it is not very well described by the draftsman. In particular, the expression 'void for remoteness' is not apt. But section 15(4) only bars the operation of the Act in cases where the rule applies to *pure purpose* trusts. So it seems that the settlor or testator *can* select an eighty-year period even for the purposes of the rule against inalienability if the trust is for *beneficiaries*, but not where the trust is for pure purposes.

[99] *Re Kelly* [1932] IR 255, 260–1.

[100] *Re Dean* (1889) 41 Ch. D 552; see Gray, n. 12 above, 529–30.

[101] *Pirbright* v. *Salwey*, n. 49 above.

[102] *Re Hooper*, n. 45 above.

[103] *Re Kelly*, n. 99 above, 261; *Re Compton* [1946] 1 All ER 117; cf *Re Budge* [1942] NZLR 350.

[104] *Re Kelly*, n. 99 above, 262–4; *Tidex* v. *Trustees Executors and Agency Co. Ltd* [1971] 2 NSWLR 453, 463; cf *Re Budge*, n. 103 above, purporting to follow *Re Kelly*.

[105] N. 41 above, Suppl., 21.

[106] N. 13 above, 177–8. See also Crampin and Thomas in Glasson (ed.), n. 26 above, B4–13, who say 'it is difficult to see why' s. 1 should not apply.

MODERN DEVELOPMENTS IN THE RULE

There are three matters which I wish to discuss here.

Re Denley's Trust Deed

First, in *Re Denley*,[107] land was given to trustees to hold on trust to be maintained and used as a sports ground primarily by the employees of a limited company and secondarily by such other persons as the trustees might allow, until the expiration of a (valid) perpetuity period. One question which arose was whether this provision was void for uncertainty or for want of a beneficiary. Goff J held that it was not. He said:[108]

I think that there may be a purpose or object trust, the carrying out of which would benefit an individual or individuals where that benefit is so indirect or intangible or which is otherwise so framed as not to give those persons any locus standi to apply to the court to enforce the trust, in which case the beneficiary principle would, as it seems to me, apply to invalidate the trust, quite apart from any question of uncertainty or perpetuity. Such cases can be considered if and when they arise. The present, is not in my judgment, of that character, and it will be seen that clause (d) for the trust deed expressly states that subject to any rules and regulations made by the trustees the employees of the company should be entitled the use and enjoyment or the land.

Apart from this possible exception, in my judgment the beneficiary principle of *Re Astor* . . . is confined to purpose or object trusts which are abstract or impersonal. The objection is not that the trust is for a purpose or object *per se*, but that there is no beneficiary or cestui que trust.

He went on:[109]

Where, then, the trust, though expressed as a purpose, is directly or indirectly for the benefit of an individual or individuals, it seems to me that it is in general outside the mischief of the beneficiary principal.

And he concluded:[110]

The trust in the present case is limited in point of time so as to avoid any infringement of the rule against perpetuities, and, for the reasons which I have given, it does not offend against the beneficiary principle; and unless, therefore, it be void for uncertainty, it is a valid trust.

He went on to hold that the trust was not void for uncertainty.

When *Re Denley* first appeared it caused much comment.[111] On one

[107] [1969] 1 Ch. 373. [108] *Ibid.* 382–3.

[109] *Ibid.* 383–4. [110] *Ibid.* 386.

[111] [1968] *ASCL* 437; (1969) 32 *MLR* 96; (1970) 34 *Conv.* 77; (1973) 37 *Conv.* 420; Gravells, n. 13 above, 399, 417. See also Gardner, n. 13 above, 187.

reading it seemed that the beneficiary principle had been liberalized. You no longer needed a beneficiary, or group of beneficiaries, in the *Saunders* v. *Vautier* sense. It was enough that there were individuals who would directly or indirectly benefit for the purpose expressed. Yet even at that level a number of criticisms can be made. One is that Goff J really did not do justice to the axiomatic requirement of the *beneficiary,* rather than a mere *enforcer,* and in particular did not deal properly with the Privy Council's decision in *Leahy* v. *A.G. for New South Wales,*[112] citing only a dictum dealing with enforcement. Secondly, the thrust of his liberalizing dicta went to the *fact* of benefit, direct or indirect, to persons. But the mere *fact* that the person receives a benefit of some kind under a (non-charitable) trust does not make him a beneficiary, nor even entitled to enforce the trust.[113]

Nevertheless, in the later case of *Re Lipinski's Will Trusts*[114] Oliver J specifically approved *Re Denley,* adopting the first two passages quoted as according 'both with authority and with common sense'.[115] But in respect of Oliver J's 'approval' there are two points to make.

The first is that Oliver J approved the *particular statements* made by Goff J. And these statements are ambiguous. In particular the last sentence of the first statement ('The objection is not that the trust') and the second statement ('Where, then, the trust') can be read to mean that a particular trust in fact *has* beneficiaries, albeit disguised or concealed. This approach is reinforced by the citation by Goff J in support of his views of *Re Bowes,*[116] a case of a bequest on trust to plant trees on an estate owned by A for life, remainder to B. North J held that, applying the rule in *Saunders* v. *Vautier,* A and B together could insist on taking the money rather than having the trees planted. As North J said,[117] it was a 'trust to lay out money for the benefit of the persons entitled to the estate'.

And there are other cases[118] to the like effect, where, although the trust may be expressed as a purpose, the intention of the settlor or testator was to benefit some person or persons, and hence the *purpose* is subordinate to the *benefit.* So if the absolutely entitled beneficiary (for that is what he is) chooses to take the money instead, no-one can complain. Indeed, that was exactly what happened in *Re Lipinski's Will Trust;* a gift of money to an unincorporated association 'to be used solely in the work

[112] [1959] AC 497.

[113] See e.g. the cases in n. 35 above. Cf *Hunt* v. *Severs* [1994] 2 AC 350, criticized in (1995) 58 *MLR* 395. There is a special statutory regime for 'charity proceedings': see Charities Act 1993, s. 33, and *Gunning* v. *Buckfast Abbey Trustees,* n. 44 above.

[114] [1976] Ch. 235.

[115] *Ibid.* 248.

[116] [1896] 1 Ch. 507.

[117] *Ibid.* 511.

[118] e.g. *Re Skinner's Trusts* (1860) 1 J & H 102; *Re Osoba* [1979] 2 All ER 393; *Wicks* v. *Firth* [1983] AC 214; cf *Gott* v. *Nairne* (1876) 3 Ch. D 278 (advowson not just for son).

of constructing new buildings for the association and/or improvements to the said buildings' was treated by Oliver J as a gift to the members of the association 'with a superadded direction'.[119] In truth, this is but an example of the deep-rooted notion of English law that you cannot make someone the owner of property and then fetter his ownership by saying what he can or cannot do with it.[120] Here equity simply follows the law.

Accordingly, the approval of Oliver J in *Re Lipinski* of the dicta of Goff J in *Re Denley* does not demonstrate that he agreed that the beneficiary principle was being in any way watered down or the rules liberalized. Indeed Oliver J went on in his judgment to point out that there were numerous cases[121] where a gift which looked like a gift for a purpose in fact had ascertainable beneficiaries.

The second point is that in *Re Grant's Will Trusts*[122] Vinelott J considered that the decision in *Re Denley* was in fact perfectly orthodox, as concerning a discretionary trust of land for the benefit of a class of beneficiaries.[123] He said:[124]

> I can see no distinction in principle between a trust to permit a class defined by reference to employment to use and enjoy land in accordance with the rules to be made at the discretion of trustees on the one hand, and, on the other hand, a trust to distribute income at the discretion of trustees amongst the class, defined by reference to, for example, relationship to the settlor. In both cases the benefit to be taken by any member of the class is at the discretion of the trustees, but any member of the class can apply to the court to compel the trustees to administer the trust in accordance with its terms.

The actual decision in *Re Grant's Will Trusts* was that a gift to a Constituency Labour Party was invalid because, by virtue of a provision in the rules of the constituency association, the members could not so vary the rules as to put all the funds in their own pockets without the consent of a third party (the Labour Party National Executive). This decision has been criticized,[125] in my respectful view rightly. In giving an orthodox solution to one problem, the judge created a further problem. The fact that the contracting parties had *agreed* not to change their contract without reference to a third party did not, in law, prevent them from later agreeing to do so. As so often happens, the Australian cases have remained more faithful to the true doctrine.[126]

[119] [1976] Ch. 235, 250.

[120] *Re Rosher* (1884) 26 Ch. D 801; *Re Brown* [1954] Ch. 39.

[121] See n. 64 above.

[122] [1979] 3 All ER 359.

[123] Cf Hackney, *Understanding Equity and Trusts*, 71.

[124] [1979] 3 All ER 359, 368g.

[125] Rickett (1980) 39 *CLJ* 88; Green (1980) 44 *MLR* 459.

[126] *Re Producers Defence Fund*, n. 25 above, 253; *Re Goode*, n. 64 above, 121–2 (neither cited in *Re Grant*).

The *Quistclose* Trust

A second modern development in the law of purpose trusts has been the so-called *Quistclose* trust. In *Barclays Bank* v. *Quistclose Investments*[127] A gave money to B solely for the purpose of paying a debt owed by B to C. Had this debt been so paid, B would have been A's debtor, and A would have had no claim to the money now in C's hands. But B (a limited company) went into liquidation before the money could be paid to C, and hence the sole purpose of advancing the funds became impossible of performance. On these facts the House of Lords held that B held the funds on *resulting trust* for A. (This mattered because the funds were in a bank account—in credit—which the bank wished to combine with and offset against another account in debit, and, as the House held, the bank had notice of the trust). The position is apparently the same, and there is a resulting interest for A, if B *does* pay C, but then C repays those funds to B because the transaction between B and C does not proceed.[128]

So far, so orthodox. But two further cases[129] suggest that in the case of such a trust, C, though having no beneficial interest in the funds, has an equitable right to compel B to carry out the purpose for which the funds were advanced. This is analogous to Goff J's notion of the person having a factual benefit under a purpose trust thereby being able to enforce that trust. Yet the decisions concerned have been congently criticized,[130] and it is submitted that the *Quistclose* kind of trust, properly analysed, is no more a purpose trust than *Re Denley* was. It all depends on the intention of A as settlor of the trust. If he intended to benefit C there would be a trust for C. If A's intention was to benefit *himself* (e.g. to create a kind of 'mandate'), or to benefit B without giving him a beneficial interest (a kind of 'factual' benefit), there will be a trust for A.[131] It will be a form of illusory trust. These two main possibilities may of course be mixed, perhaps contingent on some event(s) happening or not happening. One interest may be a security interest only, the other an interest of 'full' enjoyment. The important thing to note is that, though the mixture may be complex, the concepts employed are quite orthodox. There is no more need to think of purpose trusts here than there was, say, in *Re Bowes*.[132]

[127] [1970] AC 467.
[128] *Re EVTR Ltd* [1987] BCLC 646.
[129] *Re Northern Developments Ltd*, unreported, 6 Oct. 1978, Megarry V-C; *Carreras Rothmans* v. *Freeman Matthews Treasure* [1985] 1 All ER 155, 166.
[130] Millett, n. 28 above.
[131] Cf Gray, n. 12 above, 511.
[132] N. 116 above.

Class-closing Rules

We have already mentioned the Perpetuities and Accumulations Act 1964, with its obscure section 15(4). One other aspect of the Act deserves to be mentioned here, and that is the effect of 'wait and see' on a trust for a continuously expanding class of beneficiaries. This is, or may be, important in considering the *Re Denley* kind of trust.

Suppose a discretionary trust amongst a class of employees of a company, as in *Re Denley* (on Vinelott J's view), but not limited to the perpetuity period. *Prima facie* the trust should fail as infringing both the rule against remoteness of vesting (because interests may vest outside the perpetuity period) and the rule against inalienability (because it will not be certain that the rule in *Saunders* v. *Vautier* can apply—if the beneficiaries wish—by the end of the perpetuity period; the company *might* be wound up within the period, but may not be). The 'wait and see' principle in section 3 of the Perpetuities and Accumulations Act 1964 can be applied during the perpetuity period (ascertained by reference to section 3(4)). But at the end of the period, if the company is still in existence, the class of employees is *prima facie* still open, and the gift should fail for remoteness. But here section 4(4) of the 1964 Act comes into play. That provides:

> Where, in the case of a disposition to which sub-section (3) above does not apply, it is apparent at the time the disposition is made or becomes apparent at a subsequent time that, apart from this sub-section, the inclusion of any persons, being potential members of the class or unborn persons who at birth would become members or potential members of the class, would cause the disposition to be treated as void for remoteness, those persons shall, unless their exclusion would exhaust the class, henceforth be deemed for all the purposes of the disposition to be excluded from the class.

Despite the rather tortuous drafting of the provision, it is clear that the effect is to exclude the potential future employees of the company from the class, which in effect therefore closes at the latest by the end of the perpetuity period. Hence the 'wait and see' principle is satisfied, and the gift is not void for remoteness of vesting.

But what about the rule against inalienability? We have already seen how section 15(4) of the Act prevents the Act (including section 4) applying to the rule against inalienability in relation to trusts for *purposes*. But it seems not to exclude the Act in relation to trusts for *persons*. So section 4 can apply to our example. What is its effect? The potential members of the class, i.e. future employees of the company, have been excluded under section 4(4) 'for all the purposes of the disposition'. That must include for the purposes of the rule against inalienability.

The conclusion accordingly is that a *Denley-type* trust would be valid now even without being expressly limited to the perpetuity period, but only because of the provisions of the Perpetuities and Accumulations Act 1964. So a case like *Re Flavel's Will Trusts*,[133] where a trust to create a pension fund for employees of a company was held void for perpetuity, would now presumably be effective.

SIDESTEPPING THE RULE

The effect of all this is simple enough. It means that the astute draftsman can create a beneficiary trust that has the effect—more or less—of a purpose trust. Suppose, to take an example at random, that a settlor wishes to create a trust to encourage research into the possibility of the English language being written in a different alphabet, and to publish English language works in that alphabet. So he transfers assets to trustees on trust for the benefit of the then members of an unincorporated association having those objects (taking care that the rules do not forbid the members to wind up the society and put the money in their pockets).

Or, if he does not trust the society not to wind itself up, he transfers his fund to trustees on trust during the perpetuity period to pay out of the income to such of a large class of persons as spend money out of their own resources on the like objects sums equal to 110 per cent of such sums as they spend, until the income for a particular period be exhausted, the capital at the end of the perpetuity period to go to charity. As long as the objects are defined with precision, and the class is too large for them to agree to take the money in any other way, in practice the objects will be advanced, albeit at a slightly inflated cost.

There are other ways too. You may say that this ingenuity ought not to be necessary. Perhaps. But it does illustrate a truth about trust law, which is that fundamentally it is based on there being an equitable owner of the property or interest given.

FUNCTIONS OF PURPOSE TRUSTS

At this point my story changes. It ceases to be a history of concessions to sentiment. Instead it becomes a story of the Grail. Instead of the purpose trust being consigned to a few footnotes in equity textbooks, it suddenly springs to centre stage, ardently pursued by youthful offshore jurisdictions. How is this?

[133] [1969] 2 All ER 232.

Public Purposes

One of the functions of non-charitable purpose trusts is to enable purposes which are not *charitable* in the strict sense, but are—or may be—beneficial in a wider sense, to be fulfilled. In this respect non-charitable purpose trusts would merely supplement the law of charity, filling in some of the crevices and cracks revealed by the case law. The list of purposes intended to be carried out by purpose trusts which have failed is a long one: publishing a newspaper,[134] researching and developing a new alphabet,[135] erecting a statue,[136] and preventing vivisection[137] are just some of the examples. These and other purposes might be furthered by non-charitable purpose trusts.

But it is not these things, worthy as they may be, that have stimulated a number of offshore trust jurisdictions to enact laws specifically permitting non-charitable purpose trusts to exist. Instead these jurisdictions have seen—or think they have seen—important commercial advantages that would flow from permitting such trusts. Fundamentally, these commercial advantages all derive from one aspect of non-charitable purpose trusts.

Orphans and Old Buffers

As we have seen, the characteristic of the true non-charitable purpose trust is that it is has no beneficiaries. This means that the beneficial ownership is not in the trustees—it is after all a trust, not for their benefit—and there is no one else in whom it can be located. So—it is said—the property the subject of the trust cannot, in strict law, be said to belong beneficially to *anyone*. Now there are many estate-planning exercises and commercial transactions that can make good use of this phenomenon, which we could describe as 'orphans and old buffers'.

Private Trust Companies

Beginning with trusts, one of the burning issues in the offshore trust world of the last few years has been the growth of so-called asset-protection trusts. These are trusts designed specifically to insulate the worth of the settlor against claims from future creditors (particularly in the United States of America) or from members of his family, includ-

[134] *Re Lawlor* [1934] VLR 22, affd. (1934) 51 CLR 1; *Re Astor's ST*, n. 1 above.
[135] *Re Shaw* [1957] 1 WLR 729.
[136] *Re Endacott*, n. 39 above.
[137] *National Anti-Vivisection Society* v. *IRC* [1948] AC 31.

ing so-called 'forced heirship' claims (particularly in civil law or Islamic jurisdictions).[138]

Many offshore trust companies have been alive to the risks that they might be drawn into litigation as trustee of an asset-protection trust that became subject to attack. So they have seen the need for a 'buffer zone' of protection between them and the assets. Or again, some settlors prefer that the trustee of the trust should be a 'one-trust' company, i.e. a private trust company incorporated only for the purposes of being trustee of that trust. They are afraid of the possibility that a claim made against a trust company in respect of another trust (wholly unconnected with their own) might impinge on the assets held by that trust company on the trusts of their own trust. Again, this appeals particularly to civil law and Islamic settlors. But at the same time such settlors do not want to be directly connected with, let alone the beneficial owner of, that private trust company, for fear that it should be regarded as a sham, or because local tax legislation might consequently regard the settlor as continuing to own the trust property as a result of his control, or because they may thereby have access to information about the trust which may be extorted from them in their own country.

So (in any of these cases) a private trust company is used as a trustee of the offshore trust. But the *shares* of the private trust company are held by the offshore trust company on the trusts of a purpose trust. Typically the 'purposes' concerned are (i) to hold the shares of the private trust company and (ii) to enable the private trust company to act as trustee of the individual trust. In this way the settlor demonstrably has no control over the trust assets, and the offshore trust company is *not* the trustee of the offshore trust, nor does it own the trustee beneficially.

This is an interesting use of a purpose trust. But, were this the *only* 'offshore' use of non-charitable purpose trusts, it is doubtful that many jurisdictions would have changed their trust law specifically to cater for it. As is often the case, it is the big commercial transactions that offshore jurisdictions hope to attract.

Foreign Agencies

The simplest commercial use of a purpose trust is to provide a foreign agency. Suppose company A wishes to do business in country X, but wants to provide for as few contacts with that country as possible. If company A directly trades in country X, or even if it incorporates a subsidiary company (call it 'B'), these may be sufficient contacts to enable it to be said that company A is 'resident' or has a 'presence' there, so

[138] See generally Matthews (1995) 6 *KCLJ* 62; (1996) 5 *OTPR* 57.

as to be subject to the jurisdiction of the courts of X. If on the other hand company A finds a wholly independent agent, whom it does not control, in country X it runs the risk that the agent steals its customers for a rival company. So company A instead causes a purpose trust to be set up in offshore state Y, and the offshore trust company holds all the shares of company B (which is going to act as agent of company A in country X) upon valid purpose trusts. In this way company A has no direct connection with company B. A does not own B, which is, legally speaking, wholly independent. But at the same time company B will only act as laid down in the purpose trust. This (it is hoped) will prevent company B acting as agent for any rivals to company A.

Off-balance-sheet Transactions

A more complex use of the same idea is to structure transactions through a purpose trust so that they are 'off balance sheet'. The advantages to a company of taking large transactions—including, say, joint ventures—off balance sheet are many. You do not have to consolidate the transactions into your group accounts, making your gearing look better. You will be less likely to breach financial covenants if things go wrong, and any regulatory requirements (e.g. capital ratios) will be easier to comply with. At the same time group tax benefits will probably still be available.

To take a transaction off balance sheet of the main company requires that it be performed by a separate company which is not a 'subsidiary' as defined by the relevant legislation.[139] Usually such definitions are put in terms of control of the company or of its voting rights. So the 'subsidiary' company's shares are divided into two classes, voting shares with no economic benefits attached, and non-voting shares carrying all the economic benefits. The voting shares are held by an offshore trust company on the terms of a purpose trust, and the non-voting shares are held by the main investing company. The result is that the 'parent' company has all the economic advantages of a successful 'subsidiary', without any of the disadvantages. The same technique can be used for joint ventures between two investing companies, to similar effect.

Special Purpose Companies

A variant of the technique enables an asset to be acquired by an offshore company incorporated for the purpose (often called a 'special purpose company' or 'single purpose vehicle') whose voting (but non-economic) shares are held by the offshore trustee on a purpose trust, while the non-

[139] See e.g. Companies Act 1985, s. 258; Companies (Jersey) Law 1991, Art. 2.

voting (but economic) shares are held by the intended acquirer. The shares of the offshore company can be pledged to a bank to secure a loan to acquire the asset in the first place. Structures of this kind have become popular in Bermuda since 1989, as they can be adapted to secure the US tax benefits available to offshore companies which qualify as 'foreign sales corporations' under US law.[140]

Cross-border Debt Securitization

And more complex structures still can be devised. One would be a cross-border debt securitization. A sells goods or services to B in return for a series of payments (an income stream) by B. A sells the right to these payments to the special purpose company offshore. This company raises the capital to pay that price by issuing securities or loan notes to investors worldwide. The company is, however, owned by an offshore trust company which holds the shares of that company on the trusts of a non-charitable purpose trust. So the company belongs to no one. But everyone is happy. In such a case the advantages are legion. Risk is minimized, tax breaks are maximized. And the company appears on no-one's balance sheet.

Now, it is not my purpose to suggest that any of these uses of trusts is illegitimate, or even (perish the thought) a sinister and time-wasting exercise. On the contrary, if the structures exist, they can be made useful. In any event, one must be practical. Even if one trust jurisdiction attempted to forbid them, others would still permit them. We have the example of France[141] and the other civil law countries, vainly trying to swim against the tide of trusts rushing in from common law countries. Liechtenstein made provision for trusts in 1926.[142] Luxembourg has had a rather weak form of trust since 1983.[143] Ultimately even France will have to introduce a 'French' version of the trust,[144] if only to try to capture back some of the lucrative international financial work which has gone to common law jurisdictions.

STATUTORY NON-PURPOSE TRUST JURISDICTIONS

The number of offshore trust jurisdictions with non-charitable-purpose trust legislation, permitting the creation of such trusts, is growing apace.

140 See further Anderson (1991) 2 *OTPR* 1.

141 e.g. *Caron* v. *Odell* [1983] R 282; [1986] R 66; [1991] R 924.

142 *Personen- und Gesellschaftrecht* ('PGR') of 1926 ([1926] I LGB Nr 4).

143 *Réglement grand-ducal*, 19 July 1983.

144 'La fiducie': see Dyson [1992] *Conv.* 407; Urquhart (1993) 3 *OTPR* 35; Matthews (1995) 5 *OTPR* 31, n. 138 above, 37–9.

If we exclude Liechtenstein as a special case,[145] the first in the market were Nauru, in 1972,[146] and the Cook Islands, in 1984.[147] But the first comprehensive legislation was that of Bermuda, in 1989,[148] closely followed by the British Virgin Islands,[149] Belize,[150] Mauritius,[151] and Cyprus.[152] More recently Nevis,[153] Anguilla,[154] Niue,[155] the Seychelles,[156] and the Bahamas[157]have all introduced such legislation. And there are others who have proposed such legislation.[158] Even that most respectable of offshore jurisdictions, Jersey, has recently enacted purpose-trust legislation[159] (which received the sanction of Her Majesty in Council on 24 April 1996, and came into force when the Order in Council was registered in the Royal Court of Jersey, on 24 May 1996).

A curiosity is that non-charitable-purpose trust legislation in general[160] has not purported to answer explicitly the question where the 'beneficial' ownership of the trust property lies. But—safety in numbers—it has tended to follow a certain model. There are five main features, although it must be emphasized that not every example of such legislation makes provision for each of these features.

The five features are as follows:

(1) Restrictions on the purposes for which the trust can be established; typically the legislation says that the purposes must be both *workable*, i.e. specific or certain and possible to carry out, and *beneficial*, i.e. not immoral or contrary to public policy.

(2) Enforcement mechanism: typically there must be a person whose job it is to keep an eye on the trust and to enforce it. For this purpose he will have rights to information about the trust. He may be called the 'enforcer' or the 'protector', or something else, but he will have certain obligations to blow the whistle, apply to the Court, or notify an official (typically the Attorney General) if he thinks something wrong is going on, or if there is no enforcer in office. Sometimes these duties are backed up by criminal sanctions.

145 PGR, Art. 927; see Biedermann, *The Trust in Liechtenstein Law*, 28.
146 Foreign Trusts, Estates and Wills Act 1972, s. 6.
147 International Trusts Act 1984, s. 12(2).
148 Trusts (Special Provisions) Act 1989, ss. 12–16.
149 Trustee Ordinance, s. 84 (as amended by the Trustee (Amendment) Act 1992).
150 Trusts Act 1992, s. 15.
151 Offshore Trusts Act 1992, s. 15.
152 International Trusts Law 1992, ss. 2, 7(3).
153 International Exempt Trust Ordinance 1994, s. 8.
154 Trusts Ordinance 1994, s. 15.
155 Trusts Act 1994, s. 16.
156 International Trusts Act 1994, s. 14.
157 Perpetuities Act 1995, s. 18.
158 Including Barbados (See now International Trusts Act 1995, s. 10) and Montserrat.
159 Trusts (Amendment No 3) (Jersey) Law 1996, passed by the States of Jersey on 21 Nov. 1995.
160 Cf the Belize Trusts Act 1992, s. 27(3).

(3) Restrictions on the trustees: it is common to provide that at least one of the trustees must be resident in the jurisdiction concerned, and/or must be a professionally qualified person or body, for example a lawyer or accountant. Also, usually a trustee may not be the enforcer.
(4) Restrictions on the trust property: often such trusts are not allowed to own land in the jurisdiction concerned;
(5) Duration and termination of the trust: most of the jurisdictions have perpetuity periods or maximum duration periods,[161] and provision for what is to happen to the property at the determination of the trust.

For the sake of example, let me compare the relevant rules of the Bermudian and the (new) Jersey non-charitable-purpose trust laws, under each of the five heads.

Restrictions on Purposes

Bermudian law requires that the purposes be 'specific, reasonable and possible' and not 'immoral, contrary to public policy, or unlawful'.[162] Jersey law makes no requirement at all under this head, though the general requirements of certainty, consistency with public policy and lawfulness apply to such a trust in any event.[163]

Enforcement Mechanism

Bermudian law requires that the trust instrument provide for a person to be appointed to enforce the trust and for a successor to be appointed. It also requires one of the trustees to notify the Attorney General if there is no enforcer.[164] Jersey law makes a similar requirement, save that the trustees must apply to the Court for appointment of a new enforcer rather than merely notify the Attorney General.[165]

Restrictions on Trustees

Bermudian law requires that at least one trustee be a 'designated person', i.e. a lawyer or accountant entitled to practise in Bermuda or a licensed Bermudian trust corporation, or a person approved by the

[161] Although there is a new trend in offshore trust jurisdictions for there to be no perpetuity rule and no maximum duration. So far, Nauru, the Turks and Caicos Islands, Cyprus (for purpose trusts), the BVI, the Cook Islands, Anguilla, and Nevis have taken this step. Others will follow.
[162] 1989 Act, s. 13(1)(a), (b).
[163] 1984 Law, Art. 11(2).
[164] 1989 Act, s. 13(1)(e), (2).
[165] 1984 Law, Arts. 10A, 17(7), (8).

Minister of Finance.[166] Jersey law has no such requirement for non-charitable-purpose trusts, but the general trust law requirement will apply, so that the court has power to appoint a Jersey resident trustee if there is not one already.[167] Bermudian law does not make it express that a trustee cannot also be the enforcer, though this seems to be implied.[168] Jersey law makes it express.[169]

Restrictions on Trust Property

Bermudian law has a specific prohibition on Bermudian land being held on non-charitable-purpose trusts.[170] Jersey law has a general prohibition on Jersey land being the subject of any express trust.[171]

Duration and Termination of Trust

The general rule in both Bermuda[172] and Jersey[173] is that a trust must not endure longer than 100 years, and this applies to a non-charitable purpose trust as to any other.[174] Under Bermudian law the trust must specify the terminating event and what is to happen to the trust property then.[175] Under Jersey law there is no such specific requirement. The general trust law rule applies, that on termination the trust property should be distributed 'in accordance with the terms of the trust to the persons entitled thereto'.[176]

PROBLEMS

In considering these legislative responses to the beneficiary principle, a number of problems arise. Some of them relate to the particular form that the legislation takes. Some of them are more general.

One specific problem is that of the 'self-serving' purpose. Can it *really* be a purpose of a purpose trust 'to hold shares in such and such a company'? Must not the purpose be more substantive, for example 'to plant trees on the X Estate', 'to preserve the Cornish language', or 'to publish books on military uniforms'? In other words, the *form* of the assets held by the trust is not really a purpose; a purpose is *what you apply the assets to.* Certainly that view is consistent with the notion of the

[166] 1989 Act, s. 12(2). [167] 1984 Act, Art. 40. [168] See 1989, s. 13(2).
[169] 1984 Law, Arts. 10B(2), 10C(4)(d). [170] 1989 Act, s. 16.
[171] 1984 Law, Art. 10(2)(a)(iii).
[172] Perpetuities and Accumulations Act 1989, s. 3(1).
[173] 1984 Law, Art. 11(1). [174] 1989 Act, s. 13(1). [175] *Ibid.*, s. 13(1)(f).
[176] 1984 Law, Art. 39(1). Note, incidentally, the reference to 'persons'.

charitable trust. These purposes consist of applications of funds, not in merely organizing them. The *Helen Slater* case[177] caused trouble because it did not involve a primary application of charitable funds; it involved payment by that charity to a second charity, and hence only *secondarily* an application of the charitable funds. But, be it noted, it did ultimately involve an application of trust funds. The notion of the purpose as being to stand still and simply *be* is frankly rather odd. Yet it will have been noted that many of the commercial uses to which the non-charitable-purpose trust is nowadays put depend on this strange, narrow meaning of the word 'purpose'.

The danger is that, the moment you start declaring purposes which are more substantive, you run the risk of identifying *beneficiaries.* A trust for planting trees on a specific estate may be construed as a beneficiary trust for the benefit of the estate's owners.[178] So may a trust to publish a specific book.[179] So if the settlor's purpose is to create a fund not beneficially owned by anyone, we can see why he should resort to such feeble purposes as 'to hold the shares in X Ltd as a private trust company'. But at that level there is a danger in the opposite direction. This is that, by proclaiming so vociferously that the fund belongs to no one, whilst using it vigorously to benefit the settlor or those designated by the settlor, you draw attention to the inconsistency. The trust instrument does not record the truth. It is a sham.[180]

Another problem is that of providing information. There can be no trust where the trustee is not accountable to someone.[181] In the normal beneficiary trust, it is the beneficiary who can hold the trustee to account, and he can seek information for the purpose of doing so. With these statutory purpose trusts, there is a person whose job it is to enforce the trust. Often this person is simply called 'the enforcer'. In the Bermudan legislation, that person is expressly given power to inspect trust documents.[182] In most other forms of such legislation, the enforcer is not given specific powers, but is simply stated to be a person 'to enforce' the trust. Presumably this must involve having the right to call for all the information which a beneficiary under the same trust could have called for.[183] But it will be subject to any lawful restrictions on information which are included in the trust instrument.[184]

177 *IRC* v. *Helen Slater Charitable Trust Ltd* [1982] Ch. 49.

178 *Re Bowes*, n. 116 above.

179 *Re Skinner's Trusts* (1860) 1 J & H 102.

180 Cf *Re Marriage of Goodwin* (1990) 101 FLR 386; *Rahman* v. *Chase Bank (CI) Trust Co. Ltd* 1991 JLR 103; *Midland Bank plc* v. *Wyatt* [1995] 1 FLR 696.

181 See Hayton, *The Irreducible Core Content of Trusteeship.*

182 Trusts (Special Provisions) Act 1989, s. 12. See also the Turks & Caicos Trustee Ordinance, s. 84(11).

183 See e.g. *Re Londonderry's Settlements* [1965] Ch. 918.

184 *Tierney* v. *King* [1983] 2 Qd. R 580; cf *Jones* v. *Shipping Federation of British Columbia* (1963) 37 DLR (2d) 273, 274–5; *A.G. for Ontario* v. *Stavro* (1994) DLR (4th) 750.

Of course, we are talking of a theoretical position. In commercial practice an enforcer will be a stooge, provided by an offshore trust and corporate services organization, just like the trustee, the protector (if there is one), and any company directors and nominee shareholders that may be needed. And for all that we say and do here, in academic terms, if anything can be said with certainty, it is that the great bulk of such trusts will never come under the microscope at all, much less be subject to attacks. If one in 100 questionable 'trusts' is ever set aside, that is probably a high proportion. Indeed, the invention of these statutory purpose trusts is in part an attempt to improve the statistics, to make it less likely that any such trusts will be attacked, by removing one source of superintendence and complaint.

Let me explain. We all know that it is possible to draft a valid trust, genuinely conferring benefits on real beneficiaries, such that those beneficiaries can never in practice control what goes on, or individually have any sufficient property interest to deal with or dispose of. The long-term discretionary trust is a well tried and tested structure for this purpose. And, as we have seen from *Re Denley,* it can be adapted for use in an employment setting, and in relation to assets other than money. So if you are looking, for the purposes of a commercial transaction, for a trust where the beneficiaries are utterly independent of the settlor, yet are not in themselves in control, this should do. Yet there is still a wrinkle. The beneficiaries have significant rights: rights to information,[185] rights to prevent misuse of the trust funds,[186] rights to require the trust to be performed.[187]

Before the offshore jurisdictions rushed in with their statutory purpose trusts, such beneficiary trusts could have been—and were—used for some of the functions which I have outlined. And they would be both appropriate and realistic in some cases. If a company was to be held safe from predators, a trust of its shares for the long-term benefit of employees might have been ideal. Or you could collect together a band of down and outs and paupers and have them as your class of beneficiaries. In some cases such trusts were shams.[188] But in any event you took a risk, i.e. that the human beings in your class of beneficiaries might seek to exercise some of their undoubted rights.

So, more popular still for use in such cases was the charitable trust. No people there. In some cases, these also were just shams. It was all nominal. No one intended charity to get a penny, just like those famous offshore trusts we call 'blind' trusts, because one or two charities are the

[185] *Chaine-Nickson* v. *Bank of Ireland* [1976] IR 393; *Spellson* v. *George* (1987) 11 NSWLR 300, 315–16.

[186] Cf *Dance* v. *Goldingham* (1873) LR 8 Ch. App. 902.

[187] *McPhail* v. *Doulton* [1971] AC 424.

[188] Cf *Rahman* v. *Chase Bank (CI) Trust Co. Ltd,* n. 180 above, *Midland Bank plc* v. *Wyatt,* n. 180 above.

sole objects of a large discretionary trust, *but* there is power to add further (real) beneficiaries in the future.[189] In other—perhaps most—cases, though, these charitable trusts were genuine. There would be a small sum of money settled upon proper charitable trusts. Then significant assets would be transferred to the trustee for some of the commercial functions discussed. When the functions had been carried into effect the trust would be wound up. It would have made a little money for charity—though nothing like as much as its commercial sponsors would have made for themselves—which would be applied to charitable purposes. It was a bit like putting something in the poor box when you won on a horse.

But this too had disadvantages. First, because it was charitable, the Attorney General, or in some jurisdictions the Charity Commissioners, would have significant rights to require information about the trust, or otherwise to interfere in its administration, perhaps even to replace the charitable trustee. *Not* an attractive prospect for international businessmen trying to carry through commercial purposes that were not only complex and confidential, but also, how shall we say, economical with the taxes. It *might* be lawful, but the magician never wants to reveal to the audience how the trick is done. And moreover, there was always unease that the charitable trust was not benefiting very much, so that there was a feeling of vulnerability. Perhaps the trustees were not exploiting their position to obtain for charity as much as was their duty. Perhaps they might be sued. Perhaps—heavens above—the commercial transactions themselves might be at risk.

EUREKA

At all events, the offshore trust jurisdictions saw that there was a need for a vehicle that could truly be said to belong to no one beneficially, and which could be slotted into complicated commercial transactions without difficulty. Enter the statutory purpose trust. And this is why offshore jurisdictions are now falling over each other to offer such a facility.[190]

Yet, have the offshore jurisdictions succeeded in their quest for the non-owned entity? Is a purpose trust *really* any better in this respect than a beneficiary trust or a charitable trust? You still have a trust. You still have trustees owing fiduciary obligations to maximize benefit for

[189] *Re Gea Settlement*, 17 Mar. 1992, unreported, Royal Court of Jersey.

[190] But the statutory purpose trust is not the only vehicle. The guarantee company has for many years been used for similar purposes: see Taylor (1992) 2 *OTPR* 193; cf Ghosh (1995) 5 *OTPR* 21; what is difficult to understand is why no offshore centre has produced *the company that entirely owns its own shares*. Perhaps it is thought that this would be a try-on too far.

some *thing*, and not for themselves.[191] True, it is for a purpose, but if trustees felt uneasy about charitable trusts not benefiting much, why should they feel any easier if the purpose is not charitable? The only difference is that the Attorney General is not going to be interested. Instead, it is all down to a creature of your own making (and paying) called the 'enforcer'. So perhaps it is a practical point. *In practice, no one is going to complain.* But, if *that* is the point, it is, to say the least, rather tacky.

Of course it is possible for offshore jurisdictions, by specific legislation, to create legal institutions that can be genuinely autonomous and belong to no one.[192] The question to be asked here is whether, in the way such legislation is currently and commonly used, those trusts achieve that. If those creating such trusts do so because they do not like the consequences of using trusts for classes of paupers or charitable trusts, they should ask themselves why. I gravely doubt some of the arguments put forward by offshore jurisdictions for introducing statutory purpose trusts.

Even if courts and lawyers in these jurisdictions consider that their legislation does achieve its object in *that* jurisdiction, there is a further problem, and that is international recognition. Many—if not most—transactions carried out using this kind of legislation are international in scope and effect. They will not work (or not as well) if the purpose trust is not recognized. But the question of recognition is more likely to arise in other countries than the 'home' jurisdiction. And if the courts of other countries say that there is no trust, then the previous beneficial owner of the property will never have divested himself of ownership. Imagine the chaos (and tax bills) that *that* would cause.

Now, as we have seen,[193] adhering to the Hague Trusts Convention will involve a contracting State in undertaking to recognize a trust 'for a specified purpose'. But to date only a handful of States have ratified,[194] and amongst the non-ratifiers so far remain the USA, New Zealand, Ireland, and India (all trust States) and *all* the civil law and Islamic law States except Italy, Malta, and the Netherlands. Moreover, even where ratification has occurred, Articles 15, 16, and 18 of the Convention confer significant scope upon the courts of contracting States to refuse recognition in special cases (e.g. where public policy considerations are involved).[195] Added to this, if the question of validity and effect came before (say) an English or US court, it is true that this would involve expert

[191] This is made explicit in the Belize Trusts Act 1992, s. 27(3) (drafted by English counsel).

[192] Cf Gardner, n. 13 above, 192–3.

[193] N. 22 above. [194] *Ibid.*

[195] See e.g. Hayton (1987) 36 *ICLQ* 260.

evidence of the foreign law, but at the end of the day it would be an *English or US* court deciding the point. That court may not be so sympathetic to the needs of an offshore jurisdiction to ensure that its purpose-trust legislation is upheld as effective. In view of the problems I have mentioned, there must be a significant risk that it would not do so.

ARE YOU BEING SERVED?

Trusts came into existence because lawyers were asked to create structures to serve particular purposes: holding land whilst the owner went off to the Crusades, devising land when there was no power of testation, avoiding feudal incidents of tenure. Today the position is much the same. New and different types of trust are used to achieve particular objectives. Like it or not, the client-driven trust is as much a 'product' in the modern legal industry as is life assurance or the zero-coupon Eurobond (both of which, incidentally, are often combined with trusts).

There are arguments about when the offshore financial services industry first came into being. Was it after the First World War, the Second World War, in the 1960s? It does not matter. Different things happened at different times. But, formerly, competition between offshore centres was limited. There were not many of them, and each had its own sphere of influence. And anti-avoidance legislation in the high tax jurisdictions was a great deal less sophisticated than it is today. Few commercial enterprises—the Vestey empire was a rare example—bothered to set up offshore. So an offshore centre traded—and thrived—on straightforward tax avoidance, making huge differences to a very small number of people.

But times change. Now there is much greater competition. The number of offshore centres has grown, and continues to grow, rapidly.[196] Industrial nations have much more sophisticated anti-avoidance legislation. All trust jurisdictions—including the offshore centres—have complex rules to combat money-laundering. There is no longer the easy, large-margin business of forty years ago. Now it is cut-throat competition, and (comparatively) high volume, low-margin business, trading on what are often minute differences in tax rates and double tax treaties. Most of all, business has seen the offshore light in a big way. A high proportion of all businesses are owned, or managed, or have their profits

[196] As does the number of books and journals devoted to them, e.g. Harris (ed.), *The Use of Offshore Jurisdictions*; Withers (ed.), *International Trust Precedents*; Grundy, *Tax Havens*; Glasson (ed.), n. 26 above; *The Trident Practical Guide to Offshore Trusts* (2nd edn., 1995); *The Offshore Tax Planning Review*, *Tolley's Trust Law International*; *The Journal of International Trust and Corporate Planning*; *Trusts and Trustees*.

laundered, through offshore vehicles. Every offshore jurisdiction wants their business. Every new product in the offshore financial marketplace finds its competitors: the international business company, the asset protection trust, the limited life company, the limited liability partnership, and the purpose trust. What one jurisdiction has, they all want.

CUI BONO?

We must see trusts—and the purpose trust in particular—in this light. It is a product, serving a commercial need. To some extent, like all law and legal institutions, it is a conjuring trick. It is a way of making another legal institution—ownership—disappear, or half disappear. First it is refracted into legal ownership and beneficial enjoyment, and then beneficial enjoyment seems to dissolve into thin air.

There is nothing wrong in any of this, provided that we understand what we are doing, and that we doing it deliberately. Unlike the laws of physics, the laws of man are fully mutable. But what we must *not* do—and we are in danger of doing it—is to misunderstand and to misuse a doctrine, to think we have achieved an object when we have not. The statutory purpose trust is, or can be, a good thing. But it is not the entirely autonomous vehicle that its promoters think. It is not the Holy Grail. There are obligations—no one doubts that—but also there are rights. If the trust has background beneficiaries, like *Re Denley*, then *they* have rights. If the trust is a sham, then again there will be real beneficiaries, able to exercise rights and—more seriously—saddled with the beneficial ownership. Even if—and it is a big if—it is a genuine, substantive purpose statutory non-charitable-purpose trust, the enforcer has rights. If there is a trust, there is a benefit. And, like the *damnosa hereditas* of the classical Roman law,[197] the question can still be asked, to whom does it belong in the end?[198]

[197] See Thomas, *Textbook of Roman Law* (1976), 498–9.

[198] I am grateful to all those who were kind enough to comment on the first draft of this paper, given to the conference on 'Trends in Contemporary Trust Law', held at the University of Cambridge on 6 Jan. 1996. These include Sir Peter Millett, Professor David Hayton, Robert Venables QC, Robert Ham QC, Andrew Tettenborn, and Katie Bradford, though none of them should be taken necessarily to agree with what I have written, and I am alone responsible for the errors that remain.

2

Presumptions and Illegality

DEREK DAVIES

Presumptions are not as innocuous as they seem. They tend to become more presumptions of law than of fact and create awkwardness in the law, distorting issues and affecting adversely the manner in which cases are decided. A number of illustrations can be given.

It can happen even in the context of automatic resulting trusts. I believe it to be true of *Vandervell* v. *IRC*,[1] where an issue arose whether the entire beneficial interest in certain shares in a private company had been disposed of, or whether a resulting trust had arisen in relation to a share option derived from the transferor. A majority in the House of Lords took the view that the law of resulting trusts was attracted, there being a gap in the beneficial title. But a minority held that the real intentions were discernible, and in my view they were right. There was no gap to plug. Doctrine was used too readily and common sense relegated to second place. The moral is not to presume when one can find out.

Presumptions can also intrude when a dispute arises on the nature of a transaction. Take the simple case of money passing by cheque or a chattel by delivery, and the parties disagreeing—there being no written evidence—on whether a loan or a gift had been intended. In Australia, weight is given to the fact of payment or delivery in itself.[2] The consequence is that the onus lies on the transferor to show that only a loan was intended, and this seems sensible. Someone who has carried out an act ordinarily signifying the passing of property should have the responsibility of showing that he did not mean it to do so. Why expect the transferee to delve into the other's mind and demonstrate that the latter intended to give? The presumptions have no relevance in these cases. Transactions should *prima facie* be taken to mean what they apparently achieve. What matters is the weight of evidence. A difference in relationship between the parties at the time of transfer is part of that evidence, but it should not be isolated and given a potentially decisive effect. Yet in England the rule is the other way round: the presumptions apply, and the onus will often lie on the transferee.[3]

[1] [1967] 2 AC 291.

[2] *Joaquin* v. *Hall* [1976] VR 788, a briefly reported case but accepted by Ford and Lee, *Principles of the Law of Trusts*, para. 2111.

[3] *Sheldon* v. *Davidson* [1968] 1 WLR 1083.

Distortion occurs in a more obvious way when resulting trusts are presumed to reflect the real intentions of parties who transfer personalty voluntarily. People do not think this way any more. The issue will only rarely come to the surface when a transaction is effected orally, but when this is not the case, presumptions can cause documents to be interpreted on the basis that they do not mean what they say. There is no justification for doing so. A share transfer that is properly executed should be presumed to be transferring full beneficial title for instance. A presumption of resulting trust is misleading, and not even supportable as a long-stop.[4] Documents should be construed according to their tenor. Moreover, no encouragement should be given to practices that favour half-truths. Draftsmen should aim at making documents self-sufficient. Thus there is merit in the Court of Appeal's decision in *Goodman* v. *Gallant*,[5] giving full weight to express declarations of trust and casting doubt on earlier precedent that subjected them too readily to re-interpretation.

The position becomes totally different when contributions to the purchase of real property, usually a family home, are made by a person who does not become a title-owner expressly, and those contributions are treated as indicia of an intended shared beneficial entitlement. Here the presumption of resulting trust is not a significant factor. It is part of the technique of equity that leads to beneficial entitlement being recognized, but it is the contributions and the facts surrounding them that are vital;[6] and due to that the presumption of resulting trust does not itself mislead.

Yet because the outdated technique of resulting trusts remains embedded in the law, an antidote is needed in the form of presumptions of advancement. But they do not date well either. There may have been a time when transfers and contributions towards a purchase of property did reflect obligations to dependants, and mothers did think differently from fathers, so that it could be said with some semblance of reality that the presumption of advancement represented a 'greater prima facie probability'[7] of what was actually meant than what was expressed in documents. But such days are past; giving is as often as not today dictated by tax considerations. The presumption of advancement is not sound as a technique, and only useful as a means of limiting

[4] Note the critical tone of Nourse LJ's comment in *McGrath* v. *Wallis* [1995] 2 FLR 114 at 122 that presumptions are only to be thought of as a last resort.

[5] [1986] Fam. 106. It is different if a deliberate decision is taken to put certain matters behind a curtain, as in some modern varieties of trusts.

[6] See *Baumgartner* v. *Baumgartner* (1987) 164 CLR 137.

[7] *Per* Dixon CJ in *Wirth* v. *Wirth* (1956) 98 CLR 228 at 237.

the damage flowing from the presumption of resulting trust. Attempts to modernize presumptions of advancement are of dubious validity also.[8]

It is of course true that a presumption will only rarely in itself determine the outcome of a case, for the weight of presumptions is in practice depreciated, the presumption of advancement giving way at the present time almost as readily as the presumption of resulting trust to more persuasive inferences drawn from the facts of a case.[9] But alleviation is no solution to the manifold problems that stem from the presumptions; piling illogic on illogic only causes more confusion and artificiality. There is a strong case for dispensing altogether with the presumption of resulting trust as an indicia of intent. The presumption of advancement would cease to be needed. Documents and acts could then be interpreted on the basis that they mean what they say and do.

In one area however presumptions remain potentially decisive: where an illegal purpose underlies a contribution towards the purchase, or a voluntary transfer, of property.[10] The result, as will be shown, is unsatisfactory. Moreover, the law is in danger of becoming increasingly complex as the courts struggle to avoid the consequences of the position. On this score an interesting comparison can be made between cases in the United Kingdom and Australia.

The first case I want to mention is *Blackburn* v. *Y. V. Properties*.[11] A solicitor, Cleary, controlled a private company which had purchased land for development. His aim was to build a hotel on it, but another developer had lodged an application for permission to build a hotel on land near it. So Cleary caused the land to be transferred to Blackburn, who agreed to oppose the application before a Planning Tribunal as an apparently disinterested party. The ruse seems to have succeeded; at any rate the planning application was turned down. Then Blackburn refused to re-transfer the land. A majority in the Full Court of Victoria held that he could be made to do so. That Cleary had caused the land to be vested in Blackburn for a purpose that involved deceiving the Planning Tribunal was immaterial. Blackburn had not paid for the land, in Victorian law a resulting trust arose, and the action could succeed simply on that basis. No evidence concerning the reason for vesting the land in Blackburn

[8] As in *Calverley* v. *Green* (1984) 155 CLR 242, *per* Gibbs CJ and *Nelson* v. *Nelson* (1995) 132 ALR 133.

[9] See for a recent example *McGrath* v. *Wallis*, n. 4 above.

[10] Issues of illegality arise elsewhere in the law but I cannot here go beyond the cases discussed and into other areas. No distinction is taken in this paper between transfer and contribution cases; they are discussed interchangeably by McHugh J for instance in *Nelson* v. *Nelson*, n. 8 above.

[11] [1980] VR 290.

need be given, so it could not be said that the plaintiff was in any way placing reliance on an illegal matter.

Tinsley v. *Milligan*[12] is to similar effect. A house purchase had been financed by Miss Tinsley and Miss Milligan jointly, but they had agreed that title should be placed in Miss Tinsley alone in order to facilitate the making of fraudulent claims on the Department of Social Security, from which claims they both benefited. But then they quarrelled, and Miss Tinsley claimed possession and absolute ownership of the house. Miss Milligan wished to establish that she had a share in the ownership of the house, and a majority in the House of Lords held that she was able to do so. It was sufficient that she could show that she had contributed to its purchase; there was no need to go beyond that into questions of why the title had been put into Miss Tinsley's name alone or on the purpose of the transaction. Miss Milligan could succeed without having to rely on the illegal aspect of the transaction. It was Miss Tinsley who would have to bring any illegal element into the open. A minority in the House of Lords however took a different view, holding that the issue was not just one of whether reliance had to be placed on an illegal element. The issue was one of policy; and if regard was had to policy, Miss Milligan should not receive the aid of the court and would have to forfeit her share of the house.

I dislike the approach of the majority. It appears to regard the accomplishment of the fraud as immaterial, and I do not think that is right. Moreover its emphasis on reliance places an undesirable premium on pleadings and on who has to give evidence of what; as if it were crucial when the first whiff of illegality emerged from the witness box. It can only encourage counsel asking questions in a simplistic form that will deceive no one, least of all the court. The matter becomes even more unsatisfactory when it is realized that the majority would have arrived at a contrary conclusion if a presumption of advancement had existed between Miss Milligan and Miss Tinsley. The presumption would then have had to be rebutted by Miss Milligan and, in Lord Browne-Wilkinson's view,[13] it would have been difficult for her to do so without bringing in evidence herself that would reveal the illegal aspect of the purchase. But if this is so, presumptions are decisive; and why should they be? The illegality is the same whether it has been engineered through a stranger or a dependant, and it is the illegality that would seem the more major consideration.

More recently, this potentially decisive impact of the presumptions was noted in *Tribe* v. *Tribe*;[14] and it cannot be said that the Court of Appeal gave it a great welcome.[15] Millett LJ[16] furthermore is unwilling to

[12] [1994] 1 AC 340. [13] *Ibid.* 372. [14] [1995] 4 All ER 236.
[15] See *per* Nourse LJ at 244. [16] At 254–7.

accept that implementation of an illegal purpose is irrelevant in resulting trust cases, postulating that in certain circumstances it will be relevant. He may very well be right, but the circumstances he postulates relate less to the illegality and the facts surrounding it than to the character of the evidence given; and if this route is followed, the law can only increase in complexity without what I see as the central issues being addressed.

The ratio in *Tribe* v. *Tribe* concerns a different point however—that of non-implementation of an illegal plan in circumstances where there had been a presumption of advancement. In Lord Browne-Wilkinson's view, a transferor or contributor will ordinarily experience difficulty in rebutting such a presumption without adverting to the underlying element of illegality. But the Court of Appeal's view is that he should not be prevented from leading evidence of his underlying intention if the plan has not been implemented. Thus Mr Tribe senior, who had transferred a controlling number of shares in a private company to one of his sons in order to give a false impression to creditors, was able to recover them from the son when he reached a settlement with the creditors, who had never even known of the intention to deceive them. In these circumstances, the fact that the plan to deceive them had been carried to the stage of transferring assets did not prevent their recovery. It would be otherwise, in Millett LJ's view,[17] if the deception had been material in procuring the settlement. Accomplishment of the illegal purpose in that way would be quite different in its effect.

The Court of Appeal regarded that conclusion as compatible with the law as laid down in *Tinsley* v. *Milligan*, and technically that may be right. But it is a strange result that non-implementation counts for so much in advancement cases, while in resulting trust cases its role is not central at all. The result also adds considerably to the complexity of the law; and there is the further practical difficulty that sufficiently identifying abandonment of an illegal plan poses problems, as can be seen in the Australian cases on the topic.[18]

I fear that United Kingdom law has taken a wrong turning. One is driven to the conclusion that the minority in *Tinsley* v. *Milligan* was right to place substance and policy above reliance and tactics. But it does not follow that the conclusion of the minority that Miss Milligan must forfeit her share is the right one. The majority's view leads to bad law. But the minority's view leads to unjust law. It is unjust to Miss Milligan and over-indulgent to Miss Tinsley.

[17] At 254.

[18] e.g. in *Perpetual Executors and Trustees Association* v. *Wright* (1917) 23 CLR 185 and *Martin* v. *Martin* (1959) 110 CLR 297. In the latter case at 305, Dixon CJ puts the issue in the form of whether a party has 'recanted' or 'virtuously refrained' from carrying his illegal plan to fruition: the latter in particular is not an easy factor to measure.

In these cases involving an illegal element, there is a need for a policy that will provide a better balance between various factors that are relevant. The issue is not just about reliance or implementation, let alone the presumptions. Such a policy seems wholly lacking, and I would like to advocate one. I am not however trying to resuscitate the 'public conscience' test that attracted some support in the Court of Appeal in *Tinsley* v. *Milligan*.[19] That test was developed from rather weak precedents and lacked specific qualities. Its unanimous rejection in the House of Lords was not surprising, though the rejection was distinctly summary.

The recent Australian case of *Nelson* v. *Nelson*[20] can serve to indicate many of the factors that I believe to be relevant. It was a case where an illegal purpose was implemented, and it is to such cases that this paper is principally directed. Mr and Mrs Nelson had a son Peter and a daughter Elizabeth. In 1987 Mrs Nelson was aged 66, Peter 37, and Elizabeth 33. In mid-1987, having returned from a period living overseas, Mr and Mrs Nelson owned no home of their own. But property prices were rising and it was decided in August of that year that a house at Petersham in Sydney should be bought at a cost of $145,000. The house would need renovating, but that was a job Peter was good at. It was not intended as a permanent family home, and a profit would be made on re-sale. Mr Nelson was entitled under the Defence Service Homes Act 1918 (Cth) to a war service loan which gave him the right to borrow money at a subsidised rate for purchase of a home. As his widow, Mrs Nelson would enjoy the same right. But it was not available if a residential property was already owned, so the Petersham property was put in the names of Peter and Elizabeth as joint tenants to ensure that Mr Nelson or, as his widow, Mrs Nelson, would be able to take advantage of the right when the time came to acquire a permanent home. Completion of the Petersham purchase took place in November 1987, just a few hours after Mr Nelson had died of cancer. When the renovations were complete, the house was put on the market but it proved difficult to sell; it was eventually sold in October 1990 for $400,000. In the meantime it was decided that the time had come to acquire a permanent home for Mrs Nelson, and a house at Paddington was acquired in August 1989 for $162,000. To assist with its purchase, Mrs Nelson had applied under the 1918 Act for a subsidized loan and received one for the maximum of $25,000 that was possible. Her application was submitted in July 1989 and had been prepared by Peter, though she had signed it herself. In it she answered 'no' to the question whether she owned any other residential property. But the answer was false. Mr and Mrs Nelson's joint bank account had been used

[19] [1992] Ch. 310.

[20] (1994) 33 NSWLR 740; (1995) 132 ALR 133.

when financing the Petersham purchase, and Mr Nelson's assets had passed to Mrs Nelson under his will. In these circumstances Mrs Nelson was to be treated as the provider of the funds for its purchase and its beneficial owner. By 1991 Peter and Elizabeth had quarrelled, and Elizabeth took issue with her mother and brother on a number of matters, including the proceeds of sale of the Petersham house that remained after a loan was repaid. Elizabeth claimed beneficially a half share of such proceeds, amounting (with interest) to $232,509. But Peter denied that either she or he had ever been entitled to a beneficial share in the property; beneficial ownership had always been in Mrs Nelson alone. At first instance it was found that this had indeed been the common intention of all parties throughout. But it was then held that Mrs Nelson's false statement in her application for a loan disentitled her from claiming her beneficial entitlement. The result was that she could not recover any part of the proceeds of sale from Elizabeth.

The New South Wales Court of Appeal affirmed the decision.[21] The Court first considered whether a presumption of advancement arose when property was given by a mother to a child, and adopted as ratio earlier judicial views that today it did. It therefore fell to Mrs Nelson to rebut the presumption. The Court held she was unable to do so without adverting to the illegal purpose that underlay putting the house into Peter's and Elizabeth's names. The Court looked to the substance of the matter, holding it to be artificial to let Mrs Nelson succeed on the basis that she could lead evidence to show the common intention as to beneficial ownership without having to reveal the significance of the evidence she adduced. The Court was not impressed by the niceties adopted by the majority in the House of Lords in *Tinsley* v. *Milligan*; and indeed seemed to think that the same approach should govern presumption of advancement and presumption of resulting trust cases (though that is difficult to reconcile with the decision in *Blackburn*, which is not discussed).

There is much to be said for the Court's view. But as with the conclusion reached by the minority in *Tinsley* v. *Milligan*, the result is dismaying. The Court puts great weight on the fact that the ruse of putting the Petersham property in the names of Peter and Elizabeth had succeeded and little on any other consideration. I do not think this is right. It is possible both to breed respect for the law and to do justice to litigants, without letting the law degenerate into discretion as a consequence.

A number of factors can be identified as of particular relevance when a court is considering whether or not to refuse relief to a party who had an illegal purpose in mind when he contributed to the purchase of or

[21] See particularly (1994) 33 NSWLR at 742 and 748–9.

voluntarily transferred property. Among them I would include: the relationship between the parties; the character of the illegality; whether the parties knew that what was being done was illegal; the extent to which the illegal element in the transaction was furthered; the relationship between the illegality and the relief sought; the consequences for both parties of refusing relief; the legitimacy of a double penalty; whether a statute was involved and a sanction prescribed; the policy of the law in relation to the particular statute and also more generally.

On the relationship of the parties, which is not just a matter of presumptions, there could for instance be an issue whether one party was under the dominance of the other. The issue is not relevant on the facts in *Nelson*, but it does not require much strength of imagination to see it as a possible variant of the facts in *Tinsley* v. *Milligan*, for Miss Tinsley was nearly twenty years younger than Miss Milligan and only 19 years of age when they met.

On the character of the illegality, there is a considerable difference between putting property in the name of another so as to (a) evade tax or mislead creditors (which is *Tribe*), (b) make a party to a matrimonial cause seem less affluent (alas not uncommon), (c) make an objection to a planning application at a hearing seem to come from someone who is disinterested (which is *Blackburn*), (d) obtain sums to which one is not entitled at all from a social security fund (which is *Tinsley* v. *Milligan*), (e) obtain a subsidy to which one is *prima facie* entitled despite a temporary[22] disqualification (which is *Nelson*).

On the knowledge of the parties, it is relevant to know whether both parties were aware, or unaware, of the illegality or that one was aware of it and the other not. In *Nelson*, it is not readily to be supposed that Elizabeth, who was probably the most astute of the family, was not as involved in the illegality as her mother and brother were.

On the issue of furthering the illegal purpose, it is material to distinguish cases where steps were taken to make the illegality achievable but nothing further was done, from cases where the illegal purposes was to a greater or lesser extent carried out. In *Nelson* it was wholly achieved.

On the place of the illegality in the transaction in *Nelson*, the link between the illegally obtained subsidy and putting the title away from Mrs Nelson is obvious. So the illegality was clearly relevant to a consideration of whether the court should recognize Mrs Nelson's beneficial entitlement or not.

On the consequences for the parties, it is necessary to appreciate that Elizabeth at the age of 41 receives a windfall of $230,000 while her mother at the age of 74 suffers a major reduction in her limited free

[22] The house was not retained for longer than was necessary to obtain a satisfactory selling price.

capital. Yet Mrs Nelson's gain, given that she received not a grant but only a loan repayable in any event, could not have exceeded the amount of the element of the subsidy on a loan of $25,000. The issue of a double penalty seems relevant.

If a statute is involved, it is necessary to consider whether its provisions shed any light on the enforcement or otherwise of obligations under civil law that become relevant. This is in fact the situation in *Nelson* itself. No criminal sanction was imposed under the 1918 Act (though one might have been attracted from legislation aimed at frauds against the Commonwealth more generally), but the Act included a provision enabling the Commonwealth to recover subsidies paid under it without entitlement.

A court that is deciding whether or not to refuse relief in a case involving an illegality should have all the facts of the case before it. The matter is not only one between the litigants. And the court should then weigh the factors that emerge as relevant before coming to a decision. Proceeding in this way is not a moral free-for-all; for only factors that are relevant are weighed. There is in fact less danger of a moral free-for-all in what is being proposed than exists under the present law. What I suspect happens as a result of our existing unsatisfactory rules is that moral considerations are taken into account but then concealed behind complex and artificial reasoning that is employed to conceal the fact. It would be wiser to base decisions more openly on grounds that are relevant. Thus I would prefer the decision in *Blackburn* to be justified on the ground that refusal of relief would have been out of proportion to the wrong committed rather than on the technical ground of a resulting trust; and the decision of the majority in *Tinsley* v. *Milligan* on the ground that a decision the other way would (*inter alia*) fail to recognize the joint nature of the criminal enterprise.

It might be thought desirable however to place this weighing of relevant factors within a more general principle. If so, one is at hand. It would be possible, taking *Tinsley* v. *Milligan* as the example, to argue in this way. Miss Tinsley claims the whole beneficial ownership and possession of the property in question; Miss Milligan replies (being more interested in its proceeds of sale presumably than in joint occupation) by claiming beneficial ownership of one half of it; Miss Tinsley responds by alleging that Miss Milligan can only establish her ownership of a half by relying on an illegality and will not be allowed to do so; Miss Milligan then asserts that the result would be an unjust enrichment of Miss Tinsley that the Court should reverse. Issue would be joined on the relevant factors under the head of unjust enrichment. Some would say, however, that to use unjust enrichment in this way would be to offend the purity of the concept. But I value its protean quality more.

To return to *Nelson* v. *Nelson*, it must now be clear that I think the case was wrongly decided in the New South Wales Court of Appeal. The decision was unjust to Mrs Nelson and unjustly enriched Elizabeth. If one weighs the sizeable windfall to Elizabeth, the small gain to Mrs Nelson, the ways in which the father, mother, and both children all played their parts in the scheme, the character of the illegality, and the right of the Commonwealth to recover the amount of subsidy wrongly secured, it seems harsh indeed to turn Mrs Nelson away from the seat of justice. And that is what this paper was intended to demonstrate when drafted in the autumn of 1995. But I knew then that the High Court had heard an appeal in the case. The Court's decision was handed down in November and I can now bring the paper up-to-date due to the kindness of Gummow J in sending me a copy of the reasons given by the Court when allowing the appeal. I would like to welcome the decision and comment on those reasons, so far as they fall within the ambit of this paper. The Court was unanimous in allowing the appeal, but four opinions were delivered.

The first thing to note is that the presumptions survive. Argument in the appeal centred on the presumption of advancement, and the technique of resulting trusts was not challenged. That puts the cart before the horse, and an opportunity to bring the law into line with reality was missed. McHugh J in particular recognizes that neither presumption may now accord with 'contemporaneous practices and modes of thought'.[23] The issue involves ordinary people who, however intelligent they are, would simply be baffled if they studied what the courts talk about in these cases. When an inference has ceased to reflect reality, as the presumption of resulting trust has, it should simply be abandoned as false. *Cessante ratione, cessat ipsa lex.* It reflects no credit on the law to continue to base itself on factual inferences that are untrue. The argument is also advanced[24] that conveyancers have relied on the presumptions, but I do not find it a convincing one. It is the presumption of resulting trust that is in question, and how often is a document of transfer that does not contain words excluding a resulting trust likely to be interpreted as creating one?

The consequence is that the courts will have to continue to battle with the embarrassing distinctions that disfigure the presumption of ad-

[23] At 184. Cf *Calverley* v. *Green*, n. 8 above, *per* Murphy J at 264–5, and Kirby P (now a Judge of the High Court) in *Brown* v. *Brown*, n. 24 below.

[24] At 184. It should also be noted that, at the time when the Petersham house was bought, authority to the effect that there was no presumption of advancement between mother and child had not been repudiated, though it had been questioned: see *Scott* v. *Pauly* (1917) 24 CLR 274 at 282, *per* Isaacs J; *Brown* v. *Brown* (1993) 31 NSWLR 582. Yet Mrs Nelson was made to rebut the presumption and, in the Court of Appeal, debarred from doing so. There is a high degree of unreality in these arguments based on supposed expectations.

vancement. In the context of parent and child, the judges can derive assistance from statutes as well as common sense in modernizing the presumption. But will the judges fare equally well when faced with the need to reconsider the distinctions at present drawn in this context between husbands and wives and *de facto* partners? They will no doubt make the best of a bad job, but it is a pity that the chance was not taken to recognize that the interpretation of transfers and contributions by reference to the relationship between the parties is flawed in principle.

Having decided that both presumptions had to remain, the High Court nevertheless avoided giving them the potentially decisive effect that they possess in the United Kingdom. The Court is unanimous that the majority in *Tinsley* v. *Milligan* was misguided in making the outcome in the case dependent on the presumptions. The matter is one of policy, and not to be approached on such a technical basis. It is disingenuous to ignore the underlying illegal element in the case of the presumption of resulting trust, but not in the case of the presumption of advancement. Arguments concerning who has to give evidence of what, and when a party has to rely on an illegal aspect in a transaction, then lose their significance.[25] The Court is also unanimous in thinking that it is not appropriate to adopt a rigid rule to deal with the varied questions of entitlement and enforcement that can arise when transactions contain an illegal element. Quite a number of matters need to be taken into consideration before a decision is reached, and the minority in *Tinsley* v. *Milligan* was being simplistic in treating the matter as if it were just one of clean hands. Beyond this point however, the reasoning in the judgments diverges in emphasis.

In a joint judgment, Deane and Gummow JJ look principally to the 1918 Act for guidance on the right answer. They give weight to the power that the Act confers on the Commonwealth to recover a subsidy obtained without entitlement. In their view it would not be right, in addition to Mrs Nelson's liability to return the amount of subsidy received, to cause her to forfeit her beneficial entitlement to the proceeds of sale of the Petersham property. It was not part of the policy of the Act to make her do so, the trust was not illegal in itself, and no justification existed for such a harsh penalty. The judgment provides little indication, however, of how they would decide cases such as *Tinsley* v. *Milligan* when no statute affords the guidance that the 1918 Act provided. But the judgment contains other points of importance. They reject treating cases involving illegal elements on a different basis according to whether the

[25] In general the High Court seems to be in agreement with the Court of Appeal's view of these matters: see in particular Toohey J at 176. But note Dawson J's rather different approach at 165–6. The Court is able, of course, to utilize the finding made at first instance as to the parties' real intentions.

law of property or the law of contract is involved for instance; and observe that more than the interests of the litigants is at stake when a case involves an illegality.[26]

Dawson J places less emphasis on the statute, and attaches importance to ensuring that problems concerning obligations that arise within transactions containing an illegal element are solved by common law and equity in a similar way. He draws attention to the fact that the two parties to a case of this nature may share the illegal intention. He also points out that, until her application for a subsidy was made, Mrs Nelson would have had no difficulty in establishing her beneficial entitlement to the Petersham property, and that her claim to its proceeds of sale is not linked to her wrongdoing 'in any direct or necessary way'.[27]

Toohey and McHugh JJ both place reliance on the statute, but their judgments may provide more guidance on how the courts could choose to balance out the considerations that are relevant when no statute is involved. McHugh J suggests that 'principles'[28] can be employed to indicate what the courts' response should be to an illegal element in a case before them. It is not necessary, in order to have a flexible response to illegal elements, to resort to the 'unstructured discretion' that he sees as vitiating the view of the majority of the Court of Appeal in *Tinsley* v. *Milligan*.[29] He looks at the consequences for the parties of refusing relief, including the factor of a windfall gain, and concludes that a penalty should not be disproportionate to the seriousness of a breach. He also comments on the futility of penalties as deterrents in this area.[30] Toohey J, who regards the character of the illegality and the circumstances in which it occurred as significant, also refers to 'enrichment of one party at the expense of another'[31] as among the considerations the courts should take into account.

What then is the outcome for Australian law of the High Court's decision? It is, I fear, less easy to say what the law concerning illegality within transactions is based on than what it will not be based on. In the context of trusts, it will not be based on presumptions; and consequently, decisions will not turn on points of pleading and evidence. That could be the consequence, too, in areas where common law is involved. Policy considerations are likely to prevail over technical considerations. But how will that approach become reflected in practical terms?

Where a statute gives compelling guidance, as in *Nelson* v. *Nelson*,

[26] At 148. [27] At 167.
[28] At 192. Are such principles very different from the factors identified at 40 above?
[29] N. 19 above. McHugh J's view is to be found at 192.
[30] At 130, quoting from Millett LJ in *Tribe* v. *Tribe*, n. 14 above, at 258.
[31] At 180. The joint judgment of Deane and Gummow JJ, at 155, also contains a reference to unjust enrichment.

there is no problem. But what is the position when statute law provides less guidance or no statute is relevant? I am loth to think that the High Court's decision lacks impact where that it so. Most, if not all, of the factors identified in this paper as relevant to cases involving an illegality, in the trusts context at any rate, are mentioned in the High Court's judgments. I do not see why they should cease to be relevant when there is no statute to provide guidance or the guidance is inconclusive.

But mention of the factors is scattered among the judgments and not unified. Thus the question that to my mind arises is whether a subsequent court will want to connect them with each other and bring them under some more general principle. This is what I believe should happen. They could underpin the court's use of that principle, which could well be unjust enrichment. It then becomes interesting to speculate on how a case like *Tinsley* v. *Milligan* would now be decided in Australia. Earlier precedent[32] placing weight on non-implementation would suggest that Miss Milligan would lose. But it could be argued today that the degree of implementation or accomplishment of an illegal purpose is only one among a number of factors, albeit a strong factor, that have to be taken into account in cases both of presumptions of advancement and resulting trust. On that basis, the result in *Tinsley* v. *Milligan* could well be the same in Australia as it was in the United Kingdom.

But what is to be done about the UK law on the subject? So far as trust law is concerned, I do not think that we will easily escape the consequences of having embedded the presumptions more deeply into the law. But it may be possible to look beyond that and deal with *Tinsley* v. *Milligan* in this way. First, the ratio of the case could be isolated as one bearing, if unsatisfactorily, on resulting trusts. But then secondly, weight could be placed on the valuable part of the case, namely that there was rejection of the minority's view that a degree of indiscriminate injustice[33] has to be accepted in this area. That aspect of the case could also be projected into the common law side of the subject.

Finally, how did Mrs Nelson fare in the end? And here the High Court divided three to two. Dawson and Toohey JJ would simply have allowed the appeal, enabling her to recover the whole of the proceeds of sale of the Petersham property from her daughter. But Deane, McHugh, and Gummow JJ thought that the order of the Court should take account of the sum representing the illegally gained subsidy. In effect they gave Mrs Nelson a choice, either to repay that sum (when quantified) to the Commonwealth and recover the whole proceeds of sale from Elizabeth; or to

[32] See n. 18 above.
[33] As envisaged by Lord Goff at 364.

leave that sum with Elizabeth and recover only the remainder. She was given until 9 January to make the choice so, when this was written, the case was not quite at an end. But given the relationships prevalent within the Nelson family, I do not have much doubt of the outcome.

3

The Irreducible Core Content of Trusteeship

DAVID HAYTON

INTRODUCTION

At the core of the trust concept is a duty of confidence imposed upon a trustee in respect of particular property and positively enforceable in a Court of Equity by a person.[1] As Lord Evershed MR has stated,[2] '[n]o principle, perhaps, has greater sanction or authority behind it than the general proposition that a trust by English law, not being a charitable trust, in order to be effective must have ascertained or ascertainable beneficiaries.' The beneficiaries' rights to enforce the trust and make the trustees account for their conduct with the correlative duties of the trustees to the beneficiaries are at the core of the trust. A beneficiary will be a beneficiary under a fixed trust with a vested or contingent entitlement to income or capital (as the case may be) or a beneficiary under a discretionary trust with an entitlement[3] to put his case to be considered for a distribution of income or capital (as the case may be) by the trustees who must make such a distribution to one or more of the discretionary beneficiaries[4] (subject to any temporary power or duty to accumulate income for the benefit of capital beneficiaries[5]). Exceptionally, charitable trusts for purposes (necessarily benefiting the public) are enforceable by the Crown as *parens patriae* via the Attorney-General or the Charity Commissioners.[6]

[1] Underhill and Hayton, *Law of Trusts and Trustees* (15th edn.), 3; Lewin, *Law of Trusts* (16th edn.), 1; Hanbury and Martin, *Modern Equity* (14th edn.), 46; *Morice* v. *Bishop of Durham* (1804) 9 Ves. 399, 405; *Re Endacott* [1960] Ch. 232; *Re Denley's Trust Deed* [1969] 1 Ch. 373. This paper is concerned with the internal trustee–beneficiary relationship and not with the external relations of trustees with third-party creditors. To protect such third parties' right of subrogation to the trustee's right of indemnity (an equitable lien) against the trust fund a settlor's purported exclusion of the trustee's right of indemnity probably ought not to be effective against third parties not reimbursed by the trustee.

[2] [1960] Ch. 232, 246.

[3] Even the object of a discretionary power who is aware of the power is entitled to put his case to the trustees: *Re Manisty's Settlement* [1974] Ch. 17, 25; *Re Gulbenkian's Settlements (No 2)* [1969] 2 All ER 1173, 1179.

[4] The discretionary trustees must distribute the income within a reasonable period and a beneficiary will have a right to be considered for an income payment until all such income has been distributed to the beneficiaries.

[5] A duty to accumulate income for an accumulation period will be enforceable by the capital beneficiaries benefiting thereby.

[6] See now Charities Act 1993, ss. 1–20, 24–35.

As a matter of property law, in the rare case where all the beneficiaries are of full age and capacity and between them absolutely entitled to the whole trust property they have a power,[7] if unanimous, to terminate the trust and divide the property between themselves as they agree.[8] Otherwise, the trustees are bound to account to the trust beneficiaries for what they have done with the trust property, whether in their administrative, managerial role or in their distributive, dispositive role. The trustees will be accountable to the beneficiaries for profits made or losses flowing from a breach of fiduciary duty, except to the extent that a clause in the trust instrument ousts an otherwise applicable duty or exempts the trustees from accounting for profits or losses arising in breach of fiduciary duty.

In recent years, fears of increasingly litigious beneficiaries spurred on by their lawyers have led settlors and trustees to consider how far they can go in restricting beneficiaries' rights to information and trustees' potential liabilities. They can place reliance on the facilitative liberal laissez-faire approach of English law[9] that allows a settlor to generate his local law for his autonomous trust so long as it is not inconsistent[10] with, or repugnant[11] to, the very trust relationship that he is purporting to create or uncertain or otherwise administratively unworkable[12] or contrary to some rule of public policy.[13]

It thus becomes necessary to consider what is the irreducible core

[7] In Hohfeld's terminology: J. W. Harris (1971) 87 *LQR* 31, 62–3.

[8] *Saunders* v. *Vautier* (1841) 4 Beav. 115, *Stephenson* v. *Barclays Bank* [1975] 1 WLR 88.

[9] See S. Gardner, *An Introduction to the Law of Trusts* 13–14, 35, 38–9; *Wilkins* v. *Hogg* (1861) 31 LJ Ch. 41, 43; *McLean* v. *Burns Phelps Trustee Co. Pty. Ltd* [1985] 2 NSWR 623, 640–1, *Midland Bank Trustee (Jersey) Ltd* v. *Federated Pension Services* (Jersey CA, unreported, 21 Dec. 1995); *Armitage* v. *Nurse* (unreported, Jacob J. (High Ct.), 17 July 1995); *Roywest Trust Corporation (Bahamas) Ltd* v. *Savannah NV* (unreported, Telford Georges CJ of Bahamas, 22 July 1987); express choice-of-law possibilities under Recognition of Trusts Act 1987.

[10] A settlor cannot convert what is an equitable charge or a debtor–creditor relationship into a trust merely by calling it a trust. Thus, the right of the 'trustee' to mix 'trust' moneys with his own and use them as he likes subject to an obligation to repay a similar amount of money is inconsistent with any trust, so preventing one arising.

[11] Where there is duly segregated trust property vested in a trustee, otherwise than simply as security for a debt, and it is clear that a bare trust for the settlor was not intended to be created nor beneficial ownership in the trustee, then any exclusion or exemption clause the effect of which would be to create such a bare trust or such beneficial ownership will be struck out as repugnant to the fundamental nature of the trust: *Midland Bank Trustee (Jersey) Ltd* v. *Federated Pension Services*, n. 9 above. As stated by the Law Commission Consultation Paper No 124 on Fiduciary Duties, para. 3.3.6, 'It is clear that trustees are subject to a core level of duty from which they cannot be exempted.'

[12] e.g. *McPhail* v. *Doulton* [1971] AC 424, 457; *R.* v. *District Auditor, West Yorkshire Metropolitan CC* [1986] RVR 24, *Re Kolb's WT* [1962] Ch. 531.

[13] e.g. the rule against remoteness of vesting or against perpetual purpose trusts or the rule against a settlor effectively settling property on himself determinable upon bankruptcy.

content of trusteeship of property that sets limits to the free will of the settlor.

RIGHTS TO INFORMATION

As a necessary incident of the trustee–beneficiary relationship at the core of the trust the trustee is under a duty to find and pay a beneficiary entitled to an income or capital payment, thereby making such beneficiary aware that he is a beneficiary.[14] In the case of a discretionary trust, since the beneficiary's entitlement to put his case to the trustees for the exercise of their discretion in his favour is of no effect unless he is aware of it, and since he cannot be expected to become aware of it unless the trustees draw it to his attention it must surely be a necessary incident of the trustee–beneficiary relationship that the trustee must be under a duty to take reasonable steps[15] to make a discretionary beneficiary aware that he be such.[16] Knowledge of the trust is necessary to make the trust effectual with the trustees being accountable to the beneficiaries for their stewardship of the property: unaccountability to the beneficiaries arising from the trustees not letting them know that they are beneficiaries is inconsistent with, and repugnant to, the purposes for which the settlor transferred the trust property to the trustees or the fundamental requirement of accountability to beneficiaries before there can be duties of trusteeship.[17] Thus beneficiaries, even if discretionary, have a right to information revealing what the trustees have done with the trust property,[18] though not the reasons[19] for the exercise of distributive powers in favour of beneficiaries.

The essential ingredient of trusteeship is the duty to account which affords the beneficiaries a correlative right to have the court enforce the

[14] *Hawkesley* v. *May* [1956] 1 QB 304, 322; *Burrows* v. *Walls* (1855) 3 De G M & G 233, 253; *Brittlebank* v. *Goodwin* (1868) LR 5 Eq. 545, 550.

[15] These will require a businesslike approach depending on the size of the class and the extent to which a sub-class may be regarded as the primary object of the settlor's bounty cf. *Re Manisty's Settlement* [1974] Ch. 17, 25; *Hartigan Nominees Pty. Ltd* v. *Rydge* (1992) 29 NSWLR 405, 432; *Re Baden's Deed Trusts* [1973] Ch. 9, 20, 27.

[16] Cf. *Scally* v. *Southern Health & Social Services Board* [1992] 1 AC 294, 306–7.

[17] Cf. *Hawkins* v. *Clayton* (1988) 164 CLR 539, 553. A clause directing the trustees not to inform any discretionary beneficiary that he be such unless so directed by the settlor or the protector should either negate the trust or more likely, be regarded as repugnant to the trust: such a person should only be made the object of a power.

[18] *Re Londonderry's Settlement* [1964] Ch. 594; *Chaine-Nickson* v. *Bank of Ireland* [1976] IR 393; *Spellson* v. *George* (1987) 11 NSWLR 300, 315; *Lemos* v. *Coutts & Co.* [1992–3] CILR 460; *West* v. *Lazard Bros (Jersey) Ltd* [1987–8] JLR 414; *A.G. of Ontario* v. *Stavro* (1995) 119 DLR (4th) 750.

[19] *Re Londonderry's Settlement*, n. 18 above, *Wilson* v. *Law Debenture Trust Corp.* [1995] 2 All ER 337; *Hartigan Nominees Pty. Ltd* v. *Rydge*, n. 15 above.

trustees' fundamental obligation to account. Where there are beneficiaries with such correlative right so that there is a trust, do objects of a fiduciary power of appointment have a right to be informed that they are such objects and then have a right to make the trustees account, so providing all relevant information about their stewardship of the trust property? It would seem not.[20] Such rights are not crucial to underpinning the trust obligation because the beneficiaries entitled in default of exercise of the power have the requisite rights supporting the correlative duty of the trustees that is at the core of the trust obligation.

Thus, Templeman J, in discussing a fiduciary power in favour of the settlor's relations and the employees of the settlor's company where the trustees consider but decide not to exercise the power or exercise it only in favour of the settlor's children, stated:[21]

> During that period the existence of the power may not be disclosed to any relation or employee and the trustees may not seek or receive any information concerning any relation or employee. In my judgment it cannot be said that the trustees in those circumstances have committed a breach of trust and that they ought to have advertised the power or looked beyond the persons who are most likely to be the objects of the bounty of the settlor. The trustees are, of course, at liberty to make further enquiries but cannot be compelled to do so. . . . If a person within the ambit of the power is aware of its existence he can require the trustees to consider exercising the power, and in particular, to consider a request on his part for the power to be exercised in his favour. The trustees must consider this request, and if they decline to do so or can be proved to have omitted to do so, then the aggrieved person may apply to the court which may remove the trustees and appoint others in their place. This, as I understand it, is the only right and only remedy[22] of any object of the power.

Exceptionally, so as to give effect to the implicit wishes of the settlor, it would seem that if the ultimate beneficiary entitled in default of appointment will not be ascertainable until the end of the trust (e.g.

[20] However, in *Spellson* v. *George*, n. 18 above, it was held that objects of a power had the same rights to information as beneficiaries of a discretionary trust but, in context, the settlor could have been regarded as impliedly conferring such rights on the objects of the power primarily intended to benefit from expected exercises of the trustees' powers. Further see second following paragraph in text (after citation from Templeman J).

[21] *Re Manisty's Settlement*, n. 15 above, 25.

[22] This still seems the position for someone who is merely the object of a power (see n. 27 below) as opposed to a beneficiary under a trust in whose favour extra powers may be exercised e.g. powers of maintenance or advancement (*Re Lofthouse* (1885) 29 Ch. D 921, *Klug* v. *Klug* [1918] 2 Ch. 67) or of augmenting pensions (*Mettoy Pension Trustees Ltd* v. *Evans* [1991] 2 All ER 513, where at 549 Warner J opined that Lord Wilberforce's views in *McPhail* v. *Doulton*, n. 12 above, 456–7 as to ways for the court to execute a discretionary trust could generally be applied to carry out discretionary fiduciary powers and thus he exercised the power to augment pensions where (i) it was impossible for such power to be exercised because the employer-trustee was in liquidation and the liquidator was in an impossible conflict-of-interest situation and (ii) the beneficiaries had earned their rights and expectations). Further see n. 27 below.

settlor's issue alive at the end of the perpetuity period or such charitable organizations as the trustees shall decide upon at the end of the perpetuity period) then pragmatically, those objects of the power that are the primary objects of the settlor's bounty within the perpetuity period should have the right to make the trustees account and provide information as to their stewardship. Thus, in a trust conferring upon the trustees power to accumulate income or to appoint income or capital to the settlor's issue (or to a spouse or cohabitee of a descendant who becomes bankrupt) and, subject thereto, directing distribution at the expiry of a co-extensive perpetuity and accumulation period[23] amongst such of the issue then alive or such then existing charities as the trustees select in their absolute discretion, issue or a spouse or co-habitee thereof to whom a payment has been made[24] will be entitled to 'police' the trust and make the trustees account for their stewardship[25] unless the settlor reveals a contrary intention. After all, such a contrary intention is not repugnant to the trust concept, accountability to the default beneficiary sufficing to create the fundamental trust obligation.[26]

It is, therefore, submitted that a settlor can validly insert a clause in his trust instrument to emphasize that the objects of a power have no right to be informed that they are objects and no right to obtain information from the trustees as to their stewardship of the trust property or otherwise to make the trustees account for their trusteeship. It suffices that the default beneficiary alone has a right to make the trustees account and to impeach any exercise of their fiduciary power that is in bad faith or perverse or irrelevant to any sensible expectation of the settlor,[27] ex-

[23] Many jurisdictions have co-extensive perpetuity and accumulation periods, as did England before panicked into the Thellusson Act 1800.

[24] Ordinarily, receipt of trust property by an object of a power should not make him a beneficiary for the purposes of having a right to information, etc. In a trust a power to add persons to the class of beneficiaries will if exercised make the added person a beneficiary with rights to information etc.

[25] Cf. *Spellson* v. *George*, n. 18 above, 315–16.

[26] Even in a 'blind' trust there will ultimately be accountability once the sensitive period of office of the settlor is over or once a contingent ultimate beneficiary is ascertained at the end of the trust period.

[27] See *McPhail* v. *Doulton*, n. 12 above, 441, where Lord Hodson states, 'Whether the trust is discretionary or not the court must be in a position to control its execution in the interests of the objects of the trust. Where there is a mere power entirely different considerations arise. The trust in default controls and he to whom the trust results in default of exercise of the power is in practice the only one competent to object to a wrongful exercise of the power by the donee' and Lord Guest states (445) 'The court apart from a mala fide exercise of the power has no control over the exercise of the power. If it is not exercised the fund goes to those entitled in default.' In *Lutheran Church of Australia* v. *Farmers' Co-operative Trustees Ltd* (1970) 121 CLR 628, 639 Windeyer J states 'If it is a power the court cannot dictate to the trustees whether it should be exercised or not exercised. That discretion is committed to them', though going on to point out that if trustees refuse to consider the exercise of the power the court will remove them at the instigation of objects of the power.

cept that an object of a power, who is aware that he is such, can insist that he be considered for an appointment and seek the removal of the trustees if they refuse to consider whether or not to exercise the power.

In the case of a discretionary trust, particularly for a large class of discretionary beneficiaries e.g. for the settlor's issue, the settlor's other relations, employees of the settlor's company or any company of which the settlor is a director, the question arises whether the trust obligation can be sufficiently underpinned by an obligation to account to the primary beneficiaries of the settlor's bounty, so as to justify a court upholding an express direction of the settlor that only issue are to be informed of their rights and to have a right to information and to make the trustees account for their trusteeship. It is submitted that this is an attempt to convert a discretionary trust for a large class into a discretionary trust for a small class with a discretionary power in favour of a larger class,[28] so that the settlor's direction should be ignored as repugnant to the discretionary trust for a large class. He cannot derogate from the trustee's duty to take reasonable steps to make discretionary beneficiaries aware that they be such, though he can indicate what he considers to be reasonable steps, e.g. searching for close relatives but only putting an advert annually up on a works notice board or in a Christmas newsletter.

TRUST DOCUMENTS AND LETTERS OF WISHES

The beneficiaries' rights to inspect trust documents are now seen as better based not on equitable proprietary rights but on the beneficiaries' rights to make the trustees account for their trusteeship.[29] Thus, beneficiaries under fixed or discretionary trusts have the right to see all documents relating to the management and administration of the trust by the trustees and to the distributive function of the trustees[30] except to the extent that such documents would reveal the reasons for the exercise of the trustees' sensitive discretions[31] or are confidential e.g. letters between trustees and a beneficiary relating to the beneficiary's personal needs or a letter of wishes from the settlor to his trustees if expressly or impliedly confidential.[32]

[28] A well-advised settlor will, of course, create only a discretionary power for the larger class intended as reserve recipients of his bounty.

[29] *Hartigan Nominees Pty. Ltd* v. *Rydge*, n. 15 above; *A.G. of Ontario* v. *Stavro*, n. 18 above (beneficiaries of unadministered residuary estate legally and beneficially owned by executor subject to fiduciary duties); Ford and Lee, *Principles of the Law of Trusts* (2nd edn.), 425.

[30] See n. 18 above. Exact rights will vary depending upon whether the beneficiary is interested in income or in capital.

[31] See n. 19 above and J. D. Davies (1995) 7 *Bond. LR* 5.

[32] *Hartigan Nominees Pty. Ltd* v. *Rydge*, n. 15 above; *Tierney* v. *King* [1983] 2 Qd. R 580, *Re Londonderry's Settlement*, n. 18 above.

However, a settlor cannot, by purporting to make all trust documents (e.g. the trust instrument, trust accounts, documentary evidence of title to trust assets) confidential to the trustees and not to be disclosed to the beneficiaries (except during the course of litigation[33] when one party has a right to discovery of the other's documents that are relevant to the dispute[34]), oust the accountability of the trustees that is fundamental to the very existence of the trust. Such an overwhelming confidentiality clause would either be ignored as repugnant to the trust intended to be created by the settlor or, indeed, construed as confidential to the trustees and the settlor to whom alone the trustees are intended to be accountable so that a trust exclusively in his favour would arise.

The settlor, surely, cannot require his trustees to withhold the information without which the beneficiaries cannot vindicate the rights that the settlor purported to give them in his trust instrument.[35] He cannot wholly give with one hand and wholly take away with the other[36] if the court finds a genuine intention to give. However, there is no reason why a settlor-beneficiary while he holds a sensitive public office should not place his investments in the hands of trustees and for the duration of that office effectively give up his right to information about trust investments. Indeed, it seems a settlor-beneficiary can by contract forgo some rights to information from the trustee,[37] though regulatory rules as to minimum information rights may then be imposed in the public interest, as in the pensions trusts context.[38]

[33] There are professional restraints on lawyers pleading and particularizing that the trustees did not act in good faith or otherwise acted in breach of trust without *prima facie* evidence of such; hostile litigation will be struck out if it is merely an attempt to go fishing in the hope that something will turn up to justify the claims made.

[34] Much latitude is afforded: *Compagnie Financière et Commerciale* v. *Peruvian Guano Co.* (1882) 11 QBD 55, 63; generally, see Matthews and Malek, *Discovery* (1992).

[35] A non-binding letter of wishes (as opposed to a letter of wishes intended to prevail over a sham part of a trust instrument) does not confer any rights on the beneficiaries and so should not rank as a trust document. It is not intended to be futile but to indicate (*prima facie* and subject to changing circumstances) the purposes for which the trustees are supposed in a responsible way to exercise their discretionary powers (*Re Hay's ST* [1981] 3 All ER 786, 792) so it must be disclosed in the discovery process of litigation. Until then, beneficiaries should have no right to see it, whether because it is not a trust document or, if it is, it is impliedly confidential if given only to the trustees.

[36] Cf. in the contractual context *MacRobertson Miller Airline Services* v. *Commr. of State Taxation* (1976) 50 ALJR 348, 351 and in the property context *Green* v. *Ashco Horticulturist Ltd* [1966] 2 All ER 232, 239. A clause in the trust instrument automatically terminating a beneficiary's interest if he seeks by court action to make the trustee account should be struck out as repugnant to the interest granted and as an attempt to oust the jurisdiction of the court, though a provision making his interest terminate or empowering the trustees to terminate his interest if he seeks to impeach the trust and recover assets by virtue of forced heirship rights under the *lex successionis* of the deceased should be valid: *Rhodes* v. *Muswell Hill Land Co.* (1861) 29 Bev. 560, *Re Williams* [1912] 1 Ch. 399.

[37] *Tierney* v. *King*, n. 32 above.

[38] e.g. Pension Schemes Act 1993, ss. 113, 114, 115 and Pensions Act 1995, s. 41 and regs. thereunder; Australian Superannuation Industry (Supervision) Act 1993 and regs. thereunder.

USE OF PROTECTOR AS CUT-OFF DEVICE

Use of a 'protector' (or 'committee' or 'board') with lesser or greater powers of direction or veto is becoming increasingly popular. Can a settlor therefore use a protector as the accountable person so as to avoid the inconvenience of the trustees being troubled by 'irritating' beneficiaries? Since the settlor intends the benefit of his trust to be not for the protector but for the beneficiaries the core right to obtain information about the trustees' stewardship must be held by the protector as a fiduciary:[39] any attempt expressly to state that his rights and powers are purely personal to him for his own benefit would surely be ignored as repugnant to the nature of his irreducible core function.[40] Thus, the beneficiaries would have a right to obtain information from the trustees joining the protector as co-defendant if need be.

Would it help the settlor and beneficiaries if the trustees were expressly accountable to the protector alone, unless the beneficiaries could establish on a balance of probabilities (or a *prima facie* case) that the protector was acting in bad faith, whereupon the trustees would become accountable to the beneficiaries? It is thought not. After all, how can the beneficiaries realistically hope to establish on a balance of probabilities (or a *prima facie* case of) bad faith if they have no means of finding out anything that has been going on? The substance of the matter is that the point of such a clause is to prevent the beneficiaries from having any effective rights and so it is repugnant to the original intention to confer equitable rights upon the beneficiaries.

EXPRESS OUSTER OF ACCOUNTABILITY AS TO SOME PROPERTY

Hayim v. *Citibank*[41] is a facilitative Privy Council decision revealing that in special circumstances minimal accountability may subsist for a

[39] On usual fiduciary role of protector see J. Mowbray QC (1995) 5 *OTPR* 151, D. Hartnett and W. Norris [1995] *Private C B* 109, Underhill and Hayton, *Law of Trusts & Trustees* (15th edn.), 23–5.

[40] The terms of the trust instrument and the circumstances when the trust is created (e.g. nature of major investment, position held by original protector) will be relevant as to whether powers are personal or fiduciary and whether the fiduciary duty is greater than merely a duty to act in good faith. If the inherent nature of the protector's function (e.g. to make trustees account so as to look after the beneficiaries' interests or to appoint a new trustee as replacement for the existing trustee) relates to management of the trust property for the beneficiaries' benefit then any clause stating such functions or powers are only personal and not fiduciary should be disregarded as repugnant to the core duty of the protector. Where the protectorship is intended to be an enduring office then the Isle of Man High Court has held that the court has an inherent jurisdiction to appoint a protector: *Steele* v. *Paz Ltd*, unreported, 10 Oct. 1995, Isle of Man appeal (P. W. Smith QC and T. B. Hegarty QC) from acting Deemster.

[41] [1987] AC 730.

period. To avoid death-duty problems and putting his elderly brother and sister, A and M, (92 and 87 years old when the testator died) at the mercy of the beneficiaries under his will, the testator directed in respect of a Hong Kong house which he subjected to a trust for sale (with power to postpone sale) and which was occupied by A and M, '[m]y executors and trustees shall have no responsibility or duty with respect to such house . . . [their] only duty and responsibility shall arise upon receipt of proceeds of said residence or upon the death of the survivor of A and M whichever shall first occur.' The provision was 'understandable and explicable' and was designed to enable A and M, though not beneficiaries, to remain in the home rent-free so long as the trustee saw fit. 'If clause 10 were exploited for any other purpose the beneficiaries could complain and the court could find that [the trustee] had not properly exercised the discretion conferred on it to postpone sale either in the interests of the beneficiaries or of A and M.'[42] Thus, if the power to benefit A and M was used to benefit the trustees they would be accountable to the beneficiaries, as would fully occur on the death of the survivor of A and M.

Of course, *Hayim* concerned only a small part of the trust property. At the other extreme one often sees attempts to oust the accountability of trustees in large measure in respect of a controlling shareholding in a trading or an investment company which may represent virtually all the assets of the trust. Such attempts start by purporting to exclude any duty to make inquiry as to the running of the company or to interfere therein unless the trustees have actual knowledge that the company is being run dishonestly or by a person suffering from mental incapacity. The problem remains that a trustee still has a power to inquire and to intervene and is required[43] 'to be prudent and exercise the degree of care he would in conducting his own affairs but mindful, when making investment decisions, that he is dealing with another's property', while 'a professional person, a trust corporation, held out as an expert will be expected to display the degree of skill and care and diligence such an expert would have'.

To deal with this problem one can insert a further clause such as:

> irrespective of the position under the company law applicable to any company in which the trustees have a controlling shareholding, the trustees must treat themselves and be regarded as having no power to inquire into or intervene in the affairs of any such company unless it comes to their actual knowledge that the affairs of the company are being run dishonestly or by a person suffering from mental incapacity and must also treat themselves and be regarded as having no power to take steps to ascertain whether or not the affairs of the company

[42] *Ibid.* 746.
[43] *Per* Lord Nicholls (1995) 9 TLI 71, 75–6.

are being run dishonestly or by a person suffering from mental incapacity, so that they are entitled and bound to assume that the affairs of the company are being run honestly and by a person of full capacity until the contrary comes to their actual knowledge.

Are the trustees then, in substance, under any real duty to beneficiaries in respect of such property so as to give rise to a trust obligation, especially if the company is run by the settlor or by his nominee and no dividends are declared, the company making loans and gifts to persons, some of whom happen to be beneficiaries under the trust? It is too easy for the trustee from the outset to let the settlor (or his nominee) run the company as he likes so that the trust is alleged to be a sham. To avoid such an allegation it seems that the trustees need consciously (with some written evidence) to consider whether or not to exercise their controlling shareholding power. This will require them to make inquiries to ascertain whether or not there is any factual basis to remove the settlor or his nominee from running the company, thereby negating much of the point of the clause and indicating that the purported effect of much of the clause is repugnant to the concept of trusteeship.

USE OF THE SETTLOR OR PROTECTOR TO RELEASE TRUSTEES FROM LIABILITY

Can trustees be protected by the settlor reserving to himself an overriding power to release the trustees from any liability, such power binding the beneficiaries, and being regarded simply as making their interests defeasible or revocable at the whim of the settlor? It is thought not. A trust revocable by the settlor or a trust defeasible by the settlor exercising a general power in favour of himself or a special power in favour of someone else is different in concept from a trust created by S in favour of X, Y, and Z subject to X, Y, and Z not being entitled to sue the trustees for a breach of trust whenever S decides they cannot sue the trustees.

The latter amounts to a bare trust for S, to whom alone the trustees are accountable, with a power to benefit X, Y, and Z: neither X nor Y nor Z can have a right against the trustees if the so-called 'right' ceases to be a right whenever S decrees.[44] If the trustees are really only accountable to S, then no trust exists in favour X, Y, and Z to whom the trustees are not accountable.

Similar arguments apply if the settlor conferred the above overriding power on a protector.

[44] See n. 36 above.

EXCLUSION OF DUTIES

Exclusion of a duty is different from exemption from liability for breach of duty because it prevents any breach of duty from arising, so there can be no question of removing a trustee for breach of duty, which may arise where an exemption clause simply exempts a trustee from liability for breach of duty.

As already seen, the fundamental interrelated core duties to disclose information and trust documents and to account to the beneficiaries for the trustees' stewardship of the trust property, so as to be liable for losses or profits in relation thereto, cannot be excluded. However, duties to avoid a conflict of interest may be excluded,[45] while where investment is concerned the degree of care of a gratuitous trustee or a paid professional trustee (already adverted to[46]) can be diminished.

Clearly, a settlor who has just won £10 million in the National Lottery can transfer £5 million to professional trustees (on discretionary trusts for himself and his spouse and issue) under a duty to speculate recklessly with it with intent to treble it or lose it all in a five-year period on the basis that the £5 million is money that a sole beneficial owner can well afford to lose. It must follow that if the settlor is a starving artist who has just won a £50,000 prize which he transfers to trustees on discretionary trust for himself, his wife, and children under an express duty to speculate recklessly with it with intent to double it or lose it all in a two-year period, as if it were money that a sole beneficial owner can well afford to lose, then no beneficiary can complain if the money is lost.[47]

Thus, there is no core duty of care (other than to act in good faith[48]) that cannot be excluded in relation to investment. Only if the relevant clause in a trust instrument intended to benefit the beneficiaries purported to enable the trustee to speculate with the trust fund for its own private purposes, without being accountable therefor, would such clause be struck down as repugnant to the trust for affording the trustee uncontrollable powers of disposition i.e. absolute ownership.

The duty to act in good faith (i.e. honestly and consciously) in respect of any trust matter cannot, of course, be excluded. To do so would make a nonsense of the trust relationship as an obligation of confidence. It would make the trustees a law unto themselves free from the jurisdiction

[45] See Arts. 33 and 61, Underhill and Hayton, n. 1 above, *Re Penrose* [1933] Ch. 793, *Re Beatty's WT* [1990] 3 All ER 844, 846; *Re Hart's WT* [1943] 2 All ER 557.

[46] See text to n. 43 above.

[47] The settlor's advisers will not be liable if he took a fully informed risk.

[48] Thus, the duty to speculate recklessly will require the trustees consciously and rationally addressing their minds to the risks of particular investments rather than merely stick pins in to a list of possible investments or automatically do what the settlor tells them: *Turner* v. *Turner* [1984] Ch. 100.

of the court and the court will not recognize this if the trustees were intended to be trustees and not absolute owners.[49]

EXEMPTION CLAUSES

Similarly, an exemption from liability for breach of the duty to act in good faith cannot have effect, because that would empty the area of obligation so as to leave no room for any obligation. A trustee will not be acting in good faith if he acts fraudulently or dishonestly i.e. to benefit himself or third parties at the expense of the beneficiaries. Can a trustee, therefore, protect himself against being 'liable for any loss or damage which may happen from any cause whatsoever unless such damage shall be caused by his own actual fraud'? In the case of unpaid trustees of a family trust Jacob J, much impressed by the use of the word 'actual',[50] held[51] this clause to be effective where:

> the defendant trustees wilfully or recklessly disregarded the terms of the trust but did not do so dishonestly, [even though] it amounts to the settlor, having set out in detail all the terms of the trust, going on to say 'Actually it does not matter if you disregard any of these, provided you do so honestly' . . . 'His own actual fraud' is very strong language indeed. I do not think it can encompass honest[52] but wilful or reckless breaches. The trust was undertaken by trustees who knew they would not be liable unless they were fraudulent. It would be wrong to impose on them any liability for honest acts.

The judge was impressed by the fact that this exemption clause is found in the standard work, Hallett's *Conveyancing Precedents* at pages 796–7 where Mr Hallett observes, 'This clause is extremely wide but can reasonably be required by gratuitous trustees and has been accepted by settlors in such circumstances.'

An alternative approach would be for a clause to provide that the trustees may do anything or omit to do anything that would otherwise amount to a breach of trust if they *bona fide* consider such action or

[49] See *Re Jeffrey* [1984] 4 DLR 704, 710, endorsed in *Boe* v. *Alexander* (1988) 41 DLR (4th) 520, 527.

[50] If 'actual' is omitted then it seems a *contra proferentem* construction could be used to treat 'fraud' as including unconscionable conduct or a lack of good faith e.g. acting recklessly or deliberately committing a breach of trust expected to be in the best interests of the beneficiaries albeit with a small risk (which materializes) that it might harm a beneficiary.

[51] *Armitage* v. *Nurse* (unreported, 17 July 1995).

[52] Both counsel and judge assumed honesty to be a very subjective concept, though for dishonest assistance in breach of fiduciary duty it has objective connotations: *Royal Brunei Airlines* v. *Tan* [1995] 3 All ER 97, 105–7, endorsing fraud as including taking 'a risk to the prejudice of another's rights, which risk is known to be one which there is no right to take' as held in *R.* v. *Sinclair* [1968] 1 WLR 1246, 1249 and *Baden Delvaux* v. *Société Générale* [1992] 4 All ER 161, 234.

inaction to be in the best interests of the beneficiaries as a whole. One can see the sense of such provision to deal with unforeseeable eventualities and it does require the trustees consciously and honestly to consider seriously what they should or should not do.

This leads one to submit, with respect, that Jacobs J goes too far in so far as his view allows a trustee to act with reckless indifference to his trusteeship as if he were not a trustee. A trustee, even a settlor-trustee, must at the very least be under a duty to act conscious of the terms of the trust, though he can then be exempted from liability for negligence. In the case of a paid trustee it should certainly be the case that a clause purporting to exclude him from liability for reckless indifference should be struck down as repugnant to the core paid-trusteeship function, if indeed such reckless indifference be not regarded as dishonest.

It is clear that a trustee, paid or unpaid, can be exempted from liability if he acts in good faith[53] and from liability for negligence[54] but what about gross negligence, *culpa lata* in Roman or Scots law?[55] A distinction first needs to be made between gross negligence and recklessness. It is submitted that recklessness is worse than (gross) negligence and should be regarded as a positive, affirmative, intentional, 'could-not-care-less' attitude taken by a defendant deliberately indifferent to his responsibilities. Negligence should be regarded as a negative state, a lack of due attention, a failure to take care to a greater or lesser extent.

There seems no reason in principle why a settlor should not have freedom to exempt his trustees from liability for losses flowing from negligence, covering ordinary and gross negligence,[56] but not extending to losses flowing from recklessness in the sense of deliberate indifference to one's responsibilities because the latter would enable the trustees to act in bad faith and negate a core duty of the trustees.

[53] *Galmerrow Securities Ltd* v. *National Westminster Bank plc* (unreported, 20 Dec. 1990, Harman J).

[54] Except for trustees of unit trusts or debenture trusts or in their investment role trustees of pension trusts: Financial Services Act 1986, s. 84; Companies Act 1985, s. 192; Pensions Act 1995, s. 29. Further see P. Matthews [1989] *Conv.* 42; s. 30 Trustee Act 1925 should not prejudice the position: Underhill and Hayton, n. 1 above, 560–1.

[55] *Knox* v. *MacKinnon* (1888) 13 App. Cas. 753, 765; *Rae* v. *Meek* (1889) 14 App. Cas. 558; in context the wording of some exemption clauses may be construed *contra proferentem* as not extending to omissions considered to be gross negligence.

[56] In *Roywest Trust Corporation (Bahamas) Ltd* v. *Savannah NV*, n. 9 above, Telford Georges CJ in dealing with a clause exempting against loss from any cause whatsoever except 'actual fraud' stated, 'The words are wide enough to include gross negligence and dereliction of duty. . . . There is no good reason why this exclusion clause should be rejected. . . . This is not in any sense unreasonable . . . the parties have been bargaining on terms of equality. . . . In striking the bargain it seemed reasonable to accept a stringent exclusion clause for a *quid pro quo*. . . . The exclusion clause would not, however, cover acts which were void because of self-dealing or which did not fall within the trustee's powers.'

English and Scots cases holding that an exemption clause did not extend beyond ordinary negligence to gross negligence (in the narrow sense or in the broad sense including recklessness) depend on particular *contra proferentum* constructions as held in the 21 December 1995 reserved judgment of the Jersey Court of Appeal (in *Midland Bank (Trustee) Jersey Ltd* v. *Federated Pension Services*), stating (44) 'It follows from our consideration of earlier authorities above that a clause exempting trustees from liability for breaches of trust due to gross negligence is not to be regarded as being void for repugnancy to the nature of a trust.' Thus a clause that 'the Trustee shall not be liable for anything other than a breach of trust knowingly and wilfully committed' was *prima facie* valid to exclude liability for gross negligence, but was construed *contra proferentem* so that the trust would be liable if it knowingly and wilfully committed an act which amounted to a breach, and not only if it knowingly and wilfully committed an act which *at the time of commission was known* to the trustee to be a breach of trust.

The Court held (48) that the trustee's conduct 'was not mere negligence consisting of a departure from the normal standard of conduct of a paid professional trustee, but a serious, unusual and marked departure from that standard which amounted to "gross negligence"' within Article 26(9) of the Trusts Jersey Law 1984 (as retrospectively substituted by Article 5 of the Trusts (Amendment) (Jersey) Law 1989) which provides, 'Nothing in the terms of a trust shall relieve, release or exonerate a trustee from liability for breach of trust arising from his own fraud, wilful misconduct or gross negligence.'

Where there are two (or more) trustees it seems that the existence of one 'proper' or 'managing' trustee should enable the co-trustee to be wholly exempted from liability if in good faith obeying the directions of the 'proper' trustee upon whom the settlor has conferred complete and uncontrolled powers without the concurrence of, nor reference to, the co-trustee.[57] Thus, in such fashion a second trustee necessary to make good title to land or to hold foreign property can incur no responsibility for joining in good faith with the 'proper' trustee to carry out transactions at his direction. However, if the second 'sleeping' trustee becomes suspicious that the 'proper' trustee is probably acting improperly then he should seek the court's directions at the expense of the trust fund because he would not be acting in good faith but would be dishonestly[58] assisting a breach of trust if he proceeded to comply with the 'proper'

[57] *Re Arnott* [1899] IR 201.

[58] In *Jones* v. *Gordon* (1877) 2 App. Cas. 616, 629 Lord Blackburn stated, 'If the jury or whoever has to try the question of fact came to the conclusion that [X] must have had a suspicion that there was something wrong and that he refrained from asking questions not because he was an honest blunderer or a stupid man but because he thought in his secret mind—I suspect there is something wrong and if I ask questions and make further inquiry

trustee's directions, and so would lose the benefit of the exemption clause.

SETTLOR'S FULLY INFORMED CONSENT REQUIRED

Where a trustee benefits from reduction of the ordinary duties of trustees to lesser duties there needs to be full frank disclosure to the settlor, so that a fully informed consent can be given, because a fiduciary relationship exists even before the trust instrument is finally executed.[59] The greater the reduction in the trusteeship duties (e.g. to the bare core of duties) the greater the need to make full and frank disclosure (evidenced in writing) and to obtain the fully informed consent in writing of the settlor or a written acknowledgement that he was strongly advised to seek independent legal advice, yet voluntarily assumed the risk of not seeking such advice.[60]

The sanction for the trustee's breach of fiduciary duty is that the trustee will not be able to rely on the relevant clause because it is wholly offensive to Equity's standards of integrity that the trustee could take personal advantage of the settlor's confidence.[61] It would seem that a successor trustee will be equally disadvantaged on the basis that it is a donee of the legal title with a beneficial equitable interest to the extent of the value conferred by remuneration and exemption clauses as already vitiated in equity by the circumstances surrounding their creation.[62]

CONCLUSIONS

A settlor can validly spell out that objects of fiduciary powers are not to have any individual right to be informed that they are objects (the trustees only being under a general core duty,[63] subject to the sanction of

it will no longer be my suspecting it but my knowing it—I think that is dishonesty.' Further see *Macmillan Inc.* v. *Bishopsgate Investment Trust plc (No 3)* [1995] 3 All ER 747, 769, 783 and *Royal Brunei Airlines* v. *Tan*, n. 52 above, 105–7.

[59] *Galmerrow Securities Ltd* v. *National Westminster Bank plc*, n. 53 above, where Harman J accepted 'as a correct statement of the law' Stephenson LJ's observations in *Swain* v. *Law Society* [1982] 1 WLR 17, 26 'as establishing that fiduciary duties can exist before any trust has been created'. Also see *Jothann* v. *Irving Trust Company* (1934) 270 NYS 721, affd. 277 NYS 955.

[60] See Kessler, *Drafting Trusts and Will Trusts* (2nd edn.), para. 4.012; Prideaux, *Forms & Precedents in Conveyancing* (25th edn.), iii 158; Hallett, *Conveyancing Precedents*, 801 n. 30, *Encyclopaedia of Forms & Precedents* (5th edn.), 512.

[61] *Baskerville* v. *Thurgood* (1992) 100 Sask. LR 214, 227–30 (CA).

[62] Successor trustees should not be regarded as purchasers: remuneration clauses are regarded as gifts subject to a condition (*Re White* [1898] 2 Ch. 217, *Re Duke of Norfolk's ST* [1982] Ch. 61) and exemption clauses confer a bounty by saving trustees the costs of insuring against the liabilities excluded.

[63] See *Re Hay's Settlement* [1981] 3 All ER 786, 793.

removal, to survey the range of objects and take whatever businesslike steps they consider necessary to appropriate consideration of making appointments in favour of the reserve objects of the settlor's bounty) nor to have any rights to make the trustees provide information about their stewardship of the trust property or be otherwise accountable to the objects. It is only if a particular object becomes aware that he is an object that he then has a core right to request the power to be exercised in his favour, subject to the sanction of the court removing the trustees if they ignore him.

Where beneficiaries of a trust are concerned, the settlor cannot, even in the case of discretionary beneficiaries, oust the duty of the trustees to take all reasonable steps to inform the beneficiaries that they are beneficiaries, and to account to them. However, the settlor can effectively prevent them from seeing any letter of his wishes given to the trustees, particularly if he expressly states that such letter is confidential to the trustees until forced by litigation to make discovery of documents in their custody. He cannot prevent them, however, from having the core right to see trust documents the withholding of which would prevent the beneficiaries from being in a position to vindicate or enjoy their position as beneficiaries.

While a temporary express ouster of almost all accountability can be stipulated for in special circumstances, an exemption clause cannot oust the trustees' duties to act in good faith. If the settlor's fully informed consent be obtained a clause can exempt the trustees from liability for negligence, whether or not a great or marked departure from the normal standard of conduct, but not from liability for dishonesty which is taken to include acting deliberately with reckless indifference to the interests of the beneficiaries.

Thus, while there is a strong contract-like basis for gratuitous family trusts to be regarded as 'deals' made with trustees for the benefit of the beneficiaries,[64] any provisions apparently reducing the deal, instead, to one for the benefit of the trustees or of the settlor (or protector), entitled in default of the trustees exercising inherently revocable powers in favour of objects specified by the settlor, must either be struck out as inconsistent with, or repugnant to, the original deal for the benefit of the beneficiaries or be implemented as the real deal.

[64] J. Langbein, 'The Contractarian Basis of the Law of Trusts' (1995) 109 *Yale LJ* 625.

4

The Protector: New Wine in Old Bottles?

DONOVAN W. M. WATERS

INTRODUCTION—THE PHENOMENON OF THE PROTECTOR

Just a few years ago—*Underhill and Hayton* in its fourteenth edition in 1987[1] had nothing on the subject; it is that recent—those who had reason to see the documentation of offshore trusts noticed the appearance in those instruments of an individual named a protector. Some instruments referred to this person as an 'adviser', an 'appointor', or even a 'guardian', and in others a plurality of persons assumed this role as a 'management committee' or 'the protector group'. But these latter descriptions were not usual in the early days; then it was the individual acting alone. However, then, as now, the name of the position had no particular significance; the significance of the position lies in the fact that it is an empowerment of a person or group. An individual, natural or incorporated, or group is granted in the trust instrument, invariably *inter vivos* in offshore trusts, a power or several powers that enable the grantee to direct the trustees, or refuse consent to the trustees, in the latter's exercise of one or more of their administrative powers (or discretions), or to appoint and delete, or to consent to the appointment and deletion of, trust beneficiaries. The grantee may have powers of both kinds.

The protector in the later 1980s appeared to be little more than a watchdog of the trustee on behalf of the settlor. He would usually be a close relative or friend of the settlor, and his task was to ensure that the trustee of the trust, so many miles away from the settlor and vested with the settlor's property, was actually and efficiently discharging the various trustee duties. Such a protector would often have a power to approve or disapprove proposed trust investments, but essentially he had the power to dismiss and appoint trustees as a complement to his monitoring role. Those who drafted the offshore trust of the time, and included a protector provision, described this inclusion as providing 'comfort' for the settlor.

[1] *Law of Trusts and Trustees*, ed. David J. Hayton. Professor Hayton deals with the subject in the 15th edn. (1995), at 23–5.

The idea had an immediate appeal. Evidently it seemed not only to settlors, but to trustees and to beneficiaries, and no doubt to their legal advisers, that here was a role, an office, that might meet needs in a number of ways. Protectors began to appear in offshore trusts almost as a matter of routine, and today they are a standard feature of all offshore trusts. Protectors are commissioned to play a number of parts. To settlors they give the long arm of control or at least influence over trustee activity, but they also allow confidentiality to be enhanced, both from third parties and, if desired, beneficiaries themselves. The protector may be authorized to edit or veto information that the trustees propose to release. For professional trustees, especially those charged with considerable and sensitive discretions, as in the standard discretionary trust, the protector is welcome as one who will assume some of the onus of decision-taking. He will also interpret for the trustees the settlor's letter of wishes. He will approve investments, and sometimes be empowered to direct the acquisition of the high return, higher risk investment. He will nominate among the beneficiaries those who should receive loans or advancements. The more exercise of discretion the protector is empowered to assume, the better he can discharge his watchdog role, and where discretion and power is left with the trustees the protector empowered to subject the trustees to surveillance can at least determine for the trustees the criteria they should follow. With the power to direct the trustees, his role changes from watching over management to instructing management. Such directives may be supplementary to the trustees' similar power, or constitute an exclusive power to make decisions on the particular subject. A familiar subject-matter is investment.

Beneficiaries also will encourage the intending settlor to allow them to be consulted and to give their approval to proposed trustee action or inaction. The 'protector group' will probably constitute a committee of adult and capacitated beneficiaries. These people, otherwise as beneficiaries neutralized by the fact of the existence of other beneficiaries who are minors or unborn, now have the opportunity both to protect the beneficiaries' interests and, if so authorized, to instruct the trustees within the scope of their authority as to how they (the trustees) shall act.

In the last five years it is no exaggeration to say that at one time or another the protector has been employed to exercise every administrative and dispositive power associated with the common law concept of express trusts. Of course, no one protector will be given all these powers, if only because the settlor fears he will fall foul of a tax authority's ruling that the trust is not that at all, but a simple agency. The 'trust' will be said to be a sham, attempting to hide from view the continued control of the settlor over the assets. It is probable that the settlor will therefore have focussed upon certain objectives in creating the position of protector, and in most instances certain powers alone will have been conferred upon the position holder in order to achieve these objectives. However, if there were an instance where all these powers are so conferred, and the governing law of the trust is the law of an offshore jurisdiction, it seems more likely than not that the courts of at least some of those jurisdictions would hold there is nevertheless a trust—a fiduciary vested with property and beneficiaries to benefit from that vesting. The protectorship is regarded as merely superimposed upon that conceptual structure, and superimposition would mean that *any* administrative and dispositive power can be given to a protector.

Together these two points—whether, in some circumstances at least, the instrument has indeed created a trust, and the fact that a protector may be given any type of power—underline the vital importance of the correct analysis of the nature of the position. That analysis must include the issues of the standards of behaviour required of the position-holder, the accountability of the office-holder and to whom that accountability is to take place, the remedies otherwise available and to whom they are available when the power-holder refuses to act, at all or appropriately, or he causes loss to the trust. Then there is the problem, if the instrument is silent, of who, if the power is not personal to the original grantee, shall be the successor to the power-holder in the event of his death or incapacity, retirement or resignation, and the instances in which the responsibilities of the protector and the trustees are distinct, so that each can disclaim any obligation to be the other's keeper, and when, if at all, they are shared.

What has caused concern is that to this date none of the courts in the mainland jurisdictions has had occasion to consider these issues, and until last year none of the standard trusts texts in any common law jurisdiction had dealt with the phenomenon. The contemporary offshore trust protector seems to be a law unto himself. Meanwhile, the nature of protectorship appears to be what settlors and their advisers choose to see as the limits of this institution which has been so magnified by the practitioners, and though the courts of the offshore jurisdictions, where one would expect the litigation, are now beginning to be confronted with the hitherto unanswered questions, the first results have not been uniformly well received. The *Star Trusts*[2] decision of July 1994 in Bermuda has been subjected to the charge that there was little

[2] *In the Matter of the Star I (Revised) and Star II (Revised) Trusts, and In the Matter of the Trustee Act, 1975; Jurgen von Knieriem* v. *Bermuda Trust Company Ltd and Grosvenor Trust Company Ltd,* Civil Jurisdiction 1994, No. 162, Sup. C. of Bermuda, 13 July 1994. See for a practice note, Andrew Penney, 'Rights and Powers of Trust Protectors: Rahman Revisited' [1995] 1 *Journal of International Trust and Corporate Planning* ('*J Int.P*') 31. For further comments, see A. J. Conder, 'The Office of the Protector' (1995) 4 *Trusts & Trustees* 12; Paul

rigorous analysis. The exercise of a power to dismiss and replace trustees was evaluated solely in terms of the appropriateness of the appointment of the replacement, which leaves the impression that the reasons for the preceding dismissal of the original trustee were of no concern to the court. The power to dismiss was apparently absolute, even given that the protector was described by the court as a fiduciary.[3] Within the last two or three years some offshore jurisdictions have legislated on the subject of protectors,[4] but what legislation there has been is outline in character or strangely unperceptive of the issues protectorship raises.

Nevertheless, what has triggered this paper is the most recent development, namely, the adoption of the protector role by those drafting domestic (as opposed to offshore) trusts. In Canada it appears things are as yet at the beginning stage, but with the equally recent appearance of bankers' mailed information services to their clients commending the value of offshore asset-protection trusts the practice of the domestic usage of protectorships can be expected to grow. The powers given to domestic or onshore protectors are at this time mostly within a more narrow and familiar range, such as the power to dismiss and replace trustees, or to consent to particular investments, even if far-reaching in possible effect. But this is not uniformly so; some protectorships within domestic discretionary trusts control completely who shall receive income or capital as beneficiaries of the particular trust, and others have a right of intervention and veto in the exercise by the trustees of *any* of their portfolio-management powers, in particular when there is a favoured family business as part of the settlor's wealth. On occasion the protector evidently represents the introduction of 'settlor-friendly' intervention into trust management when tax considerations rule out both the presence of the settlor in the formal structure of the trust and the conferment upon the settlor of reserved powers.

Meanwhile, our mainland Trustee Acts[5] are silent, the published literature concerning the contemporary protectorship in a domestic setting is non-existent,[6] and the courts are evident strangers to this as yet unmet phenomenon. The reports also are silent. Nor would one readily

Matthews, 'Protectors: Two Cases, Twenty Questions' (1995) 9 *Trust Law International* 108, at 109.

[3] Some consider, contrary to the critics, that this judgment confirms what they have long understood to be the law, namely, that a power to dismiss means what it says. The power-holder is no more required to give reasons for a dismissal than is a trustee to reveal his reasons for the particular exercise of his discretion. The protector may feel it no more appropriate for him to state his reasons than it often is for trustees.

[4] See, pp. 110–114 below.

[5] Canada has 9 provincial Trustee Acts, and two territorial Acts.

[6] For a practice note on offshore trusts, see R. C. Lawrence, 'The Role of the Protector—An Insulator for Corporate Fiduciaries?' [1993] 1 *J Int.P* 88. Two valuable papers have been written on the subject of offshore trusts. Antony Duckworth, 'Protectors—Fish or Fowl?',

expect early litigation on this subject; where disagreements as to protectors' exercise of their powers or proposed exercise occur, most practitioners until serious confrontational interests arise will be successful in reaching accommodations for their clients. Litigation is likely to be both costly and uncertain in outcome. Instead, challenge is likely to occur first in a tax setting, and this has the unfortunate outcome that an answer in line with the provisions of the jurisdiction's tax legislation or regulations[7] may not be that which would have been reached for the purposes of the law of trusts. Trusts law in Canada is a matter within the sovereignty of each province.

With the confluence of the protectorships being drawn by mainland and offshore practitioners for offshore trusts, and those now being inserted into domestic trusts, the moment is perhaps timely to analyse the protectorship, and to attempt the reaching of answers, before the incoming tide carries all before it.

It may be timely for another reason. *Scott on Trusts*[8] has a paragraph on powers of others to consent to trustees' proposed administrative action, or to direct trustees in matters of administration. It has been a feature of that work since the first edition in 1939. *Scott* was referred to in the court's judgment in *Rawson Trust* v. *Perlman*,[9] a decision of the Bahamian courts in 1990, and the paragraph in question was cited and adopted as to who is a fiduciary by the court in the *Star Trusts* case in Bermuda's Supreme Court in July 1994. Curiously enough, however, there has been no systematic analysis in the literature of what *Scott* is saying in those pages, though threads he canvasses and pulls together into a theme merit the examination. This paper attempts to make that analysis, extending that examination to the subtleties of present-day law on powers of appointment. This will cover both types of powers that are given to protectors.

TWO SCHOOLS OF THOUGHT

We must appreciate at the outset that there are two opposed lines of opinion on this subject. The first school is of the view that there should

delivered at the 9th IBC Annual Transcontinental Trusts Conference, *The Offshore World in Perilous Transition*, Geneva, Switzerland, 29–30 June 1995. See now [1995] 1 J Int. P. 131 The second thought-provoking paper, 'The Role and Control of Protectors', was delivered by Maurice C. Cullity QC to a Law Society of Upper Canada seminar, *Effective Estate Planning*, Toronto, 7 July 1995. Mr Duckworth's paper is to be published in the *Journal of International Trust and Corporate Planning*. The present writer acknowledges his debt to these writers for both information and insights.

[7] In Canada this is the federal Income Tax Act (Canada), RSC 1985, c. 1 (5th Supp.).

[8] W. F. Fratcher (ed.) (4th edn., 1987), Vol. IIA, para. 185.

[9] Grand Court of Bahamas, 25 Apr. 1990.

be control by the courts over the holders of powers, and that such holders should be subject to the same level of control as the courts have over the trustees of discretionary trusts. This means that where the settlor has simply not imposed any accountability obligations upon the protector, or the settlor has clearly described the particular power as a personal privilege of the grantee though its exercise is bound to affect the existing beneficial interests of others, the law would step in. It would require the grantee to demonstrate that his act or omission is within the scope of the power, and also does not constitute an abuse of the behaviour expectations that the law imposes on those who are exercising discretions. In short, accountability is called for on all occasions, save for that very narrow band of powers that are demonstrably granted in order to further the benefit solely of the grantee.

The second school of opinion maintains that, where the opportunity to act is given to the power-holder who is not a trustee of the trust property (for example, he *may* intervene in the exercise by the trustees of their administrative discretions, or he *may* appoint or delete beneficiaries), or the settlor has described the power as a personal privilege (that is, exercisable by the holder for his own benefit), there should be accountability to no one. The law already confers upon the settlor, it is noted, the freedom to create personal privilege powers, and, if this has hitherto been sound law that has created no practical problems, it should not be changed now. This second school does not therefore challenge the duty of trustees to account; its principal perspective is the existing right of the settlor to create the personal confidence (right or privilege).[10]

The Concerns of the Accountability School

Because of the many and varied reasons for the particular instrument adopting the protectorship and the powers that in consequence are conferred, the protectorships that appear in offshore trusts are so different that generalization is a risky enterprise. However, one general observation can certainly be made. The familiar circumstance to which we now turn is that, while the protector is endowed with powers, nothing is usually said in the instrument as to who has the authority to call to task the protector who abuses or neglects those powers. The power-holder

[10] These will be referred to for present purposes as the accountability school and the no-accountability school. Mr Duckworth's paper (n. 6 above) is substantially concerned with trust instruments that contain no accountability provisions so far as the protector is concerned. Mr Cullity's paper is concerned that the courts not impose accountability requirements where the power in question is for the benefit of the donee of the power. The present writer would emphasize that neither paper wholly represents the views of the particular school with which each paper can be associated.

may act beyond the scope of his powers by doing things he has no authority to do, or he may exercise his powers in a manner that would be unacceptable in a fiduciary. Otherwise, there may be a concern as to the protector's continuing mental capacity to make the decisions for which his powers call. Moreover, when the power enables the protector to direct the trustees how they shall act, the trustees' position is an ambiguous one. To whom do they have recourse if they are concerned that, having carried out the protector's direction, responsibility for loss of trust assets or singularly poor investment return may be laid at their door? Of course, in practice the trustees' position is hardly any different if the protector's particular power is to approve or veto the trustees' proposed action or inaction. Refusal to respond in a reasonable period of time, conditional approvals, purported delegation, the unknown location of the power holder, his intervening death or incapacity, are the situations the critics have in mind; in any of these instances, and others that may be imagined, the trustees must know whether they are responsible for their own consequent delay or actual lack of response to circumstances that require action. Can they at any stage, thus ignoring the language of the instrument, take the law into their own hands, as it were, and proceed validly without approval? Indeed, must they?

There is an apprehension that settlors, their trustees, and legal advisers are unwittingly sailing in uncharted waters with this office of the protector. Indeed, the protectorship may not be intended as an office at all when a relative or close friend of the settlor is given certain powers, and nothing is said about succession. Is it then on the particular occasion an office like trusteeship, or a personal privilege given to a particular person, that is intended? The view is expressed by those who share the apprehension that this is a completely novel problem, and moreover one in which the very foundations of the trust concept are jeopardized. The argument runs as follows. Here is a totally loose cannon. The essence of the express trust is the fiduciary relationship between the beneficiary and a trustee who is vested with the trust property; it is a delicate balance of title ownership and enjoyment rights distributed between two persons, with beneficiary remedies and trustee defences to support that relationship. Though he may be in ignorance of what he does, the settlor is in a position to overturn that balance with the power or powers of intervention that he gives the protector. At one extreme the settlor can retain for himself effective control through the protector of both the assets and their beneficial disposition, and at the other the beneficiaries through a 'protector group' equally effectively run their own asset investment, administration, and disposition. In either case it is the protector, not the trustee, who administers for the benefit of another; the trustee is a depositee of title. If, says the critic, you want to grace such a 'trustee' with the description of a custodian with agency duties, you may.

The Concerns of the No-accountability School

For his protector the average settlor wants someone who will ensure the security of the transferred property and the settlor-desired operation of the trust; the settlor may wish to give the protector a commission that includes the power to determine who without specification shall benefit as beneficiaries, and how they shall benefit. The aim of the settlor is flexibility, and while structuring the trust he wishes to maintain as many options over the expected lifetime of the trust as he believes his purposes may require. Asset security established, he wants the options as to administrative decisions and original or substitute beneficiary appointment in familiar hands. This average settlor does not think in terms of controls over, and the liability of, the protector; indeed, if asked, he would likely reply that this is the very thing he does not want. He wants someone whom he knows and with whom he has ease of communication, who is outside the trust's legal structure, and who will see that the reasons he had in creating the trust are adhered to throughout the trust's existence. In any event accountability for such a role as the protector has is not easily created. Formal accounting to the settlor is not usually appropriate drafting, given the mainland tax concerns it may raise. Accounting to the beneficiaries effectively causes the protector to be a duplicate of the trustees, and therefore lessens the value of the role to the settlor. A protector as an additional trustee accomplishes only the undesired application of the law as to co-trustees. The settlor's assurance of appropriate protector operations is not legal action, inevitably in the foreign jurisdiction, but his own degree of intimacy and ongoing communication with the protector. In any event a concerned settlor can always ensure that he retains in the instrument the ability to replace the holder of the personal privilege.

The no-accountability school fears that in an age of judicial intervention, largely employing equity doctrines, the courts will ultimately require of the holder of the personal privilege that he account for his handling of the power, even though it be for his own benefit. The judicial thinking will be that, when the results of exercise or non-exercise affect other trust beneficiaries, accountability is appropriate.

The Background to the Apprehension

The reasoning behind the apprehension is not at all surprising. Historically there has been no granting of powers of beneficiary appointment, or the conferment of administrative powers upon persons who are not the trustees, to anywhere near the extent that is now occurring in offshore trusts. It is the extent that constitutes the new phenomenon.

In an earlier generation things were more simple. Powers of appointment, whether general, hybrid, or special,[11] were given to the surviving spouse or to children or, less commonly, to other family relations, often trust beneficiaries themselves. Today it is true that they are frequently seen in the hands of the trustees of *inter vivos* trusts. Indeed, the tendency of the last quarter century has been to concentrate powers, including powers of trust variation and termination, in those same hands, something which has been done largely in order to facilitate continuing tax planning. However, powers in the trustees' hands was an established practice before the arrival of the modern offshore trust protector, and essentially with the trustee having such powers the simplicity of the structure remains. Instead of the relative or friend it is a stranger who appoints, but a stranger who, as the trustee, is already subject to the remedial measures available to the beneficiary for the enforcement of the fiduciary obligations.

So far as administrative trust powers were concerned, previous generations might well confer the power of trustee appointment upon a beneficiary, instead of the existing trustees, and already in the nineteenth century the professional adviser or close friend of the settlor or testator might be given that power. Curiously no one appeared to notice that this practice came close to interposing another between the trustees and the beneficiaries, or that empowering a person other than a trustee might render irrelevant the beneficiary remedies—and trustee defences—that regulate the fiduciary relationship. On the other hand it was normally a single power that was granted, such as the power to consent to the sale by the trustees of a family home or the shares of a particular company. On occasion the power so granted might go further, both as to the nature of the intervention the non-trustee might make and the extent of the power given. For instance, the grantee is empowered to direct the trustees as to what they shall do in a specified situation. He is not merely to give or withhold consent. Again the implications for this trust, if any there were thought to be, were not apparently discussed in any common law jurisdiction.[12]

However, the empowering of a person who is not the trustee of the trust property appears clearly to have been the exceptional situation;

[11] The general power enables the donee to appoint anyone, including himself; the hybrid power (categorized as a special power for perpetuity purposes) enables the donee to appoint anyone with the exception of certain persons; and the special power enables the donee to appoint among a class of persons or among named persons. The special power is sometimes described as a fiduciary power because it requires exercise for the benefit of persons other than the donee.

[12] Save in *Re Rogers*, n. 19 below.

more frequent was it that one trustee is given a power which the other trustee or trustees do not have. And of course, whether or not it is wise in any instance, the grant of such an exclusive power does not threaten the balance of the trust structure between trustee and beneficiary and its complementary enforcement machinery. The co-trustee, faced with a decision of the empowered trustee that in the view of the co-trustee is a breach of trust, jeopardizing the best interests of the beneficiaries, must act. He seeks the advice and direction of the court. If the empowered trustee is refusing to exercise his power (e.g. to make a decision), the co-trustee as a trustee must again move to protect the interests of the beneficiaries. His own fiduciary relationship with the beneficiaries requires his own responsive behaviour.

Nor at the same time can it be said that the opponents of accountability are wrong in their assertion that an earlier age permitted (1) the opportunity power (the mere power of appointment), and (2) the power authorizing the grantee or testamentary donee to benefit himself, to be exercised or not exercised with but minimal judicial control. The only control was—and largely remains—a basic test of whether the power-holder has acted within the scope of the power.

These two schools of opinion provide the focus of this paper.

THE EXISTING LAW AS TO PROTECTOR-LIKE POWERS

How have nineteenth and twentieth century courts reacted when powers to appoint beneficiaries, and powers concerned with the administration of property, have been granted to persons other than the trustee or trustees, put in place by the instrument to play a part in administration or, more recently, the distribution or disposition of the trust property?

Powers of appointment constitute an area of law which, both in common law courts and equity courts, though principally in the latter, go back in embryo to the fifteenth century and the age of the 'use'. As an area of law it was quite distinct from trust law which began to evolve in the first half of the seventeenth century. The power of appointment was a means whereby the creator of an instrument, having title to property and conferring successive interests in that property upon other persons (and possibly himself,)[13] would delegate to one or more of those persons the opportunity and authority to determine who the subsequent successor should be. Such powers were familiar in the strict settlement at law, and in the express trust recognized and enforced by Chancery. For the

[13] The owner of the property retains for himself, e.g., a life interest, with a power of appointment over income or capital or both.

greater part of this century they have been associated exclusively with express trusts.

Traditionally these powers have been retained by the settlor or conferred both initially and by substitution upon third parties, such third parties being in the majority of instances members of the family of the settlor or testator. Special (or fiduciary) powers, hybrid powers, and general powers[14] have been known and utilized by settlement creators for many years, and the distinction between mere powers and trust powers[15] was established long before the modern protector appeared. So there are no surprises today in those respects. Moreover, for the past quarter of a century tax considerations have popularized the trust power (in the form of the discretionary trust). The discretionary trust being well-known in theory since the last century, the epoch of the employer-funded benefit trust has resulted in the courts clarifying the certainty of objects test, not only for mere powers, but for trust powers. Since 1970[16] in the Commonwealth jurisdictions, the test of certainty for all powers of appointment—whether the donee may or must determine who benefits, and how and when he or she is to benefit—has centred upon the necessary qualification of the proposed appointee who is to benefit rather than upon the numerical determination of all those who fall within the described class.

This emancipation of the discretionary trust from the confines of the test of certainty for fixed-interest trusts was both caused by, and considerably enhanced, the tax-planning possibilities of discretionary trust terms in all Commonwealth common law jurisdictions. In its turn this development brought the next stage, namely, that there might be not only a power within a discretionary trust to appoint further beneficiaries, but a power to delete any existing beneficiary's name from the discretionary trust listing of beneficiaries.[17] The power to add and delete has been seized upon by settlors who are anxious to give their tax advisers the maximum flexibility in the distribution of trust income and capital, and who wish to exclude the divorced spouses of their lineal heirs from the family trusts. That exclusion, and the creation of the separation agreement, go hand in hand. This power, too, was familiar before the contemporary protector appeared.

Powers of administration, however, have a different history. The

[14] N. 11 above.

[15] The so-called mere power is the opportunity without obligation to exercise the power or discretion; the so-called trust power is the obligation to exercise the power or discretion.

[16] *McPhail* v. *Doulton* [1971] AC 424, [1970] 2 All ER 228 (HL). See Fiona Spearing, 'Discretionary Trust and Power: Distinction without a Difference?' (1990) 4 *Trust Law & Practice* 117.

[17] *Re Manisty's Settlement* [1974] Ch. 17, [1973] 2 All ER 1203; *Re Hay's Settlement Trust* [1982] 1 WLR 202, [1981] 3 All ER 786.

power of the trustee or trustees to administer the trust property, whether it constitute interests in land or a portfolio of securities, including promissory notes, has been with us in connection with settlements and trusts for sale since the seventeenth century. Frequently, and correctly, referred to in trust instruments as the 'administration trusts', there exists the trust to sell, subject to the power of retention, and the trust to pay debts and expenses. However, we are concerned here with the general powers of administration, namely, the authorities given to the trustees in order that they may carry out their duties as described in the trust instrument. Those authorities include the powers to hold, or to hold, invest, and re-invest in a permitted manner, to sell, to repair, to insure, to grant and receive surrenders of leases and options, to compromise and waive debts owed, to borrow, to sub-divide, to exercise tax Act powers, and to make loans. A contemporary instrument, when such is envisaged as trustee activity, will give extensive powers to vote and exchange shares, to take part in corporate reorganizations, to form corporations and create trusts, and, of course, to carry on any business transferred to the trustees. Trustees will also be empowered to delegate their powers, duties, and discretions, and one expects to find the power to employ agents of enumerated and various kinds. In the 1850s in England the movement began that aimed to assist conveyancing through legislation;[18] the most familiar powers of administration were expressly incorporated by statute in trust instruments, subject to the instrument's expression of a contrary intent, and this practice has been continued to the present day, adopted in all the Commonwealth jurisdictions. But it is a movement to ensure that trustees are adequately empowered in the context of express trusts, imposing active duties upon those trustees.

The point we are seeking to make is that powers of an administrative nature have been firmly associated with trustees, even if for particular purposes an instrument confers one or more such powers upon one particular trustee to the exclusion of his or her co-trustees. The conferment of administrative powers upon third parties or beneficiaries, or even the reservation by settlors of such powers, does not seem at any time prior to this recent 'protector' phenomenon to have been other than an occasional practice, responding to the particular wish of a settlor, less often a testator, who does not prefer—like most creators of trusts—to spend time and thought on the selection of trustees, original and replacement. What we have witnessed in recent times is the move from the occasional nomination of a named person who is to consent or direct on one particular administrative matter (to the specific exclusion of all other matters) to the nomination of a specified person—and possi-

[18] The Trustee Act, 1850 (13 & 14 Vic. c. 60), was the first such Act.

bly his or her successors—who is given a number of administrative powers, and to whom the settlor does not really wish to see liabilities attach. The 'protector' is there to protect his, her, or their own interests, or the protector is to keep the trustee under surveillance to the comfort of the distant settlor. The protector's 'closeness' to the settlor is the settlor's guarantee of the integrity and good sense of the various players in the trust; no particular reliance is placed upon the possibility of legal action in a foreign, and largely unknown, jurisdiction. But the case law is not silent where there has been the occasional nomination of a named person to consent or direct on one particular administrative matter. This is where the present writer would differ from those whose apprehension he otherwise understands. There is such law, even though it not be great in quantity.

There appear from the case law to be three central concerns. First, what control have the courts over a person who is not a trustee under the instrument, but who has a power that is either administrative or to appoint (and delete) trust beneficiaries? Secondly, what standards of behaviour, if any, attach to such a person in his exercise or purported exercise of that power? Thirdly, is the trustee liable and, if so, in what circumstances, if he knows or ought to know that the donee of the power who is not a trustee of the trust property is acting, or failing to act, in breach of the power, or that that action or inaction is not in the best interests of the beneficiaries?

Control by the Courts

It is likely that most courts would react to the suggestion that the third-party donee of an administrative power is somehow beyond the reach of the courts, as the Ontario Court of Appeal reacted in *Re Rogers*[19] in 1929. The trustees of a testator's trust were required by the instrument 'to consult with and be governed by the advice of [X] in all matters relating to my investment [shares] in the [ABC Co.], and I release my said executors and trustees from all liability for any action that may be taken at the request of' X. Some time after the testator's death the trustees reached the conclusion that a sale of the shares was in the best interests of the beneficiaries, and in fact almost all the beneficiaries in question supported a sale. However, X resisted a sale, and ultimately the trustees applied to the court for directions as to what they should do. It was certainly an element in the facts, as found, that since the testator's death X himself had become a shareholder, director, and president of the ABC Co. who might have seen advantage for himself in the estate continuing to retain its shareholding. Nevertheless, without emphasizing this, Orde

[19] (1929) 63 OLR 180, [1929] 1 DLR 116.

JA described[20] X as 'a quasi-trustee (I don't know what other technical term to apply to his so-called right to control the trustees)', and added[21] 'how important it is that no one should be permitted to continue to perform a trust, and much less to exercise an anomalous power of control with no corresponding liabilities, where he has placed himself in a position where his interest may conflict with his duty'. The Court thereupon ordered the trustees to be free to sell the shares without their being concerned for X's approval.

The Ontario Court found 'quasi-trustee' status in the third party seemingly because he had a 'so-called right to control the trustees . . . an anomalous power of control with no corresponding liabilities'. No other reason was offered. Nevertheless, the decision and these words are not out of line with the trend of the cases in other jurisdictions. *Scott on Trusts*[22] says of a third party 'otherwise unconnected with the administration of the trust' that the power of that party 'is ordinarily conferred on him as a fiduciary and not for his own benefit'. And those words directly point the reader to the principal initial concern of the courts in all common law jurisdictions. Is the donee of the power a fiduciary? However, this body of law—under what circumstances a court will hold on an examination of the facts that one party is a fiduciary *vis-à-vis* another—need not be of concern here. The present context is one of construction and who is to benefit. If the settlor intends, as revealed by the trust instrument, that the power-holder may consider his own benefit, then he is not a fiduciary, and he has none of the obligations or duties associated with that status. The intention of the settlor may be express or implied; the property being settled is his by title or control, and subject to law and public policy a settlor can dispose of it to whom and in what manner he chooses.

If a power-holder is a fiduciary, that is, one who must act for the benefit of a class or enumeration of beneficiaries as a whole, he is subject to the duty of loyalty. One who undertakes, on request or by voluntary assumption, to act for another, must act selflessly for that other when acting within the scope of the undertaken task. He may not in any way seek to pursue or have in mind his own interest in what he does or declines to do. Personal advantage gained without previous authorization he must surrender. Even-hand considerations, whether delegation is possible, and the level of prudence and attentiveness required are the other familiar fiduciary obligations. However, there is no doubt, particularly in Canada as a result of judgments of the Supreme Court

[20] *Ibid.*, at 122–3 (DLR). Orde JA noted (at 118) that the power-holder was neither trustee nor executor; the learned judge did not know of any other kind of fiduciary. He therefore assumed the power-holder was intended to be a non-fiduciary.

[21] *Ibid.* 123. [22] N. 8 above, 565.

of Canada,[23] that the obligations associated with 'fiduciary' status have been expanded in recent years. The obligations the fiduciary may be held to have are now several and diffuse; those brought into play on any particular occasion will depend on the context, and the obligations will be enforced with more or less rigour depending on the degree of intensity of the particular fiduciary relationship. Later in this paper it will be seen that the courts have indeed had difficulty in determining what obligations *are* imposed when a power holder is found to be a fiduciary, one who must act for the benefit of others.

The issue will arise whether the power-holder, whoever he is (the settlor, a trustee of the trust, a beneficiary, or an otherwise disinterested third party), is intended by the instrument to be able to benefit himself, or to exercise the power for the benefit of others. Attention in each case is also given not only to who the power holder is, but to what it is the power-holder is empowered to do. *Scott*[24] is of the view that, while a beneficiary is the most likely person to have a power that it is intended he shall exercise for his own benefit, the settlor of an *inter vivos* trust 'ordinarily, it is believed, . . . is under a fiduciary duty to the beneficiary'.[25] So far as the trustee is concerned, it is 'ordinarily clear'[26] that he is a fiduciary with respect to any power that he alone has, and similarly a power is 'ordinarily conferred on [the third person who is not associated with the trust benefit or its administration] as a fiduciary and not for his own benefit'.[27] It is worth recalling at this point with regard to the present protector appointments that such a protector can be the settlor himself, but is usually a third party or less frequently a committee of adult beneficiaries. The protector is almost always someone other than an appointed trustee; the distinction between the protector and the trustee or trustees, as a practice, seems almost axiomatic.[28]

The recurrence of the word 'ordinarily' in *Scott's* assessment of who is a fiduciary in connection with 'directory powers', as American literature describes this topic,[29] is a reflection of the fact that this question is so much a question of fact.[30] On the basis of the sort of power that was

[23] The most recent, referring to all its forbears, is *Hodgkinson* v. *Simms* [1994] 3 SCR 377, 117 DLR (4th) 161.

[24] N. 8 above, at 567.

[25] In *Steele* v. *Paz Ltd*, p. 114 below, Judge Hegarty considered that a settlor's reserved powers are likely to be construed as intended for the settlor's own benefit.

[26] *Ibid.* 564.

[27] *Ibid.* 565.

[28] Unless the power given to the one trustee alone is clearly intended as a personal power that he may exercise without restraint of fiduciary obligation.

[29] That is, power to direct trustees or consent to their proposed actions.

[30] *Scott* does not say why these things are 'ordinarily' so. One would infer it is a matter of construction of the immediate trust instrument. But may one go further and assume also that the settlor is free to release the donee of the power from all fiduciary status and

granted, and the position of the person to whom it was granted, the court must interpret the instrument and thus discover the intent of the settlor or testator. When the instrument is silent, which seems to be the preponderant situation, so much surely is impression as to who was intended to benefit from the exercise of the power, and yet so much turns on the court's conclusion. If it is decided the power was granted for the sole benefit of the grantee, then the court will not consider any allegation of misuse of the power, provided the grantee has done only what he was empowered to do. Action within the scope of the power—was there fraud on the power?[31]—is the only control the court will impose.

The difficulties in characterizing the nature of a power—whether it is indeed for the sole benefit of the grantee, or is for the benefit of others—is readily imaginable. Take the case of a beneficiary of the trust. Suppose the trust instrument grants to the surviving spouse, the life tenant, the power to consent to the sale of the family residence. Most courts would probably construe this power as intended to benefit solely the donee. However, circumstances can arise which suggest that the limits of the intent of the settlor or testator have been reached. What then is the scope of the power? The house is large and of an age that calls for constant maintenance. The surviving spouse is living mostly in one room, and leaves the rest of the house vacant. It would make excellent sense, both economically and in terms of his health, for the elderly donee of the power to live elsewhere. Everyone concedes this, save the elderly person, who appears to enjoy the obstinate stance of refusing his consent. His doctor states that such an attitude is not unfamiliar in elderly people, but that the life tenant is not lacking capacity. The children of the settlor or testator are the remaindermen who are to take the capital of the trust. Did the trust creator intend the power to include circumstances like these, or was it her intention that at some point—this point—the power should terminate and the trustees' discretion with their power of sale prevail? The instrument has created this situation, of course; at the time when it was drawn no one gave apparent thought to what should happen if the refusal to consent makes no sense and seems designed simply to annoy others. In any event, when the instrument provides no express provision, the authorities suggest that no better answer is available from the courts than the unpredictabilities of a construction of that instrument in the light of such extrinsic evidence as is admissible.

An administration power given to a person who is a co-beneficiary is not readily to be characterized as for the donee's sole benefit. The power to consent, or to direct, as to the trustees' investments when granted to

consequent accountability obligation? The no-accountability school makes this assumption, as does Mr Cullity's paper (n. 6 above).

[31] *Snell's Equity* (29th edn., 1990), 562–7.

a sole life tenant who is a surviving spouse might well be thought self-evidently to have been given in order that the life tenant may ensure there is a entire portfolio of such high-income-producing securities as are compatible with prudence. Nevertheless, the case law suggests that when the terms of the trust create successive interests the court may well stipulate that more evidence than the mere conferment of the power is required that the trust creator intended to depart from the even-hand principle.[32] Clearly the capital beneficiaries will be disadvantaged by exclusive investment in high-income-producing fixed interests. However, provided the limits of the power are otherwise compatible with impartiality, it may be that the court will be prepared to condone the self-interest that is expressly permitted. An English court[33] condoned what would have been a breach of the conflict-of-interest rule when it permitted a life tenant, authorized to direct the trustees as to the securities they should purchase, to require of the trustees that they purchase from him certain shares in his personal ownership. The court demanded only that the life tenant act in good faith and offer the shares at a fair price. When one comes to reflect on the outcome of the decision, it seems apparent that the court was balancing a settlor-desired self-interest with the principle that all administration be disinterestedly objective. It was upholding what it found to be the trust creator's intent that there might be a sale by a beneficiary of his own property to the trust, but it was also assuming that the limits of the power to direct acquisition by the trustees were intended to lie short of where the donee of the power is without integrity and is seeking to take unfair advantage.

As we shall see, if the court finds that a power was not granted for the donee's sole benefit, the donee of the power is a fiduciary. That may appear self-evident, but the point being made is that, so far as private donative trusts are concerned, the case law admits of no middle ground, where the donee may properly have regard to his or her own personal benefit and at the same time have the obligation to consider and weigh the benefit of others.[34] The absence of a possible middle ground is particularly demonstrated when one examines dispositive powers. Let us look at an example. Suppose an irrevocable *inter vivos* trust with a trust company as sole trustee, and the instrument grants a power of appointment to the income beneficiary, a son of the settlor, to appoint the capital 'among [the settlor's] grandchildren'. At the time of the creation of the trust the settlor has six grandchildren, two of whom are the children of the donee of the power. There is a default gift to the settlor's two children equally. Shortly after the settlor's loss of capacity the son ap-

[32] *Scott*, n. 8 above, at 563–8.
[33] *Re Hart's Will Trusts* [1943] 2 All ER 557.
[34] This subject is examined later in greater detail. See pp. 92–98, below.

points the entire capital to his then three children. That there is need among the remaining grandchildren is indisputable. In this instance it must be concluded that the donee of the power has been authorized to have sole regard to his own family interests. That proposition excludes any degree of requirement that the donee even put his mind to what he might do in order to benefit his sibling's offspring.[35]

Not even the imposition of trusteeship upon the donee of the mere power automatically means the donee is a fiduciary with regard to the power. The power may be given to the donee in his personal capacity,[36] and this may be apparent both from the character of the donee and the persons (or objects) in favour of whom the power is granted. Take another example. Suppose a will empowers the executors and trustees to make an *in specie*, equal-in-value distribution of the testator's 'personal effects' among the testator's three children 'as my Trustees at their discretion think fit'. The named executors and trustees are the testator's son, X, and a close friend, Y. The friend dies shortly after probate has been taken out, and X continues the administration alone. There are three particular items among the deceased's effects which all the siblings would like to have; X divides the effects into three parts of equal monetary value but all three items are in his own share. If the power is personal to the named trustees, then he is entitled to do that. Would it make any difference if evidence was available and admissible that X had said that, since he wished to have all three items, that was an end of the matter, that he had no obligation to consider his siblings' position or such objective fairness as would allocate one such item to each sibling? The answer is surely no. The scope of the power includes his taking any such item for himself as is pleasing to him. Had he been given the power in his capacity as an express trustee of the instrument, he would be subject to the fiduciary rules of conduct and the duty to give his mind as to how he should exercise the power among the members of the beneficiary class or the named beneficiaries of the power.[37] His own position as a co-beneficiary would then be a consideration that he could not entertain, unless the testator could otherwise be said to have impliedly authorized the conflict of interest and duty, and waived any objection. Needless to say, when the donee of the power is not a trustee also of the trust property and is himself a possible appointee, it is difficult to imag-

[35] This example demonstrates also the difficulty of defining 'personal benefit'. It includes any advantage to the donee of the power himself, which would include the advantage of those close to the affections of the donee. *Pilkington* v. *IRC* [1964] AC 612 (HL) in another context reveals the nebulous character of the concept of 'benefit'.

[36] See, n. 28 above.

[37] *Re Hardy* (1952) 29 MPR 358, [1952] 2 DLR 768. In this case the trustee in question was a friend of the testator; the construction problem is more difficult when the trustee is a child, one upon whom the testator has leaned.

ine any circumstances when the court will find a coincidental intent of the creator of the trust that the donee should exercise the power as a fiduciary. The two positions are totally contradictory.

The Manner of Exercise of the Power

Provided he acts within the scope (and intention) of his power,[38] it seems to be generally accepted that, if the holder of a power does not hold that power as a fiduciary, the courts are not going to impose restraints or criteria as to behaviour upon him in the exercise or non-exercise of that power. That would mean that, in the case of our earlier example of an elderly person with a power to consent to the sale of the family home in which he is living, it matters not what motivates his refusal to consent. Given that he is mentally capacitated, he may effectively act within the scope of his power by withholding his consent to sale for reasons that to him alone seem best. This is precisely the judgment to which the court came in *Re Green Estate*.[39] The trial judge himself had 'no hesitation'[40] in saying that, from a practical point of view as well as in the elderly woman's self-interest, the time had come for sale, if it had not passed. However, he held he had no statutory power to overrule the donor's capacitated refusal to consent to sale, and dismissed the trustee's application. Of course, the power to consent to the sale of a house in which the donee of the power is resident constitutes perhaps one of the most familiar of these administrative powers given to a person other than the trustees. Older settlors of *inter vivos* trusts, and spouses of those making their wills, entertain so often a dread that their children will move them in their failing years to a nursing home; they seek nothing with more determination than the right to die in the home they have occupied for years. The courts naturally reflect in their judgments this very natural and innocent desire, and that is why this particular power is almost always found, as a matter of intention, to be non-fiduciary in character. Other powers, such as the power to consent to the sale of unserviced land and the power to vary or terminate a trust, do not enjoy this readiness of the courts to construe them as non-fiduciary.

However, in *Scott*'s opinion[41] American case authority leaves no doubt

[38] *Halsbury's Laws of England* (4th edn.), xxxvi, paras. 951 and 962, states that all power-holders must act within the scope of their powers, but that holders only whose powers are for the benefit of others are subject to the 'fraud on a power' rule. The latter rule (see, n. 31 above) is that the power-holder must act in good faith and therefore not appoint 'to effect some object that is beyond the purpose and intent of the power' (para. 962). In the present writer's opinion, however, that rule can be said to operate with the scope of the fiduciary power as the test to be applied. 'Abuse of the power' is essentially a scope of the power concern rather than a behaviour concern.

[39] (1983) 45 NBR (2d) 17. [40] *Ibid.* 18. [41] N. 8 above, at 569.

that, if the holder of the power in question (a power creating an *opportunity* to act) is a fiduciary (one who must act or omit to act for the benefit of others), the standard of behaviour demanded of the holder is that demanded of the express trustee. 'The principles that are applicable', writes Scott, 'are those that apply to discretionary powers conferred on a trustee.'

Those principles are, of course, well established, but in an area of law noted for its generalities it is useful to be reminded what they are, and to what extent they are of assistance to the would-be challengers of a power-holder's action or inaction.[42] A trustee who has a mere power cannot release the power, and he must apply his mind whenever it would be reasonable for him to do so, as to whether he should be exercising the power, and, if so, in what manner. The exercise must be in good faith. That is, he must entertain no irrelevant motives or considerations, such as the unpleasant character of one of the beneficiaries of the fiduciary relationship, and his attitude of mind must be that of a reasonable person who has informed himself for the particular decision he has to make and is seeking to achieve for the beneficiary or beneficiaries what seems genuinely and objectively best.

If this description of the standard of behaviour required appears amorphous to a degree, at least it appears more helpful than another approach, which is to conceive of good faith as the absence of bad faith. As a general proposition, the courts will not interfere with the exercise of discretion by the fiduciary unless bad faith is proved by those alleging it, and, should it be proved, they will merely require that the fiduciary or a court-appointed substitute undertake the *bona fide* exercise of the discretion that should have been made in the first place. A fiduciary's actual decision as to what should be done will not be successfully challenged before a court unless that decision is outside the range of decisions to which an informed, objective, and prudent person could have come. This is the reasonable person test.

How far will the court intervene if the trustee or a fiduciary holds a mere power, necessarily for the sole benefit of others, and he acts in a manner which is outside the scope of the power or he exercises the power within its scope but in a manner other than that of the informed, objective, and prudent person? It is clear that the court will not exercise the discretion given to the holder of the mere power. It is after all an *opportunity* to exercise a discretion, whether the power be administrative or dispositive. Nor, of course, will a court exercise a trust power, where the trustee (or fiduciary donee) *must* exercise the discretion.[43] Neither power can be released because, while this is evidently so when

[42] See further, pp. 101–103, below.

[43] This is most likely to be a dispositive power.

the power *must* be exercised, the trustee or fiduciary holding a mere power owes it to the power's described beneficiaries to consider whether, and, if so, how benefit to or among that class could best be achieved. In terms of what it has the means to accomplish, a court can and will remove and replace the trustee or fiduciary if the wrongful conduct and its effect justify that approach, and at the other extreme it may simply criticize the trustee or fiduciary, leaving him to correct his ways. There are a number of courses in between those two extremes that the court may take, such as the issue of an injunction against repeated wrongful conduct. And these courses of possible judicial response are common to trustee-holding and fiduciary-holding alike of both mere powers and trust powers. The only difference would be that, since a trust power is an *obligation* to exercise the discretion, it is that power which will attract the more exacting and demanding court order. Lord Wilberforce in *McPhail* v. *Doulton*[44] discussed solutions that the court might adopt when trustees have a dispositive discretion that they *must* exercise, and fail to discharge that duty. *Scott*[45] speaks of 'an abuse of discretion or [the trustee or fiduciary who] threatens to abuse the discretion conferred on him.'

If the trustee or fiduciary is within the scope of his power in what he does or fails to do, and his manner of exercise of that power satisfies the test of what a reasonable person might have done, then the trustee or fiduciary is beyond assault. It matters not that those who did benefit or might have benefited from the exercise of the power are dissatisfied with what the trustee or fiduciary has done or has not done. Provided the applicable fiduciary obligations have been honoured, whether the power be dispositive or administrative, the holder of the power is beyond challenge.

Where 'abuse of the discretion' has already occurred, as when the holder of a power to direct the trustees' investment acquisitions requires them to make a loan to himself at the going interest rate, thus breaching the no-profiteering rule, or the holder has the power to consent to the sale of commercial real property and withholds his consent when sale is obviously advantageous to the trust beneficiaries, thus acting to the detriment of the interested parties, the court can remedy the situation. It can issue an injunction against any personal unauthorized profit-taking by the trustee or fiduciary, it can require the harming trustee or fiduciary to account for loss caused to the trust capital, whether the loss is caused by an *ultra vires* act, an improper exercise of the power, or fraud or negligence, and it can order the trustees (inside whose trust a trustee or a fiduciary holds the power) to sell despite the non-forthcoming con-

[44] N. 16 above.

[45] See, nn. 8 and 38 above. 'Abuse' in this context means behavioural deviation.

sent. Courts in all common law jurisdictions possess these means to prevent further abuse and to obtain compensation for loss caused. Though the court in the New Brunswick precedent of *Re Green Estate*[46] decided the Trustee Act of that province gave it no authority—which it would have exercised—to override the refusal of the elderly holder of the power to consent to a sale, this was not the conclusion of Maugham J in *Re Beale's Settlement Trusts.*[47] Clear statutory authority to override the refusal existed in section 30 of the Law of Property Act, 1925,[48] but the judge also found authority in section 57(1) of the Trustee Act, 1925,[49] which authorizes the court to confer 'the necessary power' upon trustees where for the purposes of the 'management or supervision' of property the trustees lack such a power and their possession of it would be 'expedient'.

Breach of Fiduciary Obligation, and the Compliant Trustee

If under the terms of the trust the opinion of a majority of the trustees, or of one particular trustee (for instance, the spouse of the testator or settlor), is to prevail in the event of a difference between the trustees, the minority or the co-trustees in the case of the particular trustee have a duty to bring the matter before the court if they reasonably entertain the view that the contemplated action or inaction of the majority, or of the particular trustee, constitutes a breach of trust. At this point, of course, we are essentially concerned with administrative powers, but breach will not always exist. If the minority trustees merely cannot agree with a decision that is both authorized by the instrument and is within the range of what is reasonable, they are required to lend their formal approval to necessary documentation and other procedural requirements for the carrying out of the decision. In any minutes of meetings they may also have their dissent recorded.

It is in this way that the case law introduces a balance between the stalemate in decision-making that might otherwise occur, possibly to the injury of the beneficiaries, and the danger that the substance of the disagreement involves action or inaction that in fact constitutes breach. Again, breach may cause injury and loss to the trust beneficiaries. The role of the minority or of the co-trustees when it is a particular trustee who has the exclusive power is to ensure that decisions dictated to them are those which a court would permit trustees to take, whatever the court itself might have decided in the circumstances.

However, as we have said, trust laws are largely default rules. Suppose the testator or settlor expressly states that the minority trustees or the

[46] N. 39 above. [47] [1932] 2 Ch. 15. [48] 15 Geo. 5, c. 20.
[49] 15 Geo. 5, c. 19.

co-trustees shall not be liable for the consequences of any decision taken at the direction of the majority trustees or the particular trustee. Would this excuse the minority or co-trustees if the consequences were loss and the decision itself was a breach? Courts in the common law jurisdictions are rarely prepared to say that an exculpatory clause shall have its full possible meaning.[50] Given the breach that has occurred, and a degree of judicial condemnation of that particular act or inaction, the court may well take the view that the testator or settlor could never have intended the clause to apply and to exculpate in the circumstances that have actually happened. The very generality of exculpatory clauses facilitates this interpretation. Professional trustees are especially vulnerable to this approach, and even the more sophisticated non-professional trustee will be hard put to it to show that, though he was in a position to do something to prevent or arrest the breach, he was justified in doing nothing or too little. A trustee, after all, is a fiduciary, one who within the scope of his task will act selflessly for the benefit of others. Where he is aware of trustee wrongdoing, he will not permit his sense of oneness with his fellow trustee or trustees to restrain him from taking the course that only he can take if loss is not to be caused to the beneficiaries, however distasteful in the circumstances any public disavowal of his co-fiduciaries might be.

On the other hand the testator or settlor might be understood by the court to have meant what he said. He *is* putting the risk of loss, and non-recovery of that loss from the trustees who are responsible, upon his beneficiaries. This analysis and conclusion are most likely when the trustee is, or the trustees include, his spouse. If the trustees are not relatives or close friends, and particularly when they are professionals who charge for their trustee services, such a judicial conclusion is least likely.

The paramount duty of the trustee remains that, if he cannot prevent by his vote what he understands to be breach or possible breach, he applies to the court for advice and directions. If conduct is about to be perpetrated that will imperil the beneficiaries' best interests, he does not think first how he can avoid any blame. How far have the courts applied this thinking to trusts when the holder of a power, whether to consent or to direct, is someone other than a trustee of the trust? The most familiar situation, as we have said, is the circumstance when the holder of the power has the authority to direct the trustees' acquisition and sale of investments, or to consent to their buying and selling intentions. By direction of the power-holder securities are purchased which are speculative by any standard, and later loss is suffered; because of refusal to

[50] See e.g. D. W. M. Waters, *Law of Trusts in Canada* (2nd edn., 1984), 755–8.

consent on the part of the power-holder shares are retained that the wise investor would undoubtedly have sold.

Where the holder of the power may properly exercise it for his own benefit, he is not therefore a fiduciary with regard to the power, and the trustees are concerned only that the holder directs or consents strictly as he is authorized by the instrument and by law to do. Again, the test is whether the power-holder is acting within the scope of his power. Whenever the power-holder within his power directs, or further to his power he withholds his consent, the trustees must accept that decision, even if they regard the direction or refusal to have been made oblivious and uncaring of its effects upon others. Of course, that very state of affairs—the injurious effect on others' interests—may lead the court to conclude that the holder was actually intended to act for the benefit of others rather than himself, but this would very rarely or never be a reasonable conclusion as to the intent when the holder is a member of the class among whom he is empowered to make a discretionary distribution.[51]

The holder of a power who must exercise it for the sole benefit of others is subject to the fiduciary duties we have already discussed, and with those equitable obligations of the holder comes the correspondingly more compelling argument that the trustees of the trust in which the power appears have a positive duty to protect the interests of the beneficiaries. If the trustees know, or ought to have known, that the fiduciary holder of the power is acting beyond the scope of his power or is exercising his discretion improperly in the directions he has given or with his refusal to consent, then, it is contended, those trustees are themselves in breach. *Scott*[52] puts it this way: 'In such a case the trustee is under a duty similar to that which one trustee owes with respect to his co-trustees.' Of course, it is established that such a trustee is himself liable for breach if by his own activity he could have prevented or arrested the breach by his co-trustees. If the power-holder is not otherwise a trustee, it matters not, say the injured beneficiaries, that the trustees are expressly required by the trust instrument to accept the directions of the fiduciary holder of the power, or not to question his refusal to consent. As we have seen,[53] it may well also be no defence that the trustees are expressly exonerated from the consequences of their implementing the directions, or of accepting the refusal of consent to their considered and proposed trustee acts.

Not surprisingly the courts are divided in their response to the ques-

[51] It would certainly lead to added difficulties. Current criteria for determining whether the power-holder's conduct in exercising the power is wrongful are necessarily very general in expression. But if, additionally, conduct need not be exclusively selfless, where in any set of facts does conduct smack too much of self-concern? How do we determine objectively when legitimate self-concern has become selfish?

[52] N. 8 above, at 574.

[53] At pp.84–85, above.

tion whether trustees who know or suspect breach by the fiduciary holder of the power are responsible, together with the fiduciary, for the loss that ensues to the trust. *Scott* provides five case authorities on the point;[54] two concern the co-trustee of the trust, and are therefore strictly irrelevant.[55] Two others concern a holder who was the settlor of the trust, where the court in each instance held the trustee liable to make good the loss.[56] However, in one of these cases, as *Scott* states, this first instance decision was reversed on appeal.[57] The other[58] is particularly interesting because the trustee was held in fault for not applying to the court for an override of the settlor's refusal to consent to sale of the retained speculative investments. This is a familiar ground of liability of the trustee who is confronted with refusal to sell from his co-trustee.[59] The fifth case[60] again concerned a settlor, this time with the power to direct investments, but, though the trustee actually suggested to the settlor the purchase that was then directed by the settlor, namely, the acquisition of second mortgages from the trustee bank's affiliate, the court refused to hold the trustee liable for the loss. This was done on the ground that an express term of the trust instrument entitled the trustee to act on the written instructions of the settlor. The settlor himself, who brought action, was the life tenant, but the capital beneficiaries were his wife, nephews, and nieces. In these circumstances the power was surely fiduciary in character.

The problem of the compliant trustee has notable and particular concern today for pension plans.[61] It is a familiar practice for the pension trust documentation to entrust the custodianship of the trust fund portfolio to a trust (or trustee) corporation as trustee for this purpose. The custodian is to provide safekeeping, and to transfer and receive securities as they are traded by the plan trustee (often the employer) or the plan trustees (persons nominated as to some of their number by the employer and as to the others by the labour force). If the plan trustee or trustees are engaged in an imprudent high-risk policy in their choice of investments, is it a responsibility of the custodian trustee, whose safe-

[54] N. 8 above, at 574–5.

[55] *Matter of Cross*, 172 A 212 (1934), rev'd. 176 A 101 (1935) (NJ); *Matter of Langdon*, 277 NYS 581 (1935).

[56] *Matter of New York (Cowles)*, NYLJ, 9 Jan. 1964; *Steiner* v. *Hawaiian Trust Co.*, 393 P 2d 96 (1964).

[57] *Ibid.*

[58] *Steiner* v. *Hawaiian Trust Co.*, n. 56 above.

[59] *Fales* v. *Canada Permanent Trust Co.* [1977] 2 SCR 302, 70 DLR (3d) 257.

[60] *Reeve* v. *Chase National Bank*, 287 NYS 937 (1936).

[61] Or superannuation schemes, as they are known outside North America. The nature of the corporate employer's power to increase benefits to members from actuarial surplus in an on-going plan, or from actual surplus upon a plan termination, and the employer's consequent obligations to its employee members, is an issue which is considered later. The reference here to employee benefit plans connects such plans with the present discussion.

guarding duties are carefully delineated in the custodian trust instrument, to refuse to question this acquisition of high-risk investments? If the answers are unsatisfactory or answer is not forthcoming, should the custodian trustee inform the plan members (the active and retired employees) of what is going on, should it apply to the court for directions, or should it be content punctiliously to carry out its own delineated duties?

In *Froese* v. *Montreal Trust Company*,[62] a case recently heard in British Columbia, the issue did not concern a custodian trustee and the plan trustee (or trustees). It involved a corporate trustee of the plan which was vested with the trust fund, carried out the investment policy, and paid entitlements on direction of the corporate employer to the retired or otherwise entitled corporate employee/members. The corporate employer was required under the plan to make annual contributions to the corporate trustees in order to provide an actuarially-calculated, full funding of the current liabilities. It administered the plan, and determined the entitlements of employee members, who themselves were required to make their own contributions from salary or wages. The employer collected these contributions, and remitted them to the trustee. The trustee was expressly under no liability for the size of payments to be made to members; it was to accept the *ipse dixit* of the company on such matters. The company alone was enabled to bring action against the trustee, and the trustee was responsible to no one for the adequacy of the trust fund to fulfill the current liabilities. That was the company's obligation. The members, who dealt solely with the employer's pension committee, played no part in any aspect of the trust administration or the plan administration. As the corporate trustee knew, however, if the company was not ensuring that the plan and the funding of the benefits were being administered solely with the members' interests in mind, no one was doing that.

The company had the power of amending the plan, and in 1985, in order to pursue a more 'aggressive' investment policy and thus reduce its own contribution requirements, the company took fund investment out of the trustee's hands, as the instrument enabled it to do, and put that responsibility into the hands of consultants who would carry out this new policy. In October 1987 came the market crash, and the fund lost heavily. Thereafter, the company itself being in difficulty, company contributions to the trustee were reduced, were irregular and in odd amounts; the plan was in fact insolvent, and ultimately, when the company failed and the plan was wound up, a substantial shortfall in plan-funding became apparent. Was the corporate trustee liable to the plan

[62] (1995) 8 BCLR (3d) 262.

members for this shortfall? Had the trustee an obligation as from 1985 to inform the plan members? As of that year it knew of the change of investment policy and later it knew or could have known of the pattern of unsatisfactory contribution payments of the company. After all, the plan members were the beneficiaries of the trust, even if the trustee had business relations with the company only.

The trial judge obviously found the issue extremely difficult to determine, for his judgment only appeared nine months after argument concluded. However, he concluded there was no liability on the trustee. The trustee, he held, had no obligation to offer unsolicited opinion to the trust beneficiaries; there was nothing in the trustee's task as set out in the trust agreement that required it to be responsible for the beneficiaries or that necessitated their assistance. It was simply not the place of the trustee to monitor the performance of the plan under the company's administration. The trust deed set out the duties of the trustee; none of *those* duties had been breached in any of the post-1985 events. And there was an end of the matter. In January 1996, after this paper has been delivered, this decision comes before the British Columbia Court of Appeal, and the issue will be whether the contrary opinion of *Scott*, on the basis of the US decisions he cites, is convincing, despite the far-reaching significance of such an outcome upon the entire industry of corporate custodian trusteeship. A result for the injured pension plan members must mean that across the industry custodian trusteeship rates will be increased, perhaps dramatically, with consequent increased overhead costs for all employee benefit plans. Even given the existence of collective bargaining, employees must find that much of the increased cost is assumed by themselves, deducted from their compensation for employment services.

On the other hand in the spectrum ranging from the established liability of an express trustee for the act or omission of his co-trustee (where the negligence or inactivity of the trustee is enough to attract that liability) to the potential liability of an express trustee for the act or omission of a fiduciary[63] power-holder, where is the line to be drawn between those who are liable as trustee for the other's conduct and those who are not? Is the situation conceptually different if on behalf of the beneficiaries the trustee has expressly and solely a particular task, and the fiduciary has expressly his own task? Where does that situation differ from the private trust instrument where one trustee has a discretionary power his co-trustee expressly lacks? Logically it seems *Scott* must be right.

[63] Whether the employer was a fiduciary was not discussed in the *Froese* case, but there is no doubt in the pension law context that this would have been the finding.

Death or Loss of Capacity or Absence of the Donee of the Power

The case law appears to suggest no clear line of thinking, if the instrument is silent, as to how this situation should be dealt with by the trustees. The tenor of the case authorities suggests an application to the court for directions is appropriate, but what the court is expected to order if the donee is a fiduciary of the power, or he must exercise the discretion it confers, is not readily apparent. Moreover, in imaginable instances trustees who are mandated to obtain consent from the power-holder may have little time before investment opportunities are gone, or the circumstances in which they would otherwise have acted are gone. Of course, this is not a problem that is experienced with the express trustee of the trust property as the holder of an exclusive power. If the instrument does not provide a means of appointment of a substitute trustee, or authorize the trustees to act with a depleted number of trustees in office, the court will have statutory or inherent authority to provide a replacement.

The problem is likely to be a constructional one. Was the express trustee given a power which he or she might exercise in his or her personal capacity, or solely *ex officio*? If the donee of the power might properly benefit himself, the power was surely given to him personally, but if he was to benefit others that must be his sole concern, and the question whether his replacement in the trustee office was intended to have the same power is a real issue.

In those circumstances where the donee of the power is not a trustee of the trust property other considerations arise. Where the donee *must* exercise his discretion, either to do something administrative such as direct the investment policy or dispositive in the form of naming trust beneficiaries, that donee, though not a trustee of the trust property, *is* a trustee, albeit of the power only, and the instrument or statute or the inherent jurisdiction will no doubt afford a modus of replacement.[64] But when the power, though to be exercised for the benefit of others, is a mere opportunity to act, the law will require the donee in all likelihood to give his mind on a regular basis to whether, and if so how, he should exercise the power. However, there may well be no modus of replacement that is available. So far as the inherent jurisdiction is concerned, the courts of the State or sub-unit in question may hold there is nothing

[64] Where the holder of the power is not a trustee of the property subject to the power, it has been said that English law would regard the holder as having a trust power in those circumstances only where the power is to appoint among a class of persons, and there is a trust for those persons in default of appointment: Parker and Mellows, *The Modern Law of Trusts* A. J. Oakley (ed.) (6th edn., 1994), 152–5. *Scott* would say that he who has the power to benefit others is a fiduciary, and, the writer would add, a trustee of the power when he must exercise it. The power is an asset.

they can do. What now is to be done by the trustees of the trust in which the power is to be found?

The answer should not be too difficult. The ready solution is that the law would permit the trustees to ignore the power of the donee, and authorize the trustees to assume the holder's power to direct, where the instrument takes that power from the trustees. In the alternative the court itself would be prepared to adopt an emergency inherent jurisdiction, and make on each occasion an appropriate order. American courts, which alone seem to have had occasion to deal with the problem, regard it as primarily a matter of construction of the trust instrument whether the power terminates on the inability of the donee to exercise it or, if the power is to continue, the trustees may ignore it. If it is to continue, both the nature of the power (that is, whether it is vital to the proper administration or the dispositive structure of the trust) and the circumstances that necessitate its exercise, determine the response the court will make as to whether the existence of the power can be ignored. If any trend exists, it is that the courts will authorize the trustees to ignore the power that is in hands other than their own.[65]

American courts seem disinclined to permit the committee (guardian, trustee, etc.) of a mentally incapacitated donee to exercise the power, and presumably this disinclination would extend to the guardian (tutor or curator) of a donee who happens to be still a minor when the testamentary trust that includes that power takes effect. What would be the attitude of the courts to the donee of an enduring power of attorney who seeks to exercise the power of an incapacitated power-holder? This can occur as an issue whether the power given to the now mentally incapable person is for his own benefit, or can be exercised only for the benefit of others. Again US case law suggests the courts in that country would not be happy with an attorney exercising a power for the benefit of others in the place of the actual power-holder. A fiduciary role should not be capable of being passed to anyone the power-holder is content to see conduct with unrestricted authority the settlor's affairs.[66] But at this point we begin to speculate; the authorities are few, and evidently there is no single direction of judicial thinking.

Settlors and testators are often concerned with the future possible bankruptcy, insolvency, or criminal behaviour of their trustees. Statute

[65] *Scott*, n: 8 above, at 577–8.

[66] Legislation in all the major Commonwealth common law jurisdictions (Trustee Acts, Powers of Attorney Acts, etc.) deals in varying ways and to a varying extent with absence of, and incapacities in, *express trustees*, but not other holders of powers. As to delegation, there is authority that the holder of a power of appointment may not delegate (*Snell's Equity*, n. 31 above, 567), and the case law suggests that no administrative power can be delegated unless the power concerns only ministerial (or day-to-day administration) decisions. See as to express trustees, Waters, n. 50 above, 706–7.

in Commonwealth jurisdictions provides for removal of the trustee in these circumstances. A power-holder who is in a conflict-of-interest and duty situation gives rise to a similar concern. Nothing appears in any mainland Trustee Act, so far as donees of powers are concerned. It is supposed that powers to appoint beneficiaries naturally fall into two classes, those that need not (thus providing no further problem) and those that must be exercised. The latter are trust obligations, and that problem would seem to be readily capable of solution. The Act should apply. As for administrative powers, the Trustee Acts associate these with express trust administration, and perhaps in any event this is a less pressing problem because it is the trustees who are vested with title to the trust property. There is the ultimate security. The trust property is secure, though the power be unexercisable.[67]

Employee Benefit Plans

The spate of legislation and of case law that has occurred within the last quarter century with regard to 'trusteed' pension plans and health and welfare plans has added another area of law where both legislatures and courts have had to rule on the several liabilities of those who find divided between them the task normally associated in private trusts, *inter vivos* or testamentary, with sole trusteeship. ERISA[68] in the United States, and the federal and provincial Pension Benefits Standards Acts[69] in Canada, commonly contemplate a situation with single employer pension plans where a trust corporation assumes the trusteeship of the securities that make up the trust portfolio, and the employer or a management committee conducts the administration of the plan *vis-à-vis* the members. This 'plan administrator' will discharge all the duties, and exercise all the powers, associated with the delivery of pension entitlements to 'active' and retired members, but it will also very often assume the task of investment of the trust portfolio, for which purposes it will hire agents such as investment consultants. Those consultants will work with brokers, for

[67] Administrative powers have not been divided into those that *must* be exercised (trust powers), and those that *may* be exercised (mere powers), but clearly they could be divided in this manner. E.g., in a trust of a portfolio of investments, a power to direct the trustees as to the sale and purchase of securities is impliedly a trust power if the trustees may not make sales or purchases other than on direction. It is impliedly a mere power if the trustees may otherwise sell and purchase on their own initiative. Obviously the settlor can make express his contrary intent in either case.

[68] Employee Retirement Income Security Act 1974, 29 USC, paras. 1001–1461 (1988 & Supp. III, 1991).

[69] The federal legislation is the Pension Benefits Standards Act 1985—RS 1985, c. 32 (2nd Supp.). The provincial legislation, as in the case of Ontario, is sometimes named the Pension Benefits Act.

whom the custodian trustee makes securities available when there have been sales, and from whom or through whom the custodian receives securities on purchases taking place.

ERISA sets out the standards of behaviour that are expected of those who are described as 'fiduciaries' in the discharge of various administrative duties involved with 'trusteed' plans, and in all common law jurisdictions that know trusts of this kind and what is in effect bifurcated trusteeship the case law is heavy with the question of who is a fiduciary in the discharge of the task or tasks that he has. The corporate custodian trustee may have express duties which result in it being nothing more than a bare trustee, and otherwise it acts as an agent of the plan administrator (or investor) in supplying its services when required by the administrator to do this or that task. On the other hand the custodian may have more extensive duties than mere provision of security for the trust portfolio, but still be an agent *vis-à-vis* the administrator because it performs other tasks associated with the trust at the regular call of the administrator who decides what shall be done, and when it shall be done. In these latter instances of custodianship it will be more difficult to interpret in what circumstances the custodian makes its own decisions (as a trustee) and where (as agent) it must accept the instructions of another. The custodian will expect to be able to look to the trust instrument to determine the scope of its duties and powers as a trustee, assuming that all those tasks that are not described as trust duties and powers it fulfills as an agent. However, even where in the instance of a particular plan that distinction can be made, that is not an end of the matter of determining to what standard of behaviour he must act who would discharge a duty, or exercise a power, assigned to him by the terms of a plan. An agent too is a fiduciary within the scope of his task. Given that a line can be drawn between trust and agency duties and powers, the issue then is whether the fiduciary obligations imposed on the agent approximate in intensity to those imposed upon the trustee.

So far as the non-trustee is concerned—one who is not vested with the trust property and who *prima facie* does not have a power or discretion which he must exercise, whatever discretionary decisions he makes in exercising the power—he too may be a fiduciary. That is to say, in the circumstances he must regard it as a power to benefit others, and he therefore owes the objects of the power the obligation to consider whether, and if so how, he should exercise the power in order to benefit them. Such a fiduciary obligation will arise, not only when he is empowered to act solely for the benefit of others, but where, if he decides not to act in the exercise of his power, the property subject to the power passes under the terms of the plan to himself. In *Mettoy Pension Trustees* v. *Evans*[70] this was the position. The trustee of the plan when the bankruptcy of the employer occurred was a privately incorporated trustee company. However, in the event of any liquidation the corporate employer had a power which enabled it to appoint surplus in the form of supplementary benefits to plan members. Those members were its employees. If in its discretion the corporate employer considered such further benefits to be something it would not award or award in sufficient amount to exhaust the surplus, the employer itself took the unappropriated surplus. The court held the corporate employer to be 'a fiduciary in the full sense'.[71] That is to say, it was in the circumstances a trustee of the power. It could not point to the default interest of its own, and assert that it had no duty of any kind to the objects of the power, the employees. It did not have the freedom, like any owner of property, to decide whether or not it would make *gifts* to the employees. It had a duty. It might not consider its own advantage; it must regularly put its mind to how it might exercise the power for the benefit of the members. It followed that it could not release the power, as the holder of a mere power may do, and its receiver or trustee in bankruptcy could not take the surplus for the creditors, who are the first and foremost concern of the receiver or trustee. In the event of bankruptcy a new trustee of the power would have to be appointed. The employees had a right to be considered for discretionary benefits.

The case law on employee benefit plans is therefore addressing two kinds of problems with which we are concerned in this paper. First, when is the holder of a power that is *prima facie* unassociated with any duty upon the donee subject to the obligations that are imposed upon a fiduciary?[72] Secondly, when is the trustee vested with the trust property (or trust portfolio) liable in lieu of, or together with, the fiduciary power-holder who originally caused loss through his fraud or negligence, and of whose wrongdoing the trustee—because of his own express duties—was aware or ought reasonably to have been aware? Can a custodian trustee plead superior orders, as it were, or is trusteeship a status that requires the holder to be concerned for any injury that may be occurring to, or threatening the best interests of, the trust beneficiaries?

On the first issue, namely, powers coupled with an obligation with regard to their exercise, unfortunately limited assistance is available. This is because the English case authority[73] in question has drawn a very

[70] [1990] 1 WLR 1587, [1991] 2 All ER 513. [71] *Ibid.* 1614 (WLR).

[72] i.e., is the holder of a power (or opportunity) to benefit others nevertheless subject to fiduciary obligations with regard to the object of the power, if the holder takes the property subject to the appointment power in default of his own appointment?

[73] *British Coal Corp.* v. *British Coal Staff Superannuation Scheme Trustees Ltd* [1995] 1 All ER 912, at 925; *Re Drexel Burnham Lambert UK Pension Plan* [1995] 1 WLR 32 at 39.

clear distinction between private donatory trusts, familiar in the testamentary and *inter vivos* estate-planning setting, and employee benefit trusts. The English courts see these benefit trusts as the outcome and part of the contract of employment. The trust beneficiaries are not volunteers receiving the bounty of a donor; for these beneficiaries, whether or not they are individually required as employee members to contribute, the benefit plan is part of the consideration the employer pays for the employee services it receives. Collective bargaining between employer and union will make this state of affairs abundantly clear, but even in the absence of such bargaining the employer is purchasing services from its employees with the pension, medical, dental, disability, and similar benefits that it extends to its employees. And this is so whether such plans are generous ('Cadillac plans') or as minimal in what they offer as the market for the particular labour permits.

As a result authorities like *British Coal Corporation* v. *British Coal Staff Superannuation Scheme Trustees Ltd*,[74] carefully reasoned and analytical though they may be, are principally of value in that they precisely delineate the distinction between powers in private donative trusts and powers in employee benefit trusts. Reference to benefit that may flow back through the exercise of a power of appointment to the holder of the power must be seen against the background of a labour contract designed by the parties to provide mutual benefit.

In that case Vinelott J was concerned with whether the employer had the right to set off future instalment payments of a sum it had previously contractually obligated itself to contribute to the pension trust fund against the substantial accrued actuarial surplus in the fund. It sought, that is, a 'contribution holiday' as to amounts it was otherwise, absent an agreed instalment arrangement, bound to pay at once, a 'holiday' which it would expressly authorize by the exercise of its power in the instrument to amend the plan, following consultation—as was required—with the plan trustee. The trial judge held that no such exercise of the power was possible with regard to the employer's contractual obligation to fund fully those pension fund liabilities that already existed at the time of the application to the court. So far as future liabilities were concerned, for services not yet given or 'golden handshakes' not yet granted, that was different. Set-off against actuarial surplus might then be defensible, and the power be properly exercisable by the employer, even though the facilitating amendment to the plan directly or indirectly result in benefit to the employer.

The court also saw the decision in *Mettoy Pension Trustees* v. *Evans*, where a mere power was stepped up to a power with obligation, the

[74] N. 73 above.

holder of the power being in consequence 'a fiduciary in the full sense', as reached in the context of liquidation and plan winding-up. A power to distribute surplus, with a default entitlement in the empowered appointor, Vinelott J characterized differently in the situation where the plan was, and foreseeably would remain, a going concern. In doing this he expressly adopted Browne-Wilkinson V-C's words in *Imperial Group Pension Trust Ltd* v. *Imperial Tobacco Ltd.*[75] The power-holding employer was not there described as being a fiduciary; rather it was bound in the employment contract by an implied term that the employer as appointor would demonstrate good faith towards its employee members. This implied term was therefore the source of a duty similar to that which arose in *Mettoy Pension Trustees* from the fiduciary (trusteeship) characterization of the power-holding. The employer could not 'set limits to the benefits provided for members or pensioners for a collateral purpose without regard to their legitimate expectations'. This expression in the negative of the power-holder's duty arose from 'the relationship of confidence and trust between employer and employee' and the implied term that the employer will not knowingly injure that relationship.

The contract of employment, as noted here, permeates all the judicial statements about powers to determine directly or indirectly who, including the holder, shall have benefit from an exercise of the power. In each reported instance the trustee of the 'trust', or of the fund, is another person or is the trustee wearing the distinct other hat of a power-holder. What clearly emerges is that the type of trust under consideration will determine the character of the power. There are two separate conceptions of powers in the two settings of estate planning trusts and employee benefit trusts. What the courts are envisaging in both settings, but with different conclusions, are powers that allow the holder to consider his own advantage.

The ability of the power-holder in a private donatory trust to benefit himself, either as the default beneficiary or as one of the power objects, is regarded by these employee benefit plan cases as incompatible with a conclusion that the power-holder is a trustee of, or a fiduciary with regard to, the power.[76] It is in the operating and continuing benefit plan that one has to envisage an obligation upon the power-holder to have in mind others' interests, and yet at the same time the holder's valid entitlement to be not unaware of his own. The explanation for this approach in the benefit plan is that the contract of employment reflects an interdependence of the parties, one aspect of which is the interest of

[75] [1991] 1 WLR 589, at 597–600, [1991] 2 All ER 597.

[76] As between the trial judge in the *British Coal Corporation* case and the editors of the reports containing *Re William Makin & Son Ltd* [1991] PLR 177, quite some heat was generated on the point. See n. 73 above.

the employee in the continuing economic viability of the employer as the holder of the power.[77]

In the *Imperial Group Pension Trust* case Browne-Wilkinson V-C concluded that 'the pension trust deed and rules themselves are to be taken as being impliedly subject to the limitation that the rights and powers of the company can only be exercised in accordance with the implied obligation of good faith'.[78] That is, no more than good faith may be demanded of the corporate employer exercising a power, albeit that that power is found in the benefits trust plan. Though Canadian employers holding the same type of powers will invoke this English authority, it is not at all sure that Canadian courts will pay that authority much attention. In *Schmidt* v. *Air Products of Canada Ltd*[79] in 1994 the Supreme Court of Canada held that 'trusteed' employee benefit plans are trusts in the full sense, not to be interpreted, that is, against the background of any other legal doctrine. So, the hybrid contract and trust analysis of pension plans being apparently rejected, Canadian case authorities concerned with existing trust funds and the powers of employers to consent to benefit increases recommended by the plan administrator, or to exercise an employer choice between benefit of the employee and benefit of the shareholder, are measurably of greater interest in the present context than the English cases. It seems Canadian authorities may well come to afford guidance on the language that gives rise in private trusts to discretionary powers that must be exercised, and those that merely may be exercised.[80]

As to the second issue, namely, to what extent the benefit plan trustee, whether custodian trustee or sole trustee, is liable for the loss caused by the dishonesty, neglect, or unauthorized act of the holder of a power conferred by the trust deed or plan, the situation is different. The parallel with trustees and protectors in private *inter vivos* trusts is exact. Indeed, why should there be a difference between the law's approach to trustees of one type of express trust as opposed to another? On any particular occasion the practitioner may be concerned with the liability of the trustee who is vested with sole trusteeship of the trust property, the administrative powers and the dispositive 'trusts', but who must obtain

[77] Neither counsel in *Imperial Group Pension Trust* felt able to argue that the power in that case was fiduciary. 'If this were a fiduciary power', said the trial judge, 'the company would have to decide whether or not to consent [to the proposed amendment increasing pensions] by reference only to the interests of the members, disregarding its own interests. This plainly was not the intention': n. 75 above, at 596 (WLR).

[78] N. 75 above.

[79] [1994] 2 SCR 611, 115 DLR (4th) 631. For a valuable article on the interplay of trust law and contract principles in this decision, and subsequent lower court decisions, see Eileen E. Gillese, 'Contribution Holidays' (1995) 15 *Estates & Trusts J* 136.

[80] Unfortunately it is only the English cases that investigate powers, and do so at such depth.

the consent or accept the direction of another on the exercise of certain powers or the discharge of certain 'trusts'. Alternatively, the trust in question may be an employee benefit plan where one person is the custodian of trust property and the power of investment—among other powers—is in the 'plan administrator'. Should the power holder himself be insolvent or bankrupt, the issue is the same as to whether the risk of loss through his culpability falls upon the trustee who knew or ought to have known of the existence and likely outcome of the power holder's actions or inaction.

Opinion in the United States is divided so far as 'directory pension plans' are concerned. *Scott,* as we have seen, would impose on the custodian trustee the liability of a co-trustee as if the duties and powers of the trust were, as is usual, located jointly in both (or all) the trustees. Only when the power holder is entitled to use the power for his own benefit would *Scott* appear to free the trustee of liability,[81] which, when imposed, would presumably be on the usual joint and several liability basis. This in turn would mean that *Scott* would foresee the beneficiary being entitled to sue either the trustee or the power holder, or to join them as co-defendants. The contrary view is that, where under the terms of the trust instrument trustee and power holder have distinct roles, application of the co-trusteeship principle, without authority in the instrument, both contradicts the distinctness of the trustee and power holder roles, and introduces cost and delay into the administration of the trust. If the pension legislation of the relevant jurisdiction imposes on the power holder the fiduciary standards of care and loyalty, it is said, whether by defining the duties and subjecting the holder to those duties, or by making the holder a trustee or a fiduciary in the exercise of the power, then the co-trustee principle would not be needed. Save of course, one must add, when the power-holder is insolvent or bankrupt at the time the breach occurs, and loss cannot be made good through a tracing action.

Looking back at this 30-year-old debate so far as 'directory pension plans' are concerned, it seems that *Scott's* view has been marginally more persuasive. However, in Canada, where *Air Products* has refused to distinguish the employment benefit trust as a legal phenomenon distinct from other trusts, *Froese* v. *Montreal Trust Company,* as we have seen, did not follow the *Scott* opinion. Whether this judgment will survive the appeal, we shall see; certainly judicial opinions other than that expressed in the *Froese* decision have been suggested in recent first instance decisions in Ontario.[82]

[81] *Supra,* n. 8, at 563.

[82] D. L. Campbell, 'Record-Keepers or Whistle Blowers? A Look at the Role of Pension Fund Custodians', (1995) 15 *Estates & Trusts J* 26, at 32–6.

Freeing the Compliant Trustee: Exculpation Clauses

In *Re Rogers* the trustees were required by the trust instrument 'to consult with and be governed by the advice of' a person who was a friend of the testator, but was not a beneficiary. The trustees were to obtain this direction 'in all matters relating to any investment in the [ABC Co.], and', the testator added, 'I release my said executors and trustees from all liability for any action that may be taken at the request of' the power-holder. These trustees applied to the court for directions, when the power-holder had acquired his own sharehold position in ABC Co. and refused also to consent to any sale of the estate shares. The trustees were allowed to proceed as they thought best with the estate investment, ignoring the consent or refusal to consent of the power-holder, and therefore the exculpation clause—entitling the trustee to hold on to the estate shares so long as consent to sale was not forthcoming, whatever the outcome to the value of the estate—was not put to the test.

Exculpation or exoneration clauses are familiar in offshore trusts that confer powers on protectors, largely no doubt because the professionals that assume the trusteeship of these trusts are not prepared to act without such protection. However, settlors themselves often opt for these clauses in order to encourage the protector to act freely in the exercise of his power or powers under the terms of the trust. The thinking is that no anxious trustee will be inhibiting the protector from action if exculpation is extended generously to the trustee.

Nevertheless, granted though they may be, how effective are these clauses? Reference has already been made to this subject,[83] and it need only be underlined at this point that they are unpopular with courts, especially where professional, fee-charging trustees are involved. There is no evidence that there is a difference of attitude to exculpation clauses among common law courts across the world when it comes to the liability of trustees for the loss caused by holders of a power. Jurisdictions are of varying minds so far as the instrument is concerned that excuses the trustee's 'simple' or 'ordinary' negligence;[84] they are of one mind when the instrument seeks to free the trustee from liability for wilful or conscious breach of trust, or for acts or failures that result in loss and with

The B.C. Court of Appeal by a majority (22 May, 1996) reversed the decision below. Breaking new ground, the C.A. held the trustee was in breach of a common law duty of case (a duty to warn), and of its fiduciary duty, to the beneficiaries. An application for Leave to Appeal to the Supreme Court of Canada can be expected.

[83] At pp. 84–85, above.

[84] Hence the exculpation clause in offshore trusts that provides the trustees shall be liable only for 'wilful fraud or dishonesty' and any 'act or omission in respect of which the Trustees cannot under the proper law for the time being of this Trust lawfully be exonerated from personal liability by the terms of this Trust'.

regard to which the trustee was reckless. In these instances of wilfulness or recklessness, whether it constitutes fraud at one extreme or gross negligence at the other, courts either construe the exculpation clause strictly so that it does not apply to the particular breach,[85] or they will rule, as frequently in the United States, that it is contrary to public policy.[86] Professional trustees are increasingly made subject these days to a higher standard of care than is applied to the non-professional, and therefore exoneration from 'ordinary negligence', even if recognized as valid in the particular jurisdiction, is unlikely to be of assistance to the fee-charging corporate trustee, the lawyer, and accountant, especially those who advertise their skills.

The *Re Rogers* exculpation clause—'I release my . . . trustees from all liability for any action that may be taken [by them] at the request of' the power holder—is therefore most unlikely to be accepted in any jurisdiction at face value. If the trustee knows or could reasonably have known when accepting the direction or the refusal to consent that the grantee of the power, though required to exercise the power for the benefit of others, was in fact acting outside his authority or within it but in a manner that constituted conscious wrongdoing, self-interest, or negligence, the courts are unlikely to allow the trustee to plead an exculpation clause. If in doubt whether it should accept the power-holder's direction or condone the holder's consistent withholding of consent, the trustee has a right and a duty to seek the court's advice and direction. This is the rule so far as the acts or inaction of a co-trustee are concerned, and *Scott* is of the opinion that the same should hold true so far as trustee liability for acts or omissions of fiduciary power holders is concerned.[87]

The mood of the courts during the last quarter century has been notably hostile to exculpation clauses, especially because in all Commonwealth jurisdictions the court possesses in any event a statutory power[88] to excuse any trustee wholly or in part who has acted 'honestly and reasonably', and 'ought fairly' to be excused. Where the beneficiaries comprise, or even include, children or the unborn, the elderly or those unskilled in financial management, the courts at large seem markedly unwilling to see the risk of trustee negligence of any kind pass from the trustee. Especially is this so if there is any finding of fact that takes the circumstances of breach beyond the bland exculpation clause that speaks of 'errors of judgment', 'mistake', or 'breaches of duty or trust

[85] 'No settlor could have intended to exonerate a trustee from the consequences of behaviour of this kind.'

[86] Exculpation clauses when the trustee has profited without authorization are also invalidated on the basis of their contravening public policy.

[87] It is obviously also true when a non-fiduciary has acted in 'abuse of the power' that is non-fiduciary.

[88] E.g., see Waters, n. 50 above, 1025–31.

committed in good faith'. Errors of judgment or mistake may be the result of incompetence or inattention; it is those failings that are the courts' concern. As for 'good faith', an apocryphally indefinite term, it will rarely be found where attention to obligation, and a level of competence and sagacity, constitute the reasonable expectation from the person who accepts to act on behalf of others.[89]

Exculpation clauses applicable to power-holders will be interpreted in all likelihood in the same way. *Scott*, as we have seen, is quite emphatic that, 'if the holder of a power of control holds it in a fiduciary capacity, he is subject to liability for losses caused by his negligence'. 'The principles that are applicable are those that apply to discretionary powers conferred on a trustee.'[90] This is an important conclusion; it will be recalled that so often settlors of offshore trusts aim to give a roving licence to the protectors they introduce into their instruments, and are silent on the liabilities of the protector. A generous exculpation clause for the benefit of the protector from any consequences of his own conduct appears to some to be a natural complement to the grant of the licence.

Judicial Control of the Trustees of a Discretionary Trust[91]

If holders of powers that are exercisable solely for the benefit of others are indeed held to the same obligations that the law imposes on the trustees of discretionary trusts, the question at this point is what level of effective control the law does in fact possess over those who hold powers that they are under an obligation to exercise. The power-holder may be the trustee of a discretionary trust, or the fiduciary holder of a power that must be exercised, but who is not the trustee of the property involved.

The discretions as to *who, how much, when,* and *in what form* (or such of those discretions that are granted) are for the power-holder, but he must make those decisions and, if he does not, the court will replace him with persons who will discharge the obligation, or it will impose some other solution that gets the job done and done to appropriate standards. The courts in these cases require of trustees that from time to time, as is appropriate or required in the circumstances, they consider whether they should exercise the power and, if so, in what manner as between the objects of the power. Obviously the trustees may not commit fraud on the power by appointing to non-objects, or to objects contingent upon those appointees agreeing to benefit non-objects. But the rules con-

[89] On the judicial interpretation of good faith, see Maurice C. Cullity, (1975) 25 *U of Toronto LJ* 99.

[90] N. 8 above, 569. See also 570, n. 17, and the reference to (1959) 98 *Trusts & Estates* 1147.

[91] See Waters, n. 50 above, 758–62.

cerned with the exercise of the power are different; they supply the criteria by which we measure whether the power has been properly exercised. Did the trustees make a reasonable survey in order to learn of those who fall within the class of objects? Having carried out such a survey, did they entertain considerations that were irrelevant or prejudicial, given the purposes or ends for the trust that the instrument reveals? If they took into account such factors, then the exercise will be set aside. Beyond this there is really nothing the courts can do for the objects of the trust power. The discretions have been given to the trustees, not to the court, and as a consequence the court will not exercise them. Even if serious injury may occur to the beneficiaries' interests as a result of the trustees' failure properly to discharge their task, the court will simply void the exercise and require the trustees to act dutifully, or replace them.

This level of control of those holding a power that they must exercise suggests the potential control that can exist over protectors with a mere power. That is, while the protector is to exercise in favour of others the power that he holds, and is therefore a fiduciary, the power itself is one which, whether administrative or dispositive, he does not have to exercise. Here the analogy with the employee benefit cases may be drawn upon. Not only does the fraud on a power concept govern what the power-holder may do, he must show—as a fiduciary—that he has given his mind to the power, whatever its content may be, and has considered, when the circumstances were right, whether, and if so how he should exercise it.

The weakness of the trust power and the mere power from the point of view of the beneficiary, whether he is a potential recipient under a dispositive power, or a power beneficiary in the case of an administrative power, is the difficulty of obtaining evidence with regard to any power-holder's conduct. There is no legal requirement that the trustee of a power, even less the holder of a mere power, keep written records of his actions, and no call for 'the trust' to issue reports from time to time, as must corporate directors. It may be merely the indiscreet conversation with a third person, or a letter or memorandum that needed not to be written, that supplies the potential or other beneficiary with information. The duty of disclosure that the law demands is also in need of being reconsidered. Written materials originated in the course of conducting trust affairs must be revealed on demand, but the trustees and the holders of mere powers who write nothing, or maintain the barest 'action' minutes, are often in practice beyond the reach of the beneficiaries. And no beneficiary will be permitted to make accusations he cannot substantiate, intending thereafter to go on a 'fishing trip' for evidence by way of discoveries.

This evidentiary matter aside, however, there is a considerable armoury of rights that the object of a power has in order to ensure that the power-holder considers the opportunity or observes the obligation he has to exercise the power, and that he avoids acting in violation of that opportunity or obligation when he does exercise it.

THE CONTEMPORARY POWER-HOLDER: COURT CONTROL OF THE NEW PROTECTOR

The no-accounting school of opinion holds the view that, provided he respects public policy considerations in the governing jurisdiction, the settlor can surely intend and provide as he pleases. The old-time property lawyer's sole distinction between those who may act selfishly and those who must act selflessly remains as valid as it ever was when we are inferring the intent of the donor of assets.

Scott has made the point, as we have seen, that powers given to anyone except a beneficiary (or a number of beneficiaries together) are naturally interpreted as being for the benefit of persons other than the grantee, but, while this narrows down to a small number the administrative powers that, given silence in the instrument, are likely to be found non-fiduciary, it leaves a large number of appointment powers that are non-fiduciary. In practice so many special powers of appointment carry a gift over in default of appointment, and this fact signals to courts—and should so signal on the authority of texts no less celebrated than *Snell's Equity*[92]—that no trust power, and therefore no fiduciary duty to exercise or not exercise the power according to an accepted standard of behaviour, was intended.[93] In England it would seem to be because of the almost total absence of control the courts have over the power-holder's behaviour when exercising or not exercising such a power that Warner J's judgment in *Mettoy Pension Trustees* v. *Evans*, the employee benefit plan case, has been turned to with so much enthusiasm. That authority is now even footnoted by *Scott*.[94]

Control of trustees and fiduciaries in their observance of the scope of their powers, administrative or dispositive, and of their behaviour in exercising those powers, is evidently much more far-reaching than that accorded to powers that authorize but do not compel appointment, and which are held by non-fiduciaries. Even with the control the courts have over trustees, however, the person who invokes those controls will not find the going to be easy. What is expected of trustees who have discretions is clear in principle, but of necessity, given the number and

[92] N. 51 above, at 97.

[93] One suspects nineteenth century and earlier courts considered that the gift over clearly expressed the intent of the settlor or testator to be that action within the scope of the power was alone required.

[94] 1994 Supp., para. 185 (235).

diversity of discretions granted to trustees, the criteria governing their behaviour—what conduct constitutes 'abuse of discretion', to use *Scott*'s term—are somewhat vague and nebulous. The trustee must have acted reasonably in giving his mind to whether, and if so, how he should exercise his power. Vigilance, prudence, and sagacity were once judicially said to be what is looked for in trustees;[95] the exercise of discretions, whether held by trustees vested with the property or by third parties (or settlors) required to act as trustees of the power, calls in addition for integrity (good faith) and objectivity. In the past the criteria could be left fairly vague and general in expression because a homogeneous society innately understood how those criteria translated into specific conduct in given circumstances.

However, during the last half century all common law societies have become multi-cultural, the attitudes of today of those with the control of wealth are markedly diverse, and the global economy has materially advanced the fortunes of off-shore financial centres. The trusts of today are very different in form and provision from those of even thirty years ago, and the protector of the contemporary off-shore trust is but the latest in the doctrinal developments that worldwide investing and safekeeping of assets have brought. How far does the relatively historic case law concerning powers, both administrative and dispositive, meet the circumstances of the modern settlor and his trust-drafting lawyer with their eye on the domestic tax legislation, but also on the investment and safekeeping possibilities of places far from the same domestic turf?

The Specific Uses made Today of the Protector

Onshore (or Domestic) Trusts

In Canada, as we have said, trusts that are to be administered in Canada, where the settlor is resident together with most, if not all, of the beneficiaries, have hitherto rarely included the third-party power-holder device. Settlors have not felt the need for it, and in fact it can be a problem. It may cause the tax 'residency' of a trust to change, it may introduce a question as to the residency of the trustees, which may be held to include the protector, and it may change the *de facto* control of the trust from the trustees to this third-party holder of the power. Because of the concern that he himself might be held to control the trust if he were the power-holder, the settlor who wishes to create a power that is independent of the trustees and himself, will give it to a third party.

However, when the power is to appoint, and to delete and add, beneficiaries the settlor may select a beneficiary for that role. The most

[95] *Fales* v. *Canada Permanent Trust Co.*, n. 59 above, at 270 (DLR).

common use of the independent power in purely domestic trusts, other than to delegate the appointment of beneficiaries, including the addition of new beneficiaries and the deletion of existing beneficiaries, is the administrative power to remove and replace, or to add, trustees at discretion. Settlors are often apprehensive that their trustees will cease to follow the settlor philosophy as explained to them, or that the trustees' investment record will prove disappointing. The power to veto or consent to investments proposed by the trustees is popular. Settlors are also often fearful that with a corporate trustee charge of the trust affairs will be put in the hands of junior staff, or suffer from the passage of the file from hand to hand as the responsible staff change. The third-party holder, or the beneficiary holder, of the power to remove the trustee or trustees avoids the costs, delays, and uncertainties of applications to the court for removal.

An additional role that may be given to the power-holder is to consent to trustee distributions of income or capital or both when the trustees of the property are not dealing wholly or at all with fixed-interest beneficiaries, but have an obligation to exercise a discretion as to *who, how much, when,* and *in what manner* among a class (or an enumeration) of beneficiaries. This will be the now-classic discretionary trust. More generally, however, for reasons of 'residency' as explained, the settlor will not use the independent power-holder as a control lever on trustee distributions. Sufficient control is thought to be provided by the power to remove trustees. Yet another power met from time to time in purely domestic trusts is the authority to advise the trustees on the management of a business. The settlor will probably have transferred the business from his own management to the trustees, and through the 'adviser' he seeks not only to monitor, but to steer, the trustees' management.

All the same the scene domestically is changing; 'protectors' and 'appointors', with increasingly more extensive powers, are becoming familiar. On the other hand with his trustees close at hand in his own community, the settlor of a domestic trust can indulge his fear, if he is so inclined, that third party (or beneficiary) powers to consent to or direct trustee administration essentially add one more layer of costs and bureaucracy. Protectorships are then avoided.

Offshore (or Foreign) Trusts

When offshore trusts are drawn in Canada, and in particular when the drafting is done offshore, things are very different. Most of the change stems from the settlor concern, already mentioned in this paper, that his assets are held in title and being administered by trustees who are mostly corporate, and whom he knows only through the recommendation of his local advisers. He may or may not himself have visited the offshore jurisdiction, and he may not know in that unfamiliar setting, if he went there, what to ask. The power may have been created for any imaginable purpose, touching any aspect of the structure, operation, or termination of the trust.

The most familiar uses of the protector in mainland-drawn offshore trusts are to control the trustees through removal, approval of their remuneration, and consent to certain of their investment decisions. If the instrument creates a fully discretionary trust—and, if the settlor or the controller of the wealth is Canadian, it normally does—the powerholder will be empowered to add to, or delete from, the beneficiary class, and increasingly to consent to all capital distributions. We have already spoken of the power to keep the trustee or trustees to the settlor's non-binding 'letter of wishes'; this is increasingly common. The desire for confidentiality may keep these 'wishes' out of the instrument, but the settlor certainly expects that his 'wishes' will be adhered to without question. It seems that most mainland lawyers in drafting are now persuaded of the need to be able to move the seat of the trust or the assets swiftly from one offshore jurisdiction to another; powers to change the governing law of the trust (sometimes of the administration), and to move elsewhere the assets themselves, are now fairly standard.

Those who have considerable experience with offshore trusts, especially those practising in the offshore jurisdictions themselves, speak of powers to vary the trust terms and to resettle the assets in new or other estate-planned corporations or trusts, to remove the settlor with reserved powers who has lost capacity, to choose and instruct trust auditors, and to approve trust accounts. We have already mentioned the power to act as arbiter or mediator when trustee/beneficiary disputes occur. The power to determine tax planning of the trust is particularly welcome to trustees, it seems; this takes close liaison with the settlor's mainland tax advisers off the trustees' shoulders. However, it goes further; the power may be to assume the role to make 'aggressive' investments the trustee as a trustee hesitates over or declines, to keep information concerning the trust from the beneficiaries, to bring legal action against the trustees, and to release trustees from liability for breach.

It is evident that these latest mentioned powers are inserting the powerholder (a third party, less frequently a beneficiary or group of beneficiaries) deep into the fiduciary relationship between trustee and beneficiary that is the doctrinal heart of the common law trust concept. And, of course, the writer is assuming that the offshore jurisdictions here in question are either historically common law jurisdictions or they have statutorily and in detail adopted the common law trust. All are likely to be in close and continuing touch with London and New York for the purpose of trading securities through asset custodians there, and to be drawing their clientele from both major common law and civil law countries.

It has been questioned[96] whether the settlor can effectively confer powers that give to a disinterested third party the beneficiary's right to information and to receive accounts, to sue for breach of trust or to release the trustee from liability. If we say the essential characteristics of a trust are the fiduciary relationship between the trustee and the beneficiary, and property under the control of the trustee, then these powers arguably do violate that dichotomy of rights and duties that connect beneficiary and trustee. These powers do not make the power-holder a delegate or agent of the beneficiary; the power-holder, like the trustee and the beneficiaries themselves as to their duties and rights, looks to the instrument as the sole source of his authority. He answers to no beneficiary, and therefore can be called to account in a court of law by none, unless he himself independently is a fiduciary towards the beneficiary. The remedies of the trust beneficiary against the trustee to compel both good quality administration, and the performance of property disposition obligations as set out in the instrument, are otherwise not available against the power-holder. At the same time, the non-fiduciary power-holder is subject to the judgment of the courts only in that anything he does must lie within the scope of his power. Beyond that he accounts to no one. A fertile judicial mind might be able to find within the notion of 'equitable fraud' an application of the fraud on a power doctrine that sees abuse of a power in the poor standard of behaviour of the power-holder. It is unlikely, however, that this level of behaviour control could be reached; if a power is non-fiduciary, the grantee may certainly regard his own self-interest in whatever way he will. Does that freedom from accounting extend to behaviour in exercise that would be substandard in a trustee or fiduciary, but that in its nature has nothing to do with the pursuit or consideration of self-interest?[97] No clear answer is available.

WHAT RESPONSE SHOULD BE MADE TO THIS STATE OF THE LAW?

Reworking our Present Conception of the Trust

As the writer has sought to argue elsewhere,[98] contention over whether the settlor has violated the concept of the trust in the powers he has

[96] By Antony Duckworth, n. 5 above.

[97] E.g., can the power-holder absent himself for a protracted period of time, and make no attempt—even if he may do so—to delegate his authority to another?

[98] *The Institution of the Trust in Civil and Common Law*, lectures delivered at The Hague Academy of International Law (Martinus Nijhoff, 1995).

created is not likely to be productive. Apart from the fact, which we consider later, that the power-holder is seen by many people who are drawing or recommending offshore trusts as one empowered but not obligated, it is increasingly evident that what are the essential attributes of a trust, even as understood in the legal system that created it, is itself an issue.[99] The writers decline to define it, and the courts adopt a descriptive sentence or two only if it is essential to the litigation. They then limit the adoption of that description to the purposes of the particular litigation in hand. Though this largely reflects the flexibility the concept has, it must be said that none of this inspires confidence in his understanding by the lawyer of another tradition, however ultimately wise the writers and the courts of the common law tradition may later be shown to have been. Worldwide the term, 'trust', is understood in a number of ways, extending from contractual relationship[100] to some form of juristic entity, and, of course, it is in the global setting, with settlors, beneficiaries, and assets in several countries and jurisdictions, that the offshore trust is operating. Those of us whose education commenced with settlements of land and trusts for sale, and who continue occasionally to twitch at the newest twist or turn the accountants have produced with the 'tax driven' discretionary trust, may find the global scene almost overwhelming.

South Africa, for instance, enacted legislation in 1988 which recognizes as a trust an arrangement whereby ownership of the trust property is in the beneficiary, but the trustee has administrative powers over the property, allowing the beneficiary no right of objection to what is done.[101] Lawyers in The Netherlands have informed the writer that they regard this *bewind* trust (or agency trust) as no trust at all. Then again the new Civil Code of Quebec[102] describes the property of the 'trust' (the English translation) as a patrimony that is owned by no one, but in or over which the trustee and the beneficiary each has personal rights of his own.[103] South African lawyers have previously described such a solution

[99] A moment ago this paper suggested fiduciary relationship between trustee and beneficiary, and control of the trust property in the trustee's hands, are to be described as the essential attributes. One offshore commentator very recently described those attributes as 'two types of ownership interest in property, legal and beneficial, and the former is held for the latter by a trustee': David R. McNair, 'Cook Islands International Trusts Act, 1995—Amendments', a paper delivered to a Canadian Institute conference, *International Estate Planning*, Toronto, 4 and 5 Dec. 1995. For a statutory 'interpretation' of *trust*, see the Trusts (Jersey) Act 1984, as amended, Art. 1, and for a description of when a trust exists, see Art. 2.

[100] See e.g. John Langbein, 'The Contractarian Basis of the Law of Trusts' (1995) 105 *Yale LJ* 625: 'The trust straddles our categories of property and contract, because it embodies a contract about how property is to be deployed' (at 671).

It is civilians who are the principal exponents of the argument that a trust is essentially a contract.

[101] See T. Honoré and E. Cameron, *Honoré's South African Law of Trusts* (4th edn., 1992), 3–8.

as unacceptable theory. Some American scholars are wondering whether the time has come for the trust to be rationalized as a legal person. It is observed that tax legislation has already made the move, and it is thought that many practitioners who already name each trust that they draw would find this expression of the trust idea more amenable for all purposes. A Liechtenstein friend of the writer regards this American reflection as 'altogether puzzling', given the added versatility he finds so valuable in his having access both to the foundation and the statutory common law trust (the *Treuhanderschaft*).

The issue, perhaps the problem, raised by the range and the far-reaching effect of powers in trust instruments is better seen, it seems, as a practical one. As is witnessed by the contemporary offshore trust, protectors can be empowered to do anything, and some are given such types or number of powers that their control is truly more complete than that of the trustees. Yet one thing appears consistently to be absent from the trust instrument—what obligations has the power-holder, and to whom are they owed? The immediate answer, of course, is that the courts have described those obligations in the law concerning powers. However, is that law able to meet the need? It was developed for another age so far as powers of appointment are concerned, and is still in the process of being worked out in its application to today's usages. As for the law concerning administrative powers, it can hardly be said there is much case law to be consulted other than that concerning administrative powers vested in express trustees. The link between the trustee and the power-holder is currently the subject of litigation,[104] but other questions are being asked beyond those being canvassed in that litigation. If the trustee vested with the trust property is sued by a disappointed beneficiary, when the refusal to consent or the directive of the power-holder was the originating case of the loss, can the trustee join the power-holder as a constructive trustee under the rule in *Barnes* v. *Addy*?[105] Recent case developments in both England[106] and Canada,[107] but particularly in the former, encourage the thought that, regardless of the law concerning powers, liability might be established through this route. But then if the power-holder is not a fiduciary in exercising the power—that is, he may properly indulge a sole concern for his own interests—does this constitute in part or in whole a defence available to the power-holder against *Barnes* v. *Addy* would-be liability?

[102] The Code was proclaimed on 1 Jan. 1994.
[103] Art. 1260. See further n. 98 above, 398.
[104] The *Froese* v. *Bank of Montreal* dispute, text to n. 62 above.
[105] (1874) 9 Ch. App. 244.
[106] *Royal Brunei Airlines Sdn. Bhd.* v. *Philip Tan Kok Ming* [1995] 2 AC 296 (PC).
[107] *Air Canada* v. *M & L Travel Ltd* [1993] 3 SCR 787, at 818 ff. and 829, 108 DLR (4th) 592.

Then there is the question of the relevance of trust law, in particular the law governing trustees. If the power-holder is also a beneficiary, but the power itself is administrative and fiduciary exercise is intended by the settlor, does the power-holder out of his own beneficial interest have the first obligation to indemnify for loss caused by him? Can his co-beneficiaries trace into his assets, should he be insolvent? Can they trace through him into the hands of knowing others? If the power holder *is* held to be a fiduciary (not, we will assume, a co-trustee, either *de son tort* or constructively appointed as such by the instrument, in which case the answer is clear), what obligations does this status impose upon him? This seems to be the nub of much of the problem with the current law. Even the court in the *Star Trusts* case in Bermuda appeared to be having some difficulty in determining which obligations are alluded to by the term, and what is added when that status is given to the holder of a power. The particular protector had removed the incumbent trustee as his power expressly authorized him to do, responsibly exercised his power to appoint a new trustee, and the exercise of the power did not involve any issue of the holder pursuing his own interest. But was he the voice of the settlor defending the settlor's interests? And, if that *was* his task, does a holder of the power to remove owe no obligation at all to a trustee whom he cannot fault as a trustee? Most settlors who have adopted this power would reply, one suspects, that they know of no obligation owed to the trustee.

Isolating the obligations and liabilities of the power-holder, therefore, is where we have to start if we are to understand the power-holder as a rounded legal creature, capable of being analysed in a manner that reveals both the rights and the obligations of the office. Rights and obligations are complementary; as Hohfeld reminds every law student, one cannot exist without the other.

A Statutory Response

With response in mind, it is illuminating that, despite the flood of trust legislation from this source in the last six years, only three offshore jurisdictions make any reference to the protector. None of the three has considered statutory codification is appropriate. That would have involved a developed treatment of the protector office along the lines of codified trustee legislation. There are several possible models, but the contents would be fairly standard. One might here suggest a possible model.

Part 1 would describe the nature of the office, and embrace types of powers and who may be a power-holder. Part 2 would deal with appointment, resignation, and removal of power-holders by private act. Part 3 would either list the most familiar powers, or leave settlors to draft their own. The preferable approach in the writer's opinion is to avoid listing, but describe the nature of a power that may be held independently of the trustee. Powers that may not be conferred, in the interests of protecting the fiduciary relationship, would also be described, or in this instance non-definitively listed. Part 4 would be concerned with the obligations of the power-holder. This covers to whom obligation is owed, in particular when the instrument confers upon the power-holder rights that traditionally belong to the beneficiaries. It also covers the requirement that the power-holder act within the scope of the power, the standards of conduct required, whether delegation may be made, and the extent of exculpation the instrument may grant. Part 5 would deal with remedies available against the power-holder—compensation or damages for loss caused, injunction, and constructive trust for knowing assistance, while Part 6 would be concerned with joint and several liability of the power-holder and the trustee of the property affected, where implementation of decisions taken under a power require trustee participation. Finally, Part 7 would cover all relevant court orders that might be sought, namely, to give advice and direction to the power-holder on questions of law and construction, to relieve the power-holder from responsibility for breach, to vary any power vested in the holder, and to appoint and remove power-holders when private appointment or removal is not possible or court assistance is necessary.

Belize, the British Virgin Islands, and the Cook Islands have each taken a much more limited approach to what is necessary in the legislation. Each appears to be responding to particular concerns of local practitioners and the local legislature. Belize has the most developed treatment of the subject. It outlines in its Trusts Act 1992[108] the office of 'protector' (powers, who may be a protector, the obligation of the office, and, when two or more are the occupants of the office, that they may act by a majority). Thereafter it provides that the trust property shall not be attachable by the protector's creditors, that the protector also may apply for a court variation of the trust, and that the court may make orders in respect of the protector, including the appointment of a protector.

The British Virgin Islands in its Trustee Ordinance 1994 authorizes the conferment of the power to consent (directives are not mentioned), but does excuse the trustee from responsibility for loss when consent was given. It permits 'any powers' to be given, and lists seven of the most familiar. There is a final subsection in the Ordinance, section 86, concerning the obligation of the 'protector'. The Cook Islands define a 'protector' in their International Trusts Amendment Act 1989,[109] as

[108] Ss. 16, 23, 48, and 58. [109] S. 3, Interpretation.

amended. The power to remove and appoint trustees appears in the definition, as it expressly appears in the legislation of Belize and the British Virgin Islands. Clearly this is seen as a prime protector power.

The common element in the legislation, or proposed legislation, of all three jurisdictions concerns the obligation (or liability) of the 'protector'. Belize provides that the protector 'shall not be accounted or regarded as a trustee',[110] and that, 'subject to the terms of the trust, in the exercise of his office a protector shall owe a fiduciary duty to the beneficiaries of the trust or to the purpose for which the trust is created'.[111] The British Virgin Islands provides that the protector 'shall not by virtue only of the exercise of the power be deemed to be a trustee; and unless otherwise provided in the instrument creating the trust, is not liable to the beneficiaries for the *bona fide* exercise of the power'.[112] The Cook Islands are about to enact a further amendment to their legislation, 'reducing the risk the Protector's functions can be determined to be those of a fiduciary in relation to trust matters'.[113] The proposed amendment to the International Trusts Act reads, '[s]ubject to the trust instrument, a protector of a trust shall not be held liable as a fiduciary in relation to any act or omission by the protector in performing his obligations under the trust instrument.'[114]

These provisions surely send a clear signal, particularly in the case of the BVI and the Cook Islands, that they are moving away from much of the body of law on 'directory powers' presented by *Scott on Trusts* in paragraph 185, and rejecting the Canadian judicial description in 1929 of this power-holder as 'a quasi-trustee'. *Scott* writes, it will be recalled,[115] that when a power-holder is a fiduciary, 'the principles that are applicable are those that apply to discretionary powers conferred on a trustee'. Orde JA in the Ontario Court of Appeal spoke of the 'quite unknown position of a super-trustee who is neither responsible to the trustees or the beneficiaries nor subject to the control or direction of the Court'.[116] The learned judge concluded, 'He cannot surely have a status superior to that of a trustee'.

In providing that the protector shall not be 'accounted or regarded as a trustee', Belize would appear to be apprehensive, like the BVI, that the behaviour control imposed upon a trustee in the exercise of his powers will be applied to the analogous circumstances of a protector who is acting for the benefit of others. Both Belize and the BVI are saying that none of the obligations and liabilities of an express trustee shall attach to

[110] S. 16(4). [111] S. 16(5). [112] S. 86(3). [113] N. 101 above.

[114] S. 20(5). S. 20(1)–(9) otherwise adopts (and adds to) the provisions in s. 16 of the Belize Trusts Act. An added element (s. 20(8)) is to the effect that, so long as no protector is appointed, the *statutory* powers or functions of the protector are vested in the Cook Islands court.

[115] N. 8 above, at 569. [116] N. 19 above, at 118.

or be imposed upon a protector. However, this leaves one in doubt as to what obligations are being referred to by the 'fiduciary duty' that is owed to the beneficiaries. Loyalty, integrity, and impartiality are the hallmark obligations of both trusteeship and the fiduciary status. At least, however, Belize—whose Act was drafted with the advice of New York and London counsel—does facilitate the applicability of a fiduciary duty, even if the settlor is free to exclude it should he choose to do so. The BVI legislation goes further down this road. It puts the onus on the settlor to require expressly that, as to his behaviour in exercising his power, the protector shall act with the exclusive benefit of others in mind. Or does this mean that the power-holder has a personal privilege, unless the settlor provides expressly that it is to be for the benefit of others? That would be to reduce accountability to the lowest possible minimum of scope of the power control. Suppose the case of a professional corporate protector. If the settlor wants the trust beneficiaries to be able to challenge the protector for any reason it had in exercising the power, or for the manner in which it exercised its power, then the settlor must draft his own terms to that effect. The Cook Islands are presented as seeing fiduciary responsibility of the protector to anyone as a 'risk' the legislation will seek to 'reduce' for the settlor. Their proposed legislation pointedly reverses the onus created by Belize as to the fiduciary role of the protector.

Far from comprehensive codification being acceptable, it seems an inescapable conclusion that at least some offshore jurisdictions are travelling in the opposite direction. Surely, responding to market demand, they *do* wish to offer settlors a roving watchdog or a super-trustee giving his own directives, in each case responsible to no one, except perhaps informally to the settlor.

In noting this, however, the writer seeks to imply no judgment. Anyone conscious today of the world scene, with 'trusts' appearing in what might be described as unusual conceptual forms in surprising locations,[117] is not likely to be confused by doctrinal experimentation or novelties in common law jurisdictions whose continued economic viability turns in large part on their ability to provide a product which investors and would-be asset-protection clients from around the world will regard as adequate. The writer's reaction to the obligation-free power-holder is different. The question is whether a trust that contains such a roving, unaccountable power-holder will work. Will it work when the beneficiary's remedies are given to the power-holder to the exclusion of the beneficiary, and it is the power-holder who determines what shall be done if the trustee of the property is in breach? It is really a very

[117] The latest being likely developments in mainland China and South Korea.

practical issue. The whole history of the common law trust is the story of a remedy. The personal right of action of the trust beneficiary, and his ability on behalf of the 'trusts' undertaken by the vested trustee to trace the trust property, have always been at the heart of the trust. This is so whether one cares to define the essential element of a trust as a fiduciary relationship between a property controller and a beneficiary or, as legal and beneficial ownership, the former held for the latter by a trustee.

It is when exception is taken by a beneficiary to the failure of the power-holder to act, or to how the power was exercised, that the difficulty surfaces. Alternatively, it may be that the beneficiary seeks to visit injury caused by the irresponsible power-holder upon the hapless trustee who did what he was told to do under the terms of the trust instrument. If the power-holder, further to the power, directs the trustee not to disclose to the beneficiaries that they *are* beneficiaries, is that a defence to the trustee as a trustee? Is a power to discuss and appoint trustees when given to a beneficiary (e.g. the settlor's spouse) an opportunity assigned to her in her personal capacity that she may then exercise for any reason that is pleasing to her? And who is to compensate the beneficiaries for the loss when the power-holder releases the trustee from liability for breach? The power-holder purports to decide for the trustee questions of law. Does the trustee retain the ability to seek advice and direction from a court, and to take his costs and remuneration from the trust fund?

Another practical risk, of course, is that mainland jurisdictions, in whose territory the trust assets have their *situs*, will refuse to recognize the so-called trust, albeit that the trust is expressly governed by the law of the particular offshore jurisdiction. They may regard the would-be trust as a 'cover' for continued settlor control, or an arrangement that constitutes agency and deposit with title.

STEELE V. *PAZ LIMITED*, AND THE JUDICIAL CONTROL OF PROTECTORS

The concern of this paper is whether, and if so to what extent, the courts will control protectors in their exercise or non-exercise of their powers. On the eve of delivery of the paper the writer's attention was drawn to an unreported decision of the Court of Appeal of the Isle of Man, delivered on 10 October 1995. The subject of protector powers, their nature and enforceability, was discussed at length in this case, and considered here are the judgments delivered so far as they speak to the concern addressed in this paper. In *Steele* v. *Paz Ltd* the issue before the Court was whether the trust failed because no protector had been appointed to carry out the protector powers and, due to disagreements among the parties involved, none could be appointed. It was held by P. W. Smith QC and T. B. Hegarty QC[118] in separate judgments that the trust did not fail. When those powers are fiduciary, a court will take steps to see that the protector considers whether he should exercise his powers and, if appropriate, exercises them as it was intended in the instrument. Failing other means, the court will itself carry out the task associated with the particular power.

The case concerned a discretionary trust where almost all of the corporate trustee's beneficiary appointment and administrative powers were subject to the protector's consent to any proposed exercise. The beneficiaries of the trust were the Irish Red Cross and such individuals, other than residents of the Isle of Man, as the corporate trustee should nominate provided the protector consent to nominations made during his lifetime. While the instrument declared that this particular power was 'collateral and non-fiduciary', both members of the Court accepted that the additional power of the protector to consent to the trustee's proposed distribution of income and capital among the Red Cross and nominated beneficiaries was fiduciary, as was each of the protector's consent powers to the trustee's administrative decisions. Each of these fiduciary powers constituted the opportunity to consent to the trustee's exercise of discretion, and they were seen by the Court as opportunities rather than obligations to consent or deny consent. On the other hand each Court member recognized these powers as of 'vital assistance' in the trustee's carrying out of its trust duties.

Both members of the Court concluded that there was no problem of uncertainty of trust objects, as the trial judge had decided in holding the trust invalid; the trust was completely constituted. What was missing was the means whereby the trustee could discharge its duties and exercise its powers. Judge Smith gave as his reasons for court intervention that the protector in this case had a fiduciary duty to the beneficiaries of the trust; the settlor could not prevent him from exercising any of his powers as he chose. 'The Protector', he added, 'must bona fide consider the exercise of his powers from the point of view of the beneficiaries under the Trust.' He concluded that in his opinion the court should and would appoint a protector 'as it would appoint a Trustee if a Trustee were neither appointed or declined to act'. Judge Hegarty entertained the same views as his colleague, but he approached the matter somewhat differently. In his opinion the court has jurisdiction to appoint a person to exercise the protectorship powers, or as a last resort to exercise

[118] The writer understands that the judges of the CA of the Isle of Man are drawn from senior counsel ('silks') of the English Bar, the Northern Circuit.

the powers itself, because of the applicability of Lord Wilberforce's words in *McPhail* v. *Doulton*.[119] There his Lordship had described how the court would act when trustees decline to exercise their discretions. Judge Hegarty was of the view that those words were intended to apply not only to trustees of the trust property having dispositive or administrative powers, but to other donees who hold their powers for the benefit of the beneficiaries. Those words were also intended to apply not only to powers that the holders are obligated to exercise, but to powers affording the holder the mere opportunity to exercise the discretion. Similarly Judge Hegarty considered that Megarry V-C's words in *Re Hay's Settlement Trust*—that the holder of a power for the benefit of others must make a survey of the possible beneficiaries (or trust objects) and consider who, if anyone, should receive what—applied to holders of powers, whether they are obligated to exercise their discretions or have merely the opportunity to exercise them.

As to how the court would intervene, Judge Hegarty obviously adopted Lord Wilberforce's description of how this would be done. The court can appoint new trustees, direct or authorize the beneficiaries to prepare a scheme for distribution, or itself direct the trustees how to distribute if this is apparent. Judge Smith was of the view that the court could (1) sanction under its inherent jurisdiction (statutory in England) the carrying out by trustees of transactions not expressly authorized, (2) itself exercise the powers of the protector, or substitute its own machinery where the instrument's machinery has broken down and is of a supportive nature to implementation of the trust terms, and (3) refuse to allow a trust to fail for want of a protector, as of a trustee, where the role of the protector is not so unique that only the settlor can select the holder. The court would then appoint a protector.

Judge Hegarty in an extended judgment expanded considerably on the thinking that appears to have underlain his colleague's judgment, and which certainly constituted the background to his own analysis. He distinguished what he described as powers where the donee has an obligation to exercise his discretion (trust powers), powers where the donee has an opportunity to act, necessarily on behalf of the beneficiaries (fiduciary powers), and so-called 'mere' or 'bare powers'.[120] The last is the personal confidence; the holder is subject to the sole control that he act within the limits of his power as required by the fraud on a power doctrine. This description of powers was necessitated, said the judge,

[119] N. 16 above. See also, p. 83, above.

[120] This reference to mere or bare powers is expressly taken from Lord Upjohn's words in *Re Gulbenkian's Settlements* [1970] AC 508, 521.

It should be noted that the term, mere power, is used in this paper to describe the situation where the donee of the power has an *opportunity* to exercise the power (or discretion), whether for his own benefit or the benefit solely of others. N. 15 above.

both by his argument that Lord Wilberforce's words apply to fiduciary powers, and by the requirement that he (the judge) show that only in the last category is there no room for finding a court power of intervention.

Two points emerge from this appellate decision, a decision which reversed the trial judge, and found a completely constituted trust where a court might intervene to appoint a protector as it would a trustee. First, that a donee of a power intended for the benefit of others, whether that power must be exercised or may be exercised, is a fiduciary and the court will require not only that the donee act within the scope of the power, but that his behaviour in the exercise or non-exercise of the power is in the best interests of the beneficiaries. This means that the power-holder will consider, when it is appropriate, whether he should exercise the power, and, if he concludes that he should, how he is to exercise it.

This fully supports *Scott's* position in paragraph 185—the first time it has happened in any Commonwealth jurisdiction, though the judge makes no reference to *Scott*—and is in line with the arguments of the control school of thought.

The second point is that Judge Hegarty's judgment is also in line with the no-control school that argues the settlor is always free to create powers for the exercise or non-exercise of which the holder is not accountable.

Judge Hegarty is alone in commenting upon the power that is non-fiduciary, that constitutes a personal privilege. His comments are *obiter dicta*, and Judge Smith for his part is totally silent on the subject. Nevertheless, they are a central feature of Judge Hegarty's reasoning, and they fully agree with the inference that *Scott* leaves, namely, that the settlor is at liberty to declare 'a power collateral and not a fiduciary or trust power' if and when he will. The settlor did this in the *Steele* case with regard to protector consent to trustee exercise of the discretion to nominate beneficiaries. The instrument specifically stated, as the above words show, that that particular power was not conferred on the protector other than as a personal privilege or confidence.

Where nothing is express, when will the court imply such an intention? Judge Hegarty thought that what must be shown is that the protector has been selected because of his personal characteristics. Those characteristics or who that person is are of such central importance to the settlor that, as settlor, he is prepared to see the powers exercised in 'an individual, subjective, and even idiosyncratic way', something that would not be permitted to a fiduciary. 'Such powers', he continues, 'will normally arise when the intention of the settlor is to confer some individual benefit or protection or right of patronage upon the donee.' Later he describes the power-holder as likely to have something in the nature of a property right, a right vested in him as a particular person, natural or corporate, not as an office holder. The so-called 'Gisborne clause'[121]—where the instrument states that the power in the hands of the donee is to be an authority that is not controlled—may be enough to show a personal confidence was intended, he says, because it purports 'to remove all restraints upon the exercise of the power'. As Lord Cairns LC had put it,[122] 'supposing that there is no *mala fides* with regard to its exercise, [the power] is to be without any check or control from any superior tribunal'.

THE AFTERMATH OF THE *STEELE* CASE

It is evident that Judge Hegarty is prepared to go further than the present writer in inferring a settlor's intent to create a personal confidence. It is difficult for the writer to believe that a modern court, particularly in Canada, would regard 'uncontrolled authority' as enough to turn an otherwise fiduciary power into a personal confidence, and remove the power of the court to intervene when non-exercise is due to 'indolence, indifference, or obstinacy'. Alternatively, a court today would hold that *mala fides* in the exercise of the power, in which circumstances Lord Cairns himself presupposed judicial intervention, is a very wide net. Nevertheless, it is likely, as Judge Hegarty suggests without expressing a concluded view, that where the power is held to be personal a court would not appoint a substitute protector when no such protector is in place, or the protector in place ignores or declines for no credible reason to exercise the power. In other words in principle the behaviour of the power-holder is not subject to court review.

This leaves one last question, and *Steele* v. *Paz Ltd* does not answer it. If the drafting lawyer has clear instructions from a settlor, who understands the possible consequences, that the protector as to his powers is not to be accountable to a court at the suit of anyone, what language should he use and how far can he go to obtain this result for the instructing client? The power in question might appear for all purposes to be for the benefit of others; it is not reasonably arguable, that is, that the settlor intended the sole benefit of the power-holder in conferring the particular power, nor can the power in itself reasonably be said to be for the 'protection' of the holder. The right of patronage, to which Judge Hegarty refers, would seem to be more associated with a dispositive power than administrative powers, and even then there must surely be some degree of personal relationship between patron and recipient for

[121] A reference to a clause which was the issue in *Gisborne* v. *Gisborne* (1877) 2 App. Cas. 300 (HL).

[122] *Ibid.* 305.

the power to be capable of description as a personal confidence or privilege. This is only likely to exist when the protector is a parent, grandparent, or spouse of the recipient.

So can the drafting lawyer achieve the desired result for the settlor by saying simply that the power, whatever is thereby authorized, is granted to the grantee, 'as a personal confidence and privilege, a power collateral and not as a fiduciary or trust power'? Or would a court, concerned that without such words the power would be construed as fiduciary, regard them as improperly seeking to oust the jurisdiction of the court? And, if the court would rule in this way, how far can the settlor carry further or broaden the meaning of 'benefit', 'protection', and patronage' so that what is authorized is recognizable by the court as indeed a personal confidence and privilege, advancing in some manner, that is, the interests of the power-holder?

These questions await answers from common law courts across the world. As previously said, Canadian courts with their inclination towards the appropriateness of fiduciary obligation can be expected to give personal confidence or privilege a very narrow range of operation. On the other hand English and Australian courts are likely to be more traditional in the degree to which they will recognize and uphold the settlor's intention to create the personal right. The legislation of Belize and the British Virgin Islands, and the prospective legislation of the Cook Islands, suggests those jurisdictions are uncertain about when their courts, left to the case law, would find the protector to be a trustee of his power or powers, or at least one who holds his powers for the benefit of others and is therefore subject to the fiduciary obligations of avoiding conflict of interests and of acting with care. The legislation therefore removes the threat of a ruling in those local courts that the protector is a trustee, and with varying policies as to whether he is *prima facie* a fiduciary[123] draws to the settlor's attention that he must make his position clear in the trust instrument. Meanwhile the Isle of Man, lacking such legislation and being so close to England, appears likely to take the traditional position concerning the availability to the settlor of the personal right.

CONCLUSION

The notion of the protector has brought many benefits to the administration of trusts. A trusted relative, close friend, or long-time business or legal adviser on the spot can provide ease of mind to the settlor that there is someone in the far-off administration centre of the trust who is advis-

[123] Is the legislation speaking of one who acts for the benefit of others, or of fiduciary obligations?

ing the corporate trustee with regard to suitable distributions and who is keeping an eye on the way in which the trustee is investing and administering the trust. The unsatisfactory or uncommunicative trustee can be removed quickly and inexpensively. Liaison between trustee and distant beneficiaries can be made smoother and intervention prevent discord from festering. A corporate trustee is a bureaucracy; a power-holder on the spot can step usefully between this form of trusteeship and the family. Trust assets may consist of, or include, an active offshore business; the local power-holder is the mainland family's supervisor who deals with employee problems and the emergencies. Emergencies may also arise when movement elsewhere of the trust or the administration of its assets is most desirable, and should take place quietly and quickly. The power-holder on the spot is best for this task; the trustees may be unable to carry out the move themselves because of a local ordinance, or a difficulty of that kind.

There is a significant, if somewhat historic and otherwise oriented, body of law on powers of appointment, and some law on powers of administration in the hands of persons other than the trustees of the property. In the view of one school of thought, this law has not been analysed in terms of its applicability to the contemporary 'protector' phenomenon; the majority of settlors and their advisers have not considered the lessons that law affords. Those lessons are, first, that the nature and scope of the administrative power must be tailored to the circumstances of each trust. Boilerplate powers are rarely appropriate, and the broad, wide-ranging power as to what may be done by the holder is usually less appropriate than the carefully-considered power of known and calculated narrow dimension. Secondly, the consequences of introducing such a power, whether a beneficiary appointment and deletion power or an administrative power, should be considered, and that consideration be reflected in some degree of obligation imposed on the power-holder. There ought to be someone to whom remedy or relief is available with regard to the power-holder, and how the power-holder proposes to exercise or has exercised its discretion. In the small circle of settlor, trustee, and beneficiaries it will often be difficult to determine who should have the remedy, and tax laws in the settlor's home jurisdiction—plus the desire to keep too much control from beneficiaries—lead to the familiar adoption of yet another, a fourth party, as protector. Nevertheless, whoever is to be the protector, the conferment of power without imposing responsibility creates only a 'fair weather trust'.

Scott's paragraph 185 underlines that courts have normally found the power-holder is intended to be a fiduciary—one who must account—and *Steele* v. *Paz Ltd* suggests that English law has also reached the position that a power that must be exercised, or offers the opportunity of exercise, in favour of persons other than the grantee, is fiduciary. That is, the court will intervene to ensure the trust machinery operates efficiently, including that the power-holder properly consider the exercise of his power. On the other hand, as the second school of thought emphasizes, the settlor remains free, both in the view of *Scott* and now of the *Steele* court, to create a power that is personal to the grantee.

A power is an authority, it is said, and settlors on the international scene want in their power-holders authority—to consent and direct. They do not want to incur the expense of a protector only to find that he, like the trustee, is constantly looking over his shoulder because of accountability. Accountability is appropriate for trustees, who are vested with the trust property; it makes no sense for mere holders of powers, especially those who are simply to ensure the settlor's objectives are being met.

The second school might also add that when accountability is to be made by the trustees to the protector to the exclusion of the beneficiaries, or the protector may require information concerning the trust administration to be withheld from the beneficiaries, when the protector is to bring any action for breach against the trustees and may settle with or release the trustees, and when the protector may act as binding arbiter in trustee/beneficiary disputes, it is a little hollow, if not contradictory, to say the protector must account to the beneficiaries.

Nevertheless, if the personal confidence (right or privilege) may be created to achieve such a number of goals, as readily, and with such minimal judicial control, as Judge Hegarty suggests in the *Steele* case, the observation is not unfair that the trust in question may simply break down. This surely it is the task of the settlor's adviser to avoid. Clauses to deal with death or loss of capacity are not difficult to draw, though the appointment of a corporate protector to hold the personal confidence can obviate that problem at once. So far as the problem of the indolent, capricious, or unreasonable protector is concerned, whether at one extreme it is a simple matter of consistent neglect to give consent or at the other extreme a demand for excessive fees or expense reimbursements from the trust fund, it is naïve for the settlor to provide no solution.

The *Re Rogers* court thought a power-holder accountable to no one was preposterous. However, that was a case where the power-holder was in an obvious conflict situation which was proving equally obviously to be contrary to the best interests of the beneficiaries. Clearly the court conceived of the power-holder as one required to act for the benefit of others, and that state of affairs (the power holder as fiduciary) both *Scott* and the *Steele* court regard as fully enabling judicial intervention, even when a power-holder is not a trustee of the trust property and has a mere opportunity to act. The problem stems from the existence of a personal confidence, in particular when the non-exercise of the power or its mode of exercise is in fact unreasonably contrary to the interests of others, though done in the name of the grantee's authorized self-interest. In the first place the existence of such a power, as opposed to a power for the benefit of others, turns on the often impressionistic outcome of construction and, in the second place, where the intention of the settlor is expressly stated, the case law is not clear about what characteristics must be absent from a power that purports to be benefiting the grantee alone.

In these circumstances, as it seems to the present writer, use by the settlor of the personal confidence (right or privilege) should be limited to those situations only where the indolence or capriciousness, the self-concern or idiosyncrasy of the power-holder in the exercise or non-exercise of the power cannot harm the interests of others. At that point where such harm does begin to take place, the power should expressly become one when the grantee can no longer consider his own interest—it should become a fiduciary power.

Whatever be the purpose for having a protector, the art of drafting must surely be to capture for the settlor the advantages of the position, and at the same time to build in breakdown prevention and remedy that are likely both to be effective and, with explanation, acceptable. Solutions after the event are rarely solutions. Perhaps there is no more lonely and desperate cry in history than that attributed in 1170 to Henry II of England, who totally failed to foresee how his own nominee as Archbishop of Canterbury would cross him at every turn, '[a]re there none of the cowards eating my bread who will rid me of this turbulent priest?' The results were disastrous.

5

Some Trust Principles in the Pensions Context

SIR ROBERT WALKER

The social and economic importance of occupational pension schemes has been apparent for many years[1] but it is only in the course of the last ten years that pension schemes have come before the court in significant numbers. Recently, however, the court has begun to work out how far trust-law principles that were established and developed largely[2] in the context of family trusts are appropriate, with or without modification, to pension schemes. This process is very far from complete: there are only four important decisions of the Court of Appeal,[3] and none yet of the Lords. In this paper I want to look at two areas which have already produced a certain amount of authority: judicial review[4] of decisions by pension-fund trustees (including disclosure of documents relevant to such decisions), and problems of conflict of duty and interest affecting trustees and other fiduciaries concerned with pension funds. But I will venture to begin with some very general and elementary points about pension schemes.

The essential characteristic of the schemes with which I am concerned is that they are funded: a fund (typically consisting of quoted investments or a group policy) is held in trust to provide, in due time, the pensions which an employer has promised to its employees on their

[1] The modern history of pension schemes can conveniently be treated as starting in 1921, as the Finance Act of that year first conferred important income tax exemptions and gave a strong impetus to the growth of approved schemes, at least for salaried staff. Their extention to weekly- and hourly-paid employees has mostly come since the Second World War. The 1970s brought a mass of legislation with much confused political marching and counter-marching. The Maxwell scandal has now brought the Pensions Act 1995, referred to further below.

[2] But *Re Beloved Wilkes' Charity* (1851) 3 Mac. & G 440, which influenced the development of the modern discretionary trust, was concerned with a charitable trust. That case is referred to further below.

[3] *Kerr* v. *British Leyland (Staff) Trustees*, 26 Mar. 1986; *Milhenstedt* v. *Barclays Bank International* [1989] IRLR 522; *Stannard* v. *Fisons Pensions Trust* [1992] IRLR 27; and (on pre-emptive costs orders) *McDonald* v. *Horn* [1994] OPLR 281. In *Brooks* v. *Brooks* [1995] 3 WLR 141, the HL decided that an insured pension arrangement for a single individual was a post-nuptial settlement.

[4] Not of course judicial review under RSC Order 53; but the principles of judicial review in the administrative law sense provide an interesting contrast.

retirement. I find it hard to see the point of debate on whether occupational pension schemes should continue to be regulated by trust law. If private-sector pensions are to be funded at all, it seems inescapable that there should be a pool of investments which someone holds and manages for the benefit of the scheme pensioners and members. It also seems inescapable that someone should be a fiduciary, whether his obligations are imposed specially by statute or generally by non-statutory trust law. It is odd that Parliament, which since the Trustee Act 1925 has shown little inclination to legislate for trusts, has now in the Pensions Act 1995[5] set about modernizing trustee investment powers and codifying trustee investment principles for pension schemes only; but trust law remains the foundation.

A family trust can be envisaged as a simple linear process: the settlor's or testator's bounty proceeds through the trustees to the beneficiaries. A pension trust is more aptly envisaged as a triangle. The trustees are at the apex, the employer and the employees (in whom I include former employees who have become current or deferred pensioners) are at the other corners. The employer and the employees are linked to the trustees by both fiduciary and contractual obligations. The nexus between the employer and the employees is normally only contractual[6] but it imports a basic duty of good faith which may influence the exercise of an employer's non-fiduciary powers under a pension scheme: the landmark judgment on this point is that of Sir Nicolas Browne-Wilkinson V-C in *Imperial Group Pension Trust* v. *Imperial Tobacco.*[7] The members of the pension scheme are not volunteers and that has influenced the court's attitude to the obligations of trustees as well as employers.[8]

In earlier drafts of this paper I referred at this point—by way of introduction to the most important decisions which pension-fund trustees have to take or participate in—to the controversy over beneficial ownership of actuarial surplus in a pension fund. But I found that, try as I might, the topic expanded in so many directions (including an excursion into the influence of tax law and Inland Revenue practice) that I was going to run out of time before I had even got to the end of my introduction. So I shall limit myself to two comments.

The best short summary of the current development of the law (refer-

[5] Ss. 34–6.

[6] In *Mettoy Pension Trustees* v. *Evans* [1990] 1 WLR 1587 (discussed below) Warner J held that a power over ultimate surplus exercisable by an employer was, in the circumstances, fiduciary. See also Pensions Schemes Act 1993, s. 121(2)(b), to be replaced by s. 25 of the Pensions Act 1995.

[7] [1991] 1 WLR 589.

[8] See especially the first three CA decisions at n. 3 above. In *Stannard* (at 233) Dillon LJ quoted the summary of the relevant law by Fox LJ in *Kerr*. But if trustees have a fiduciary discretion do they not owe even to volunteers a duty to give 'properly informed consideration' to its possible exercise?

ring to recent decisions in British Columbia, New South Wales, and New Zealand,[9] as well as in England) is by Knox J in *LRT Pension Fund Trustee* v. *Hatt*.[10] Knox J quoted with approval the words of Sir Robin Cooke P in the Court of Appeal of New Zealand:[11] 'considerations of the merits are of little importance. What must be decisive are the terms of the trusts constituted by the particular scheme.' Knox J recognized[12] that the terms of many schemes are constructed so that surplus is 'in baulk': that is, it cannot be resorted to without the concurrence of both the employer and the trustees. This leads to the sort of negotiations referred to by Millett J in *Re Courage Group Pension Schemes*.[13]

My other comment is that the current importance of beneficial ownership of actuarial surplus is a direct result of recent events, that is the long bull-market of the Thatcher years and its economic concomitants: massive gains on portfolio investment, massive takeovers, and massive redundancies in many older industries. Pension-fund surpluses have themselves become significant targets for predators. Hence the importance of trustees getting it right when they hold one of the dual keys to surplus which is in baulk.

Where trustees have a discretion they must from time to time consider exercising it; and if they exercise it they must do so in good faith, and in a responsible and reasonable manner, and within the scope of the particular discretion. If they fail to do so and loss is occasioned to the trust fund, they are liable to compensate the fund for the loss. But apart from hostile actions for breach of trust (where indemnity clauses may influence the outcome)[14] there was until fairly recently little authority on how strict a test was to be applied to trustees' decisions: in other words, how far they could fall short of the ideal of a fully informed, wholly rational decision-making process before the court would intervene.

The classic formulation of the court's general attitude of non-intervention was by Lord Cairns in *Gisborne* v. *Gisborne*.[15] That case, decided in 1877, was one in which the trustees were expressly given a 'discretion and uncontrollable authority'. At the other extreme is *Turner* v. *Turner*[16] where the trustees did not realize that they had any duty to exercise their own judgement at all: a sort of equitable *non est factum*. No pension trustees, one hopes, would ever be in that position. A more

[9] *Hockin* v. *Bank of British Columbia* (1990) 46 BCLR (2d) 382; *Lock* v. *Westpac Banking Corporation* (1991) 25 NSWLR 593; *Re UEB Industries Pension Plan* [1992] 1 NZLR 294.

[10] [1993] OPLR 225.

[11] N. 9 above, at 298.

[12] N. 10 above, at 267.

[13] [1987] 1 WLR 495, at 515.

[14] But see now the restrictions on some indemnities imposed by Pensions Act 1995, ss. 31 and 33.

[15] (1877) 2 App. Cas. 300.

[16] [1984] Ch. 100.

technical error was considered by the Court of Appeal in *Re Hastings-Bass.*[17] That case was concerned with the exercise of a power of advancement by a transfer to a new settlement, in order to save estate duty. But the trustees (or their advisers) misunderstood the operation of the rule against perpetuties and managed to create only a life interest. But that partial resettlement, though unintended, was held valid. The Court of Appeal said that where[18]

> a trustee is given a discretion as to some matter under which he acts in good faith, the court should not interfere with his action notwithstanding that it does not have the full effect which he intended, unless (1) what he has achieved is unauthorised by the power conferred on him, or (2) it is clear that he would not have acted as he did (a) had he not taken into account considerations which he should not have taken into account, or (b) had he not failed to take into account considerations which he ought to have taken into account.

The cases cited in argument in *Re Hastings-Bass* suggest that the very distinguished counsel in the case found it difficult to produce any direct authority on this issue. The most interesting authority which was cited is the decision of the House of Lords in *Dundee Hospitals* v. *Walker.*[19] That case concerned a will by which a Scottish testator made a bequest conditional on his trustees being in their 'absolute discretion' satisfied that an infirmary was not at his death under public control. It came under public control as a result of retrospective legislation which received the Royal Assent a month after the testator's death. It is therefore an unusual case which might have turned on the issue of conceptual certainty, or even on ouster of the court's jurisdiction, and it is not clear how far the Lords' robust non-interventionist attitude was linked and limited to its special facts. But the speech of Lord Reid contains some general observations on the circumstances in which the court will intervene in trustees' decisions. Those observations are in terms reminiscent of Lord Greene's much-quoted judgment in an administrative law decision of the same period, *Associated Provincial Picture Houses* v. *Wednesbury Corporation.*[20] In trust law as in administrative law, *ultra vires*, procedural irregularity, and unreasonableness tend, in Lord Greene's phrase,[21] to run into each other.

The most interesting authority which was not cited in *Re Hastings Bass* is a New South Wales decision, *Hill* v. *Permanent Trustee.*[22] As Sir Donald Nicholls said in *Sinclair* v. *Lee*[23] that case was a sequel to the decison of the Privy Council in the earlier case of the same name.[24] Trustees had refrained from liquidating a pastoral company, and had voted for a

[17] [1975] Ch. 25. [18] *Ibid.* 41. [19] [1952] 1 All ER 896.
[20] [1948] 1 KB 223. [21] *Ibid.* 229. [22] (1933) 33 SR (NSW) 527.
[23] [1993] Ch. 497, at 512. [24] [1930] AC 720.

change in its articles instead, on the strength of advice from chancery counsel that a capital dividend paid by the company would be capital as between tenant for life and remainderman. The decision of the Privy Council was that the distribution was income for trust purposes. The Chief Justice in Equity held (in subsequent litigation for which the Privy Council left the door open) that the trustees' exercise of their voting rights had been flawed and that, to avoid injustice, the dividend must be treated as capital.

The decision in *Re Hastings Bass* has been considered and applied in two pension cases. The first was *Mettoy Pension Trustees* v. *Evans.*[25] The employer had been a successful toy manufacturer but in the early 1980s competition from the Far East and an unfortunate venture into home computers put it into serious financial difficulties. At the end of 1983 it went into receivership and then into liquidation. There was at that time a substantial surplus in its pension scheme.

Under the original trust deed and rules, on the winding-up of the scheme (which had to follow on the winding-up of the employer company) the surplus could have been used at the trustees' discretion to augment pensioners' and members' benefits (this discretion being exercisable without reference to the employer or its receiver or liquidator, though subject to Inland Revenue limits). In 1980 (when the employer's financial position was not yet serious) the trustees purported to adopt lengthy new rules which (among many other changes) had the effect of transferring this discretion to the employer. Later however doubt arose (because of section 37(1)(c) of the Trustee Act 1925[26]) whether the trustees had been properly constituted when they changed the rules. In March 1983, when the employer's finances were (in the words of Warner J[27]) 'precarious though not dire' the new rules were re-adopted.

On neither occasion were the trustees given any adequate advice about the significance of the transfer of discretion over surplus; and in 1983 at least the winding-up of the employer (and the consequential winding-up of the scheme) were more than a theoretical possibility. Warner J's conclusion on the facts was that, had the trustees been aware of the change in the discretion over surplus, had the employer's new discretion over surplus been non-fiduciary, and had the trustees been properly advised on these matters, they would not (either in 1980 or in 1983) have made the change. But since the employer's new discretion was (as Warner J held[28]) fiduciary in nature, the trustees might well not have objected, and so the rule in *Re Hastings Bass* did not apply.[29]

[25] N. 6 above.

[26] Whether s. 37(1)(c) can be excluded has now been decided (positively) by Knox J in the *LRT* case, n. 10 above, at 260–2.

[27] N. 6 above, at 1607. [28] *Ibid.* 1613–6. [29] *Ibid.* 1629–30.

Before reaching this conclusion Warner J touched on several points which help to clarify the scope of the rule. First, it is not limited to cases of 'excessive execution' where trustees act beyond the scope of their powers.[30] That seems clearly right: otherwise the second limb of the rule would add nothing. In *Re Hastings Bass* the issue was not whether part of the resettlement offended the rule against perpetuities—that was common ground—but whether that admitted mistake tainted the part of the resettlement which was within the trustees' powers.

Secondly, those who challenge the exercise of a discretion by trustees must show that, if properly directed, they would have acted differently. But the test seems to be objective, and there is less need for examination of the parties' actual intentions than on a claim for rectification.[31]

Thirdly, Warner J rejected the submission that a valid exercise of discretion by trustees must be an 'all or nothing' issue. There may, he said,

> be cases where the court is satisfied that the trustees would have acted in the same way but with, for instance, the omission of a clause in a deed. I do not see why, in such a case, the court should not declare only that provision void. It seems to me that the remedy to be adopted by the court must depend on the circumstances of each case.[32]

This shows a flexible approach, and reflects what was said in *Re Hastings Bass*[33] about 'monolithic' benefits. But it is easy to imagine cases in which such an approach could produce grave uncertainty,[34] either in a pension scheme or in a family trust. For instance, trustees of a family trust who have executed a deed of appointment might a year or two later say with perfect truth, '[h]ad we been more fully and more expertly advised about the tax position, we would have acted differently.' Can trustees or beneficiaries get the court, in effect, to give a second opinion on technical aspects of deeds which have already been executed? If so is the jurisdiction limited to the blue pencil of partial avoidance, or can it include the positive correction of errors? These are questions which may have to be explored a good deal further in future cases.

The other pension case in which this sort of problem was considered is *Stannard* v. *Fisons Pension Trust*.[35] It was also a decision of Warner J, but it went to the Court of Appeal, which upheld the decision at first

[30] N. 6 above, at 1623.

[31] *Ibid.* 1624 and cf at 1629; but see below as to *Stannard* v. *Fisons Pension Trust*, reference at n. 3 above.

[32] *Ibid.* 1624–5.

[33] N. 17 above, at 41.

[34] See n. 6 above, at 1622, where the submissions of Mr E. G. Nugee QC on this point are recorded.

[35] It is understood that a compromise has avoided the need for a further contested hearing.

instance. It has to be said that it is a difficult case to evaluate, partly because Warner J heard and decided only some of the questions raised in the originating summons. Consequently, the case has some resemblance to a preliminary issue in which the facts are not fully explored. The case was concerned with a decision by the trustees of the Fisons pension scheme to make a transfer payment of about £31.7 million to another scheme, following the sale of Fisons' fertilizer division to a subsidiary of Norsk Hydro. The decision was attacked on various grounds, notably (first) the trustees' ignorance of a substantial rise in the value of the pension fund between the sale (in June 1982) and the transfer (in December 1982); and (secondly) the incorrect advice given to the trustees as to which rule authorized the transfer (the two rules being in similar but not identical terms). Dillon LJ (with whom Ralph Gibson LJ agreed) and Staughton LJ attached importance to the first point; Staughton LJ alone attached much importance to the second. The nub of Dillon LJ's judgement[36] was that 'it *might* materially have affected the trustees' decision in December 1982 if they had been properly informed as to the then current value of the fund and the implications of its value'. It is not clear whether this represents a significant relaxation of the *Hastings Bass* test ('unless . . . it is clear that he would not have acted as he did') or whether it simply reflects the incomplete state of the evidence on the first part of the originating summons. If the *Hastings Bass* test is to be relaxed it will be hard for trustees to be confident—even when they are thoroughly conscientious and have thoroughly competent advisers—that their decisions may not be open to challenge, perhaps years later. There is an important balance to be struck here between the pursuit of perfectly informed decision-making and the need for practical certainty.

If pension scheme members are considering a challenge to a decision by their trustees—for instance, as to a partial repayment of surplus to the employer or the size of a bulk transfer payment—they will wish to have access to written advice given to the trustees and to minutes of the trustees' meetings. The decision of the Court of Appeal in *Re Londonderry*[37] establishes that the court will not normally direct trustees to disclose to beneficiaries documents setting out the reasons for trustees' decisions. But that was in the context of a family settlement of a discretionary nature: thus Salmon LJ said:

> Nothing would be more likely to embitter family feelings and the relationship between the trustees and members of the family, were trustees obliged to state their reasons for the exercise of the powers entrusted to them. It might indeed

[36] *Ibid.* 233, emphasis supplied. [37] [1965] Ch. 918.

well be difficult to persuade any persons to act as trustees were a duty to disclose their reasons, with all the embarrassment, arguments and quarrels that might ensue, added to their present not inconsiderable burdens.[38]

The differences between running a discretionary trust for members of a family—or, I might add, selecting a young man to be trained for Holy Orders as in *Re Beloved Wilkes' Charity*[39]—and running a pension scheme for employees of a company or a group of companies are obvious. The beneficiaries of a pension scheme are not volunteers; and the most important decisions which the trustees have to make generally concern participation in surplus as between the employer (on the one hand) and the members and ex-members (on the other hand); and within the latter class, as between continuing members, transferring members, and current and deferred pensioners. There are, it seems to me, strong arguments that in such circumstances the trustees should be ready to justify their decisions to those whose interests they represent, subject to protection for what is truly confidential (whether for commercial or personal reasons). Whatever their strict obligations pension trustees would in my view be well advised, in almost all circumstances, to adopt a policy of the utmost openness. Secrecy breeds suspicion, and suspicion can lead to speculative actions for breach of trust, often at the expense either of trade union funds or of the legal aid fund. Once litigation is on foot, the process of discovery imports a separate set of rules: as Lord Wrenbury said in *O'Rourke* v. *Darbishire*,[40] '[t]he right to discovery is a right to see someone else's documents. The proprietary right is a right to access to documents which are your own.' But by the time litigation is on foot, the parties are in entrenched positions and costs are mounting.

In *Wilson* v. *Law Debenture Trust Corporation*[41] Rattee J followed *Re Londonderry* and declined to order the trustees of the Chloride Group pension scheme to produce all documents showing the basis on which the quantum of a bulk transfer payment had been calculated. Advice to the trustees from their actuaries and solicitors had been disclosed during the course of the proceedings, but with some passages obliterated.

After referring to *Re Beloved Wilkes' Charity* and *Re Londonderry* Rattee J said:[42]

Of course I accept that a pension scheme is different from a private trust in that, in particular, the members of a pension scheme have purchased their interests, but the question is what is the nature of the interest which they have purchased. . . . It would in my judgment be wrong to hold that the long-established principles of trust law as to the exercise by trustees of discretions

[38] *Ibid.* 936. [39] N. 2 above. [40] [1920] AC 581 at 626–7.
[41] [1995] OPLR 103. [42] *Ibid.* 113.

conferred on them by their trust instruments, in the context of which parties to a pension scheme such as the present entered into those schemes, no longer apply to them. . . . I accept Mr Warren's submission that if any such amendment to the law of trusts as applied to pension schemes is to be made it should be made by the legislature, either by regulations made under or by extension of section 113 of the Pension Schemes Act 1993.

This conclusion seems, with great respect, to treat *Re Londonderry* as a rather more precise and definitive statement of principle than it may be. It may also run counter to the important general observation by Lord Browne-Wilkinson in *Target Holdings* v. *Redferns*:[43]

It is important, if the trust is not to be rendered commercially useless, to distinguish between the basic principles of trust law and those specialist rules developed in relation to traditional trusts, which are applicable only to such trusts and the rationale of which has no application to trusts of quite a different kind.

It remains to be seen how the law will develop, either by case law or by further legislative intervention.[44] In administrative law the tide is running towards a general duty to give reasons for decisions, and decisions of pension trustees have at least as much in common with those of official bodies as with those of family trustees, as regards the degree to which they depend on objective, rather than subjective, judgement.

It may also be pertinent to reflect that in the Scottish appeal already referred to Lord Normand commented:[45]

It was said for the appellants that the courts have greater liberty to examine and correct a decision committed by a testator to his trustees, if they choose to give reasons, than if they do not. In my opinion that is erroneous. The principles on which the court must proceed are the same whether the reasons for the trustees' decision are disclosed or not, but, of course, it becomes easier to examine a decision if the reasons for it have been disclosed.

It would certainly be odd if the court were more ready to intervene against trustees who are careful enough to obtain full written advice and keep full written minutes, and candid enough to disclose them to their members' scrutiny.

The other area that I want to refer to briefly is conflict of interest. In an ideal world, a fiduciary's single-minded concern for his beneficiaries' interests would never be distracted, even in the slightest, by self-interest. In practice, in the pensions field, conflicts of interest are endemic. Normally the trustees are constituted (either directly or as the board of

[43] [1995] 3 WLR 352, at 362.

[44] Pension Schemes Act 1993, s. 113 will remain in force but s. 114 will be replaced by Pensions Act 1995, s. 41. For the present position see Occupational Pension Schemes (Disclosure of Information) Regs. 1986 (SI 1986/1046) as amended.

[45] N. 19 above, at 900.

directors of an in-house corporate trustee) wholly or mainly by employees of the employer company. The finance director will generally be there, and so will the the company secretary and the pensions manager. There will be blue-collar employees as well, often selected or approved through trade-union channels. Current pensioners are seldom found among the trustees, and deferred pensioners (that is, early leavers) hardly ever.

In my experience the vast majority of pension trustees do perform their duties carefully, conscientiously, and on occasion courageously, sometimes in anxious and difficult circumstances. But it would be unrealistic to deny that there are often feelings of 'us' and 'them' threatening the collegiate character which trustees' decisions ought to have. No amount of skill in drafting indemnity clauses can remove these difficulties. Legislative intervention might of course seek to put the balance of power in the hands of independent trustees. At present that happens only when the employer is insolvent.[46] A general statutory requirement for control by independent trustees would be a drastic step, and might cause or hasten a move away from final-salary schemes. Sections 16 to 21 of the Pensions Act 1995 (which comes into force in 1997) will ensure that there are normally some workers or workers' representatives among the trustees (or on the board of a corporate trustee). But that change will not by itself improve the position on conflict of interest: if anything, it will exacerbate feelings of 'us' and 'them'.

When the affairs of a pension scheme come before the court, a small number of beneficiaries may be made parties to the proceedings in order to represent the interests of others in the same class. (The class might consist of active members, current pensioners, or deferred pensioners, with further separate representation for any sub-class with special rights, or for the sexes where there are issues under Article 119 of the Treaty of Rome.[47]) In *Re William Makin & Sons*[48] a situation had arisen similar to that in *Mettoy*, but with the further complication that the employer company (then in liquidation) had been sole trustee of the pension scheme. Vinelott J would have preferred to appoint new trustees to prepare proposals for distributing the pension fund surplus, but was persuaded that in order to save time and costs a scheme could be prepared by the representative beneficiaries (both former directors) for approval by the court at a further hearing. Vinelott J added that the representative beneficiaries[49] 'will be entitled to full indemnity against

[46] Pension Schemes Act 1993, Pt. VII, Ch. 1, to be replaced by Pensions Act 1995, ss. 22–26.

[47] It is inappropriate to go into the mass of European Union litigation following *Barber* v. *Royal Exchange Assurance* [1990]ECR 1–1889 except to say that it has greatly added to the burdens of pension trustees and their advisers.

[48] [1993] OPLR 171. [49] *Ibid.* 179.

any costs incurred in preparing the scheme in just the same way as if they were trustees; they must, of course, accept that they themselves will have to be excluded from any benefit under the scheme'.

This last observation may not have been the subject of any considered submissions to the judge and it seems to have come as something of a shock both to the parties and (after publication of the report) to pensions law practitioners. It was criticized by some commentators, and in *British Coal Corporation* v. *British Coal Staff Superannuation Scheme Trustees*[50] Vinelott J replied to the critcism. He said:

> I find the idea that a person who has a power to distribute a fund amongst a class which includes himself should be able to apply the fund or any part of it for his own benefit equally outrageous. This does not rest on any technical rule of trust law; common sense dictates that no man should be asked to exercise a discretion as to the application of a fund amongst a class of which he is a member.

I yield to no one in my respect for Sir John Vinelott, but I think that these observations must be read in the context of the particular (and unusual) facts of *Makin*—where the representative beneficiaries were former directors. My next remarks are directed, not to that particular case, but to the generality of cases. The trustees of a pension scheme are often beneficially interested under it, and representative beneficiaries joined as parties in legal proceedings invariably and necessarily are. Their whole function is to do their best for themselves and those whom they respectively represent, and their duty to those whom they represent makes them fiduciaries. But if on the compromise of proceedings the representative of (say) current pensioners negotiates a once-for-all 10 per cent increase in pensions then in payment, he is getting nothing for himself that he does not get for his constituency; and what he gets for himself he gets because he is a pensioner, not because he happens also to be a fiduciary. That is so even if the compromise involves the exercise of a discretion. Moreover, any scheme or compromise arrived at in the negotiations is no more than provisional until approved by the court, which will take account of the interests not only of current and prospective pensioners, but also of creditors of an insolvent employer (see *Thrells Ltd (1974) Pension Scheme* v. *Lomas*[51]). The Chancery Division has an ancient and much-used inherent jurisdiction, partly enlarged and partly replicated by statute, to enable fiduciaries to enter into transactions despite any conflict of interest.

All these points were considered by Lindsay J in *Manning* v. *Drexel Burnham Lambert Holdings*[52] in which the judge held that he possessed, and went on to exercise, jurisdiction to approve augmentation of benefits on the winding up of a pension scheme, even though the four

[50] [1994] OPLR 51, at 62. [51] [1992] OPLR 21, at 29–30. [52] [1994] OPLR 71.

plaintiff trustees were scheme members who would benefit from the augmentation. Lindsay J's judgment contains a careful review of the 'general rule of equity' stated by Viscount Sankey in *Regal (Hastings)* v. *Gulliver*,[53] 'that no one who has duties of a fiduciary nature to perform is allowed to enter into engagements in which he has or can have a personal interest conflicting with the interests of those whom he is bound to protect'. The general rule is, as Lindsay J noted,[54] 'riddled with exceptions'. The whole judgment deserves close study, not least as a tactful exercise in judicial comity.

In *Manning* v. *Drexel Burnham Lambert Holdings* Lindsay J made it quite clear that the court has a dispensing power enabling conflicts of interest to be avoided or resolved with the court's approval. But legal proceedings about pension schemes are often slow and expensive, even when relatively uncontroversial. The judge noted[55] that some trust deeds might be incapable of amendment so as to avoid such problems without the need for legal proceedings. That is a difficult area which has, so far, been little explored in reported cases.[56] For trustee-beneficiaries the point will become academic in 1997 with the coming into force of section 39 of the Pensions Act 1995, but it is not at all clear that the absolving effect of that section would apply to a representative beneficiary who is a fiduciary but not an express trustee exercising a power.

Pension schemes resemble cricket, or horse racing, or poker—the list could be extended almost indefinitely—in that either you are fascinated by them or you find them stupifyingly boring: there is no middle ground for 'don't knows'. It will be apparent that I am not ashamed to be counted among the former faction. I hope I may have persuaded some of you that there is real interest in seeing how some long-standing trust principles are being tested in this relatively new and very important field.

[53] [1967] 2 AC 134, at 137. [54] N. 52 above, at 78. [55] *Ibid.* 80.
[56] But see Millett J in *Courage*, n. 13 above at 505.

6

Self-dealing Trustees

HON. MR JUSTICE B. H. M^c^PHERSON, CBE

In *Tito* v. *Waddell (No 2)*,[1] Sir Robert Megarry V-C distinguished between two rules applicable to trustees. The first, which he called the 'self-dealing rule', is that 'if a trustee purchases trust property from himself, any beneficiary may have the sale set aside ex debito justitiae, however fair the transaction.' The second, labelled the 'fair-dealing rule', is that 'if a trustee purchases his beneficiary's beneficial interest, the beneficiary may have the sale set aside unless the trustee can establish the propriety of the transaction, showing that he had taken no advantage of his position and that the beneficiary was fully informed and received full value.'

The descriptions 'self-dealing' and 'fair-dealing' have been adopted by modern textwriters on trusts and fiduciary relations in their treatment of the topic.[2] Although the terminology is novel, the underlying dichotomy itself is not. It has antecedents going back to the early part of the last century. Its scope and effect have, however, recently been the subject of challenge or question. In *Holder* v. *Holder*,[3] it was suggested that the self-dealing rule may not apply if the trustee purchases for himself at public auction. In *Tito* v. *Waddell (No 2)*[4] itself, and in the later case of *Re Thompson's Settlement*,[5] it was submitted by counsel that there was really only one rule, which was the 'fair-dealing' rule; or else that the self-dealing rule should be restrictively applied.[6] In both cases the submission was rejected. If accepted, it would leave the purchase of trust property by the trustee to be regulated exclusively by the general equitable principle which renders a transaction voidable for conflict of duty and interest. That would have the effect of making the fair-dealing rule exhaustive and the self-dealing rule largely, if not entirely, redundant.

Most textwriters approach the matter of trustees' purchases of trust property in that way. After referring to the self-dealing rule, they proceed

[1] [1977] 1 Ch. 106, 224–5.

[2] Parker and Mellows, *The Modern Law of Trusts* (6th edn., by A. J. Oakley), at 232–7; P. H. Pettit, *Equity & the Law of Trusts* (7th edn.), 424–8.

[3] [1968] 1 Ch. 353, 398, 402. Contrast *Glennon* v. *Federal Commissioner of Taxation* (1972) 127 CLR 503, 572–3.

[4] N. 1 above, 224–5.

[5] [1986] 1 Ch. 99.

[6] *Ibid.* 114–15.

to treat the matter as being governed by the general equitable principle applicable to all fiduciaries,[7] citing as authority the decisions of Lord Eldon in *Ex parte Lacey* (1802)[8] and *Ex parte James* (1803).[9] There is, of course, no doubt about the applicability of that principle to trustees in the strict or traditional sense. Quite apart from it, however, the reported cases disclose four separate reasons why a trustee is unable to purchase the trust property from himself. These reasons, or the rules which flow from them, are distinct, although there is a tendency at times to run them into one another. The four reasons are that a person cannot make a contract with himself; that a trustee's power of sale cannot validly be exercised in his own favour; that a person cannot convey to himself; and, if all these obstacles are surmounted, that a purchase by a trustee of the trust property has, in any event, no effect on the beneficial ownership of that property, which simply remains where it always was. On this footing there can be no question of a beneficiary having to set aside the transaction, whether as a matter of right or otherwise. The purchase by a trustee of trust property is invalid without action being taken by the beneficiaries to set it aside.

CONTRACTING WITH ONESELF

In *Tito* v. *Waddell (No 2)*,[10] the self-dealing rule was said to apply 'if the trustee purchases trust property from himself'. This accords with orthodox formulations in standard English texts.[11] In the United States the rule is stated in substantially the same form.[12] What it overlooks is that you cannot make a contract with yourself. The procedural objection to an action in which one of the opposing parties appears on both sides of the record is not the source of the problem. The rule precluding a person from contracting with himself is one of substance, not procedure.[13] It is true that it is a rule of law; but it is not one that attracts the statutory provision that equity prevails over the common law,[14] which applies only

[7] See n. 2 above, and also *Lewin on Trusts* (17th edn.), at 693–4; *Snell's Equity* (29th edn.), at 249–51; Ford and Lee, *Principles of the Law of Trusts* (2nd edn., 1990) §900, at 400–2; Finn, *Fiduciary Obligations* §430, at 184–5; Waters, *Canadian Law of Trusts* (2nd edn.), 718–24. Contrast *Jacob's Law of Trusts in Australia* (5th edn., 1986) §1737, at 424-5.

[8] 6 Ves. Jun. 625, 31 ER 1228.

[9] 8 Ves. Jun. 338, 32 ER 385.

[10] N. 1 above, at 225.

[11] *Lewin on Trusts*, n. 7 above, at 693–4; *White & Tudor's Equity Cases* (7th edn.), ii, at 709–51; *Snell's Equity*, n. 7 above, at 249–51.

[12] 76 Am. Jur. 2d §§578–90.

[13] *Mainwaring* v. *Newman* (1800) 2 Bos. & Pul. 120, 126 ER 1190; *Ellis* v. *Kerr* [1910] 2 Ch. 529, at 534–6.

[14] Judicature Act 1925, s. 44, replacing Judicature Act 1873, s. 25(11).

where there is a conflict or variance between equity and common law. There is no such conflict or variance here. In this respect equity follows the law. It does not insist that there is a contract where the law denies it. It follows that a trustee cannot purchase the trust property from himself; or, which is the same thing, sell it to himself.

Formerly it made no difference that there was another party on one side or the other. The rule preventing a contract with oneself applied to a contract by a person with himself and one or more others. Such a contract was a nullity in the same way as a contract with that person alone, which is why a contract between two partnerships having a common partner was void,[15] or a lease by one person to himself and another.[16] At least that was so if the covenant or promise was joint,[17] as it ordinarily is in the case of co-trustees, rather than joint and several. In England the common law has never adopted the American expedient of recognizing a contract made by two or more persons with themselves 'acting as a unit' in some other capacity, such as trustees or partners.[18]

Section 82 of the Law of Property Act 1925, improving on earlier legislation which had proved inadequate,[19] now permits the enforcement of a covenant or agreement entered into by a person with himself and one or more other persons 'in like manner as if the covenant or agreement had been entered into with the other person alone'. The legislation has been widely adopted in other common law jurisdictions.[20] As a result, an agreement, for example between two partnerships with a common member,[21] is now enforceable. So is any other contract by a person with himself and another.[22] Whereas formerly a trustee could not validly agree to buy from himself and a co-trustee,[23] the reform introduced by section 82 of the Law of Property Act 1925 means that there is now at least no contractual obstacle to doing so. Although, however, a contract like that is no longer void, section 82 has not affected the other reasons that invalidate such a purchase, and which operate independently of the equitable principle making the contract voidable as involving a breach of

[15] *Mainwaring* v. *Newman*, n. 13 above; *Ellis* v. *Kerr*, n. 13 above; *Stewart* v. *Hawkins* [1960] SR (NSW) 104, 106, 108–9.

[16] *Grey* v. *Ellision* (1839) 1 Giff. 436, 444, 65 ER 990, 993; *Napier* v. *Williams* [1911] 1 Ch. 361.

[17] *Ibid.*

[18] See *Corbin on Contracts* (revd. ed.) §3.1; Restatement (2d) Contracts §§9, 11; *People's Bank* v. *Allen*, 344 Mo. 193, 125 SW 2d 829 (1939).

[19] *Napier* v. *Williams*, n. 16 above, 367.

[20] See *Jacob's Law of Trusts in Australia*, n. 7 above, §1737, at 424.

[21] *Stewart* v. *Hawkins*, n. 15 above, not adopting Glanville Williams, *Joint Obligations*, at 47.

[22] *People's Prudential Assurance Co. Ltd* v. *Australian Federal Life & General Assurance Co. Ltd* (1935) 35 SR (NSW). 253, 265.

[23] *Williams* v. *Scott* [1900] AC 499; *Re Boles & British Land Company's Contract* [1902] 1 Ch. 244, 246.

fiduciary duty.[24] However, apart from agreements now specifically covered by section 82, it remains the rule that a person cannot contract with himself alone. Section 82 does not affect that case. Indeed, the principle appears to have been the underlying justification for the decision in *Rye* v. *Rye*[25] that two persons together cannot lease to themselves,[26] which might itself be thought to involve an extension of the original rule.

EFFECT OF THE SELF-DEALING RULE

Some time seems to have elapsed before the rule which precludes a contract with oneself received full recognition in the case of a trustee seeking to buy the trust property from himself.[27] One of the first occasions on which it was given effect was in *Lewis* v. *Hillman*[28] in 1852, where Lord St Leonards said:

> There was no contract. To be a contract there must be two persons. Two minds are essential to constitute a contract. For a contract of this sort, there must be not only a buyer but a seller; and upon this occasion there was a buyer, no doubt, in one sense of the term, but there was no seller. . . . No man in a court of equity is allowed himself to buy and sell the same property. He cannot sell to himself. Even in the case of a fair trustee, he cannot sell to himself. If he has the power or the trust to sell, he must have someone to deal with.

Following upon that decision, Romilly MR in *Denton* v. *Donner*[29] in 1856 explained the distinction between the self-dealing rule and the fair-dealing rule in a way which, it is suggested, accurately states the position:

> No doubt where a person is trustee for sale, and he sells the estate to himself, the transaction is absolutely and *ipso facto* void; but if a trustee purchases from his cestui que trust his reversionary interest . . . I do not assert it is absolutely void, but certainly the burden of proof lies on the trustee to show that every possible security and advantage were given to the cestui que trust, and that as much as possible was gained from the transaction as could have been gained under any circumstances.

The case involved the purchase by a mortgagee of a reversionary interest in settled property, which was conveyed to him absolutely after default

[24] On the ground of conflict between the duty and interest of the trustee: see *Jacob's Law of Trusts in Australia*, n. 7 above, §1737, at 434; *People's Prudential Assurance Co. Ltd* v. *Australian Federal Life & General Assurance Ltd*, n. 22 above, at 265.

[25] [1962] AC 496.

[26] *Ibid.* 505, 514.

[27] Even now, it tends to be overlooked in discussions of the self-dealing rule. Cf Finn, *Fiduciary Obligations* §430, at 184–5; Ford and Lee, n. 7 above, at 400.

[28] (1852) 3 HLC 607, 629–30.

[29] (1856) 23 Beav. 285, 290, 53 ER 112, 114.

in making the mortgage payments. Reconveyance was ordered to enable the mortgagor to redeem.[30]

In *Denton* v. *Donner* the mortgagee who purchased also happened to be the mortgagor's solicitor. For that reason, the Master of the Rolls treated the transaction as a purchase of the equity of redemption, which he held exposed it to the fair-dealing rule. An opportunity to apply the self-dealing rule directly to a trustee purchasing from himself came before the same learned judge only few years later in *Ingle* v. *Richards (No 1)*.[31] Henry Richards devised the remainder of his estate to his brothers, John and Thomas Richards, on trust for his sisters and their children. The trustees offered for sale at public auction some land at Doddington forming part of the estate. Acting through a nominee, John Richards bought it for himself. Before conveyance he died intestate, upon which his next-of-kin claimed to be entitled to the land against Thomas and the other beneficiaries under Henry's will, arguing that the sale had converted the land to personalty. In rejecting that contention, Sir John Romilly said it made no difference that the sale had been by public auction. The result would have been exactly the same if John Richards had signed a document saying that he agreed to buy and sell the Doddington estate. Such a document, said the Master of the Rolls, would be a 'mere piece of waste paper', something which the Court would never enforce specifically.[32]

The question was considered again in *Franks* v. *Bollans*,[33] where the trustee for sale contrived to sell and convey to himself land forming part of a deceased estate held in trust for himself and his brothers and sisters. In the Court of Appeal in Chancery, Selwyn LJ said:[34] '[h]ow can we say that there has been a sale here? The trustee could not sell to himself. To every sale there must be two parties, and they must both be competent to contract'. After that, the contractual invalidity of a trustee's purchase from or sale to himself was raised with increasing frequency. In *Farrer* v. *Farrer's Limited*[35] Chitty J said:

> A mortgagee cannot sell to himself, nor can two mortgagees sell to one of themselves, nor to one of themselves and another. The reasons for this are obvious, and are not merely formal but substantial. A man cannot contract with himself, and in the cases supposed there cannot be any independent bargaining as between opposite parties.

[30] *Ibid.* 291 (Beav.), 114 (ER).
[31] (1860) 28 Beav. 281, 54 ER 405.
[32] See also *Luff* v. *Lord* (1864) 28 Beav. 220, 226, 55 ER 619, 622, affd. (1865) 11 LT 695; *Hodson* v. *Deane* [1903] 2 Ch. 647, 653.
[33] (1868) 3 Ch. App. 717.
[34] *Ibid.* 719.
[35] (1888) 40 Ch. D 395, 404.

On appeal the proposition was indorsed by Lindley LJ:[36] '[a] sale by a person to himself is no sale at all, and a power of sale does not authorise the donee of the power to take the property subject to it at a price fixed by himself, even although such price be the full value of the property.' *Farrer* v. *Farrer's Limited* was an instance of sale by a mortgagee, although not to himself personally but to a company in which he was interested.[37] The validity of a sale by someone directly to himself was considered by the Privy Council on appeal from Jamaica in *Henderson* v. *Astwood*.[38] Speaking of a purported sale by a person to his agent, Lord Macnaghten was explicit: '[t]he so-called sale was of course inoperative. A man cannot contract with himself. A man cannot sell to himself, either in his own person or in the person of another.' As his Lordship's observations show, it is not possible to evade the rule by employing an agent to purchase on behalf of the trustee. If the principal is incompetent, his agent cannot do what the principal himself is precluded from doing.[39]

Henderson v. *Astwood* was yet another instance of sale by a mortgagee. In case it be supposed that the rule is peculiar to mortgage transactions, a further decision of the Privy Council, this time on appeal from New South Wales, illustrates its application to a trustee. In *Williams* v. *Scott*[40] the testatrix, having appointed her son David Austin and her daughter Catherine as executors, left to them her estate on trust to sell and divide among her eight children. The estate included land near Sydney. In 1889 David sought to purchase the land for himself under a deed to which the parties were David and Catherine as trustees and vendors, Catherine's husband, a solicitor named Bull to whom the property was conveyed in trust for David, and David himself as purchaser. Having bought the property in this way, in 1897 David mortgaged it to the respondent, Scott, who in exercising his power of sale as mortgagee later agreed to sell it to the appellant Williams. The appellant refused to complete on receiving advice from his solicitors that the mortgagee's title was defective, having as it did its source in the deed of 1889 by which David and Catherine purported to sell to David, who, the solicitors objected, was incapable of purchasing from himself and his co-trustee.[41] In giving the opinion of the Privy Council discharging an order for specific performance of Scott's contract to sell to Williams, Sir Ford North took as the

[36] *Ibid.* 409; applied in *Hodson* v. *Deane*, n. 32 above, 652.

[37] See also *Tse Kwong Lam* v. *Wong Chit Sen* [1983] 1 WLR 1349, 1354–5.

[38] [1894] AC 150, 158.

[39] *Re Bloye's Will Trust* (1849) 1 Mac. & G 488, 494–5, 41 ER 1354, 1357. See also *Campbell* v. *Walker* (1800) 5 Ves. Jun. 678, 31 ER 801; *Randall* v. *Errington* (1805) 10 Ves. Jun. 423, 32 ER 909; *Ex parte Bennett* (1805) 10 Ves. Jun. 381, 32 ER 893, 900; *Watson* v. *Toone* (1820) 6 Madd. 153, 56 ER 1050.

[40] [1900] AC 499. See also *Union Trustee Co.* v. *Gorrie* [1962] Qd. R 605, 614.

[41] N. 40 above, 501.

starting point that[42] '[i]t is clear undisputed law that a trustee for the sale of property cannot himself be the purchaser of it—no person can at the same time fill the opposite characters of vendor and purchaser.' In the result, it was held to be inequitable to force such a title on the purchaser Williams. If the rule was that the contract was merely voidable, the decision should have gone the other way. Only the beneficiaries had power to avoid the contract in that instance, and they had never elected to do so.

CONVEYING TO ONESELF

It will be necessary to return to *Williams* v. *Scott* in considering whether an invalid sale by a trustee to himself can survive as a purchase by the trustee of the beneficial interest of the cestui que trust. Before doing so, mention must be made of the conveyancing implications of a sale by a trustee to sell to or purchase from himself. At common law a person could not convey real or personal estate to himself directly.[43] However, various other devices could be and were resorted to. An extreme example is afforded by *Franks* v. *Bollans.*[44] Only the decision on appeal is given in the Law Reports, where the reporter contented himself with saying that the deed employed in that case was 'of a somewhat singular character, into the particulars of which it is unnecessary to enter'. The conveyancing form resorted to is, however, reported in full in the Law Times account of the suit at first instance. The testator devised his estate to his son William Bollans on trust for the testator's widow for life, and then to sell and divide among his five children. In 1842, after the death of the widow and a co-trustee, William Bollans executed a deed to which he and his brothers and sisters, together with their husbands and one Hodgson, were all parties, by which William affected to purchase the fee simple in land forming part of the estate for a price of £200. In the same deed Hodgson acknowledged receipt of the sum of £200 as agent for William, who was expressed to have 'granted, bargained, sold, aliened [and] released' to Hodgson all the 'estate, right, title, interest, use, trust, equity of redemption, inheritance, property, claim and demand whatsoever, both at law and in equity' of the beneficiaries and their wives, leaving Hodgson to have and to hold to the use of William for life, and then to his heirs and assigns.

Recognizing it as an attempt to override the beneficial interests under the trust, Stuart V-C said[45] of the deed generally, and the provision in it

[42] *Ibid.* 503.

[43] *Rye* v. *Rye*, n. 25 above, 507, *per* Lord MacDermott.

[44] N. 33 above, affg. (1867) 17 LT 309.

[45] N. 33 above, at 17 LT 309, 311.

for payment of the purchase moneys to Hodgson as agent for William: '[a]nything more absurd than this, in the way of conveyance, can hardly be imagined. It is a contract by a man with himself; and in contracting with himself he appoints an agent to pay himself the purchase-money. It is simply nonsense, and can operate as nothing.' Contract apart, it was perhaps not quite as absurd as it seemed. Although at common law a person could not grant or convey to himself, it was possible to convey to a grantee for uses,[46] whereupon the Statute of Uses of 1535 executed the use and revested the property in the grantor. The Statute of Uses was repealed by the Law of Property Act 1925, which, however, provided in section 72(3) that thereafter 'a person may convey land to or vest land in himself'.[47] Correspondingly, under section 72(4) of the Act a person may now convey to himself alone or jointly with another or others. A conveyance to oneself, or to oneself and others, may thus be valid even if the precedent contract is not.

POSITION AFTER CONVEYANCE

The fact that it is possible to convey to or to vest in oneself makes it necessary to examine the effect on the beneficial ownership of the sale of trust property by a trustee to himself, or by a trustee to himself and another, or by other combinations of a similar kind, followed by a conveyance or vesting in favour of that person or persons. Vesting property in oneself was possible under the Statute of Uses, and may now be effected by conveying directly under section 72(3) of the Law of Property Act 1925, but it can have no impact on the trust. Taking the legal title out of the trustee and then vesting it in him again plainly has no effect on the beneficial interests in the property conveyed.[48] The trust continues to attach to the trustee and to the property after, precisely as it did before, the conveyance or vesting. The trust and its incidents are not extinguished by passing the property through a legal hoop. So much was recognized in *Frank* v. *Bollans,* where Stuart V-C said:[49]

> The situation of William Bollans being that, before the execution of the deed the property was vested in him in trust for sale, and that after its execution it was still so vested in him, how can it be said that any trust connected with the property was extinguished by the deed? There is no release to him by any of the cestuis que trust in respect of their interest. He had still the control of the property, and

[46] *Rye* v. *Rye,* n. 25 above, 511, *per* Lord Radcliffe.

[47] In passing it may be noticed that in *Rye* v. *Rye,* counsel for the appellant suggested that s. 72(3) 'deals with the occasions when a man acting in one capacity wishes to convey land to himself in another capacity'.

[48] *Glennon* v. *Federal Commission of Taxation* (1972) 113 CLR 503, 513.

[49] N. 45 above, 312, 313.

was able to sell it in execution of the trust, and in my opinion was still as much bound to sell it as he was before he executed the deed . . . he was still possessor of the land upon trust to sell, and had not acquitted himself of the trust in any way.

Likewise, on appeal, Page Wood LJ (as Lord Hatherley then was) said:[50]

The defendant, being a trustee for sale, could not acquire the beneficial ownership of the property except by gift or sale from the cestuis que trust; he was under an absolute disability to acquire it otherwise. He is a trustee of it still, for the plaintiff [beneficiary] never disposed of her interest to him.

Once a trustee, always a trustee. Even if the trustee can convey to himself, he cannot by doing so destroy the beneficial interests in the trust property. That a trustee can never assert a title of his own to trust property is said to be 'an elementary proposition'.[51] Being a trustee, he can never claim to be a *bona fide* purchaser for value without notice. The trust will survive all manner of conveyancing tricks practised on it, whether or not the property afterwards remains in precisely the same condition, or is transformed wholly or partly into something else.[52] The beneficiary can therefore continue to claim the property if, after the conveyance, it remains vested in the trustee.[53] In a simple case like that it may be unduly sophisticated to speak of the process as one of tracing. A trustee who sets out to keep the property for himself remains bound by the trust as he was before it was conveyed to him.[54]

CONVEYANCE TO NOMINEE

It would, however, be only an exceptionally foolish trustee who tried to make off with the trust property by selling and transferring it to himself in his own name. More often the method adopted is to arrange for an agent or nominee to purchase and take the conveyance, sometimes openly but usually secretly, on the trustee's behalf.[55] As we have seen, however, the prohibition against a trustee purchasing for himself cannot be evaded by employing an agent to contract on his behalf. The conse-

[50] N. 33 above, 718.

[51] *Frith* v. *Cartland* (1865) 34 LJ Ch. 301, 303. For qualifications on the proposition, see Ford and Lee, n. 7 above, §927, at 414–16.

[52] *Buckeridge* v. *Glasse* (1841) Cr. & Ph. 128, 41 ER 438; *Carson* v. *Sloane* (1884) 13 LR Ir. Eq. 139.

[53] *Re Hallett's Estate* (1879) 13 Ch. D 696, 708–9; *Silkstone & Haigh Moor Coal Co.* v. *Edey* [1900] 1 Ch. 167, 171, adopting *Lewin on Trusts*, n. 7 above, at 558.

[54] *Gordon* v. *Holland* (1913) 4 WWR 419, 426–9; 10 DLR 734, 741–4 (PC).

[55] *Rye* v. *Rye*, n. 25 above, 511; Waters, n. 7 above, 720–1. For a sale to the trustee's wife, see *Robertson* v. *Robertson* [1924] NZLR 522.

quence of doing so would still be a contract by the trustee with himself, which is no contract at all.[56]

Even if the contractual dimension is ignored, a device like that cannot nullify the trust or the beneficial interests subsisting in the property. In *Lewis* v. *Hillman*[57] in the House of Lords,[58] a sale to an agent or nominee in the guise of a *bona fide* purchaser was held to render the trust for sale, as Lord St Leonards put it, 'powerless for that purpose'.[59] This is to characterize a sale by a trustee to himself as an excess of power, which incidentally accords with the statement, mentioned earlier, by Lindley LJ in *Farrer* v. *Farrer's Ltd*[60] that a power of sale does not authorize the donee of the power to take the property at a price fixed by himself.[61] If the sale is beyond power, transferring title to a nominee cannot extinguish the trust.[62] The only result is that the transferee himself holds the property as trustee for the original cestuis que trust. As was recognized in *Denton* v. *Donner*,[63] merely conveying trust property to a new trustee does not affect the rights of the beneficiaries in or to it. It would be rare indeed for a nominee, to whom the property was conveyed by the trustee, to succeed in taking without notice of the subsisting trust. Apart from notice, the equitable rights of the beneficiaries under the trust also have the advantage of priority in time.[64] To express it in another way, the beneficiaries are, after conveyance, entitled to follow the trust property into the hands of the nominee.

EXTINGUISHING THE TRUST

In the end, the problem confronting a trustee who sells, or affects to sell, to himself, or to an agent, nominee, or trustee for himself, or even directly to himself and another, is that, regardless of whether the contract or the conveyance is valid or void, the trust continues to attach to, and the interests of the beneficiary continue to subsist in, the trust property. It is only if the trust property is transferred to a *bona fide* purchaser for

[56] See the authorities cited in n. 39 above.

[57] (1852) 3 HLC 606, 10 ER 239.

[58] For proceedings below, see *Re Bloye's Will Trusts*, n. 39 above.

[59] N. 57 above, at 630 (HLC), 249 (ER). See also *Latec Investments Ltd* v. *Hotel Terrigal Pty. Ltd* (1965) 113 CLR 265, 273. An anomalous exception at one time allowed a tenant for life to lease to himself: *Boyce* v. *Edbrooke* [1903] 1 Ch. 836, 844–7. See now Settled Land Act 1925, s. 68.

[60] N. 35 above. See also Farwell, *Concise Treatise on Powers* (3rd edn., 1916), at 631.

[61] N. 36 above. *Glennon* v. *Federal Commissioner of Taxation*, n. 48 above, 513.

[62] *Nelson* v. *Larholt* [1948] 1 KB 339, 342–3. Cf also *Eddis* v. *Chichester Constable* [1969] 2 Ch. 345, 358.

[63] (1856) 23 Bear. 285, 287, 53 ER 112, 113.

[64] Cf *Latec Investments Pty. Ltd* v. *Hotel Terrigal Pty. Ltd*, n. 59 above, 278; Meagher Gummow and Lehane, *Equity Doctrines and Remedies* (3rd edn., 1992) §803, at 226.

value without notice that the equity of the beneficiary is, in *Scott's* phrase,[65] 'effectively cut off'. From the nature of things, it is quite improbable, in any circumstances in which (to adopt what was said in *Tito* v. *Waddell*[66]), 'a trustee purchases the trust property from himself', that the sale or the ensuing conveyance will ever be effective in equity to destroy subsisting beneficial interests.[67]

Apart from transferring to a purchaser without notice, the only other way in which the beneficial ownership in trust property can be extinguished is, as Lord Hatherley said in *Franks* v. *Bollans*,[68] for the trustee to acquire it from the cestuis que trust by gift or sale. A transaction like that attracts the second or 'fair-dealing' rule in *Tito* v. *Waddell (No 2)*,[69] which does not make the contract void but throws upon the trustee the burden of establishing the propriety of the transaction by demonstrating that the beneficiary was 'fully informed and received full value'. The effect of the purchase, if the beneficiaries do not elect to challenge it, is that equitable interests in the trust property are extinguished by transfer to and merger with the legal title of the trustee, who in consequence becomes the absolute owner, both at law and in equity, of the property in question.

On rare occasions it may be possible to construe a trustee's invalid attempt to sell to himself as an effective acquisition by him of the equitable interest in the property from the beneficiaries. The courts have seldom been receptive to such arguments, at least where the transaction savours of an attempt to override the beneficial interests. In *Ingle* v. *Richards (No 1)*[70] the attempt failed because the invalid contract was held to be incapable of converting the land into personalty. In *Franks* v. *Bollans*[71] the release in the deed was ineffectual, because, although all the beneficiaries executed it, some of them were married women under coverture, who failed to acknowledge in accordance with the Fines and Recoveries Act 1833.[72] Because of their general contractual incompetence, infant beneficiaries invariably raise problems of a similar kind.

It is only in an exceptional case that a trustee's unsuccessful attempt to purchase from himself will result in a valid agreement to purchase from the beneficiaries. *Williams* v. *Scott*,[73] to which it is now necessary to return, is an instance in which the trustee tried to have it both ways. He not only sought to purchase from himself but also tried to buy from the

[65] *Scott on Trusts* (4th edn.), iv, para. 316, at 218.
[66] N. 1 above, 225, 241.
[67] *Glennon* v. *Federal Commissioner of Taxation*, n. 3 above, 513.
[68] N. 33 above, 718.
[69] N. 1 above, 225, 241. See also *Thomson* v. *Eastwood* (1877) 2 App. Cas. 215, 236.
[70] N. 31 above. Contrast *Denton* v. *Donner* (n. 26 above), where the purchase was viewed as a sale of the equitable interest.
[71] N. 33 above. [72] 3 & 4 Will. 4, c. 74, s. 77. [73] N. 23 above.

beneficiaries. A few weeks before the deed of purchase by the trustee in 1889, the beneficiaries had been persuaded to execute another deed purporting to operate as an absolute release of the trustees by all of them. The deed was treated as effective by the Full Court of New South Wales[74] but not by the Privy Council. Viewed as a purchase of the equitable interests of the beneficiaries in the trust property, it needed to satisfy the fair-dealing rule. In this it failed because, in their Lordships' opinion, the evidence did not show that the beneficiaries had full knowledge of all the circumstances.[75] A trustee for sale of property, said Sir Ford North:[76]

> cannot sell to himself. If notwithstanding the form of the conveyance, the trustee (or any person claiming under him) seeks to justify the transaction as being really a purchase from the cestui que trust, it is important to remember upon whom the onus of proof falls. It ought not to be assumed, in the absence of evidence to the contrary, that the transaction is a proper one, and that the cestuis que trust were all informed of necessary matters. The burden of proof that the transaction was a righteous one rests upon the trustee, who is bound to produce clear affirmative poof that the parties were at arms' length; that the cestui que trusts had the fullest information on all material facts; and that, having this information, they agreed to and adopted what was done.

Because the executed release could not be regarded as bringing the trust to an end, the property remained, as it was before execution of the deed, vested in the trustees for sale.[77] The case illustrates, perhaps better than any other, the relationship between the two rules.

LEAVE TO PURCHASE

Before a trustee can purchase for himself he must, as Lord Eldon said, in *Ex parte Bennett*[78] first 'shake off the character of trustee'[79] by putting himself in a position in which he is no longer a person entrusted to sell. Apart from selling to a purchaser without notice, or validly acquiring the equitable interests of the beneficiaries in the trust property, a trustee can effectively 'shake off' the trust only by virtue of a specific authority in the trust instrument authorizing him to acquire the property himself,[80] or by obtaining leave of the court to purchase. There is a long line of authority recognizing that, on fulfilling stringent conditions, a trustee may be

[74] 20 LR (NSW) Eq. 102. [75] N. 23 above, at 503–5. [76] *Ibid.* 508.
[77] *Ibid.* 504.
[78] N. 39 above, at 394 (Ves. Jun.), 897 (ER).
[79] See also *Ex parte James*, n. 9 above, at 345, 353 (Ves. Jun.), 384, 391 (ER).
[80] Cf *Wright* v. *Morgan* [1926] AC 788. For later proceedings, see *Morgan* v. *Wright* [1928] Gaz. LR 525.

given leave to bid for the trust property at auction, or even to buy it privately.[81]

The reported cases do not identify the precise mechanism by which such a purchase is carried into effect. It may be largely academic now that a person can convey to himself. However, in the case of a sole trustee, it is possible for someone other than the trustee to be appointed to purchase and receive the conveyance on behalf of the trustee, upon his paying the purchase money into court, or as directed to or by the beneficiaries.[82] An order vesting the equitable interest in the trustee upon receipt of the payment would serve the purpose equally well; alternatively, the trustee might be removed and another appointed in his place before sale. Presumably the procedure that is chosen varies according to whether the trust itself is intended to continue, or is to be brought to an end by distributing the proceeds of sale to the beneficiaries.

The effect of judicial leave to buy is to divest the intending buyer of the character of trustee,[83] and so place him in the position of an ordinary purchaser.[84] Sometimes the rationale is said to be that, in doing so, the trustee is relieved of his obligation of avoiding a conflict of duty and interest,[85] which is usually identified as the dominant principle in this context. But if a trustee is incapable of making a contract with himself, or of exercising power of sale in his favour, something going beyond mere breach of fiduciary duty is being eliminated by the order giving leave to purchase.

DIFFERENCES BETWEEN THE TWO RULES

Complying with the fair-dealing rule puts an end to a trust. If the trustee validly acquires the interests of the beneficiaries in the trust property, the trust itself is terminated. The interests of the beneficiaries are extinguished by union with the trustee's legal title. Self-dealing does not and cannot produce that result. If the trustee presumes to purchase the trust property himself, whether in his own name or that of an agent or nominee, the trust survives unless and until the property finds its way to a

[81] See G. W. Hinde, 'Purchase of Trust Property by a Trustee with the Approval of the Court' (1961) 3 *Melbourne University LR* 15. S. 57 of the Trustee Act 1925 may now provide a statutory source of power to grant such leave.

[82] As is the practice with sales in lieu of partition, or property held by co-owners on the statutory trust for sale: *Re Cordingley* (1948) 48 SR (NSW) 248.

[83] *Campbell* v. *Walker*, n. 39 above, at 681 (Ves. Jun.), 802 (ER); *Boswell* v. *Coakes* (1883) 23 Ch. D 302, 311; *Throp* v. *Trustee Executors & Agency Co.* [1945] NZLR 483.

[84] *Boswell* v. *Coakes* (1886) 11 App. Cas. 232, 245, affg. 23 Ch. D 302.

[85] *Boswell* v. *Coakes* (1883) 23 Ch. D 302, 311.

bona fide purchaser for value without notice. Meanwhile the beneficiary may follow it into the hands of any transferee with notice and successfully lay claim to it by asserting his equitable ownership.[86]

The beneficiary nevertheless has an option.[87] Instead of following the trust property into the hands of the transferee, he may, if he wishes, elect to take the proceeds of sale.[88] By doing so, he acquiesces in the transaction, and so affirms[89] the purchase, which has the practical consequence that he cannot thereafter complain of it as a breach of trust. The early cases tended to approach the matter as giving rise to an election to rescind or avoid the trustee's purchase. Many of them involved fiduciaries in whom the trust property was not vested.[90] However, a trustee who appropriates the trust property to purposes of his own necessarily misapplies it. Such conduct is a breach of trust, which means that in equity it is ineffective unless with full knowledge the beneficiary elects to ratify it,[91] or is estopped from asserting his beneficial interest in the property.

The distinction between the self-dealing rule and the fair-dealing rule entails something more than a difference in what must be established by a beneficiary wishing to avoid the transaction. A fundamental difference of theory is involved. Self-dealing, as Professor Waters notices,[92] amounts to a breach of trust. Unless ratified by the beneficiaries, it has no effect in equity. The property in the hands of the trustee or his nominee remains subject to the trust. Even if the beneficiary does elect to ratify the transaction, or the original trust property passes to a *bona fide* purchaser for value without notice, the trust will fasten on the proceeds of sale. The beneficiary's interest is overreached but the trust survives. By contrast, fair-dealing extinguishes the trust. If the trustee fulfils the requirement of full disclosure to the beneficiaries and obtains their informed consent, he acquires beneficial ownership of the property. If he already holds the legal title, it means that he becomes the absolute owner both in equity as well as in law. What he is purchasing, however, is not the legal title to the trust property (which as trustee he already holds), but the equitable ownership. Statute apart, no one but the beneficiaries are able to sell that interest.

86 *Silkstone & Haigh Moor Coal Co.* v. *Edey* [1900] 1 Ch. 167, 171.

87 *Ex parte James*, n. 9 above, at 351 (Ves. Jun.), 390 (ER); *Price* v. *Blackmore* (1843) 6 Beav. 507, 49 ER 922; *Frances* v. *Frances* (1854) 5 De G M & G 108, 43 ER 811.

88 *Ibid.*; *Carson* v. *Sloane* (1884) 13 LR Ir. Eq. 139.

89 *Holder* v. *Holder* [1968] 1 Ch. 353, 305.

90 The starting point is *York Buildings Co.* v. *Mackenzie* (1795) 3 Bro. Parl. Cas. 42, 3 ER 432, which concerned a Scots 'common agent' (as to which see *Wright* v. *Morgan*, n. 80 above, 797–8).

91 *Morse* v. *Royal* (1806) 12 Ves. Jun. 355, 374, 33 ER 134, 141; *Re Sherman* [1954] Ch. 653, 658.

92 Waters, n. 7 above, 720–2. Contrast Ford and Lee, n. 7 above, §1825, at 809, who say that a trustee purchasing trust property 'has not committed a breach of trust as such'.

HISTORICAL EVOLUTION

It is common to ascribe both the self-dealing rule and the fair-dealing rule to a series of decisions dating from the beginning of the last century, in which Lord Eldon applied the principle that a trustee or a fiduciary must not place himself in a position where his interest and duty conflict.[93] In doing so, his Lordship had two objects in mind. One was to suppress a practice, widespread at that time, under which assignees in bankruptcy and their solicitors bought up parts of the insolvent estate for themselves.[94] The other was to dispel a suggestion in some of the earlier cases[95] that transactions like that were assailable only on proof of a loss to the beneficiaries[96] or of a profit or advantage to the trustee.[97] Lord Eldon treated *Keech* v. *Sandford*,[98] to which he referred, though not by name, as illustrating a wider principle that, however fair and honest it might appear to be, purchases by trustees, assignees, and other persons having a confidential character, must be 'destroyed'.[99] The justification was said to lie in the difficulty faced by beneficiaries in knowing whether or not the transaction was to their advantage, compared with a trustee who in the course of his duties might have acquired special information about the property which he knew would enhance its value.[100]

Adopting conflict-of-duty and interest as a unifying single principle had the advantage that fiduciaries, such as solicitors and agents, and not only trustees in the traditional sense, were brought within the rule. So much was settled by Lord Eldon's decision in *Ex parte James*[101] in 1803; but it must not obscure the fact that, in *Ex parte Lacey*[102] in the previous year, his Lordship had been speaking of trustees as such (who in that case were assignees of the bankrupt's property) when he said:[103]

The rule I take to be this; not, that a trustee cannot buy from his cestui que trust, but, that he shall not buy from himself. If a trustee will so deal with his cestui que trust, that the amount of the transaction shakes off the obligation that attaches to him as trustee, then he may buy. If that case [*Whichcote* v. *Lawrence*] is rightly understood, it cannot lead to much mistake. The true interpretation of what is there reported does not break into the law as to trustees. The rule is this. A

[93] *Ex parte Lacey*, n. 8 above; *Ex parte James*, n. 9 above; *Downes* v. *Grazebrook* (1817) 3 Mer. 200, 36 ER 77.

[94] *Ex parte Bennett*, n. 39 above, at 391 (Ves. Jun.), 897 (ER).

[95] Notably *Whelpdale* v. *Cookson* (1747) 1 Ves. Sen. 9, 28 ER 440 and *Whichcote* v. *Lawrence* (1798) 3 Ves. Jun. 740, 750, 30 ER 1248, 1253.

[96] *Ex parte James*, n. 9 above, at 349 (Ves. Jun.), 389 (ER).

[97] *Ex parte Lacey*, n. 8 above, at 627 (Ves. Jun), referring to an interpretation (which Lord Eldon said he 'disavowed') of a doctrine of Lord Rosslyn. See also, *ibid.* at 628 (Ves. Jun.), 1227 (ER), referring to *Whelpdale* v. *Cookson* (1747) 1 Ves. Sen. 9, 28 ER 440.

[98] (1726) Cas. T. King 61, 2 Eq. Cas. Abr. 741, 25 ER 223.

[99] *Ex parte James*, n. 9 above, at 345–6 (Ves. Jun.), 388 (ER).

[100] *Ibid.* at 349 (Ves. Jun.), 389 (ER).

[101] See n. 9 above.

[102] N. 8 above.

[103] *Ibid.* 626 (Ves. Jun.), 1228 (ER).

trustee, who is entrusted to sell and manage for others, undertakes in the same moment, in which he becomes a trustee, not to manage for the benefit and advantage of himself. It does not preclude a new contract with those who have entrusted him. It does not preclude him from bargaining that he will no longer act as a trustee. The cestuis que trust may by a new contract dismiss him from that character; but even then that transaction, by which they dismiss him, must according to the rules of this Court be watched with infinite and the most guarded jealousy.

It is, it is submitted, plain enough that in this passage Lord Eldon was directing attention principally to the fair-dealing rule applicable to agreements with cestuis que trust to purchase their interest in trust property. By contrast, what he had to say about the self-dealing rule is contained in his introductory statement that 'a trustee shall not buy from himself',[104] to which elsewhere in his judgment he added[105] that he considered it 'perfectly clear' that 'an assignee under a commission of bankruptcy, [being] a trustee to sell for the benefit of the creditors and the bankrupt, cannot buy for his own benefit.' It would be wrong to assume that the learned Lord Chancellor was expressing himself with uncharacteristic inaccuracy, or that he was ignorant of the general rule that a person cannot contract with himself. Only shortly before, he had given the judgment of the Exchequer Chamber in the leading case on the subject.[106] Statements that a trustee may be a purchaser of the trust property are therefore to be understood (as at that time they were[107]) as meaning that the trustee may contract with the cestuis que trust to remove himself from the position of trustee[108] by acquiring from them the beneficial ownership in the trust property.

CONCLUSION

The result, it is submitted, is that there really are two separate rules, a self-dealing rule, which is prohibitory, and a fair-dealing rule, which is regulatory. At a certain point they may intersect. That point is, however, reached only where, after full disclosure, the beneficiaries assent to, and so ratify, a purported sale of the trust property by the trustee to himself, or more likely to his nominee. If they do ratify it, the transaction is then viewed as a purchase by the trustee of the beneficial interest in the trust property which puts an end to the trust. If they do not elect to do so, the sale remains a breach of trust, which means that the transaction can

104 See also *Morse* v. *Royal*, n. 91 above, at 373 (Ves. Jun.), 140 (ER), *per* Lord Erskine LC.
105 *Ex parte Lacey*, n. 8 above, at 628 (Ves. Jun.), 1228–9 (ER).
106 *Mainwaring* v. *Newman*, n. 13 above.
107 *Sanders on Uses and Trusts* (4th edn., 1841), vi, 362.
108 *Sanderson* v. *Walker* (1807) 13 Ves. Jun. 601, 33 ER 419, 420.

have no effect in equity. In those circumstances, the beneficiaries, if not barred by laches or estoppel, may maintain their right to the trust property. If it has passed to a *bona fide* purchaser for value without notice, they may claim the proceeds of sale, following them, if need be, into other property into which they have passed.

No doubt this is all quite elementary; but it is in some danger of being overlooked. Perhaps the explanation is the relative ease with which, since the 1925 legislation, the interests of beneficiaries can now be overreached.[109] Even that process, however, presupposes a sale that is 'proper',[110] which would not include a sale by a trustee to himself or to a nominee for himself. What needs to be firmly kept in mind is that self-dealing involves a misappropriation or misapplication of the trust property. It remains misapplication even when it is carried out, as it sometimes is, from the best of motives. When it is dishonest, it is called misappropriation. Dishonest appropriation is a criminal offence.[111] Without more, it can never effect a transfer of title to the trustee. A trustee cannot purchase trust property from himself. What he can do, if he goes about it in the right way, is to buy it from the beneficiaries. To do that, he must comply with the fair-dealing rule.

[109] *City of London Building Society* v. *Flegg* [1988] 1 AC 54.
[110] Megarry and Wade, *The Law of Real Property* (4th edn., 1975), at 377.
[111] Theft Act 1968, ss. 1(1), 5(3), which speak of an intention to 'defeat the trust'.

7

Moulding the Content of Fiduciary Duties

R. P. AUSTIN

INTRODUCTION

In 1991 P. D. Finn J began his essay on the commercial application of fiduciary principles by remarking that there were five questions of moment in contemporary fiduciary law.[1] They were: first, what are the criteria for finding that a fiduciary relationship exists; secondly, how and to what extent do fiduciary principles apply in commerce; thirdly, how does fiduciary law regulate multi-function business and professional enterprises; fourthly, what kinds of monetary compensation are available for breach of fiduciary duty; and fifthly, what role does fiduciary law have in regulating the actions of government?

The point of my essay is to add a sixth issue to the list of contemporary problems, emerging from Finn's first and fourth. This is the issue of content of fiduciary duties. Is the hallmark of a fiduciary relationship simply that one party owes a duty of loyalty to another, or are there separate fiduciary duties of care, disclosure, and (where relevant) strict adherence to the charter (such as a trust instrument or memorandum and articles of association) which constitutes the relationship? What precisely do we mean by 'loyalty'? Does it extend beyond narrowly defined conflict and profit rules to encompass positive duties to act in the interests of the principal and in good faith?

These are large questions which can only be touched upon in this essay, but doing so may help to redress what I see as an imbalance. The focus of contemporary scholarship is on Finn's first question.[2] This is an understandable response to the great fiduciary cases of the 1980s, which were cases about the extension of fiduciary duties beyond the recog-

[1] P. D. Finn, 'Fiduciary Law and the Modern Commercial World', in E. McKendrick (ed.), *Commercial Aspects of Trusts and Fiduciary Obligations* (Clarendon Press, Oxford, 1992), 7.

[2] A question of 'legal taxonomy', according to Professor D. A. DeMott, 'Fiduciary Obligations under Intellectual Siege: Contemporary Challenges to the Duty to be Loyal' (1992) 30 *Osgoode Hall LJ* 472. See J. C. Shepherd, *Law of Fiduciaries* (Carswell, Toronto, 1981) and 'Towards a Unified Concept of Fiduciary Relations' (1981) 97 *LQR* 51; P. D. Finn, 'The Fiduciary Principle', in T. G. Youdan (ed.), *Equity, Fiduciaries and Trusts* (Carswell, Toronto, 1989); R. Flannigan, 'The Fiduciary Obligation' (1989) 9 *OJLS* 285 and 'Fiduciary Obligation in the Supreme Court' (1990) 54 *Sask. LR* 45.

nized fiduciary categories.[3] But in an important sense this is a secondary question, given that there are, after all, many categories of recognized fiduciary relationships for which the issue of definition does not arise. It may not be mere coincidence that the first round of leading cases in modern fiduciary law, preceding *Hospital Products* by at least a decade, were cases about the primary question of content of the duties.[4]

The relative importance of the question of content was emphasized by Frankfurter J in 1943: 'to say that a man is a fiduciary only begins analysis'.[5] Until recently, however, judges approached the question with circumspection. Fletcher-Moulton LJ's warning[6] against assuming that 'every kind of fiduciary relationship justifies every kind of interference' may have been more influential than was justified or intended.[7] Clearly there is significant discretion to be exercised in tailoring remedies for breach of duty to fit the circumstances, especially on such questions as allowances for skill and effort and accountability for business gains. Undoubtedly the fiduciary's precise duty in a given case must be accommodated to any relevant contracts,[8] including any implied contractual terms.[9] But as the High Court of Australia has demonstrated in the *Warman International* case,[10] these considerations should not inhibit us from identifying in general terms the basic principle of liability.

In the *Warman International* case the High Court held that a plaintiff who has established a breach of fiduciary duty is entitled to elect the remedy of account of profits and should not be required to settle for equitable compensation. This conclusion flowed from an analysis of the nature of fiduciary duties. A breach of fiduciary duty may occur notwithstanding that the defendant has acted honestly, or that the plaintiff was unable to exploit for himself a profit-making opportunity which the defendant took up, and consequently it is no defence that the defendant has suffered no loss. It follows that, at least in the normal case, the plaintiff should be allowed to opt for an account of profits, and can be expected to choose equitable compensation only when his loss is greater than the defendant's gain.

Obviously this reasoning only works if the defendant's fiduciary duties

3 Most notably *Hospital Products Ltd* v. *US Surgical Corporation* (1984) 156 CLR 41 (HC) and *LAC Minerals Ltd* v. *International Corona Resources Ltd* (1989) 61 DLR (4th) 14 (SCC).

4 *Boardman* v. *Phipps* [1967] AC 46 (HL); *Canadian Aero Services Ltd* v. *O'Malley* (1973) 40 DLR (3d) 37 (SCC).

5 *SEC* v. *Chenery Corporation*, 318 US 80, 85–6.

6 In *Re Coomber* [1911] 1 Ch. 723, 728.

7 Lord Wilberforce's emphasis on a factual analysis (*New Zealand Netherlands Society 'Oranje' Inc.* v. *Kuys* [1973] 1 WLR 1126, 1129) may have its origin in this idea.

8 *Hospital Products Ltd* v. *US Surgical Corporation*, n. 3 above, 97, *per* Mason J (HCA).

9 *Kelly* v. *Cooper* [1993] AC 205.

10 *Warman International Ltd* v. *Dwyer* (1995) 69 ALJR 362, esp. at 368.

are given reasonably precise definition. If 'fiduciary duties' were to encompass such things as a duty to act honestly in the interests of others and a special duty of care, the argument would be less than compelling.

Warman International exemplifies a trend in case law, in which the fiduciary concept is coming to designate specified duties rather than an entire relationship. The same trend is evidenced in recent cases which have re-assessed the trustee's duty to restore the trust fund after breach, culminating in the decision of the House of Lords in the *Target Holdings* case.[11] The trend may also be identified in recent case law on equitable compensation for breaches of non-trust fiduciary duties.[12] Those cases are of interest in the present context because their cumulative effect is to suggest that there is no special measure of recovery against the negligent fiduciary (as opposed to the fiduciary who makes an improper profit or places himself in a position of conflict), and consequently that there is no special standard of 'fiduciary care'.[13] Some Australian company law cases which re-assess the director's duty of care in light of the expansion of the tort of negligence point in the same direction.[14]

Attempts by various appellate courts to answer Finn J's first question, namely the question of definition of the fiduciary relationship, are not directly relevant to this paper. However, they might become indirectly influential. Until the *Warman International* case it was arguable that:[15] '[e]mphasis has shifted from defendant to plaintiff, from the notion of selflessness which is of the essence of the traditional duty of a fiduciary to features such as the "vulnerability" of his beneficiary, a trend which could in time mean that the principle loses vital links with its roots.' If this were so, we could expect to see the development of a much more

[11] *Target Holdings Ltd* v. *Redferns* [1995] 3 WLR 352 (HL); *Bishopsgate Investment Management Ltd (in liq.)* v. *Maxwell (No 2)* [1994] 1 All ER 261 (CA); *Jaffray* v. *Marshall* [1994] 1 All ER 143 (CA); *Nestlé* v. *National Westminster Bank Plc* [1993] 1 WLR 1260 (CA); *Hagan* v. *Waterhouse* (1991) 34 NSWLR 308 (Kearney J); *Bartlett* v. *Barclays Bank Trust Co. Ltd* [1980] 1 Ch. 515 (CA); *Re Dawson dec'd.* [1966] 2 NSWR 211 (Street J).

[12] *Henderson* v. *Merrett Syndicates Ltd* [1994] 3 WLR 761 (HL), 798–800, *per* Lord Browne-Wilkinson; *Clark Boyce* v. *Mouat* [1994] 1 AC 428 (PC) and *Mouat* v. *Clark Boyce* [1992] 2 NZLR 559 (CA); *Gemstone Corporation of Australia Ltd* v. *Grasso* (1994) 12 ACLC 653 (Full SCSA); *Nimmo* v. *Westpac Banking Corporation* [1993] 3 NZLR 218 (Blanchard J); *Wan* v. *McDonald* (1992) 105 ALR 473 (Burchett J); *Commonwealth Bank of Australia* v. *Smith* (1991) 102 ALR 453 (Full FC); *Norberg* v. *Wynrib* (1992) 92 DLR (4th) 449 (SCC); *Canson Enterprises Ltd* v. *Boughton & Co.* (1991) 85 DLR (4th) 129 (SCC); *Aquaculture Corporation* v. *NZ Green Mussel Co. Ltd* [1990] 3 NZLR 299 (CA); *Hill* v. *Rose* [1990] VR 129 (Tadgell J); *Day* v. *Mead* [1987] 2 NZLR 443 (CA); *Girardet* v. *Crease & Co.* (1987) 11 BCLR (2d) 361 (SCC); *Guerin* v. *R.* (1984) 13 DLR (4th) 321 (SCC); *Capp* v. *Marac Australia Ltd* (1987) 9 NSWLR 639 (Rogers J).

[13] The principles of equitable compensation are discussed in Professor C. E. F. Rickett's essay in this series. My essay touches on the implications of the cases for the content of the fiduciary duties.

[14] *Daniels* v. *AWA Limited* (1995) 16 ACSR 607 (NSWCA); *Permanent Building Society (in liq.)* v. *Wheeler* (1994) 14 ACSR 109 (Full SCWA).

[15] L. S. Sealy, 'Fiduciary Obligations, Forty Years On' (1995) 9 *JCL* 37 ,40 .

flexible concept of fiduciary duties, in which the fiduciary duty would have a significance in the law of obligations on the same level as the duty of care, and the boundary between the two would then tend to dissolve. The High Court's insistence in *Warman International* that fiduciary duties remain prophylactic should mean, for the time being at least, that British Commonwealth law will continue to treat fiduciary duties as special and distinctive, even if their definition shifts in focus from the defendant's improvidence to the plaintiff's vulnerability.

My thesis, relying on the work of Finn J, is that the case law to which I have referred has provided us with the basis for a much more limited and more precise use of the concept of 'fiduciary duties' than ever before. The fiduciary duties relate to improper profits and the avoidance of conflicts of interest, and we should no longer use fiduciary terminology to describe other duties to which fiduciaries and others may be subject. I shall begin by contrasting this view with the more traditional understanding of fiduciary duties, and then offer a few notes on the differences between fiduciary duties strictly so-called and other duties which are frequently but inaccurately described as 'fiduciary'. I shall pay particular attention to the duty of 'strict compliance' and the duty of care.

TRADITIONAL UNDERSTANDING OF FIDUCIARY DUTIES

Professor Sealy has recently contrasted the relatively stable and undeveloped state of fiduciary law forty years ago with the sophistication and refinement, and occasional abandonment of principle, to be seen in the contemporary British Commonwealth law.[16] Forty years ago fiduciary law had received practically no sustained academic attention outside the United States. The first step in judicial analysis was to identify and classify the entire relationship of the parties, rather than to identify the particular duty to which the facts give rise. The fiduciary relationships included trustee and beneficiary, personal representative and beneficiary, director and company, partner and partner, solicitor and client, agent and principal, and financial adviser and client. The last two were of uncertain scope.[17] It was assumed that a relationship was either wholly fiduciary as a matter of law, or not fiduciary at all.

If a relationship was fiduciary, that characteristic was taken to be at the heart of the entire relationship, identifying more than merely one or a few duties amongst many. Broad moral precepts were applied to fiduciary relationships, the courts being more inclined to articulate

[16] L. S. Sealy, 'Fiduciary Obligations, Forty Years On' (1995) 9 *JCL* 37, 37.

[17] Generally, see P. D. Finn, *Fiduciary Obligations* (Law Book Company, Sydney, 1977), esp. at 201 ff.

high-minded exhortations than detailed rules.[18] Generally, fiduciary terminology was applied, often loosely, to standards of good faith, disclosure standards, limits on the proper exercise of discretionary powers, and even 'fiduciary care'.

Fiduciary relationships were assumed to lie in equity's exclusive jurisdiction and hence to be amenable to the full range of equitable remedies. It was recognized that a particular fiduciary relationship might, by virtue of additional facts, be subject to common law duties and remedies in tort or contract. However, the additional facts necessary to give rise to common law duties appeared to be unlikely to occur, or at least to be regarded as significant, in the relationships which were most categorically fiduciary, such as the relationships of trustee and beneficiary and director and company. In those cases all aspects of the relationship were developed in equity, including the duties of good faith, disclosure, and care.[19]

This traditional structure has generated some strong reactions:[20] '[f]or some observers . . . fiduciary obligation seems an anachronism, a fusty relic of an earlier era, evoking more the world of Bleak House than that of The Bonfire of the Vanities.' Notwithstanding radical departures from the traditional structure in New Zealand and Canada,[21] some commentators still defend most aspects of the traditional structure as it applies to established fiduciaries such as trustees[22] and company directors.[23] A principal focus of attention has been on whether the fiduciary standard should be set at a high, prophylactic level which disregards whether the fiduciary was honest, whether the principal was capable of exploiting the opportunity and whether the fiduciary made a gain.[24]

[18] In *Meinhard* v. *Salmon*, 249 NY 456 at 464 (1928), Cardozo J justified equity's 'uncompromising rigidity' by observing that 'only thus has the level of conduct for fiduciaries being kept at a level higher than that trodden by the crowd.' According to Lord Herschell, '[h]uman nature being what it is, there is danger . . . of the person holding a fiduciary position being swayed by interest rather than by duty,' and accordingly it has been 'deemed expedient to lay down this positive rule' (*Bray* v. *Ford* [1896] AC 44, 51–2—the 'positive rule' being, in the end, another moral exhortation).

[19] I have extrapolated from Sealy's account here. He may not fully agree.

[20] DeMott, n. 2 above, 476.

[21] See the cases cited at n. 12.

[22] D. J. Hayton, *Underhill & Hayton: Law Relating to Trusts and Trustees* (14th edn., London, Butterworths, 1987), esp. 498, 740.

[23] The notion that the company director's duty of care is an equitable duty exclusive of common law negligence was supported by H. A. J. Ford and R. P. Austin, *Ford's Principles of Corporations Law*, up to the 6th edn. (1991) but two of the three judges in the CA of NSW in *Daniels* v. *AWA Limited* (1995) 13 ACLC 614 held that a company director has a common law duty of care which is coextensive with his equitable duty.

[24] Professor Jones' essay, 'Unjust Enrichment and the Fiduciary's Duty of Loyalty' (1968) 84 *LQR* 472 is still the seminal contribution. The burgeoning scholarship of unjust enrichment has added substantially to the literature: see, in particular, P. B. H. Birks, *An Introduction to the Law of Restitution* (Clarendon Press, Oxford, 1985), esp. at 338. For a different

Greater problems have arisen, and more uncertainty has been generated by the case law, outside the traditionally recognized fiduciary categories. In particular, difficulties have arisen in those fiduciary relationships which are characteristically accompanied by a contractual relationship as well as the potential for tort liability for negligence. For example, a solicitor stands in a recognized fiduciary relationship with his or her client, and there is also a contract of retainer, though the express content of the contract is frequently minimal. Moreover, the solicitor owes a duty of care to the client and sometimes others,[25] breach of which will sound in damages in tort. Much the same pattern of liabilities applies to other advisers if their relationship to their clients is fiduciary. In all these cases, the overlapping duties and remedies have led to great confusion.

THE CONTENT OF FIDUCIARY DUTIES

When the traditional fiduciary duties came to be subjected to analysis, two distinct rules were distilled from the fiduciary incantations of the earlier judges.[26] It is now generally accepted that:[27]

> a fiduciary
> (a) cannot misuse his position, or knowledge or opportunity resulting from it, to his own or to a third party's possible advantage; or
> (b) cannot in any manner falling within the scope of his service, have a personal interest or an inconsistent engagement with a third party—
>
> unless this is freely and informedly consented to by the beneficiary or is authorized by law.

The former is conveniently called 'the profit rule', and the latter is 'the conflict rule'. While originally formulated in academic commentary, the conflict and profit rules have been expressly adopted in the High Court of Australia, first by Deane J[28] and recently by the Full Court.[29]

Finn J has made a prodigious contribution to the academic formula-

view, see R. P. Austin, 'Fiduciary Accountability for Business Opportunities' in P. D. Finn (ed.), *Equity and Commercial Relationships* (Law Book Company, Sydney, 1987), at 177 ff.

[25] *White* v. *Jones* [1995] 2 WLR 187 (HL).

[26] The process of analysis was initiated by Professor Sealy in three articles, 'Fiduciary Relationships' [1962] *CLJ* 69; 'Some Principles of Fiduciary Obligation' [1963] *CLJ* 119; 'The Director as Trustee' [1967] *CLJ* 83. Meagher, Gummow and Lehane's treatise, *Equity Doctrines and Remedies*, now in its 3rd edn. (Butterworths, Sydney, 1992) built on that analysis, as did P. D. Finn's book, *Fiduciary Obligations*, n. 17 above.

[27] P. D. Finn, n. 1 above, 9; see also P. D. Finn, n. 2 above, 27.

[28] In *Chan* v. *Zacharia* (1984) 154 CLR 178.

[29] *Warman International Ltd* v. *Dwyer*, n. 10 above, at 368.

tion of the duties, and has taken the analysis one stage further. His thesis, in effect, is that the conflict and profit rules are the complete content of the fiduciary's duties, and that other rules claimed to be fiduciary are on proper analysis non-fiduciary.[30]

The importance of the thesis is obvious. Once the fiduciary duties are confined to these two, we can be more comfortable with the idea that the appropriate remedies for breach of fiduciary duty are an account of profits or the imposition of a constructive trust (or equitable compensation, the plaintiff's election). Conversely, if we allow the fiduciary concept to meander into other areas, such as the law of negligence, the rigour of the remedies is bound to be reduced. Moreover, clarity about the consequences of discovering a fiduciary relationship should assist us to refine the criteria by reference to which a fiduciary relationship is discovered. Underlying those criteria will be the question, is this an appropriate case for imposing the conflict and profit rules and the rigorous remedies which flow from their contravention?

Converting the judges' high-sounding phrases in the old cases into these two rules has been a significant achievement. Finn J's thesis that the two rules are an exhaustive account of fiduciary duties has not yet been accepted by the courts, although case law may provide a foundation for taking that step. One wonders whether judges who speak about the fiduciary's strict duty of loyalty will accept that the conflict and profit rules capture the full breadth of their concept. There are seven problem areas which will need to be resolved before the move from fiduciary relationship to fiduciary duties can be seen as complete. Their resolution could add several new chapters to the common law of obligations.

The 'Positive' Duty of Loyalty

First, the conflict and profit rules take no account of the positive side of fiduciary duties, usually expressed as the duty to act in good faith for the benefit of the principal.[31]

Some commentators, including Finn J,[32] argue plausibly that this so-called 'positive' fiduciary duty is really a duty of *good faith* and is not strictly a fiduciary duty at all. Such a view would revolutionize the formulation of trustees' and company directors' duties and may in time lead to a more flexible evolution of the content of those duties.

Broad development of a notion of good faith in common law and

[30] P. D. Finn, n. 2 above.

[31] See, e.g., L. C. B. Gower, *Gower's Modern Company Law* (5th edn., Stevens, London, 1992), 312; H. A. J. Ford and R. P. Austin, *Ford and Austin's Principles of Corporations Law* (7th edn., Butterworths, Sydney, 1995), Ch. 8.

[32] N. 2 above, 10 ff.

equity could clarify and rationalize some very fuzzy areas, including the rules of formation of contract and implied warranties as well as the fiduciary concept. In company law, it would make sense to say, for example, that the duty of company directors to act in good faith for the benefit of the company as a whole is not strictly a duty of absolute loyalty, but tells us to whom the company director must have regard when exercising powers and discretions while absolutely avoiding unauthorized conflicts and profits. To a degree, the perennial agonizing of company lawyers over such questions as whether directors owe duties to creditors and employees can be alleviated if we are sure that the answer will not entail absolute loyalty but merely an obligation to have regard to the interests of the selected class.

The trouble with the notion of good faith is that it is recognized in British Commonwealth law only in limited circumstances. Attempts to re-interpret established doctrines as illustrations of the notion of good faith are no more compelling than other exercises in legal revisionism. For example, Finn treats the duty of directors to make full and fair disclosure to shareholders of the nature of resolutions to be put at a meeting of shareholders as an example of 'good faith and . . . reasonable standards of fair dealing'.[33] But, historically at least, it is better regarded as a detailed explication of the requirements of the typical article of association under which the convener of a meeting must give notice of 'the general nature' of the business of the meeting,[34] and hence enforceable as part of the 'statutory contract' to which companies legislation elevates the articles of association. That there are also fiduciary duties in the strict sense, and duties of care, owed to the company by directors who recommend a course of action to shareholders, merely illustrates that the same facts can generate different obligations owed to different people.[35]

Thoughts such as these have led observers to describe the notion of good faith as 'a fifth column waiting for its moment',[36] or, perhaps more gloomily, 'an answer waiting for a question'.[37] However, there are many judicial pronouncements to the effect that people such as trustees, company directors, and others owe a positive duty to act in good faith for the benefit of another. Were it not for the fact that the duty is commonly described as 'fiduciary', no imagination would be needed to regard these statements as a recognition that certain relationships (including most or all fiduciary relationships) imply or are associated with a separate duty

[33] P. D. Finn, n. 2 above, 16 ff.

[34] See esp. *Bulfin* v. *Bebarfald's Ltd* (1938) 38 SR (NSW) 423.

[35] Generally, see P. L. Davies, 'Directors' Fiduciary Duties and Individual Shareholders', in E. McKendrick (ed.), n. 1 above, 83.

[36] F. M. B. Reynolds, 'Drawing the Strings Together', in P. B. H. Birks (ed.) *The Frontiers of Liability* (Oxford University Press, Oxford, 1994), ii, 157.

[37] An oral remark by Gleeson CJ (NSW) cited by Reynolds, *ibid.*

of good faith. Judges have recognized from time to time that there is a difference between one party putting faith in and trusting another, and the latter becoming a fiduciary to the former.[38] Arguably all that is missing is express confirmation of the existence of an intermediate legal category between contract and fiduciary relationship.

For the time being, we must regard the status of the 'positive duty of loyalty' as uncertain and problematic in concept as well as in application. But the reconstruction of the 'fiduciary' cases as more accurately involving a relationship of good faith the breach of which attracts remedies focussing on rescission and restitution rather than accounting and constructive trust, may not be far away.

'Fiduciary' Discretions

Secondly, the conflict and profit rules do not cater for the principles which limit the exercise of a fiduciary's discretions, by requiring that discretions must not be fettered and must be exercised for proper purposes.[39] These principles are commonly regarded as fiduciary.

However, there is once again a plausible argument for the view that the principles about discretions are not fiduciary by nature. They can be seen as a manifestation of the equitable doctrine of fraud on a power, which may apply to powers vested in fiduciaries but may also apply to powers vested in non-fiduciaries,[40] and hence of distinguishable derivation and content.

The 'Business Opportunity' Doctrine

The conflict and profit rules do not specifically cater for more specialized applications of fiduciary principle which may apply in certain circumstances. For example, there are grounds for saying that a full-time commercial fiduciary is subject to a special duty not to divert a business opportunity from the principal if it falls within the principal's present or a contemplated line of business.[41]

I contend that the emerging law about business opportunities is best treated as a sub-rule of the conflict and profit rules not warranting separate status. In their application to the diversion of business opportunities by a commercial fiduciary, the conflict and profit rules are supplemented by a special principle which assists in more precisely identifying the circumstances in which the fiduciary must account and

[38] For a recent example see *Re Goldcorp Exchange Ltd* [1995] 1 AC 74, 98 (PC).

[39] See, e.g., P. D. Finn, n. 17 above, Pt. I, esp. Chs. 7 and 10 and App. A; H. A. J. Ford and R. P. Austin, n. 31 above, Ch. 8.

[40] *Mills* v. *Mills* (1938) 60 CLR 150, 164, *per* Dixon J.

[41] R. P. Austin, n. 24 above.

the measure of accountability. The reasoning in the 'business opportunity' cases, especially in the British Commonwealth, supports this analysis, because the judges typically draw on the conflict and profit rules in reaching their conclusions about accountability.[42]

Conflict between Duties

Fourthly, it might be argued that the formulation of the conflict rule does not fully take account of the differences between a conflict between duty and self-interest and a conflict between duties. This is a problem evidently encountered by the English Law Commission, which found it necessary to elevate the 'conflict of duties' proposition to the status of a separate rule, which it has called 'the undivided loyalty rule'.[43] Not only must the fiduciary be loyal by giving priority to the principal's interest over his own, but his loyalty must be undivided by loyalty to someone else.

Given the Law Commission's focus on the interaction of fiduciary duties with statutory and self-regulatory rules in the financial services industry, their attention to this matter is not surprising. Financial advisers in both the wholesale and retail sectors typically act for many clients. A duty to avoid conflict between their responsibility to one client and to another can become a matter of daily concern, in circumstances where a conflict between duty and interest cannot plausibly be alleged.

As a practical matter, however, it seems unlikely that a fiduciary who stands in a commercial contractual relationship with his client, such as a financial adviser, can be said to owe the client a duty of loyalty which is 'undivided'. The Privy Council's decision in *Kelly* v. *Cooper*[44] has given considerable comfort to financial advisers on this question. Their Lordships found that where an agent's business was to act for numerous principals who might have competing interests, there was an implied term in the contract of engagement qualifying the agent's fiduciary duty. Consequently the agent was entitled to act for other clients and to keep confidential any information obtained from other clients in confidential circumstances.

That being so, one must question whether there is any point in elevating 'undivided loyalty' to the status of a separate fiduciary rule. Finn J's formulation of the conflict rule, set out above, refers to 'an inconsistent engagement with a third party'. The engagement is 'inconsistent' if the

[42] The best examples are in the speeches in *Regal (Hastings) Ltd* v. *Gulliver* [1967] 2 AC 134n and *Phipps* v. *Boardman* [1967] 2 AC 46.

[43] *Fiduciary Duties and Regulatory Rules,* Consultation Paper No 124 (1992), 32.

[44] N. 9 above.

contractual relationship between the parties does not authorize it to be undertaken. The conflict rule as formulated seems adequate to cover the conflict between duties with which the Law Commission was concerned, as well as conflict between interest and duty.

Duty of Disclosure

Fifthly, it is not uncommon for fiduciary circumstances to be analysed as giving rise to a duty on the fiduciary's part to disclose information to the principal. It may be said that by defining the fiduciary standard solely by reference to the conflict and profit rules we overlook the important duty of disclosure.

Finn J has plausibly contended[45] that an adviser's duty to disclose material facts to a client, if it exists, is a duty which 'inheres in the advisory function itself' and is not a fiduciary duty unless the advisory position is used to advance the adviser's own or a third party's interest. It is interesting to compare Finn's views with the Law Commission's analysis.[46] As a result of their survey of industry participants, the Law Commission identified some examples of conflicts within conglomerate financial services firms. Some of those conflicts obviously relate to self-interest. They arise as a consequence of the abolition by the London Stock Exchange in October 1986 of its single capacity requirement which segregated broker (agency) and dealer (principal) functions, thus permitting brokers to trade on their own account in the market in which they also trade in an agency capacity for clients. But some of the typical conflicts problems related to conflict between duty and duty rather than duty and self-interest.

In the Law Commission's view, a practical consequence of the adviser's obligation to avoid a conflict of duties to clients is that the fiduciary must make available to each client all the information which comes to the adviser and is relevant to the client's affairs.[47] The adviser must therefore face up to some ticklish problems in distributing valuable information to those clients entitled to expect it without spreading the information so widely that it loses its value.

While different in focus, the Law Commission's analysis is consistent with Finn's view that the fiduciary principle does not directly impose on the adviser a duty to disclose information to the client. The Law Commission merely supplements legal analysis with a practical observation, namely that fiduciary advisers may have no practical alternative but to disclose information even-handedly to their clients in order to comply with the conflict rule.

[45] N. 2 above, 25 ff. [46] N. 43 above. [47] N. 43 above, 32.

'Strict Compliance' and Care

There are two other matters commonly claimed to be attributes of the fiduciary relationship. One is the duty of 'strict compliance' according to which trustees and company directors are absolutely liable for breach of duty if they fail to comply strictly with the terms of the charter of their relationship (the trust instrument or the memorandum and articles of association), or otherwise act illegally or *ultra vires*. In these circumstances, their 'fiduciary' obligation is to restore the trust fund or company property or its money equivalent, even if they have acted honestly and with due care. The other is the duty of care of fiduciaries, first developed in equity's exclusive jurisdiction and sometimes referred to a 'fiduciary care'. Recent case law has affected both of these areas, and they therefore warrant separate treatment.

TRUSTEES AND COMPANY DIRECTORS: THE DUTY OF STRICT COMPLIANCE

According to the traditional law of trusts, trustees and personal representatives must comply strictly with the terms of any relevant charter (trust instrument or will). A corollary is that a trustee or executor who distributes the estate to the wrong person or to the right persons in the wrong proportions is *ipso facto* in breach of duty even if acting honestly and with due care, and must restore to the estate the funds which have been misapplied. The *Diplock* litigation stands testimony to equity's rigour,[48] though a provision based on section 61 of the Trustee Act 1925 (UK) authorizes the court to relieve from liability a trustee who has acted honestly and reasonably and ought fairly to be excused for the breach and for omitting to obtain the directions of the court.

It is sometimes forgotten, even by textwriters, that company directors are subject to a similar duty. Their position is well explained by Professor Pennington:[49]

> directors must not do any act or enter into any transaction which is illegal or *ultra vires* the company, nor, without the sanction of the members in general meeting, any act or transaction which is beyond the powers conferred on directors by the articles. If they do any such act or enter into such transaction and the company suffers loss in consequence, the company can recover the amount of its loss from them, and it is not necessary for it to show that they acted negligently.

[48] *Chichester Diocesan Fund* v. *Simpson* [1944] AC 341 (HL); *Re Diplock* [1948] 1 Ch. 465 (CA).

[49] *Pennington's Company Law* (6th edn., Stevens, London, 1990), 583–4. See also R. R. Pennington, *Directors' Personal Liability* (1987), 37–9; P. L. Davies, n. 35 above, 96.

This principle has been applied not only where directors have committed the company to *ultra vires* activity or have acted contrary to the articles, but also where their conduct on the company's behalf is illegal (for example, under the 'financial assistance' provisions of company law[50] or possibly where they cause an unlawful dividend to be paid[51]).

Liability arises because the courts treat company directors as indistinguishable from trustees in this respect, namely that the property in their hands or under their control must be applied for the specified purposes of the company or the settlement. In both cases, the duty of strict compliance is said to arise out of their fiduciary position.[52] Once again, as with trustee legislation, companies legislation typically allows the court to relieve the company director who has acted honestly and ought fairly to be excused.[53]

Proposals are made from time to time to remove this head of liability on the ground that, even with the potential for judicial dispensation, the standard is too onerous.[54] Arguably, however, the House of Lords has taken steps towards confining the doctrine to a sub-group of trusts, and possibly even dismantling it, without needing any particular statutory authorization. If that development is consolidated, it will at least be clear that if anything remains of the duty of strict compliance, it is not an integral component of fiduciary relationships, which arise over a much wider spectrum.

In *Target Holdings Ltd* v. *Redferns*[55] Target, which was a finance company, received loan applications for £1,706,000 from Crowngate to assist it to purchase property for £2 million. They were supported by a valuation. In fact the arrangement between Crowngate and the owner of the property, Mirage, was that Mirage would receive £775,000, under a scheme in which Mirage would sell the property to a Jersey company for that figure, the Jersey company would sell to an English company associated with Crowngate for £1,250,000 and that company would then sell to Crowngate for £2 million.

Redferns, solicitors, acted for Crowngate and Target. They incorpo-

[50] e.g. *Selangor United Rubber Estates Ltd* v. *Cradock* (No 3) [1968] 2 All ER 1073, 1048–9 (Ungoed-Thomas J).

[51] *Re Exchange Banking Co., Flitcroft's Case* (1882) 21 Ch. D 519; *Re Sharpe* [1892] 1 Ch. 154; *Blackburn* v. *Industrial Equity Ltd* [1979] CLC 40–588. It is not clear whether the duty of strict compliance continues to apply to unlawful dividends: R.R. Pennington, n. 49 above, 37–9.

[52] *Selangor United Rubber Estates Ltd* v. *Cradock (No 3)* n. 50 above, 1092 (Ungoed-Thomas J).

[53] In Australia the reference to acting 'reasonably' has been removed: Corporations Law, s. 1318(1).

[54] See, e.g., Second Corporate Law Simplification Bill, Exposure Draft (A. G.'s Dept., Canberra, June 1995) ii, 10.

[55] [1995] 3 WLR 352.

rated the Jersey company and documented the transactions. They did not inform Target of the scheme.

Target accepted the loan application and paid £1,525,000 to Redferns with authority to pay that money on the direction of Crowngate once the property had been conveyed to Crowngate and it had executed charges in Target's favour. However, without seeking Target's consent, Redferns paid £1,250,000 to the Jersey company, representing the purchase money payable by the English company. They wrote to Crowngate saying, untruthfully, that the purchases and mortgages had been completed. Subsequently contracts of sale, transfers, and charges were executed, so that ultimately Crowngate acquired the property for £2 million and charged it in favour of Target.

It was taken to be clear that the money paid by Target to Redferns was held in trust, and that Redferns breached the trust by paying out the money before Target's security was in place. But within two weeks of their doing so, Target obtained exactly the security which it intended to obtain.

Crowngate became insolvent and was wound up two years later, and Target sold the property as mortgagee for £500,000. Target took proceedings against Redferns and others, alleging against Redferns that they had breached their duty of care as Target's solicitors in failing to alert Target to the suspicious circumstances of the transactions, and also that Redferns were in breach of trust in parting with the mortgage moneys without authority.

The issue before the House of Lords was confined to the allegation of breach of trust. It arose in an appeal from the Court of Appeal's decision to give summary judgment to Target for the amount of its loan less the net proceeds of realization.

One obvious issue for the House of Lords was whether recovery of such a loss depends on a finding that the breach of trust caused the loss. In the Court of Appeal Peter Gibson LJ (with whom Hirst LJ agreed) held, that in cases where the trustee has paid away trust moneys to a stranger, there is an immediate loss to the trust fund when the payment is made; the causal connection between breach and loss is obvious; and consequently the trustee comes under an immediate duty to restore the moneys to the trust fund.[56] But one has a different perspective on causation if one looks at the matter two weeks after the payment. By that time the security has been obtained and the beneficiary has achieved what it purported to achieve by the creation and performance of the trust. It is thus more difficult to say that the premature payment out of the fund

[56] See [1994] 1 WLR 1089.

caused the loss which subsequently occurred when the borrower became insolvent for reasons unconnected with the breach of trust.

In Lord Browne-Wilkinson's view, the question in those circumstances is whether the transaction would have proceeded but for the premature payment in breach of trust.[57] Since that is a triable issue, an appeal on an application for summary judgment must proceed on the basis that the transaction would have taken place even if no breach of trust had occurred. Consequently, the causal link between breach and loss could not be established in the present proceedings for summary relief.

While his Lordship's approach to the test of causation departs from some earlier views,[58] it is an orthodox interpretation of the authorities.[59] What makes the *Target Holdings* case both interesting and difficult is that Lord Browne-Wilkinson (with whom the other members of the House agreed) responded to counsel's argument by going beyond the question of causation in ways which could undermine traditional thinking about trusts. His most challenging proposition is this:[60]

> in my judgment it is important, if the trust is not to be rendered commercially useless, to distinguish between the basic principles of trust law and those specialist rules developed in relation to traditional trusts which are applicable only to such trusts and the rationale of which has no application to trusts of quite a different kind.

It followed, in his Lordship's reasoning, that if a bare trust is established as an incident of a wider commercial agency transaction, and the commercial transaction is completed, the trustee no longer has any obligation to make restitution by reconstituting the trust fund, even though he breached the trust by paying money out of the fund during the course of the transaction. If trusts for successive interests have come to an end, or

[57] N. 55 above, 358.

[58] *Brickenden* v. *London Loan and Savings Co.* [1934] 3 DR 465 (PC). Street J said in *Re Dawson dec'd.*, n. 11 above, that 'considerations of causation . . . do not readily enter into the matter'. However Street J may have been referring only to the common law rules of causation. Lord Browne-Wilkinson agreed that the common law rules of remoteness and causation do not apply, at any rate to a 'traditional trust': [1995] 3 WLR at 360. *Gemstone Corp. of Aust. Ltd* v. *Grasso*, n. 12 above, is a good illustration of facts to which a 'but for' analysis of causation should not be applied. There a company director breached his fiduciary duty by nominating an asset-less family company as the allottee of partly-paid shares in the company. It was argued that the directors would still have issued the shares to the family company even if the defendant had disclosed its financial position, and consequently the defendant's conduct had not caused a loss to the company. The South Australian Full Ct. held that if a director has placed himself in a position of conflict between interest and duty, it is neither here nor there to speculate whether, if he had performed his duty, he and the company would have been left in the same position.

[59] D. J. Hayton, n. 22 above, 498, 740.

[60] N. 55 above, at 362.

the trust was never for successive interests in the first place, the trustee's duty is governed by the commercial terms of the transaction. It would be entirely artificial to oblige the trustee to restore the fund once the transaction has been completed in order to enable the beneficiary to recover from the trustee more than he has lost. In such a case, 'the basic equitable principle applicable to breach of trust is that the beneficiary is entitled to be compensated for any loss he would not have suffered but for the breach'.[61] It appears that after completion of the transaction, the beneficiary's proprietary rights have evaporated and he has no more than a claim *in personam* against the defaulting trustee for compensation. The measure of compensation is not necessarily the same as at common law[62] but it is evidently not a restitutionary measure.

It is too early to assess the status and significance of Lord Browne-Wilkinson's observations. Much will depend on the meaning attributed in later cases to his concept of 'completion' of the commercial transaction in a case where the whole or part of the trust fund has been paid away before that event occurs. But one can see in his observations more than a hint of reductionism—in certain events commercial trusts will not generate for their beneficiaries the full panoply of equitable proprietary and personal rights designed to make restitution.

If the duty to restore the trust fund on breach of trust is confined to 'traditional trusts', it follows that the duty of strict compliance is similarly limited. Lord Browne-Wilkinson thought that payment out of a trust fund due to an honest and non-negligent error would not lead to liability, though perhaps this was because such a breach would not be regarded as causing the beneficiaries' loss.[63] His Lordship's observation that 'under both systems [equity and common law] liability is fault-based'[64] may leave little scope for the continuation of a duty of strict compliance even in traditional trusts. Certainly his Lordship's reasoning makes it very difficult to assert that if a fiduciary relationship arises out of some constitutive document, there is inherently a fiduciary duty to comply strictly with that document.

A FIDUCIARY DUTY OF CARE?

Earlier in this paper I outlined the commonly understood structure of fiduciary law forty years ago. One of the features of that structure was that the fiduciary characteristic was a central component of the entire relationship, and consequently influenced the content of all of the duties inhering in the relationship. This analysis might suggest that the duty of

[61] *Ibid.* 362. [62] *Ibid.* 364–5. [63] *Ibid.* 358–9. [64] *Ibid.* 359.

care owed by the fiduciary to the principal is a special duty of care having 'fiduciary' characteristics. The significance of the duty of care being 'fiduciary' might arguably be that the standard of 'prudence' in managing the investments and affairs of others must be set at a higher level than in a non-fiduciary case.[65]

In fact, however, the standard of care for various categories of fiduciaries seems to have developed without regard to their fiduciary status. While trustees came to be treated as being subject to a special standard of prudence with respect to trust investments, this cannot have been derived from their fiduciary status as such, because another fiduciary, the company director, was decidedly not subject to that conservative standard. Except as regards trustee investments, the standard of care for fiduciaries such as trustees and company directors was set at a low level, hardly 'fiduciary' in character. In recent cases the standard of care of fiduciaries is increasingly being treated as merely an application of the common law of negligence with no special equitable measure of damages, in the absence of breach of the conflict or profit rules.

Trustee

Since the law of trusts has always been the paradigm for all fiduciary relationships, it is appropriate first to investigate whether there is any direct connection between the trustee's fiduciary office and his duty of care.

Almost all of the main characteristics of the trustee's duty of care were established by the end of the nineteenth century. Thus:

(a) the trustee's duty is to conduct the business of the trust with the same care as an ordinary prudent man of business would apply to his own affairs;[66]

(b) but 'the duty is not to take such care only as a prudent man would take if he had only himself to consider; the duty is rather to take such care as an ordinary prudent man would take if he were minded to make an investment for the benefit of other people for whom he felt morally bound to provide';[67]

[65] *Daniels* v. *AWA Limited*, n. 14 above, 658, *per* Clarke and Sheller JJA. In the United States, the duty of loyalty and the duty of prudence have recently been described as the 'two great principles' of the law of fiduciary administration: J. H. Langbein, 'The Contractarian Basis of the Law of Trust' (1995) 105 *Yale LJ* 625, 655. Granted the significance of the duty of prudence, one wonders what is added by describing it as 'fiduciary'. Langbein notes (at 656, n. 159) that the official comment to the Uniform Prudent Investor Act describes the standard as resembling the 'reasonable person' rule of tort law.

[66] *Re Speight* (1883) 22 Ch. D 727, 739, *per* Jessel MR, 762, *per* Bowen LJ; applied *sub nom. Speight* v. *Gaunt* (1883) 9 App. Cas. 1, esp. 19, *per* Lord Blackburn.

[67] *Re Whitley* (1886) 33 Ch. D 347, 355, *per* Lindley LJ. See also *King* v. *Talbot*, 40 NY 76 (1869).

(c) the trustee is not bound to avoid all risks and act as an insurer of the trust fund;[68]
(d) a trustee is not liable for mere errors of judgment provided he acts with reasonable care, prudence, and circumspection.[69]

These principles appear to have been developed by Chancery judges *sui generis,* seeking to balance the need to protect the trust fund against their evident desire not to discourage honest individuals from undertaking the responsibilities of trusteeship by setting the standard too high.[70] The common law did not generally recognize equitable interests[71] and in any case, the law of negligence at that time did not offer any close analogies. Nor did equity, since the trust was by far the most developed of the fiduciary relationships.

While the trustee's duty of care was developed as an equitable duty, the courts did not find it necessary, in setting the standard of care, to refer to the fiduciary nature of the trustee's position. The fiduciary nature of the trustee's office may have been indirectly significant, but probably only to a limited extent. Thus, a relevant consideration in the minds of those judges who set the standard of care may well have been the fact that equity imposed a high standard of loyalty and in the absence of other arrangements, required trustees to act gratuitously. The absence of remuneration may have pointed towards a relatively low standard, with the implication eventually being drawn that a higher standard is expected of professional trustees, particularly with respect to the management of investments.[72] In addition, since the restitutionary nature of equitable compensation for breach of trust was made clear as early as 1801,[73] the nature and measure of equitable relief may also have influenced judicial thinking about the content of the duty of care. But these considerations do not seem to have produced a special or distinctive standard of care, and certainly not (for the non-professional trustee) a distinctively onerous standard, even in relation to trustee investments.

Company Director

The development of the strikingly lenient standard of care for company directors bears some obvious analogies with trust law. This is not the

[68] *Re Godfrey* (1883) 23 Ch. D 483, 493, *per* Bacon V-C.

[69] *Re Chapman* [1896] 2 Ch. 763, 778, *per* Lopes LJ.

[70] e.g., in *Ex parte Belchier* (1754) Amb. 218, Lord Hardwicke said 'if Mrs Parsons is chargeable in this case, no man in his senses would act as assignee under commission of a bankrupt. The Court has laid down a rule with regard to the transactions of assignees, and more so of trustees, so as not strike a terror into mankind acting for the benefit of others, and not for their own.'

[71] Meagher, Gummow and Lehane, n. 26 above, 22ff.

[72] *Bartlett* v. *Barclays Trust Co. Ltd (No 1)* [1980] Ch. 515.

[73] *Caffrey* v. *Darby* (1801) 6 Ves. 488; see also *Ex parte Adamson* (1878) 8 Ch. D 807.

right occasion for a full exposition.[74] The company director's duty was developed principally in Chancery, though after the judicature reform and the introduction of the statutory misfeasance procedure, a misfeasance summons alleging negligence was sometimes heard in the King's Bench Division.[75] It is possible that the fiduciary position of directors, which constrains them from receiving remuneration without specific authority (an authority invariably given, in fact) may have been a factor in the development of the low standard. It is possible that the company director's duty of strict compliance was also influential. Certainly the more entrepreneurial nature of the company director's office was a relevant point of distinction between directors and trustees, the latter being subject to a requirement of caution from which the former were exempt.[76] However, generalizations are difficult because proceedings against directors for breach of their duty of care were rare, perhaps because of the procedural limitations imposed by the rule in *Foss* v. *Harbottle* though perhaps also because of problems of proof.

After the introduction of the judicature system, it was not uncommon for courts to refer to the liability of a director for 'negligence', and to the 'legal duties' which the director owed to his company.[77] In the *Lagunas Nitrate* case, Lindley MR made the surprising remark that he was not aware 'that there is any difference between their legal and their equitable duties'.[78] An Australian text on company law maintained, nevertheless, that 'there is no judicial acceptance yet that the common law tortious duty of care involved in the tort of negligence applies to non-executive directors. However, a breach of the duty of care and diligence arising from a director's fiduciary role is often referred to as "negligence" '.[79] The ambiguity of the status of the director's duty of care, and the relevance of

[74] The best overall account is probably still by M. J. Trebilcock, 'The Liability of Company Directors for Negligence' (1969) 32 *MLR* 499.

[75] Generally, see *Joint Stock Discount Co.* v. *Brown* (1869) LR 8 Eq. 381 (James V-C); *Great Eastern Railway Company* v. *Turner* (1872) LR 8 Ch. App. 149 (HL); *Re Forest of Dean Coal Mining Co.* (1878) LR 10 Ch. D 450 (CA); *Re Denham* (1883) 25 Ch. D 752 (CA).

[76] The cases were recently analysed by Finn J in *Australian Securities Commission* v. *AS Nominees Ltd* (1995) 13 ACLC 1822, on the way to reaching the controversial conclusion that the directors of a professional trustee company are subject to the same higher duties as the company which they direct.

[77] *Lagunas Nitrate Co.* v. *Lagunas Syndicate* [1899] 2 Ch. 392, 435, *per* Lindley MR; *Re National Bank of Wales* [1899] 2 Ch. 629, 672, *per* Lindley MR, Sir F. H. Jeune, and Romer LJ; *Re Brazilian Rubber Planations and Estates Limited* [1911] 1 Ch. 425, 430–1, 436–7; *Ammonia Soda Co. Ltd* v. *Chamberlain* [1918] 1 Ch. 266; *Re City Equitable Fire Insurance Co. Ltd* [1925] Ch. 407.

[78] [1899] 2 Ch. 392, 435. In *Castlereagh Motels Ltd* v. *Davies Roe* (1966) 67 SR (NSW) 279 at 285, Jacobs and Asprey JJA said that Lindley MR's dictum was not related to any submission that there was a cause of action at law for breach by a director of his duties as they had been established by the authorities.

[79] H. A. J. Ford and R. P. Austin, n. 23 above, para. 1537, citing *Kimberley Mineral Holdings Ltd* v. *Triguboff* [1978] 3 ACLR 624; *Re Claridge House Ltd* (1981) 28 SASR 481.

common law principles, have remained in the United Kingdom and Australia until recent times. Recently, however, two Australian cases have held that, though there may still be an equitable duty of care for fiduciaries, strictly separate from the fiduciary duty itself, there is also a duty of care at common law, arising either in tort or contract.[80] In view of the remaining differences between equitable compensation and common law damages, this view obviously requires the development of new law to determine how the choice between the two forms of relief is to be made.[81]

Other Cases

Outside trust and company relationships, the leading case of *Nocton* v. *Ashburton*[82] embodied an element of confusion. The facts and the findings at first instance are not fully presented in their Lordships' speeches, but it appears that a central allegation at the time of Lord Ashburton's release of his first mortgage security was that Nocton made a misrepresentation that the remaining security would be sufficient. It was alleged that Nocton was aware that the remaining security would be inadequate, since he knew that the valuation upon which Lord Ashburton relied took into account some additional properties. However, it appears from the reported case that Nocton did not read the valuation before making the alleged representation, and that the judge at first instance found that Lord Ashburton's release might have enabled his mortgagors to raise more money for development of the land and consequently enhancement of Lord Ashburton's remaining security.[83] In these circumstances the finding of the judge at first instance that Nocton had failed in his duty and had given bad advice must be ambiguous, and could on the facts be as plausibly based on negligence as on equitable fraud.

Viscount Haldane's speech preserves some of this ambiguity, by addressing the topic of 'liability for negligence in word' and referring seductively to 'a special duty of care in statement'.[84] Nevertheless, his Lordship's central reasoning is fairly plainly based on a breach of fiduciary duty which he distinguishes from negligence, since he places the claim in the exclusive jurisdiction and observes that a demurrer for want of equity would have lain to a bill in Chancery which did no more

[80] *Permanent Building Society (in liq.)* v. *Wheeler*, n. 14 above; *Daniels* v. *AWA Limited*, n. 14 above.

[81] See G. H. Brandis in M. Cope (ed.), *Equity Issues and Trends* (Federation Press, Sydney, 1995), 20, discussing the judgments of the CA of the Sup. Ct. of Queensland in the *Warman International* case, prior to the High Ct.'s judgment, n. 10 above.

[82] [1914] AC 932 (HL).

[83] *Ibid.* 988 and 945.

[84] *Ibid.*, esp. at 948.

than seek to enforce a claim for damages for negligence against a solicitor.[85] Hence, on balance, it is correct to treat Viscount Haldane's speech as directed to a breach of fiduciary duty in the sense conveyed by the conflict and profit rules, rather than a breach of a duty of care, fiduciary or otherwise.[86]

The distinction ultimately to be drawn from Viscount Haldane's speech between the fiduciary duty and the fiduciary's duty of care has been accepted, by and large, in later cases.[87] However, there is still substantial support for the view that a duty of care of fiduciaries exists in equity's exclusive jurisdiction, a conclusion which may have some significance with respect to limitation of actions and measure of damages.[88]

Eventually, however, the progress of the law of negligent misstatement is unlikely to be impeded by an apparently rootless equitable duty. Lord Browne-Wilkinson's remarks in *Henderson* v. *Merrett Syndicates Ltd*[89] are a persuasive attempt to clear up some of the confusion produced by the earlier cases. He said that an alternative claim put forward in that case on the basis of breach of fiduciary duty was misconceived, the essential complaint being based upon negligence. That is consistent with the view discussed above, according to which a claim based in negligence is not a claim for breach of fiduciary duty.

His Lordship added that the liability of a fiduciary for negligence is the paradigm of a general duty to act with care imposed by those who take it upon themselves to act for or advise others, and that the duty of care imposed on bailees, carriers, trustees, directors, agents, and others is the same duty, arising from the circumstances in which they were acting, not from their status or description.[90] It would be wrong to regard these remarks as an attempt to do away with the remedy of equitable compensation in the exclusive jurisdiction. If the complaint in the case had been of breach of a true fiduciary duty, rather than negligence, his Lordship would presumably have accepted the availability of equitable compen-

[85] At 956.

[86] This is the conclusion reached by I. E. Davidson, 'The Equitable Remedy of Compensation' (1982) 13 *Melb. ULR* 349; W. M. C. Gummow, 'Compensation for Breach of Fiduciary Duty' in T. G. Youdan (ed.), n. 2 above, 57; J. D. Davies, 'Equitable Compensation: Causation, Forseeability and Remoteness', in D. Waters (ed.), *Equity, Fiduciaries and Trusts* (Carswell, Toronto, 1993), 297.

[87] *Girardet* v. *Crease & Co.* (1987) 11 BCLR 2d 361 (SCC), *per* Southin J at 362; *Lac Minerals Ltd* v. *International Corona Resources Ltd* (1989) 61 DLR 4th 14 (SCC), at 28, *per* LaForest J; *Commonwealth Bank of Australia* v. *Smith* (1991) 102 ALR 453 (Full FC); *Permanent Building Society (in liq.)* v. *Wheeler* n. 14 above.

[88] See esp. *Bennett* v. *Minister of Community Welfare* (1992) 176 CLR 408, 426, *per* McHugh J.

[89] N. 12 above, at 798ff. See also his Lordship's remarks in *White* v. *Jones* [1995] 2 WLR 187.

[90] N. 12 above, at 799.

sation measured differently from common law damages.[91] His point, rather, was that the common law should apply exclusive of the equitable measure where the claim is merely for damages for negligence.

This approach moves well beyond the recent Australian company law cases, but can be seen as a logical progression from them. The potential confusion created by a choice of measures of damages for negligence (whether the choice be made by a litigant or the judge) should be avoided if possible. All in all, the cases now point powerfully to the view that the duty of care owed by a fiduciary to his principal is not to be regarded as a special 'fiduciary' duty; and that where equitable and common law duties of care have been found to co-exist, it is likely that the equitable duty will eventually be folded into the common law to produce a single standard of care and a single measure of recovery for breach of it. Where, however, the true complaint is of a breach of fiduciary duty (that is, of the conflict or profit rule) rather than a duty of care, the equitable measure of recovery applies exclusively.

CONCLUSIONS

We have not yet securely reached the stage where specified fiduciary obligations have replaced all-embracing fiduciary relationships. The attempt to set the fiduciary standard exclusively by reference to the conflict and profit rules will succeed only if the notion of good faith can take up the positive side of the fiduciary's duty. But already the propounding of a tighter fiduciary concept is clarifying our thinking about the common law duty of care of fiduciaries, and may be contributing to some rethinking on the strict compliance duties of trustees and company directors.

There seems to be an inevitability about the developments to which this essay refers, and it is not implausible to suggest that their combined significance is greater than the sum of the significance of each. If we move comprehensively from fiduciary relationship to fiduciary duties, a momentum will have been generated to reduce fiduciary law into the general law of obligations. We may eventually come to speak about 'fiduciary duties' rather than 'fiduciary relationships' just as we speak of the duties of care, skill, and diligence—indistinguishable milestones along the road to discretionary relief. The eventual outcome may be the

[91] See his remarks in *Target Holdings Ltd* v. *Redferns*, n. 11 above, 360. Compare the criticism of Lord Browne-Wilkinson's remarks in *Henderson* by Heydon, (1995) 111 *LQR* 1.

reshaping of tort, contract, and equity and their separate remedial regimes into integrated laws of civil wrongs and civil remedies.[92]

Some would applaud such a result as real progress and would tolerate additional uncertainty along the way. Others would feel that a structured system of civil wrongs and civil remedies abandons part of the genius of a system of judge-made law (and, especially, of equity) in which new rights are constantly evolving out of the repeated demand for remedies. They would take comfort from cases such as *Warman International*,[93] which imply that fiduciary obligations are distinctive both in their origins and in their demands. They would say that the movement from relationship to obligation need not cause the fiduciary standard to be diluted from a proscriptive, prophylactic rule to a prescriptive but less demanding one.[94]

[92] P. B. H. Birks, *Civil Wrongs: A New World* (Butterworths Lectures, 1991); R. Cooke, 'The Condition of the Law of Tort', in P. B. H. Birks (ed.), *The Frontiers of Civil Liability* (OUP, Oxford, 1994), 59 ff.

[93] N. 10 above.

[94] See L. S. Sealy, n. 15 above, at 51 ff.

8

Where are We Going with Equitable Compensation?

C. E. F. RICKETT*

In the last decade or so, in Australia, Canada, and New Zealand in particular, equitable compensation has truly awoken from the slumbers it had been in since *Nocton* v. *Lord Ashburton*.[1] It is now an important part of the remedial armoury available in the context of breaches of equitable obligations. However, its true nature, its potential reach, and the particularities of its scope are matters of confusion and dispute on which a good number of judges, practitioners, and academics have already put pen to paper.[2] Some of those have also contributed to this book. I hope I will be forgiven for daring to add again to the literature. What I intend to argue is that the full dimensions of the equitable compensation remedy as it is awarded in any particular case must be defined through an articulation of the interplay between the nature of the breach of duty or wrong complained of, which forces us to consider the real substance of the plaintiff's claimed interest, and the content of the compensatory remedy which would most appropriately provide for monetary satisfaction for the loss at issue. In my view, it would be both conceptually wrong and practically unfortunate to define the nature and reach of the remedy in too formal and static a manner, so as to deny it the degree of flexibility it needs if it is adequately to carry out the task of truly compensating

* I wish to acknowledge the debt I owe my colleague Julie Maxton. I have benefited from numerous discussions with her, and much that is in this paper is the product of joint activity. That is not to say that she takes any responsibility for errors, nor that she agrees with all I have written.

1 [1914] AC 932.

2 See I. E. Davidson, 'The Equitable Remedy of Compensation' (1982) 13 *Melb. ULR* 349; The Hon Mr Justice Gummow, 'Compensation for Breach of Fiduciary Duty' in Youdan (ed.), *Equity, Fiduciaries and Trusts* (1989), 57; L. Aitken, 'Developments in Equitable Compensation: Opportunity or Danger?' (1993) 76 *Aust. LJ* 596; J. D. Davies, 'Equitable Compensation: Causation, Remoteness and Foreseeability' in Waters (ed.), *Equity, Fiduciaries and Trusts 1993* (1993), 297; C. Rickett and T. Gardner, 'Compensating for Loss in Equity: The Evolution of a Remedy' (1994) 24 *Vict. U Well. LR* 19; N. Ingram and J. Maxton, *Equitable Remedies: New Zealand Law Society Seminar* (1994), 85; Keith Mason and J. W. Carter, *Restitution Law in Australia* (1995), 607–8 and 670–6; and J. D. McCamus, 'Equitable Compensation and Restitutionary Remedies: Recent Developments' in *Special Lectures of the Law Society of Upper Canada 1995: Law of Remedies* (1995), 295.

plaintiffs who have interests recognised in equity, but whose interests have been violated and who have suffered loss as a result.

GENERAL COMMENTS FROM A NEW ZEALAND PERSPECTIVE

Let me begin, however, with some general comments from my New Zealand background. The New Zealand Court of Appeal has in recent times handed down a number of decisions in the area, *inter alia*, of equity and equitable remedies, which decisions have often been pilloried as unprincipled and therefore heretical, and in no small number these decisions have been overturned by the Privy Council. Although I have not come here overtly to defend the Court of Appeal, I do think that there is rather more principle in its decision-making than the Court is sometimes given credit for. Two aspects of its attitude, in particular, seem to me to be of central relevance to the issue to be canvassed in this paper.

First, there has been a tendency revealed in an increasing number of New Zealand decisions of an intention to move away from a formalistic and historical approach to the identification of causes of action, to a more *substantive interest-based approach*. Nowhere has this been more clearly expressed than in recent comments of the President of the Court, Sir Robin Cooke (as he then was), and Tipping J in *Lockwood Buildings Ltd* v. *Trust Bank Canterbury Ltd*.[3] Both judges in effect stated that the substance of the right claimed by a plaintiff is where the true cause of action is to be found and then accurately articulated, rather than in the historical formulation of the cause of action, which often brings with it unhelpful baggage. What is the plaintiff's complaint? Is it that she has suffered injury to some legitimate interest? If so, the Court will protect the plaintiff's interest by recognizing a cause of action. The consequence of this approach has been to maintain a considerable degree of flexibility and discretion in setting the parameters wherein the Court is prepared to recognize a cause of action or right in the plaintiff. This has caused more trenchant critics to rail against what is seen to be the abuse of power by unelected judges. Other more circumspect critics suggest that the Court is not following precedent. For both groups, it seems that what is at stake is the legitimacy of the interest sought to be recognized and then promoted by the Court. At root the problematic issue in the entire exercise is the socio-economic-political dimension of the recognition by the common law (which here includes equity) of interests requiring protection, or worthy of protection, in a multi-cultural, multi-faceted,

[3] [1995] 1 NZLR 22, at 26 and 34 respectively.

multi-values-based, technologically sophisticated, and increasingly internationalized society. It may well be that terms like 'fairness' and 'reasonable expectations', so often used by Sir Robin Cooke, are as close as one can get to defining a basis on which those interests should be and are recognized. The width given to the cause of action in negligence in New Zealand is perhaps the most notable private law example of the substantive interest-based approach.[4] It seems to me that there are signs in many cases from other Commonwealth jurisdictions,[5] including some of the equitable compensation cases, that a similar approach is being taken there too, even if perhaps not articulated quite so openly. From the point of view of equity, the most dramatic developments—outside England—where plaintiffs' interests have been recognized, and where such recognition has had enormous effect in requiring development of a relevant compensatory remedy to deal with loss caused when those interests have been violated, have occurred in respect of the fiduciary principle. Millett LJ, writing extra-judicially,[6] has recently suggested that a statement by McLachlin J in *Norberg* v. *Wynrib*[7] 'is a significant statement which has great potential for the future', by which I assume he means the future in England. Clearly McLachlin J's statement is significant, but for such an extended fiduciary concept to have more than symbolic value, the equitable compensation remedy which will follow a breach of a fiduciary duty in cases falling within the extended notion, must be, as has been discovered already in Canada (and to a lesser extent in Australia), very flexible indeed.

This substantive interest-based approach leads to, and is also itself in part the result of, a second notable aspect of some New Zealand judicial reasoning. This is what I call the *appropriateness of remedy principle.* This principle borrows heavily from Canadian decisions, where it has been developed largely in the context of remedies in unjust enrichment actions. Once a claim (or cause of action) in unjust enrichment has been recognized on any particular set of facts, it does not follow that the matter of the remedy to be awarded is *pro forma.* That matter is itself a substantive issue, because the court has a responsibility to award the most appropriate remedy, after the application of a variety of criteria of appropriateness to the facts. The Canadian cases often deal with the

4 See now *Invercargill City Council* v. *Hamlin* [1996] 2 W.L.R. 367.

5 e.g., in Australia the High Ct. (Mason CJ, Deane, Dawson, and Toohey JJ) has expressly stated that, in respect of the principle of unjust enrichment, 'regard [should] be paid to matters of substance rather than technical form': see *Dart Industries Inc.* v. *Decor Corp. Pty. Ltd* (1993) 179 CLR 101, at 111. See also *Baltic Shipping Co.* v. *Dillon* (*'The Mikhail Lermontov'*) (1993) 176 CLR 344, at 376 (*per* Deane and Dawson JJ).

6 'Equity—the Road Ahead' [1995] *King's College LJ* 1, at 5.

7 (1992) 92 DLR (4th) 449, at 499: 'Fiduciary principles are capable of protecting not only narrow legal and economic interests, but can also serve to defend fundamental human and personal interests.'

matter whether a proprietary or personal remedy is the more appropriate,[8] but there is no reason why other matters should not be dealt with, as, for example, the issue whether a gain-based or loss-based remedy is the most appropriate, or whether some punitive element is appropriate. Some further explanation of this development is warranted, since it is my contention that equitable compensation, as with any other remedy, equitable or common law, falls to be dealt with under this principle. It should further be said at this point that although 'equitable compensation', when awarded, appears simply as a sum of money payable to a plaintiff, the quantum of that sum is itself subject to appropriateness criteria, some of which are inherent in the equitable nature of that remedy and will thus be relevant in every case, but others of which are introduced into any case because of factors peculiar to that case. It is in respect of these latter criteria that the link with the substantive interest-based approach to identifying a cause of action becomes obvious.

The appropriateness of the remedy principle made its first clear appearance in New Zealand in the context of the Court of Appeal's articulation of the extent and impact of the intermingling of law and equity. In *Aquaculture Corporation* v. *New Zealand Green Mussel Co. Ltd*,[9] a case where a plaintiff was claiming that the improper revelation of confidential information had injured its commercial prospects, Cooke P was not prepared to let the uncertain historical and jurisdictional genesis of the action for breach of confidence prevent the Court from providing a suitable remedy. His Honour said:[10]

> For all purposes now material equity and common law are merged or mingled. The practicality of the matter is that in the circumstances of the dealings between the partners the law imposes a duty of confidence. For its breach a full range of remedies should be available as appropriate, no matter whether they originated in common law, equity or statute.

This is not the place to rehearse the 'fusion fallacy debate', although I do recognize that, as *Aquaculture* itself illustrates, the appropriateness of remedy principle, if it is taken to its logical extreme, must include permitting the awarding of either equitable and common law remedies in any case irrespective of its jurisdictional birthplace. The point was expressed in a radical fashion by Tipping J in a breach of contract case decided in 1991. In *New Zealand Land Development Co. Ltd* v. *Porter*, his Honour stated:[11]

[8] See in New Zealand the decision of the CA in *Investors Protection Co. Ltd* v. *Ray Courtney Architects Ltd* (1993) 7 PRNZ 1, where there was a clear intimation that 'the usual remedy for unjust enrichment is personal in the form of restitution by a money award' (at 3, *per* Gault J, speaking for the Court).

[9] [1990] 3 NZLR 299.

[10] *Ibid.* 301.

[11] [1992] 2 NZLR 462, at 468.

Incidentally there is in my respectful view no longer any value, except for historical purposes, in seeking to distinguish or to keep conceptually separate common law damages and damages in equity whether under Lord Cairns' Act or otherwise. The Court should now award such damages as are a proper and fair reflection of what the plaintiff has lost by reason of the failure of the defendant to perform the contract. It no longer matters whether the damages are called common law or equitable damages. Any residual distinction has now gone and perhaps serves more to confuse than to assist. Let us carry the fusion of law and equity into the area of damages.

For further discussion on the fusion issue, I would simply refer you to a very full analysis of this matter, including its consequence for the appropriateness of remedy principle, by my colleague Professor Julie Maxton.[12] Even if one is not prepared to buy into the fusion or intermingling school of thought, it nonetheless remains true that the appropriateness of remedy principle still has a field of operation when determining the most appropriate equitable remedy to be awarded in any case where an equitable cause of action is recognized. Further, the quantum of equitable compensation to be awarded in these more limited circumstances is likewise susceptible to an appropriateness test.

The most forthright New Zealand exponent of the appropriateness of remedy principle is Hammond J. In *Butler* v. *Countrywide Finance Ltd*,[13] his Honour drew on his own earlier published material on 'Rethinking Remedies: The Changing Conception of the Relationship Between Legal and Equitable Remedies'[14] and 'The Place of Damages in the Scheme of Remedies'.[15] He propounded the following view:[16]

In my view, the law of civil remedies in this country is, as it should be, steadily evolving into a regime in which what is appropriate of a court is a context specific evaluation of which remedy is most appropriate in the circumstances of a given case, rather than doctrinaire or a priori solutions. The problem then becomes one of informed remedial choice. . . . It will be recalled that the starting point of any remedial enquiry is the principle of compensation. The principle of the law of civil remedies is to put the person whose rights have been found to have been violated in the same position—so far as can be done—as if those rights had been observed. This rule finds expression in tort in the proposition that we endeavour to put the plaintiff in the position that person would have been in had the tort not been committed; in contract, the object is to put the plaintiff in the position

[12] 'Intermingling of Common Law and Equity' in Cope (ed.), *Equity: Issues and Trends* (1995), 25. Other interesting contributions to the debate, which also include discussion of the development of the compensation remedy in equity, are those of Martin, 'Fusion, Fallacy and Confusion; a Comparative Study' [1994] *Conv.* 13, and Burns, 'The "Fusion Fallacy" Revisited' (1993) 5 *Bond LR* 152.

[13] [1993] 3 NZLR 623.

[14] In J. Berryman (ed.), *Remedies—Issues and Perspectives* (1991).

[15] In P. Finn (ed.), *Essays on Damages* (1992).

[16] N. 13 above, at 631–2.

that person would have been in had the contract been performed according to its terms. Those general objectives can be achieved in various ways, the most obvious being a choice between some kind of performance-based remedy (for instance, specific performance or a mandatory injunction): or, by compensatory damages.

His Honour went on to list and discuss a range of factors which he said would be relevant in remedial selection.[17] These are: plaintiff autonomy (the plaintiff's choice); the economic efficiency of the relevant remedies; the relative severity of the remedy on the parties (proportionality); the nature of the right being supported by the remedy;[18] the moral view to be attached to the interests at stake; the effect of a given remedy on a third party (or the public); difficulties of calculation; the practicabilities of enforcement; and the conduct of the parties.[19] Hammond J concluded:[20]

All of this leads to a conclusion that what is involved in the allocation of the 'appropriate' remedy in a given case is a matter of informed choice, bearing in mind the general compensation principle and the factors I have listed above. Those considerations do not lead to a wholesale abandonment of much of the traditional learning. They simply point to a more open remedial system; and a requirement for articulation and candour as to why the relevant choices are being made, rather than the formalistic application of (in many cases) somewhat arid doctrinal rules drawn from some far distant time.

Hammond J returned to the matter of the appropriateness of remedy principle in *Brown* v. *Pourau*, in a dictum which perhaps sums up the thrust of the New Zealand approach:[21]

Whether these English authorities are entirely compatible with contemporary New Zealand jurisprudence on remedies is open to question. Essentially, English legal theory and practice on remedies is monistic. That is, right and remedy are perceived to be congruent. But, in the United States, and increasingly in Canada and New Zealand, our courts proceed on a dualistic basis. The court first makes enquiries as to the obligation the court is asked to uphold; it then (and only then) makes a context-specific evaluation of that remedy which will best support or advance that obligation.

[17] *Ibid.*, at 631–3.

[18] This is, together with the next factor, the equivalent of the substantive rights-based approach: *ibid.* 632: 'In part, the function of the law of civil remedies is that it should be rights enhancing, or rights maximising. To put it another way, remedies realise rights. But, of course, not every right has the same strength. Free speech, for instance, is generally heralded in common law jurisdiction as being a nearly absolute right. The stronger the court's perception of the relevant right, the stronger the remedy which may be required. This is, of course, particularly true of constitutional litigation, but it is also true of private law litigation.'

[19] 'This has, of course, always been one of the great cornerstones of equitable relief. In a system in which common law and equitable remedies now inform each other, it is surely now also relevant to a wide range of causes of action': *ibid.* 633.

[20] *Ibid.* 633. [21] [1995] 1 NZLR 352, at 368.

More recently still, in *Dickie* v. *Torbay Pharmacy (1986) Ltd*, Hammond J made the following comments about the constructive trust:[22]

> As to the nature of a constructive trust, there has been a great deal of juristic debate as to whether such is a substantive institution, or a remedial device. And, is such declaratory of something that always existed—and hence is more like an express trust? Or, it is 'constituted', and hence essentially a remedial vehicle? Or, is there more than one kind of constructive trust? My own view is that, functionally, constructive trusts can (and do) serve a variety of purposes and whether such should be decreed must turn less on abstract theory than on the facts of a given case; the nature of the 'wrong' committed; whether proprietary relief is appropriate; and the variety of discretionary considerations which routinely attend an exercise of this kind.

How then do we confront the law of equitable compensation if we are committed to the general approach as just outlined? Indeed, are some of the puzzles of equitable compensation better understood, if not solved, by adopting that general approach? Are we trying to achieve the impossible unless we permit such flexibility?

EQUITABLE COMPENSATION AS COMPENSATORY

Historically, courts of equity did not award damages, but orders for monetary compensation were made in cases where a breach of trust gave rise to a loss to the trust estate. The language used in respect of this remedy included the term 'restitution', as in the concept that the breaching trustee was liable to make restitution of the trust property, or to restore the trust property. This use of the term 'restitution' must be distinguished clearly from the meanings assigned the term by those who theorize about the law of restitutionary recovery. In this latter context, the term means either recovery of an unjustified enrichment gained by the defendant in respect of a receipt of wealth subtracted from the plaintiff, or disgorgement of a gain or profit made by means of a civil wrong committed by the defendant against the plaintiff. Restitutionary recovery in these terms is perfectly possible in breach of trust cases, but that is not the recovery which is the focus of an award of equitable compensation. 'Restitution' in this latter context is used of a remedy which is more closely related to compensatory damages at common law than it is to gain-based or property-based restitution.

This important conceptual point was reiterated, in effect, by Lord Browne-Wilkinson in his recent speech in *Target Holdings Ltd* v. *Redferns*.[23] His Lordship referred to what he saw as two principles funda-

[22] [1995] 3 NZLR 429, at 441.

[23] [1995] 3 WLR 352.

mental to an award of (compensatory) damages at common law, being, first, that the defendant's wrongful act must cause the damage complained of, and, secondly, that the plaintiff was to be placed in the same position as he would have been in if he had not sustained the wrong for which he was now to be compensated. His Lordship continued:[24]

> Although, . . . , in many ways equity approaches liability for making good a breach of trust from a different starting point, in my judgment these two principles are applicable as much in equity as at common law. Under both systems liability is fault-based: the defendant is only liable for the consequences of the legal wrong he has done to the plaintiff and to make good the damage caused by such wrong. He is not responsible for damage not caused by his wrong or to pay by way of compensation more than the loss suffered from such wrong. The detailed rules of equity as to causation and the quantification of loss differ, at least ostensibly, from their application at common law. But the principles underlying both systems are the same.

To return for a moment to the historical development of equitable compensation, in the context of its initial appearance as a remedy against defaulting trustees, it is important to observe that the principles used in calculating the compensation payable were, and are, very generous to the plaintiff. This plaintiff-sided generosity was summed up by Street J (as he then was) in *Re Dawson*,[25] a case concerned with a breach of an express trust causing loss to the trust estate, in a passage which has since been often cited as the *locus classicus* on the law of equitable compensation. The main parts of the passage are cited again here for ease of reference:[26]

> The obligation of a defaulting trustee is essentially one of effecting a restitution to the estate. The obligation is of a personal character and its extent is not to be limited by common law principles governing remoteness of damage. . . . *Caffrey* v. *Darby, supra*, is consistent with the proposition that if a breach has been committed then the trustee is liable to place the trust estate in the same position as it would have been in if no breach had been committed. Considerations of causation, foreseeability and remoteness do not readily enter into the matter. . . . The principles embodied in this approach do not appear to involve any inquiry as to whether the loss was caused by or flowed from the breach. Rather the inquiry in each instance would appear to be whether the loss would have happened if there had been no breach. . . . The cases to which I have referred demonstrate that the obligation to make restitution, which courts of equity have from very early times imposed on defaulting trustees and other fiduciaries is of a more absolute nature than the common law obligation to pay damages for tort or breach of contract. . . . Moreover, the distinction between common law damages and relief against a defaulting trustee is strikingly demonstrated by reference to the actual form of relief granted in equity in respect of

[24] *Ibid.* 359. [25] [1966] 2 NSWR 211. [26] *Ibid.* 214–16.

breaches of trust. The form of relief is couched in terms appropriate to requiring the defaulting trustee to restore to the estate the assets of which he deprived it. Increases in market values between the date of breach and the date of recoupment are for the trustee's account: the effect of such increases would, at common law, be excluded from the computation of damages; but in equity a defaulting trustee must make good the loss by restoring to the estate the assets of which he deprived it notwithstanding that market values may have increased in the meantime. The obligation to restore to the estate the assets of which he deprived it necessarily connotes that, where a monetary compensation is to be paid in lieu of restoring assets, that compensation is to be assessed by reference to the value of the assets at the date of restoration and not at the date of deprivation. In this sense the obligation is a continuing one and ordinarily, if the assets are for some reason not restored *in specie*, it will fall for quantification at the date when recoupment is to be effected, and not before.

The following points are notable for present purposes from these observations of Street J. First, the defendant was a defaulting trustee or fiduciary who had control over assets which formed a trust estate; ie the equitable obligations of the trustee to the plaintiff beneficiaries related to an estate. Secondly, from this first factor, there followed the concentration on the 'restitutionary' or 'restoratory' character of the relief. The primary liability of the defaulting trustee is to restore the property *in specie*, but if that is not possible then the monetary compensation payable in lieu (equitable compensation) must reflect the economic position had restoration *in specie* been possible. In this light, it is not surprising that the equitable compensation remedy awarded in *Re Dawson* has little in common with the common law compensatory remedy, and with matters such as causation, foreseeability, and remoteness. Even its basic compensatory nature looks a little suspect. The issue is whether the *Re Dawson* approach to the equitable compensation remedy holds good across the board whenever that remedy is to be awarded, or whether *Re Dawson* is itself a context-specific decision which does not traverse the full scope of the remedy. I think it is the latter, and I suggest that the reasoning of Lord Browne-Wilkinson, speaking for their Lordships, in *Target Holdings* strongly supports this view.

In *Target Holdings*,[27] the plaintiff was a finance company which instructed the defendant firm of solicitors to act for it in the provision of a loan as mortgagee on a commercial property to a proposed mortgagor. The same solicitors were instructed by the proposed mortgagor. The latter had told the plaintiff that the property had been valued at £2 million. In fact, unknown to the plaintiff, the proposed mortgagor was paying only £775,000 for the property. The plaintiff gave the solicitors over £1.5 million to be held on a bare trust, and then transferred to the

[27] N. 23 above.

mortgagor once the property had been purchased and charges over the property in favour of the plaintiff had been executed by the mortgagor. The solicitors actually paid out most of the £1.5 million before the mortgagor had purchased the property and thus before any charges had been executed, informing the plaintiff that all was in order. All this was admittedly in breach of trust. A short time later, the property was in fact charged to the plaintiff. The mortgagor later became insolvent, and the charged property was sold by the plaintiff as mortgagee, but fetched only £500,000. The plaintiff claimed 'restitution' of the entire sum it had transferred to the solicitors on the basis of the latter's breach of trust. In the Court of Appeal,[28] a majority found in favour of the plaintiff. Peter Gibson LJ stated that 'a trustee or other fiduciary [who] in breach of trust disposes of trust property to a stranger comes under an immediate duty to make restitution.'[29] No inquiry as to causation was necessary. The 'loss' was immediate, and the causal connection was obvious.[30] The loss here was £1.5 million, which the plaintiff could recover from the solicitors, subject only to giving credit for the £500,000 recovered on the sale of the charged property. The House of Lords allowed an appeal by the solicitors.

The structure of Lord Browne-Wilkinson's argument is most instructive. He referred to the fact that rules of equitable compensation for breach of trust were largely developed in relation to traditional trusts. As we have already seen, in such a trust the basic rule is that a trustee in breach must restore or pay to the trust estate either the assets which have been lost to the estate by reason of the breach or compensation for such loss. Courts of equity did not award damages but, acting *in personam,* ordered the defaulting trustee to restore the trust estate. If specific restitution of the trust property is not possible, then the liability of the trustee is to pay sufficient compensation to the trust estate to put it back to what it would have been had the breach not been committed. Even if the immediate cause of the loss is the dishonesty or failure of a third party, the trustee is liable to make good the loss to the trust estate if, but for the breach, such loss would not have occurred. (Thus, although the common law rules of remoteness of damage and causation do not apply, there does have to be some causal connection between the breach of trust and the loss to the trust estate for which compensation is recoverable, namely, the fact that the loss would not have occurred but for the breach.)

His Lordship continued that it is clear that these rules will not apply to every breach by a trustee of a traditional trust. For example, if a trustee commits a breach of trust with the acquiescence of one beneficiary, that

[28] [1994] 1 WLR 1089. [29] *Ibid.* 1104. [30] *Ibid.* 1102–03.

beneficiary has no right to complain and an action for breach of trust brought by him would fail. Further, if a trustee makes an unauthorized but profitable investment, the investment might be sold at the insistence of the beneficiary and the funds applied towards authorized investments, but the trustee would be under no liability to pay compensation either to the trust fund or to the beneficiary because the breach had caused no loss to the trust fund. Crucially, Lord Browne-Wilkinson emphasized that 'in each case the first question is to ask what are the rights of the beneficiary: only if some relevant right has been infringed so as to give rise to a loss is it necessary to consider the extent of the trustee's liability to compensate for such loss'.[31] As an aside, might it not be said that this remark looks very much like an acceptance of a substantive interest-based approach?

What is made plain by Lord Browne-Wilkinson's analysis is that it is wrong to lift out wholesale the detailed rules developed in the context of traditional trusts and then seek to apply them to trusts of a quite different kind.[32] The trust in *Target Holdings* was a bare trust. As such it was simply an aspect of a wider commercial transaction involving agency. The commercial objective of the plaintiff was to lend money on security. One step in that process involved the plaintiff depositing money in the defendants' trust account. Until the money was loaned in accordance with the plaintiff's instructions, it was undoubtedly trust money. Thus, if it had been paid away other than in accordance with the plaintiff's instructions, and the commercial transaction anticipated had not been finalized, general equitable principles applicable to trusts would demand that the fund be restored to the plaintiff's account. However, once the commercial transaction had been completed Lord Browne-Wilkinson considered it 'entirely artificial' to import into such a trust an obligation to restore the trust fund.[33] His Lordship continued:[34]

> The obligation to reconstitute the trust fund applicable in the case of traditional trusts reflects the fact that no one beneficiary is entitled to the trust property and the need to compensate all the beneficiaries for the breach. The rationale has no application in a case such as the present. To impose such an obligation in order to enable the beneficiary solely entitled (i.e. the client) to recover from the solicitor more than the client has lost flies in the face of common sense and is in direct conflict with the basic principles of equitable compensation. In my judgment, once a conveyancing transaction has been completed the client has no right to have the solicitor's client account reconstituted as a 'trust fund'.

In my view, the readiness of their Lordships in *Target Holdings*, through Lord Browne-Wilkinson, (i) to articulate as foundational in equitable compensation awards the two compensatory principles, (ii) to

[31] N. 23 above, at 360. [32] *Ibid.* 362. [33] *Ibid.* [34] *Ibid.*

adopt a substantive interest-based approach, and (iii) to apply both the principles and that approach in such a way as, in effect, to characterize the rather strict 'restitution by compensation' stance propounded by *Re Dawson* as relevant only where traditional trusts are breached, may herald a much greater prominence in English law for the remedy of equitable compensation. Equitable compensation has been accepted in breach of confidence actions, and very occasionally elsewhere: see, for example, *O'Sullivan* v. *Management Agency Ltd.*[35] In particular, of course, the distinction acknowledged in *Target Holdings* between traditional trusts and bare trusts does not describe the entire range of equitable obligations for breach of which compensation might be in issue. There are other equitable obligations, beyond truly trust-type or confidentiality obligations. On a continuum, beyond traditional trust, bare trust, and confidence, may be placed non-trustee fiduciary obligations as well as other types of equitable obligations, founded perhaps on the unconscionability principle. In other words, the continuum of equitable obligations stretches from trust and fiduciary duties at one end, owed in respect of property of or the economic interests of the beneficiary, to fiduciary duties and duties of care owed in respect of other non-economic interests, and then on to duties at the other end, owed to others, but whose focus is on the prevention of unconscionable behaviour by the obligee. Identification of the differences between different types of equitable obligations, as undertaken in a very limited context at one end of the spectrum in *Target Holdings*, is essential from a remedial perspective. Once the nature of any particular equitable obligation is identified, it becomes much easier to develop equitable compensation in a manner which properly reflects that loss suffered by the plaintiff which, consistent with the nature of the obligation, ought to be compensated. This is to suggest no more than that a substantive interest-based approach be adopted in recognising the plaintiff's claim, and that the appropriateness of remedy principle be applied both in choosing which remedy and in defining its reach in the case at hand.

Let us return to *Target Holdings* to make one further point. Not only was a substantive interest-based approach taken therein to the issue of the plaintiff's position, but Lord Browne-Wilkinson also discussed the matter of quantification of any compensation payable. His Lordship agreed with the majority of the Court of Appeal that the trustee's duty to remedy the breach—even in the case of a bare trust—arose immediately, and thus, had proceedings been brought before the conveyancing transaction had been completed, an order requiring restoration would have issued. However, in the events which occurred, and in view of the real

[35] [1985] 1 QB 428.

interest of the plaintiff, he could not agree with the view taken by Peter Gibson LJ that 'events which occur between the date of breach and the date of trial are irrelevant in assessing the loss suffered by the breach'.[36] This rejection of Peter Gibson LJ's position is, of course, to bring equitable compensation into line with the approach generally taken at common law to assessing compensatory damages in tort. Since the quantum of compensation was to be assessed at the time of judgment, not at an earlier date,[37] that quantum 'would be the figure then necessary to put the trust estate or the beneficiary back into the position it would have been in had there been no breach'.[38] Compensation would 'make good a loss suffered by the beneficiary and which, using hindsight and common sense, can be seen to have been caused by the breach'.[39] The plaintiff, it was assumed for the purpose of argument (since the substantive matter still had to be tried), obtained exactly what it would have obtained had no breach occurred, and accordingly the loss suffered was not compensable because it was not *caused* by the breach.[40] Had there been no breach, the plaintiff would have experienced the very same loss. This examination of causation in *Target Holdings* was the consequence of adopting a truly compensatory approach in equity and then applying it to a case dealing with loss arising from the breach of a non-traditional trust.

EQUITABLE COMPENSATION AS A REMEDY OF SIGNIFICANCE

I have already suggested that *Target Holdings* should mean that equitable compensation will take on a more important role in English equity. In other jurisdictions it has shown it has the capacity to become a remedy of considerable significance, not least because it aids in extending the utility of existing equitable obligations, in that it enables equity to meet loss as well as to strip gain. Likewise, it provides equity with an increased flexibility of approach which can easily feed back into the recognition of a wider range of obligations. In other words, it can be used to give substance to the concept of the continuum of obligations introduced earlier. Professor Finn (as he then was) warned that the revitalisation of equitable compensation meant that '[a]s far as England is concerned a particularly potent, fiduciary-based, surrogate "tort" awaits in the wings—and it is one having the advantages of those presumptions, reversals in the onus of proof, etc. that fiduciary law confers.'[41]

[36] N. 23 above, at 363. [37] *Ibid.* 364. [38] *Ibid.* 363.
[39] *Ibid.* 365. [40] *Ibid.* 366.
[41] See 'Fiduciary Law and the Modern Commercial World' in McKendrick (ed.), *Commercial Aspects of Trusts and Fiduciary Obligations* (1992), 40.

Some examples of potential future developments come to mind. There is, for instance, need to develop a compensatory remedy to be applied in cases of equitable accessory liability, after *Royal Brunei Airlines Sdn. Bhd.* v. *Tan.*[42] It is difficult to believe that, in the face of the often complex circumstances giving rise to accessory liability claims, argument on matters of foreseeability of loss, causation, remoteness, contributory negligence, and mitigation will remain suppressed for too much longer. There is also the potential for unconscionability-based equitable wrongs and breaches of equitable duties of care requiring compensation (developing from doctrines discussed in *Commercial Bank of Australia Ltd* v. *Amadio*,[43] *Boustany* v. *Pigott*,[44] *Barclays Bank plc* v. *O'Brien*,[45] and the growing line of Australian and New Zealand decisions on the reach of equitable estoppel as an unconscionability-based doctrine). And there is scope for the recognition of compensatory awards in place of constructive trust awards in *de facto* break-up cases (*Peter* v. *Beblow*,[46] and dicta in *Lankow* v. *Rose*[47]).

Outside the arena of trust law proper, it has been in the context of loss suffered by a breach of fiduciary duty that the remedy has seen its most potent and controversial development. There are increasing numbers of cases from Australia, Canada, and New Zealand which have formed the focus of much of the analysis in the literature referred to at the outset of this paper, and the future extension of the remedy to other contexts depends upon its sustainability in the breach of fiduciary duty context. A breach of the core fiduciary duty of loyalty, which duty imposes on a fiduciary a requirement not to engage in unpermitted self-dealing and a requirement not to make a profit by virtue of his position, would be unlikely to lead to loss requiring a compensatory response. The focus of this core duty, on preventing gain through exploitation and profiteering, is more usually met by restitutionary (in the proper sense of the word) responses of constructive trust or accounting for profits. Further, where a fiduciary causes loss to a beneficiary through misconduct of some form which falls short of exploitation or profiteering, particularly through careless advice-giving, the loss is these days often compensable by a common law damages award in tort. In *Nocton* v. *Lord Ashburton*,[48] a paradigm case of such fiduciary misconduct, the House of Lords awarded compensation in equity for the loss arising from the fiduciary's misconduct. The plaintiff could not on the facts satisfy the requirements for the tort of deceit, and was statute-barred in respect of a contractual claim, and, with hindsight of course, an action in tort for negligent mis-

[42] [1995] 3 WLR 64. [43] (1983) 151 CLR 447 (HCA).
[44] (1993) 69 P & C R 298 (PC). [45] [1994] 1 AC 180 (HL).
[46] (1993) 101 DLR (4th) 621 (SCC). [47] [1995] 1 NZLR 277 (NZCA).
[48] N. 2 above.

statement had not yet been articulated. What is interesting about *Nocton* is that the non-availability of a common law action for negligent mis-statement did not prevent their Lordships from providing relief in equity for loss caused by such conduct. The full purport of *Nocton* was not understood, and it remained a largely unexplored goldmine, for both equity and the common law, until 1963. Since *Hedley Byrne & Co. Ltd* v. *Heller & Partners*,[49] the need to resort to equity—both for a cause of action and a remedy—in such misconduct cases has become even more remote. When all these factors are taken together, it is not surprising that there were (until recently) relatively few cases dealing with equitable compensation claims for breach of fiduciary duty. However, that is now changing.

Perhaps at this point, it might be of some value if, in front of an English audience, I were to try and sketch my understanding of the fit between equitable duties and common law duties, centring on the analysis offered by Lord Browne-Wilkinson in his important speeches in *Henderson* v. *Merrett Syndicates Ltd*[50] and *White* v. *Jones*.[51] My view is that these speeches are insightful contributions towards the integration of equity into the broader scheme of civil liability, and that this integration, if carried through and accepted, must bring with it a more prominent role for equitable compensation, and perhaps ultimately the adoption of the holistic position with respect to the damages remedy proposed by Tipping J in the *New Zealand Land Development* case, cited earlier.[52]

In *Henderson* the House of Lords held that underwriting agents owed Lloyds' Names concurrent duties in contract and tort. Whether fiduciary obligations were also owed by the agents was discussed only by Lord Browne-Wilkinson. His Lordship considered such a claim was 'understandable' but 'misconceived', commenting:[53]

> The liability of a fiduciary for the negligent transaction of his duties is not a separate head of liability but the paradigm of the general duty to act with care imposed by law on those who take it upon themselves to act or advise others. Although the historical development of the rules of law and equity have, in the past, caused different labels to be stuck on different manifestations of the duty, in truth the duty of care on bailees, carriers, trustees, directors, agents and others is the same duty: it arises from the circumstances in which the defendants were acting, not from their status or description. It is the fact that they have all assumed responsibility for the property or affairs of others which renders them liable for the careless performance of what they have undertaken to do, not the description of the trade or position which they hold.

[49] [1964] AC 465. [50] [1994] 3 WLR 761.

[51] [1995] 2 WLR 187. See further Nicholas J. McBride and Andrew Hughes, '*Hedley Byrne* in the House of Lords: An Interpretation' [1995] *Legal Studies* 376.

[52] N. 11 above. [53] N. 50 above, at 799.

In *White* v. *Jones,* Lord Browne-Wilkinson elaborated upon his earlier statement in *Henderson. White* v. *Jones* considered 'the much discussed question whether an intended beneficiary under a will is entitled to recover damages from the testator's solicitors by reason of whose negligence the testator's intention to benefit him under the will has failed to be carried into effect'[54] and decided that such a beneficiary was so entitled. In the course of his speech, Lord Browne-Wilkinson said:[55]

> The paradigm of the circumstances in which equity will find a fiduciary relationship is where one party, A, has assumed to act in relation to the property or affairs of another, B. A, having assumed responsibility, pro tanto, for B's affairs, is taken to have assumed certain duties in relation to the conduct of those affairs, including normally a duty of care. Thus, a trustee assumes responsibility for the management of the property of the beneficiary, a company director for the affairs of the company and an agent for those of his principal. By so assuming to act in B's affairs, A comes under fiduciary duties to B. Although the extent of those fiduciary duties (including duties of care) will vary from case to case some duties (including a duty of care) arise in each case.

Lord Browne-Wilkinson appears to distinguish between different types of duties recognized in equity. The core, and arguably the most important, equitable duty, itself exemplified in the trust, is the fiduciary duty of loyalty, by which the paramountcy of the beneficiary's interest is ensured. But other duties, as in *Nocton* v. *Lord Ashburton,* have been developed to serve the interests of beneficiaries. Historically, duties of care in equity and at common law have evolved independently of each other, although they influenced each other, as can be seen from a reading of their Lordships' speeches in *Hedley Byrne.* Lord Browne-Wilkinson appears to be suggesting that the point has now been reached where in respect of obligations of care which cover the same or very similar conduct, although developed separately at common law and in equity, the substance of those obligations matters rather more than their particular historical genesis.[56] This would certainly find support in New Zealand jurisprudence. As in *Target Holdings,* this looks very much like the articulation of a substantive interest-based approach.

[54] N. 51 above at 191 (*per* Lord Goff).

[55] *Ibid.* 209–10.

[56] The approach adopted by the PC in *Downsview Nominees Ltd* v. *First City Corporation Ltd* [1993] 2 WLR 86 is quite consistent with this observation. The New Zealand Court of Appeal had held that debenture holders and receivers owed duties of care in tort to the debtor and subsequent charge-holders. Lord Templeman, speaking for their Lordships, rejected this view on the basis that the historical genesis of the duties of a receiver was in equity, and the extent of those equitable duties was more limited than the extent of a tortious duty of care. Thus, in effect, a subsumption of the limited equitable duties into a more general tortious duty of care would be to create new obligations in receivers rather than merely to rationalize their position by recognition of a single duty of care applicable interchangably in equity and at common law.

It cannot be contradicted that the institutional separation of courts of law and courts of equity has played a very major part in the separate development of equitable and common law (particularly tortious) duties of care. It is clear from *Nocton* v. *Lord Ashburton* itself that, quite apart from its obvious jurisdiction over a fiduciary's breaches of the core duty of loyalty, the exclusive jurisdiction of equity extended to 'a defendant in a fiduciary position in respect of matters which at law would also have given rise to damages for negligence'.[57] So stated Viscount Haldane LC, who also said:[58]

Although liability for negligence in word has in material respects been developed in our law differently from liability for negligence in act, it is none the less true that a man may come under a special duty to exercise care in giving information or advice. I should accordingly be sorry to be thought to lend countenance to the idea that recent decisions have been intended to stereotype the cases in which people can be held to have assumed such a special duty. Whether such a duty has been assumed must depend on the relationship of the parties, and it is at least certain that there are a good many cases in which that relationship may be properly treated as giving rise to a special duty of care in statement.

It is also clear, however, that the dualism of law and equity has not, since *Nocton*, prevented the recognition of a commonality of interests in some substantive matters at least. It is this link which Lord Browne-Wilkinson is concerned with. In *Hedley Byrne*, the breadth of the principle articulated in *Nocton* by Viscount Haldane was recognized by Lord Devlin, who stated:[59]

[The House in *Nocton*] considered that outside contract . . . there could be a special relationship between parties which imposed a duty to give careful advice and accurate information. The majority of their Lordships did not extend the application of this principle beyond the breach of a fiduciary obligation, but none of them said anything at all to show that it was limited to fiduciary obligation.

Similarly, Lord Reid in *Hedley Byrne*, referring to Viscount Haldane's speeches in both *Nocton* and *Robinson* v. *National Bank of Scotland*,[60] said:[61]

Lord Haldane did not think that a duty to take care must be limited to cases of fiduciary relationship in the narrow sense of relationships which had been recognised by the Court of Chancery as being of a fiduciary character. He speaks of other special relationships, and I can see no logical stopping place short of all those relationships where it is plain that the party seeking information or advice was trusting the other to exercise such a degree of care as the circumstances

[57] N. 2 above, at 957 (*per* Viscount Haldane LC). [58] *Ibid.* 948.
[59] N. 49 above, at 523. [60] 1916 SC (HL) 154.
[61] N. 49 above, at 583.

required, where it was reasonable for him to do that, and where the other gave the information or advice when he knew or ought to have known that the inquirer was relying on him.

Lord Browne-Wilkinson is not introducing fundamentally new and heretical thoughts. Quite the contrary. His analysis in *Henderson* and *White* v. *Jones* is a natural continuation of the theme begun in *Nocton* and then developed further in *Hedley Byrne. Hedley Byrne* grew out of *Nocton.* The dominance since 1963 of *Hedley Byrne* common law liability must not be allowed to warp our appreciation of the true scope of equity jurisprudence. In particular, it must not be thought that the trustee and fiduciary duty of loyalty is where the scope of equitable obligation starts and finishes. Lord Browne-Wilkinson is correct to recognize that the duty of care (and with it the term 'assumption of responsibility') is neither an exclusively tortious concept nor a concept unrecognized in equity. This has enormous potential for the future, in respect both of the recognition of a wider range of equitable obligations—the continuum I referred to earlier is much closer to becoming a reality—and of the development of the compensation remedy in equity.

It is trite learning now, particularly in the light of the scholarship of Professor Finn, that the concept 'fiduciary' has become, by its extension to cases where the true focus is not a duty of loyalty but some other interest, rather more confused than it should be. The term 'fiduciary' now embraces a spectrum of obligations, ranging from trust-like obligations to tort-like obligations. Some seem prepared to make the necessary analysis of what is at stake from within the terminology of 'fiduciary'. Some suggest, however, that 'fiduciary' is a term to be confined to the trust-like obligation of loyalty, and that other terminology be used to define non trust-like equitable obligations, such as 'equitable duty of care'.

SOME AUSTRALIAN DEVELOPMENTS

There have been a number of decisions from Australian courts in recent times touching on equitable compensation. Three recent decisions, however, two from the Full Court of the Supreme Court of Western Australia and one from the High Court, are of particular interest.

The first is *Dempster* v. *Mallina Holdings Ltd.*[62] This was a case where there was a fiduciary duty of loyalty, which was breached, but where there was no trust asset as such. Mallina and Dempster Nominees (a company owned by Dempster) were in association as partners or joint

[62] (1994) 15 ACSR 1. Leave to appeal to the High Ct. was refused.

venturers in respect of a mining operation in Western Australia. In breach of a fiduciary duty owed to Mallina, Dempster misrepresented the facts to Mallina, which in consequence sold its share in the venture to Connell. Connell and Dempster formed a company to continue the operation, and later sold the company for a sizable amount, Dempster's share being $50 million. Mallina sought recovery of Dempster's 'profit'. The trial judge assessed equitable compensation by starting with the $50 million, then deducting a sum to cover fees as part of the cost of the business. This left $38 million. The trial judge made his award on the basis of the loss or detriment suffered by Mallina, which he quantified on the basis that Mallina had 'lost the opportunity to make the kind of profits that the other venturer eventually made'.[63] The judge held that Mallina had a 60 per cent chance of making the same profit of $38 million. He awarded $22.8 million which included interest. Dempster appealed, arguing that the purpose of equitable compensation was restitution of a trust estate, which estate was the relevant asset the subject matter of the fiduciary obligation. Here that was, it was argued, no more that the true value of Mallina's interest sold to Connell at the date of sale. The asset value should not be expanded by engrafting onto it a notion of loss of opportunity. The appeal was dismissed. Rowland J gave the leading judgment, which was concurred in by Pidgeon and Seaman JJ. As a first step, his Honour examined carefully not only whether a fiduciary relationship existed between the parties, but what the precise duty was that arose, and what the consequences of a breach of that duty would be. He held:[64]

> The duty was fiduciary in nature. The breach occurred. It was aimed at, and had the effect of, enabling Dempster Nominees to advance its own interests contrary to its duty. Equity will grant relief to the fullest extent that it properly is able. . . . [T]he fiduciary not only breached the duty but also claimed for himself and another innocent person the continuing benefits that would have flowed to his partner had the breach not occurred, equity will not permit him to retain the benefits he received. . . . There are many examples of cases where, in strictness, there is a trust asset which can be followed and restitution *in specie* is given, together with all accrued benefits. And there are cases like the present where the breach is such that it can be seen that the plaintiff suffers loss in the *Hill* v. *Rose* sense [no gain at all by the defendant], or can simply seek an account of the profit made by the defendant.

Although Rowland J was quite prepared to sustain the trial judge's focus on the loss of the plaintiff, he was also ready to provide a proprietary constructive trust remedy aimed at disgorgement of the defendant fiduciary's gain. He indicated that the matter had not been debated, but

[63] *Ibid.* 9–10 (*per* Pidgeon J in the Full Ct.).
[64] *Ibid.* 50, 57, and 58.

that the award based on the gain made might well have been higher than the compensation awarded. Little was said in the judgment of Rowland J as to the method adopted by the trial judge in quantifying the award, other than a suggestion that the modern tendency towards obliteration of traditional distinctions between remedies in contract, tort and statute ought perhaps to be extended to include damages in equity.[65]

In similar vein to *Dempster* is the High Court's decision in *Warman International Ltd* v. *Dwyer*.[66] Dwyer was the general manager of the Queensland branch of Warman. Amongst its activities, Warman had an agency for the distribution of gearboxes manufactured by an Italian company, Bonfiglioli. The Queensland branch controlled the agency, and sold more gearboxes than any other branch. By 1986 Warman had extensively reduced its agencies for Bonfiglioli products, and the Queensland branch was effectively the only one involved with such products. Even it too was downsizing its involvement. At some time during this period, Bonfiglioli offered Warman a joint-venture opportunity for the manufacture if its products in Australia. Warman declined involvement. Dwyer became concerned and anxious about his future. Warman considered selling off its agencies division and asked Dwyer if he was interested. Dwyer declined, but entered into secret negotiations with Bonfiglioli about a joint venture. In June 1988 Bonfiglioli terminated its agency agreement with Warman. Dwyer left Warman's employ in the same month. In September 1988 Dwyer entered into a joint venture agreement with Bonfiglioli to assemble and distribute gearboxes in Australia for a twenty-year term via two companies Dwyer had set up. These business were very successful, with net profits of some $1.6 million in the four years preceding the trial. Warman brought proceedings against Dwyer and the two companies. The trial judge held that Dwyer's conduct amounted to a breach of the fiduciary duty he owed Warman. He used his knowledge and his position as a senior executive officer of Warman to advance his own interests to Warman's disadvantage by offering himself as an attractive alternative for Bonfiglioli's business.

The trial judge stated that it was open to Warman to recover 'equitable damages' for 'the loss of Warman's chance of retaining the agencies business'.[67] Warman, however, wanted an account of profits and the judge acceded to this request. In determining the appropriate basis for such an account, the judge attempted to determine the proportion of the business of Dwyer and his companies which flowed to them by reason of the breach of fiduciary duty. All members of the Queensland Court of Appeal agreed there had been a breach of fiduciary duty. The majority of the Court, however, held that instead of taking an account of profits,

[65] *Ibid.* 57. [66] (1995) 69 ALJR 362. [67] *Ibid.* 365.

Warman was only entitled to recover its loss flowing from the breach of fiduciary duty.

In the High Court, their Honours agreed in a single judgment that Dwyer was in breach of a fiduciary duty. The Court then examined the relevant remedial possibilities. An account of profits is one of the primary remedies potentially available after a breach of fiduciary obligation. Thus in *Nocton* v. *Lord Ashburton*, Viscount Haldane LC said:[68]

> Courts of Equity had jurisdiction to direct accounts to be taken, and in proper cases to order the solicitor to replace property improperly acquired from the client, or to make compensation if he had lost it by acting in breach of a duty which arose out of his confidential relationship to the man who had trusted him.

Whether a fiduciary has to render an account of profits or make compensation to the plaintiff is a matter to be determined by the plaintiff. If the loss suffered by the plaintiff exceeds the profits made by the fiduciary, it is naturally more likely that the plaintiff will seek compensation. The clear distinction between the two remedies was adverted to by the Court in its acknowledgement that 'the liability of a fiduciary to account for a profit or gain made in breach of fiduciary duty does not depend upon the person to whom that obligation is owed suffering a loss or injury'.[69] The Court went on to examine the basis for an account of profits.

For present purposes, however, the decision is of value in that it accepts that equitable compensation is an available remedy, at the plaintiff beneficiary's election, for loss caused by breach of a core fiduciary duty of loyalty. It also demonstrates once again, with *Dempster*, that most cases of breach of the core duty of loyalty, aimed to prevent exploitation and profiteering, will result not in compensation, but in profit-stripping, which is a form of restitutionary relief in the proper sense of the term 'restitutionary'.

The third Australian decision is perhaps the most interesting of the three. It is the decision of the Full Court of the Supreme Court of Western Australia in *Permanent Building Society (in liq.)* v. *Wheeler*.[70] The case concerned allegations by a company now in liquidation of breaches of fiduciary duties owed to it by its directors, causing loss to the company for which compensation was now sought. The appeal concerned, *inter alia*, the trial judge's dismissal of a claim in respect of one of the directors. In delivering what was effectively the judgment of the Court, Ipp J held that the director in question had not acted improperly *vis-à-vis* the company, but that he had breached his duty to exercise skill and care as a director of the company. It is in respect of the latter finding that Ipp J's reasoning is of interest and importance. Relying in part on *obiter dicta* of

[68] N. 2 above, at 956–7.
[69] N. 66 above, at 370.
[70] (1994) 14 ACSR 109.

judges of the High Court in *Bennett* v. *Minister of Community Welfare*,[71] his Honour drew a clear distinction between an equitable duty to exercise reasonable care and skill, and the fiduciary duty. His Honour stated:[72]

> There are indeed many difficulties inherent in the concept of 'fiduciary wrongs'. . . . It seems to me that many of those difficulties stem from equating an equitable duty to exercise care with a fiduciary duty to take care. It is essential to bear in mind the existence of a fiduciary relationship does not mean that every duty owed by a fiduciary to the beneficiary is a fiduciary one. In particular, a trustee's duty to exercise reasonable care, though equitable, is not specifically a fiduciary duty. . . . Similarly, in my opinion, a director's duty to exercise reasonable care, though equitable (as well as legal) is not a fiduciary obligation. . . . The directors' duty to exercise care and skill is nothing to do with any position of disadvantage or vulnerability on the part of the company. It is not a duty that stems from the requirements of trust and confidence imposed on a fiduciary. In my opinion, that duty is not fiduciary, although it is a duty actionable in the equitable jurisdiction of this court.

Since the plaintiff company was owed an equitable duty of care, breach of that duty giving rise to loss could be met with an award of equitable compensation. However, the breach of duty must cause the loss. His Honour's findings in this respect are extremely instructive. They support the notion that different types of duties in equity will be treated differently when it comes to the application of a causation test. Thus, there are claims for equitable compensation for breaches of fiduciary duty where the court does not inquire into aspects of causality. These, however, are cases of true fiduciary obligation, where 'the fiduciary has abused the control of the trust, there is a substantial potential for gain through such wrongdoing, the fiduciary has superior information concerning his or her acts, and there is a need "to keep persons in a fiduciary capacity up to their duty" . . .'[73] Such factors are not applicable to a breach of an equitable duty of care. Likewise, where the basis of the duty breached was that a person in a fiduciary position could not place himself in a situation where his duty and interests conflicted, there was no need for investigation into causation. Where, however, the duty breached is a duty to exercise reasonable care, that basis does not apply to rule out a causation investigation. Thus, his Honour stated:[74]

> [T]here is no reason to apply to the latter [a breach of a duty to exercise care] the rules of causation that govern the obligation of a fiduciary to account for such a breach. There is a fundamental distinction between breaches of fiduciary obligations which involve dishonesty and abuse of the trustee's advantages and the vulnerable position of beneficiaries, on the one hand, and, honest but careless

[71] (1992) 107 ALR 617. [72] N. 70 above, at 157–8.
[73] *Ibid.* 165. [74] *Ibid.* 166.

dealings which breach mere equitable obligations, on the other. There is ample justification on policy grounds for more stringent rules in the case of breaches of fiduciary obligations, but not where there has been honest but careless dealing. Further, in my opinion, a court of equity, applying principles of fairness, should not require an honest but careless trustee to compensate a beneficiary for losses without proof that but for the breach of duty those losses would not have occurred. . . . It is also significant, as regards matters of policy, that the tortious duty not to be negligent, and the equitable obligation on the part of a trustee to exercise reasonable skill and care are, in content, the same. There is every reason, in my view, in such circumstances, to apply the maxim that 'equity follows the law'.

Wheeler is significant in the following respects. It is a case where loss was suffered by the plaintiff, with no gain by the defendant. If an equitable remedy were to run, it would need to be compensation. Had it been held that the director in question had breached a true fiduciary duty, the content of that duty would have made an award of equitable compensation without reference to causation quite appropriate. However, the breach of equitable obligation did not involve the duty of loyalty. Rather, its content was akin to the common law duty of care. Thus, the award of compensation was appropriately subject to a test of causation—which Ipp J actually gleaned from *Re Dawson*—namely, would the loss have occurred had there been no breach? The decision is illustrative of both the substantive interest-based approach and the appropriateness of remedy principle as found in New Zealand jurisprudence.

SOME CANADIAN DEVELOPMENTS

Equitable compensation has been discussed in the Supreme Court of Canada on a number of occasions in recent years, and it is suggested that these decisions are also consistent with these features. There is little point in rehearsing other than in outline all these decisions, except for the most recent one.

First, in *Guerin* v. *The Queen*,[75] a majority of the Court found that a fiduciary obligation owed by the Crown to members of an Indian band with respect to dealings with reserve land on behalf of the band had been breached by a failure to consult with the band before leasing the land to a golf club. The Court held that the principles applicable to a claim for equitable compensation against trustees proper were also applicable to non-trustee fiduciaries whose breach of duty caused the beneficiary to suffer loss. The loss was the chance of profit. Although the duty was characterized as one of loyalty, the breach was simply a failure to follow

[75] (1984) 13 DLR (4th) 321.

the instructions of the band. The Crown did not exploit or profit. The severity of the award against the Crown may be explained by the particular nature of the parties.

The second decision, *Canson Enterprises Ltd* v. *Boughton & Co.*,[76] has already had much written about it. The defendant solicitor acted for both parties to a property purchase. He failed to disclose to the plaintiff purchaser a material fact concerning the transaction. The failure to disclose was a breach of a duty of loyalty. After the purchase the plaintiff proceeded with an unsuccessful warehouse development. The negligence of soil engineers and a contractor resulted in massive loss. The plaintiff was unable to recover fully on a judgment against these negligent parties, and sought to recover for breach of fiduciary duty against the solicitor. It was agreed between the parties that the plaintiff would not have purchased the property had disclosure of the material fact been made. A majority in the Supreme Court accepted two arguments put forward by the solicitor, as a result of which the loss claimed by the plaintiff was held to be non-recoverable from the solicitor. First, the approach used in *Guerin* should be applied only in cases where a fiduciary exercises control over property of the beneficiary; thus, where the fiduciary's role is trustee-like. Secondly, there was an intermingling of law and equity which had the effect of introducing common law requirements, such as remoteness and causation, into equitable compensation claims. The minority, while concurring in the result, differed as to the reasoning. The minority affirmed the independence of legal and equitable concepts, and stated that the enforcement of a fiduciary duty of loyalty set fiduciary law apart from contract and tort. There should be no intermingling. Nonetheless, there did need to be a link between the breach and the loss for which compensation was sought, and there was no link on the facts. The breach of the duty of loyalty did not lead to exploitation or profiteering by the fiduciary. The relevant breach of duty was by a material non-disclosure which caused loss.

Norberg v. *Wynrib*[77] concerned a claim by a patient against a doctor. The patient was addicted to a drug, and the doctor offered prescriptions of the drug only if sexual favours were granted. Favours were given on a number of occasions, and some years later the patient sought damages for assault and battery, and, in the alternative, equitable compensation for breach of fiduciary duty. Whilst the other judges dealt with the claim on the assault and battery basis, McLachlin J, speaking for herself and L'Hereux-Dubé J, preferred to adopt the fiduciary analysis. Her Ladyship concluded that the societal and personal interests at stake constituted a type of practical interest which should be protected by a fiduciary duty of loyalty. The duty was breached

[76] [1991] 3 SCR 534.

[77] (1992) 92 DLR (4th) 449.

> when [the doctor] prescribed drugs which he knew she should not have, when he failed to advise her to obtain counselling when her addiction became or should have become apparent to him, and most notoriously, when he placed his own interest in obtaining sexual favours from [her] in conflict with and above her interest in obtaining treatment and becoming well.[78]

Her Ladyship was prepared to award damages for suffering and loss during the plaintiff's period of prolonged addiction, damages for sexual exploitation, and punitive damages.

In *M (K)* v. *M (H)*,[79] the plaintiff was an incest victim who brought claims in assault and battery, and in breach of fiduciary duty against the perpetrator, her father. La Forest J, speaking for the majority, held that there was a fiduciary duty in a parent to protect a child's health and well-being, and that the duty had been breached. However, the differences that had emerged in *Canson* in respect of the approach to be taken to the award of equitable compensation resurfaced. La Forest J stated that the policy considerations underlying both the common law and equitable claims were the same, and that the same remedies would thus normally follow. McLachlin J could not agree. She believed that the action for breach of fiduciary duty encompassed damage to a trust relationship, which the common law actions did not. Thus, at this point, it appeared that the Supreme Court was prepared to recognize equitable protection of interests of a wider non-economic type by extending to them the fiduciary duty of loyalty. However, a disagreement as to the nature and content of such protection, even if referred to as a duty of loyalty, had created some confusion and division on the implications for remedial issues.

These decisions were followed in late 1994 by *Hodgkinson* v. *Simms*.[80] The Court analysed the jurisdiction to grant equitable compensation for breach of fiduciary duty and appears to have laid the foundation for what could arguably become a much more expansive availability of this form of relief. The facts were as follows. In January 1980 Hodgkinson was a 30-year-old stockbroker working for a Vancouver investment firm. He had recently moved from a more conservative firm dealing primarily with blue-chip securities to one dealing with speculative underwritings in the oil and gas and mining industries, and his income had increased dramatically. Prior to the move, he had grossed between $50,000 and $70,000 per year. In the year following his move, his gross income was $650,000. A year later, it was in excess of $1 million. Until this time, Hodgkinson had never employed an accountant. He had always prepared his own income tax returns and arranged his own investments. These included an interest in a ski chalet, two units in a Multiple Unit Residential Building ('MURB'), and some shares. The growing complex-

[78] *Ibid.* 495. [79] [1992] 3 SCR 6. [80] [1994] 3 SCR 377.

ity of his financial position caused Hodgkinson some concern, and, in an effort to 'shelter' his money from immediate taxation and to secure sound long-term investments, he sought advice from Simms, a partner in a firm of chartered accountants. Simms agreed with Hodgkinson that real estate would be a sound investment, and recommended four MURB projects in which Hodgkinson duly invested. Simms, however, had not disclosed to Hodgkinson that he had professional arrangements with developers of these projects. These arrangements (termed 'bonus billing') entitled Simms to larger fees from his developer clients if their MURBs were sold to other clients of Simms. In 1981 the real estate market crashed and Hodgkinson suffered losses of approximately $350,000 on the four MURB investments recommended by Simms.

Hodgkinson brought an action against Simms alleging breach of fiduciary duty, breach of contract, and negligence. The claim in negligence was dismissed at trial and not pursued in the British Columbia Court of Appeal. The trial judge accepted that Hodgkinson would not have invested in the MURBs if he had known of Simms' involvement. Hodgkinson had sought independent advice from Simms: he had looked to him as an independent professional adviser, not a promoter.

The trial judge concluded that Simms was in breach of an implied term in his retainer with Hodgkinson which imposed a contractual duty of material disclosure. The judge also held that Simms was in breach of his fiduciary duty, not having disclosed his personal interest. As a consequence, the judge awarded damages for the full amount of the loss sustained. The British Columbia Court of Appeal upheld the trial judge on the contract point but reduced the damages award to the amount of the fees received by Simms from the developers with respect to the 'bonus billing' arrangement. In the Court's view, the loss sustained as a result of the collapse of the real estate market was unforeseeable and, therefore, not recoverable. The Court rejected the judge's finding of fiduciary liability.

A majority of the Supreme Court found a fiduciary relationship on the facts, and then discussed the matter of remedial response. La Forest J, writing for the majority, considered the proper approach to damages for a fiduciary breach to be 'restitutionary', although by this he meant that Hodgkinson 'is entitled to be put in as good a position as he would have been in had the breach not occurred'.[81] On the facts before the Court, La Forest J's view entitled Hodgkinson to be restored to the position he was in before the transaction, by recovery equal to the loss of capital as well as all consequential losses. In reaching this conclusion, his Lordship rejected two arguments mounted by Simms.

[81] *Ibid.* 440.

The first argument was that Hodgkinson, had he known the true facts, would still have invested in real estate tax shelters. As to this La Forest J stated:[82]

> The main difficulty with this submission is that it flies in the face of the facts as found by the trial judge. . . . What is more, the submission runs up against the long-standing equitable principle that where the plaintiff has made out a case of non-disclosure and the loss occasioned thereby is established, the onus is on the defendant to prove that the innocent victim would have suffered the same loss regardless of the breach.

The second argument was as follows. Even assuming that Hodgkinson would not have invested had proper disclosure been made, the non-disclosure was not the proximate cause of his loss. Rather, the loss was caused by the impact of the general economic recession on the real estate market. As to this, La Forest J remarked that, since Simms' breach of fiduciary duty initiated the chain of events leading to Hodgkinson's loss, it was 'right and just that [Simms] account for this loss in full'.[83] On the facts, there was therefore a material distinction from the *Canson* case. In *Canson*, the loss was caused by the acts of third parties unrelated to the fiduciary breach, whereas in *Hodgkinson* 'the duty [Simms] breached was directly related to the risk that materialized and in fact caused [Hodgkinson's] loss'.[84]

Although it was not strictly necessary to do so, La Forest J considered how damages for breach of contract should be calculated. In his view, 'damages in contract follow the principles stated in connection with the equitable breach'.[85] The relevant contractual duty breached by Simms was of 'precisely the same nature as the equitable duty considered in the fiduciary analysis, namely the duty to make full disclosure of any material conflict of interest'.[86] And, since it was reasonably foreseeable that if the contract was breached, Hodgkinson would not have invested and therefore would not have been exposed to the market risks in connection with the four MURBs which Simms recommended, the risk which eventuated was therefore a reasonably foreseeable consequence of the breach. It was enough that the type of loss, if not the extent, was foreseeable.

The minority (McLachlin and Sopinka JJ, with whom Major J concurred) held that a fiduciary relationship did not arise. They thus discussed the remedy matter only in respect of the contract claim. However, in discussing causation, they rejected the literal application of a 'but for' compensation principle in the context of both equitable and common law claims. *Canson* was cited as establishing that 'the results of supervening events beyond the control of the defendant are not justly

[82] *Ibid.* 441. [83] *Ibid.* 443. [84] *Ibid.* 445. [85] *Ibid.* 454. [86] *Ibid.* 454.

visited upon him/her in assessing damages, even in the context of the breach of an equitable duty'.[87]

Hodgkinson is a decision of first importance. In effect, the majority's opinion was that on the facts before the Court equitable compensation and damages for breach of contract were to be calculated in the same manner. This conclusion reveals the two influences at work in the jurisprudence of some members of the Court. First, there is a willingness to develop equitable compensation as flexibly as necessary to reflect different types of fiduciary (or equitable) breaches.[88] Secondly, La Forest J's judgment reveals a desire to 'strive to treat similar wrongs similarly, regardless of the particular cause or causes of action that may have been pleaded'.[89] Thus, 'the courts should look to the harm suffered from the breach of the given duty, and apply the appropriate remedy'.[90] This is on all fours with the two developments identified from New Zealand jurisprudence.

WHERE ARE WE GOING?

The Canadian decisions, perhaps most starkly, but certainly not on their own in this respect, open up for us Professor Finn's 'surrogate tort' issue. Professor McCamus has raised the matter in this way:[91]

> If it is not misleading to characterize tort law as the body of private law doctrine that defines liability for compensatory damages arising from unprivileged or wrongful conduct, there is a very real sense in which these recent cases are reinventing an equitable body of doctrine with the same objective and policy foundations.

The effective recognition of equitable duties, the content of which is a responsibility on the duty-holder to take proper care in carrying out a task, whether those duties be called 'fiduciary' or 'merely equitable',

[87] *Ibid.* 475.

[88] '*Canson* . . . recognizes the fact that a breach of fiduciary duty can take a variety of forms, and as such a variety of remedial considerations may be appropriate . . . Huband J.A. of the Manitoba Court of Appeal recently remarked upon this idea, in "Remedies and Restitution for Breach of Fiduciary Duties" in *The 1993 Isaac Pitblado Lectures*, 21–32, at p. 31: "A breach of a fiduciary duty can take many forms. It might be tantamount to deceit and theft, while on the other hand it might be no more than an innocent and honest bit of bad advice, or a failure to give a timely warning." *Canson* is an example of the latter type': *ibid.* 443.

[89] *Ibid.* 444.

[90] *Ibid.*

[91] 'Equitable Compensation and Restitutionary Remedies: Recent Developments', *Special Lectures of the Law Society of Upper Canada 1995: Law of Remedies* (1995), 318.

coupled with the increasing recognition by equity of non-economic interests as being worthy of protection,[92] go hand in hand with the revitalized remedy of equitable compensation. The revitalized remedy must undoubtedly have potential for considerable overlap with compensation at common law, particularly in tort, but also in some instances in contract.

Where are we going, therefore, with equitable compensation? There are those who welcome the move towards an integrated law of obligations, where the historical bases of obligations and remedies play a rather less prominent role than the issues of substance and appropriateness. There are those whose stance suggests a belief that history has answered all the questions of substance and appropriateness already. And there are probably those who are attracted to different aspects offered by the disciples of both extremes.

No matter where one stands, the issues of the future will be the same, although the answers given may be different. If equity is to be used to define duties of care, will these duties be subtly different from common law duties of care, reflecting to some degree the 'higher' duty expectation of equity? Or are they no more than tactical manœuvres around limitation, burden of proof, and other problems? In respect of the latter, can 'reform' be better achieved by a direct focus on the inadequacies of the common law? In what circumstances should an overlap be allowed between equitable duties and contractual duties? What kind of loss—pecuniary and non-pecuniary, such as for emotional distress—will be compensable in equity? Are aggravated damages available in equity? Are exemplary or punitive damages available? What focus determines the correct test of causation to be applied in defining the loss for which equitable compensation will awarded—is the focus on physical injury and property damage, or economic loss, or a stricter test from traditional equity (as that applied in *Re Dawson*)? Is there a role for foreseeability? And what of matters such as mitigation, contributory negligence, the time for assessment, and the place of equitable discretions and assumptions? These questions have begun to be addressed in both the cases and the academic literature, but there is, as the Canadian cases demonstrate, no clear set of rules, even looking likely to emerge. What can, I think, be said is that the courts are feeling their way forward, and in doing this are making use of the substantive interest-based approach and the appropriateness of remedy principle, even if in some instances that fact remains unexpressed. Perhaps this means we shall end up only with guidelines, rather than rules.

[92] See, for an attempted extension in Australia, the judgment of Kirby P, as he then was, in *Williams* v. *Minister, Aboriginal Land Rights Act 1983* (1994) 35 NSWLR 497, at 511.

A NEW ZEALAND EPILOGUE

Lest it be thought that there be nothing of recent interest from New Zealand, I shall conclude with reference to four decisions.

First, in *Witten-Hannah* v. *Davis*,[93] the Court of Appeal faced a case of breach of a fiduciary duty of loyalty owed by a solicitor to his client. The client was not independently advised in respect of a financial arrangement entered into between herself and the solicitor, and suffered loss as a consequence. Both Richardson and McKay JJ gave judgments in which they characterized the duty owed as one of loyalty. As such, in respect of establishing causation of the loss claimed, both judges held that the onus was on the solicitor to establish that the breach did not cause the loss. The Court held that equitable compensation was appropriate, since, as Richardson J (as he then was) stated:[94]

> One can only conjecture as to what would have happened had she been fully informed and properly advised as to the risks in proceeding. That is not enough. It would surely have given her pause and she might well have decided not to proceed. The [solicitor] cannot show that his breach of duty was not a factor in her decision making. It follows that she is entitled to equitable relief.

Secondly, *Haira* v. *Burbury Mortgage & Savings Ltd (in receivership)*[95] also concerned a claim against a solicitor. The plaintiff borrowed money from a finance company, secured by a mortgage against her house, which money she invested, with encouragement from her brother, in a scheme. The solicitor acted for both parties in the loan and mortgage transaction. The scheme failed. At no time had the solicitor advised the plaintiff to seek independent advice, and the plaintiff brought an action for alleged breach of fiduciary duty. The Court of Appeal held that there was a breach of the fiduciary duty of loyalty, and then applied its earlier reasoning in the *Witten-Hannah* case in concluding that, once it had been shown that the conduct of the fiduciary in breach of his obligations was material to the transaction from which the loss resulted, the Court would not speculate on what might have happened had a different course been followed.

Thus far, the cases do not offer much that is new. They both dealt with compensation for loss caused by a breach of the core fiduciary duty of loyalty, which is very much towards the trust end of the continuum of equitable duties. It is not surprising therefore that a rather plaintiff-friendly approach was taken to the issue of causation of the loss.

The third case I mention largely to whet the appetite for the substantive judgment, which is due in May or June of this year. The case consists

93 [1995] 2 NZLR 141.

94 *Ibid.* 150. See also 157 (per McKay J).

95 [1995] 3 NZLR 396.

of a number of claims based on, *inter alia*, equitable accessorial and recipient liability, brought by the statutory managers of a number of failed companies, including Equiticorp companies, against the Crown in respect of a commercial contract for the sale of Crown-held shares in an Equiticorp company. The case took over a year to be heard, and the complexity of the facts and legal issues means that the High Court judgment has the potential to be of considerable interest to both equity and restitution lawyers. The sums involved may also mean that the case will be appealed 'all the way up'. Whether that will be as far as the Privy Council will depend, I suspect, on whether the abolition of the right of appeal covers only litigation not already commenced as at the date of abolition. In any event, of some interest to our discussion here, there have been two interlocutory judgments where issues of equitable remedies have been traversed. The first instance decision, *Equiticorp Industries Group Ltd* v. *The Crown (No 38)*[96] has been reported, and the Court of Appeal's decision in the same matter was handed down on 11 December 1995. It will undoubtedly also be reported in due course.[97] The Crown attempted to plead a defence to the plaintiffs' equitable claims. The claims related to monies transferred to the Crown by virtue of a contract now said to be illegal and/or in breach of fiduciary duties owed to the plaintiff companies by the transferor company. The Crown's defence argument centred on benefits alleged to have been received by the plaintiffs themselves in respect of an earlier contract with the Crown. The Crown suggested that in order for equitable discretions to be exercised meaningfully in respect of the equitable claims, and in particular in respect of the quantification of any monetary award issued in the plaintiffs' favour, the two separate contracts needed to be looked at as a single transaction, and furthermore that the separate identity of the companies involved should not be allowed to stand in the way of the court's assessment of the economic reality of what was going on. McKay J, speaking for the Court of Appeal in its rejection of the Crown's argument, rather cuttingly said: 'It is not enough for a party to cry "equity" and expect to be compensated. One must identify the relevant principle of equity on which a claim can be properly founded.'[98]

The last case to which I make reference is the advice of the Privy Council, on appeal from the New Zealand Court of Appeal, in *Rama* v. *Millar*, delivered by Lord Nicholls of Birkenhead on 30 November 1995.[99] The case concerned quantification of equitable compensation. The par-

96 (1995) 7 NZCLC 260.
97 Since reported at [1996] 1 NZLR 528.
98 *Ibid.* 537
99 Since reported at [1996] 1 NZLR 257.

ties were involved 'as partners, owing to each other corresponding fiduciary duties',[100] in a scheme to make profits by taking advantage of different rates of interest for loans of New Zealand dollars in different parts of the world. In respect of one complicated transaction, things began to fall apart and, in breach of fiduciary duty owed to the plaintiff, the defendant entered into a settlement with a bank whereby he gave up all claims he had against the bank in return for a payment of $1.5 million. This was over $105,000 less than was needed simply to break even. The most interesting feature of Lord Nicholls' advice is the manner in which he analysed closely the interests and duties of the parties in determining the extent of the plaintiff's loss attributable to the breach of duty, and hence the quantum of compensation payable. His Lordship stated[101]:

> This is not a case of a claim that a fiduciary should account for an unauthorised profit. The claim is for the loss Mr Millar is said to have sustained by Mr Rama's breach of fiduciary duty. This calls for consideration of what would have happened if Mr Rama had fulfilled his fiduciary duties and kept Mr Millar informed of the further negotiations he was having with the [bank] and told Mr Millar in advance of his wish to do a deal with the bank in return for $1.5 million. The problem in this case in that in two respects the interests of the partners were not the same. Both were interested in maximising the profits. But Mr Rama was financially exposed in a way Mr Millar was not. . . . So Mr Rama had a greater financial interest than Mr Millar in bringing the dispute to a speedy end.
>
> Secondly, Mr Rama had an interest in maintaining a good relationship with the [bank]. In his family and other dealings with the bank he received concessions and the like offered to a valuable customer. He stood to lose these if he pushed the [bank] too hard. Mr Rama made no secret of this at the time.

In light of the financial exposure of the defendant, Lord Nicholls held that the defendant was not in a position where he could not settle with the bank unless his partner agreed. 'Partners must act honestly and fairly towards each other, but this does not mean that one partner can require another to undertake a financial risk to which he has not agreed.'[102] Nonetheless, his Lordship indicated that the defendant, while entitled in settling with the bank to give weight to a reluctance to expose himself financially, could not prefer his other interests (standing as a good customer) over the interests of the partnership. Whether he had done so was a question of fact. In the result, their Lordships refused to uphold the quantum of compensation awarded in the Court of Appeal, since that sum was based on a perception that the duty breached by the defendant was stricter than it actually was. Their Lordships simply restored the much lesser sum awarded by the trial judge, on the basis, it appears, that

[100] *Ibid.* 259. [101] *Ibid.* 260–261. [102] *Ibid.* 261.

the defendant had made no attempt to challenge the award. That lack of challenge was a pity. It would have been interesting to see how, in the context of Lord Nicholls' assessment of the extent of the duty owed (and, one assumes, breached), their Lordships went about assessing the loss caused by the breach. The decision rendered is quite consistent with the theme promoted in this paper—a substantive interest-based approach to the cause of action, followed by application of the appropriateness of remedy principle.

9

A Comment

PAUL FINN

This short paper is somewhat in the nature of a postscript to the fiduciary-related ones that have preceded it. While I will refer to some matters raised in them, my purpose is not to provide a commentary on those papers. For the most part I will merely touch on a number of trends and shifts in the common law of the countries represented in this collection and I will suggest how these have impacted on what I will misleadingly call 'fiduciary law'.

The first matter I would note is two rediscoveries made in equity jurisprudence in the last two decades. I say rediscoveries because there is nothing novel about them. All that is surprising is that we forgot they were there. The first of these is the undoubted capacity possessed by equitable doctrine to impose protective or tutelary responsibilities for the protection of persons in positions of vulnerability or disadvantage. The second rediscovery was of equity's compensatory jurisdiction.

Before I look at each of these in turn I should say that because I am speaking in generalities I will not differentiate sharply between the common law countries of concern to us. I would note, though, that there are discernible differences in emphasis, ethos, and, I would add, technique between us. There has been a maturing in equity jurisprudence in Australia, New Zealand, and Canada in some number of fields which has not yet occurred in England. For this reason some of what I have to say is more a matter of contrast than of comparison for an English audience.

PROTECTING THE VULNERABLE

This is one of the grand themes of contemporary law and, I should say, not merely of equity. It is an interesting question why, in the face of over a century of reticence and restraint, the judges in a relatively short period of time have been so minded to impose a broadening range of obligations to care for others—to have regard to the interests of others—in our relationships and dealings with them. I simply pass by that engaging question, large and important though it is. My concerns are more prosaic.

The idea of neighbourhood—of good faith and fair dealing—is abroad in our law today. As Sir Robin Cooke has observed, legal obligation is being asked to match 'the now pervasive concepts of duty to a neighbour and the linking of power with obligation'.[1] The effects of this are particularly evident in developments both in tort law and in contract. There is no need to exemplify these, though I would note the fascination with the implied duty of good faith and fair dealing in contract now shared by some number of Commonwealth countries.[2]

In equity the predominant thrust has been to prevent the exploitation or manipulation of a person in a position of vulnerability. And so we see the revitalization of doctrines concerned with unconscionable dealing, mistake, estoppel, and the like.[3] This same protective idea is also reflected in the broadening of the ambit of fiduciary law beyond its traditional domains. This is evident, for example, in emerging case law on child sexual abuse by parents,[4] in the large body of very recent law (outside the United States) on the relationship of the State and indigenous peoples,[5] and in the re-emergence of the Lockean idea that the relationship of the State and the people is itself a fiduciary one.[6]

Having noted this effect in fiduciary law, I would add that for the most part there is nothing particularly fiduciary about much of the neighbourhood preoccupation. The usual purpose of the law here is not to impose a fiduciary-type obligation to act in another's interests, but rather to qualify self-interested action by duties to have regard in some way to the interest of those with whom we are dealing. This may require recommending that independent advice be taken; may oblige the disclosure of material information; may necessitate the correction of known errors; and so on.

Two effects on modern fiduciary law of this neighbourhood preoccupation should, perhaps, be marked. The first is that it has led more than

[1] *Nicholson* v. *Permakraft (NZ) Ltd* (1985) 3 ACLC 453, 459.

[2] See e.g., J. Beatson and D. Friedman, *Good Faith and Fault in Contract Law* (Clarendon Press, Oxford, 1995).

[3] Purely for reasons of convenience I here refer to major decisions in this area in my own country. Comparable developments in some instances more, in some less, pronounced can be found in the jurisprudence of New Zealand and Canada. See e.g., *Commercial Bank of Australia Ltd* v. *Amadio* (1983) 151 CLR 447 (unconscionable dealing); *Taylor* v. *Johnson* (1983) 151 CLR 422 (mistake); *Waltons Stores (Interstate) Ltd* v. *Maher* (1988) 164 CLR 387 (estoppel); *Baumgartner* v. *Baumgartner* (1987) 164 CLR 137 (constructive trusts).

[4] See e.g., *K. M.* v. *H. M.* (1993) 96 DLR (4th) 289.

[5] See e.g., *R.* v. *Sparrow* (1990) 70 DLR (4th) 385; *Te Runanga o Wharekauri Rekohu* v. *A. G.* [1993] 2 NZLR 301 and the cases referred to therein. There is a plethora of articles on this issue: see e.g., M. J. Bryant, 'Crown–Aboriginal Relationships in Canada: The Phantom of Fiduciary Law' (1993) 27 *UBC LR* 19; C. Hughes, 'The Fiduciary Obligations of the Crown to Aborigines' (1993) 16 *UNSW LJ* 70.

[6] See e.g., P. D. Finn (ed.), *Essays on Law and Government* (Law Book Co., Sydney, 1995), Vol I, Ch. 1.

occasionally to cases being forced into the fiduciary mould when no other convenient or available doctrine can be found to provide a desired solution—and cast in that mould notwithstanding that the standard of care (if I can so call it) being imposed is less than the loyalty standard imposed traditionally on fiduciaries.[7] I would note that there are quite some number of Canadian examples of this process. Throughout the common law world it has been particularly prevalent in cases involving banks—*Lloyds Bank Ltd* v. *Bundy*[8] is an obvious example—and, less commonly, the relationship of franchisor and franchisee.

The second effect is itself simply part of a more general issue we are having to confront in equity jurisprudence. That is the role to be given individual responsibility as a countervailing factor in this world of neighbourhood. The question here is one of the proper balance to be struck between my own responsibility to look after my own interests and my right to expect some level of responsibility for this to be exhibited by a person with whom I am in a relationship or dealing.[9] It is now becoming apparent that issues such as contributory negligence and *volenti* and questions of risk assumption and risk allocation are as important to equity as they are to tort and contract law.

In the fiduciary arena the issue of individual responsibility and its translation into notions such as contributory negligence is perhaps most apparent in case law involving advisers, and particularly financial advisers. In relation to this I would simply refer to decisions such as *Day* v. *Mead*[10] in New Zealand and, in Canada, to *Hodgkinson* v. *Simms*,[11] and note that in the latter the question of individual responsibility went beyond contributory negligence to the issue of whether or not a fiduciary relationship existed at all.

Let me turn now to the compensatory jurisdiction. We are all well aware of the extraordinary steps that were taken in the second half of the nineteenth century to prevent equitable doctrine from interfering with the serene flow of both contract and tort law. Such memorably unconvincing decisions as *Jorden* v. *Money*,[12] *Maddison* v. *Alderson*,[13] and *Derry* v. *Peek*[14] were in consequence to disfigure our law for over 100 years.

Now the citadels are under seige. The threat, for example, that estoppel poses for orthodox bargain theory in contract is well known and is being realized in Australia. The decision of the High Court in *Walton*

[7] This idea is explored at some length in P. D. Finn, 'The Fiduciary Principle' in T. G. Youdan (ed.), *Equity, Fiduciaries and Trusts* (Carswell, Toronto, 1989).

[8] [1975] QB 326.

[9] See e.g., *Austotel Pty. Ltd* v. *Franklins Selfserve Pty. Ltd* (1989) 16 NSWLR 582, esp. *per* Kirby P; see also on this theme P. D. Finn, 'Unconscionable Contract' (1994) 8 *Jo. Contract L* 37.

[10] [1987] 2 NZLR 443.

[11] (1994) 117 DLR (4th) 161.

[12] (1854) 5 HLC 185.

[13] (1883) 8 App. Cas. 467.

[14] (1889) 14 App. Cas. 337.

Stores (Interstate) Ltd v. *Maher*[15] is the epitome of this in contemporary Commonwealth jurisprudence. Much more significant, though, is the collision which is now occurring with tort law. In my view, we are witnessing the emergence of what can properly be characterized as a new body of economic tort law. The compensatory jurisdiction is, after all, usually invoked for the purpose of providing recompense for economic loss.

It is orthodox that compensation can be awarded for breaches of fiduciary duty, of confidence, and of trustees' and directors' duties of care. Awards of damages or pecuniary amounts are being made in estoppel cases, at least in Australia.[16] More importantly there is the question whether damages can be awarded as adjuncts to the unconscionability-based doctrines—unconscionable dealing, misrepresentation, and so on. In Canada this step has been taken.[17] I would have to say that the objection based on historical practice that is raised against this last development is one that I have difficulty in accepting. There is, furthermore, everything to be said for arming courts with that amplitude of remedy advocated in the *Aquaculture* case to which Professor Rickett refers.

It doubtless is the case that with this rediscovery of compensation and with its interaction with tort and contract law we are confronted with a plethora of issues. Here I merely note a few. Is the award of compensation to be a discretionary matter or is it to be a matter of election by the plaintiff, or will different rules apply in the case of different doctrines?[18] What rules should govern the assessment of damages?[19] It is obvious, for example, that in cases of breach of confidence the one doctrine is capable of applying to a very diverse range of circumstances and of protecting an equally diverse range of interests. This in turn raises the question whether a uniform approach to assessment can be taken even in relation to the same doctrine. Relatedly, when do you use a common law analogue in assessment and when do you not? To continue the breach of confidence example, in cases where personal confidences have been violated, is the appropriate analogy with the law of defamation?[20] Indeed is there a danger of equity being used to subvert defamation? And then there are those difficult questions about when plaintiffs should be able

[15] N. 3 above.

[16] *Commonwealth of Australia* v. *Verwayen* (1990) 170 CLR 394.

[17] See e.g., *Dusik* v. *Newton* (1985) 62 BCLR 1.

[18] Compare *Seager* v. *Copydex Ltd* [1967] 1 WLR 923, and *Warman International Ltd* v. *Dwyer* (1995) 128 ALR 201.

[19] See e.g., *Canson Enterprises Ltd* v. *Broughton & Co.* (1991) 85 DLR (4th) 129.

[20] See e.g., *Stephens* v. *Avery* [1988] 2 All ER 477 where the relief claimed was damages for breach of confidences concerning a personal friendship.

to avail themselves of presumptions that fiduciary law can offer when seeking to make out a compensatory claim.[21]

There is a final matter which bears on fiduciary law to which I would like to advert briefly. It is what Dr Austin calls the content of fiduciary obligation. Whether that content is limited merely to that of loyalty, or whether it extends to issues of care and of disclosure of information is a large matter. I have elsewhere written at some length on this matter.[22] Simply to illustrate the point let me take the example of the doctor–patient relationship.

It is not open to question that this relationship is capable of being a fiduciary one.[23] It has, for example, been held that the fiduciary character of the relationship can provide justification for the informed-consent doctrine and hence for damages claims for failure of a doctor to make full disclosure to a patient before undertaking treatment of the patient.[24] It equally has been used to justify the provision of patient access to his or her own medical records.[25] Both of these outcomes may appear positively desirable. The informed-consent use of fiduciary law, for example, has arisen in cases where there is a need to get under statutes of limitation. But neither case seems to raise any loyalty issue as that notion is traditionally conceived. The question I pose is whether it is appropriate to recast what were once accepted orthodoxies simply to produce desirable outcomes? Is it not more appropriate, for example, to accept that some relationships in their very nature give rise to *sui generis* obligations? In my view the doctor–patient relationship is one of these. But then we live in times where grand generalizations are impatient with the survival of innominate duties. This, perhaps, explains our preparedness to give new and in my view distorting content to the obligation of a fiduciary.

[21] The most problematic of these is that expounded by the Judicial Committee in *Brikenden* v. *London Loan & Savings Co.* [1934] 3 DLR 465.

[22] See n. 7 above.

[23] See e.g., *Norberg* v. *Wynrib* (1992) 92 DLR (4th) 449.

[24] See e.g., *Krueger* v. *San Francisco Forty Niners,* 234 Cal. Rep. 579.

[25] See *McInerney* v. *MacDonald* (1992) 93 DLR (4th) 415; cf *Breen* v. *Williams* (1994) 35 NSWLR 522, now on appeal to HC of A.

10

The Liberalising Nature of Remedies for Breach of Trust

A. J. OAKLEY

During the last thirty years a number of types of disposition which would not previously have given rise to a relationship of trustee and beneficiary have been held to have created valid trusts. Thus trust powers whose beneficiaries are not all capable of ascertainment,[1] and purpose trusts which are directly or indirectly for the benefit of individuals,[2] have both for the first time been held to be valid express trusts. Payments made for specific purposes have for the first time been held to be capable of giving rise to trusts, variously classified as express, resulting, and constructive,[3] in favour of the payer until the payee has carried out the purpose in question.[4] Bribes received by fiduciaries have for the first time been held

[1] Until 1970 such trust powers were void by virtue of the decision of the CA in *IRC* v. *Broadway Cottages Trust* [1955] Ch. 20 that the whole range of objects available for selection had to be ascertained or be capable of ascertainment. However in *McPhail* v. *Doulton* [1971] AC 424 the majority of the HL held that such trust powers are valid if it can be said of 'any given postulant' that he is or is not a member of the class of potential beneficiaries. This test, originally formulated for mere powers by Harman J in *Re Gestetner Settlement* [1953] Ch. 673 and confirmed definitively as applicable to such powers in *Re Gulbenkian's Settlement* [1970] AC 508, is therefore now applicable to discretionary trusts and almost certainly also to powers in the nature of a trust (see Parker and Mellows, *The Modern Law of Trusts* (6th edn., 1994), 103–4; for a contrary view as to the applicability of the test to powers in the nature of a trust, see Hanbury and Martin, *Modern Equity* (14th edn., 1993), 111.

[2] Until 1968 it was not possible to create a trust for a social experiment falling outside the confines of the law of charity if it was defined in terms of purposes, no matter how certain those purposes might be, unless they fell within the categories of anomalous cases listed in *Re Endacott* [1960] Ch. 232. However, in *Re Denley's Trust Deed* [1969] 1 Ch. 373 Goff J held that this rule was confined to purpose trusts which were 'abstract or impersonal' so that a trust, even though expressed as a purpose, which directly or indirectly was for the benefit of an individual or individuals is valid, provided that the individuals were ascertainable and the trust was not otherwise void for uncertainty. This decision was the subject of some criticism from commentators; however, it was followed by Oliver J in *Re Lipinski's Will Trusts* [1976] Ch. 235 and was accepted as correct by Megarry VC in *Re Northern Developments (Holdings)* (1978) unreported (see (1985) 101 *LQR* 280) but in *Re Grant's Will Trusts* [1980] 1 WLR 361 Vinelott J expressed the view that *Re Denley's Trust Deed* did not involve a purpose trust at all but rather a discretionary trust. These four first instance decisions urgently require a review by the CA.

[3] See Sir Peter Millett, pre-judicially: (1985) 101 *LQR* 269 and C. E. F. Rickett, (1991) 107 *LQR* 608 and in Waters (ed.), *Equity, Fiduciaries and Trusts 1993* (1993) 325.

[4] The first case of this type was *Barclays Bank* v. *Quistclose Investments* [1970] AC 567 and for this reason such trusts are often known as '*Quistclose* Trusts'; in this case the

to be subject to constructive trusts in favour of the person to whom the fiduciary duty is owed.[5] It has also been accepted that, despite the rejection of the 'new model'[6] constructive trust pioneered by Lord Denning MR in the years immediately before and after 1970,[7] 'there is a good arguable case' for the existence of a 'remedial constructive trust'.[8] All these developments, together with the recently consolidated distinction between fiduciary and non-fiduciary donees of mere powers,[9] which has

payment in question was made to enable a company to pay a dividend on its shares and, when the company went into liquidation before the dividend had been paid, the payer was held to be beneficially entitled under a trust of the payment, which had been segregated from the company's other assets. This decision was applied in *Re EVTR* [1987] BCLC 647 where part of the funds advanced had indeed been used for the specific purpose in question, the court holding that the payer was entitled to recover what was left, and in *Carreras Rothmans* v. *Freeman Matthews Treasure* [1985] Ch. 207 where the funds, although advanced for a specific purpose, were paid not, as in the two other cases, by way of loan but rather in satisfaction of a contractual debt.

[5] This was in *A.G. for Hong Kong* v. *Reid* [1993] 3 WLR 1143 (a decision of the PC on appeal from the CA of New Zealand). Until this decision which, although not formally binding on English courts, will undoubtedly be followed, fiduciaries were regarded merely as debtors of their principals in respect of the sum received; this was in accordance with the much criticized decision of the CA in *Lister & Co.* v. *Stubbs* (1890) 45 Ch. D. 1, which the PC held to have been wrongly decided (see Sir Peter Millett, extra-judicially, [1993] *Restitution Law Review* 7, on which the PC expressly relied, M. Cope in Cope (ed.), *Equity Issues and Trusts* (1995), 91, and [1994] *CLJ 31.*

[6] This expression was coined by Lord Denning MR in *Eves* v. *Eves* [1975] 1 WLR 1338.

[7] At that time, a number of decisions emanating from the CA suggested that a constructive trust 'is a trust imposed by law whenever justice and good conscience require it . . . it is an equitable remedy by which the court can enable an aggrieved party to obtain restitution' (*Hussey* v. *Palmer* [1972] 1 WLR 1286 at 1290)—see (1973) 26 *Current Legal Problems* 17. However, subsequent decisions have rejected the approach manifested in this series of cases and English law seems for the moment to have reverted to its traditional attitude towards the constructive trust, an attitude which has perhaps been most accurately described by the statement that in England 'the constructive trust continues to be seen as an institutional obligation attaching to property in certain specified circumstances' (D. W. M. Waters in Goldstein (ed.), *Equity and Contemporary Legal Developments* (1992) 457).

[8] This was accepted by the CA in *Metall und Rohstoff AG* v. *Donaldson Lufkin & Jenrette* [1989] 3 WLR 563 at 621 and may well indicate the possibility of a move towards a more remedial approach, but this is likely to be of a much more limited nature than the attempt made in the years immediately before and after 1970 to convert the constructive trust into a general equitable remedy capable of doing justice in any individual case.

[9] This distinction is not new but its earlier enunciations did not exactly commend themselves to Lord Upjohn who, as recently as 1969, felt able in *Re Gulbenkian's Settlement Trusts*, n. 1 above, 521, 524–5 to deny that the donees of mere powers of appointment ever owed any duties to the objects of those powers. However, some remarks of Lord Wilberforce in *McPhail* v. *Doulton*, n. 1 above, 449 set the scene for the authoritative statement of the distinction by Megarry VC in *Re Hay's Settlement Trusts* [1982] 1 WLR 202 at 209–10, which established a clear distinction between a mere power held by the trustees of the property in question (or other persons classified as a fiduciary donee), who 'must "take such a survey of the range of objects or possible beneficiaries" as will enable him to carry out his fiduciary duty', and a mere power held by any one else, who is not obliged to do anything at all. Subsequently in *Mettoy Pension Trustees* v. *Evans* [1990] 1 WLR 1587 Warner J held that all the remedies available to the court to enforce discretionary trusts were also available in the case of mere powers held by fiduciary donees.

already been discussed by Sir Robert Walker at this Conference, have given rise to the possibility of the imposition of remedies for breach of trust in a number of situations where fiduciary obligations would not previously have been held to exist. This has not, until very recently, produced any parallel discussion of the nature of remedies for breach of trust and the measure of recovery available to the victims of breaches of trust; the courts have generally continued to apply principles based on the nineteenth century rules developed in the context of family settlements, rules which have become increasingly inappropriate as trusts have increasingly been utilized for commercial and social purposes.[10] However, opportunities have now arisen for a number of these principles to be discussed at the highest level. Issues which have been the subject of recent judicial consideration include: the extent to which liability for breach of trust extends beyond whatever loss is suffered by the beneficiaries;[11] the extent to which fiduciary relationships will be held to arise as a result of commercial relationships;[12] the extent to which fiduciaries have to surrender benefits which, although obtained through their fiduciary position, were not made at the expense of their principals[13] and the extent to which the victims of breaches of trust can recover compensation from those who have been accessories to the breach of trust in question.[14] It is these areas of the law concerning remedies for breach of trust which have arguably now been liberalised; they, together with other analogous areas which would benefit from similar treatment, form the subject matter of this paper.

THE RECOVERY OF LOSSES CAUSED BY BREACHES OF TRUST

Where a trust has suffered a loss as the result of a breach of trust, there has never been any doubt that the 'obligation of a defaulting trustee is

[10] To the well known commercial purpose of minimizing the incidence of taxation and the commercial and social purposes of providing pensions for retired employees and their dependants and of facilitating investment through unit trusts and investments trusts must now be added the social purpose of protecting the environment. In other jurisdictions the trust has developed a role in environmental protection law both in the United States of America under the so-called 'public trust doctrine' and, more importantly, in Canada by virtue of 'the "trusteed" environmental fund' which guarantees adequate financing for post-closure land reclamation following the termination of some environmentally harmful activity (see D. W. M. Waters, n. 7 above, 383).

[11] This was considered by the HL in *Target Holdings* v. *Redferns* [1995] 3 WLR 352.

[12] This was considered by the PC on an appeal from the CA of New Zealand in *In Re Goldcorp Exchange* [1995] 1 AC 74.

[13] This was considered by the High Ct. of Australia (on appeal from the CA of Queensland) in *Warman International* v. *Dwyer* (1995) 128 ALR 201.

[14] This was considered by the PC on appeal from the CA of Brunei Darussalam in *Royal Brunei Airlines* v. *Tan* [1995] 3 WLR 352.

essentially one of effecting restitution to the estate. The obligation is of a personal character and its extent is not to be limited by common law principles governing the remoteness of damage'.[15] 'The remedy afforded to the beneficiary by equity is compensation in the form of restitution of that which has been lost to the trust estate, not damages'.[16] In *Clough* v. *Bond*[17] Lord Cottenham LC held, summarising the earlier authorities, that if

> any part of the property be invested by any such [trustees] in funds or upon securities not authorised, or be put within the control of persons who ought not to be entrusted with it, and a loss be thereby eventually sustained, such [trustees] will be liable to make it good, however unexpected the result, however little likely to arise from the course adopted, and however free such conduct may have been from any improper motive.

It is thus apparent that in such circumstances the trustees are not under any immediate liability to reconstitute the trust fund but only to make good whatever loss is eventually suffered.[18] Is this also the case when the trustees have made a wrongful disposal of trust property, causing an immediate loss to the trust, or does such a wrongful disposal place the trustees under a duty to reconstitute the trust fund immediately? The House of Lords has recently had to consider this question, which arose in connection with 'the novel point'[19] whether the trustees are 'liable to compensate the beneficiary not only for losses caused by the breach but also for losses which the beneficiary would, in any event, have suffered even if there had been no such breach'.[20]

In *Target Holdings* v. *Redferns*,[21] the plaintiff finance company seems to have been a victim of mortgage fraud.[22] On the strength of valuations prepared by the second defendants, a firm of estate agents which was in insolvent liquidation and took no part in the proceedings,[23] it had agreed

[15] Street J in *Re Dawson decd.* [1966] 2 NSWR 211 at 214 (Sup. Ct. of NSW).

[16] Peter Gibson LJ in *Target Holdings* v. *Redferns*, [1994] 1 WLR 1089 at 1101, citing Viscount Haldane LC in *Nocton* v. *Lord Ashburton* [1914] AC 932 at 952 and *Bartlett* v. *Barclays Bank Trust Co. (Nos. 1 and 2)* [1980] Ch. 515 at 543.

[17] (1838) 3 My. & Cr. 490 at 496–7.

[18] Apart from *Clough* v. *Bond* (1838) 3 My. & Cr. 490, see also *Nestlé* v. *National Westminster Bank* [1993] 1 WLR 1260, *Canson Enterprises* v. *Boughton & Co.* (1991) 85 DLR (4th) 129 (Sup. Ct. of Canada), *per* LaForest J (speaking for the majority) at 146, *per* McLachlin J (speaking for the minority) at 160.

[19] Lord Browne-Wilkinson in *Target Holdings* v. *Redferns*, n. 11 above, at 354.

[20] *Ibid.*

[21] N. 11 above.

[22] The judges were extremely careful not to say that there *had* been a mortgage fraud. Lord Browne-Wilkinson merely said (n. 11 above, at 356) that the plaintiff 'believes itself to have been the victim of a fraud' while Ralph Gibson LJ stated (n. 16 above, at 1092) that '[the plaintiff's] case is that . . . a mortgage fraud was carried out'.

[23] The plaintiff obtained judgment for negligence in default of appearance against the second defendant, from whom '[l]ittle, if anything, will be recovered' (n. 16 above, at 1092, *per* Ralph Gibson LJ).

to lend £1,706,000 to a third party, Crowngate Developments, on the security of two properties which were apparently being purchased for £2,000,000. In fact, unknown to the plaintiff, the properties were being acquired for £775,000 by a Jersey company formed specifically for the purpose,[24] which was to sell the properties on for £1,250,000 to one of Crowngate Developments' minority shareholders, which was in turn to sell them to Crowngate Developments for the £2,000,000. The first defendants, a firm of solicitors who were ostensibly acting in the normal way both for Crowngate Developments and for the plaintiff were necessarily aware of all the relevant facts since they themselves had arranged for the incorporation of the Jersey company. They duly received £1,525,000 of the mortgage advance,[25] which they were obviously holding on bare trust for the plaintiff with authority to release it to Crowngate Developments only upon receipt of the duly executed land transfers and mortgages of the properties. However, the day before the day on which contracts were exchanged (when the vendor also immediately completed those contracts by executing the land transfers), the solicitors released £1,250,000 of the plaintiff's funds to the Jersey company; subsequently, before the land transfers and the mortgages had been executed by Crowngate Developments, they released a further £240,000 to the minority shareholder.[26] When all the documents were finally executed, all the land transfers bore the date on which the first transfers had been executed by the vendor, while the mortgages bore a date exactly one month later.[27] Crowngate Developments subsequently went into insolvent liquidation and the plaintiff sold the properties as mortgagee for only £500,000.[28]

The plaintiff claimed from the solicitors the reconstitution of the fund of £1,525,000 paid away in breach of trust[29] and sought summary judg-

[24] It may be that the Jersey company was incorporated for the benefit of those interested in the vendor company rather than for the benefit of those interested in Crowngate Developments. When £1,250,000 was transferred to the Jersey company (in fact out of the plaintiff's advance but doubtless as a notional payment of the purchase moneys due from the minority shareholder), the balance which remained after payment of the £775,000 to the vendor was paid to a number of persons who appeared either to be the vendor's directors or to have no obvious connection whatever with the transaction.

[25] The balance was used to pay the premiums on certain insurance policies.

[26] They then compounded this breach of trust by sending a letter bearing the date on which the vendor had executed the transfers informing the plaintiff, quite untruthfully, that the purchases and the mortgages had been completed on that day. This was obviously in order to prevent the plaintiff from exercising the right which it undoubtedly had to withdraw its funds at any time before actual completion of the purchase.

[27] The insertion of this subsequent date (one month after the date on which the mortgages had supposedly been executed according to the letter from the solicitors to the plaintiff) was probably an oversight and must presumably have been the means by which the plaintiff eventually discovered what had actually happened.

[28] The loss suffered by the plaintiff was compounded by the general fall in land values which had occurred since the date of the transaction.

[29] It also sought damages for negligence and breach of contract and/or duty.

ment under RSC Order 14.[30] The solicitors did not dispute their breach of trust but contended that their liability for this breach was nil since the plaintiff had obtained, albeit late, the legal charges in return for which they were entitled to release the money. At first instance Warner J gave leave to defend conditional on the payment of £1,000,000[31] (effectively the entire amount paid away by the solicitors less the proceeds of sale of the properties), stating that he was 'not against' the plaintiff's contention that a defaulting trustee's obligation to restore the trust fund cannot be limited by the application of principles relating to the causation of damage.[32] The solicitors appealed, seeking unconditional leave to defend, and the plaintiff cross-appealed, seeking summary judgment for the full amount paid away in breach of trust with interest thereon. The Court of Appeal[33] unanimously dismissed the appeal[34] but, by a majority, allowed the cross-appeal. Peter Gibson LJ, with whom Hirst LJ agreed, held that there is a distinction between cases in which a breach of trust consisted of some failure in the administration of the trust, where the trustees are only liable to make good whatever loss is eventually suffered, and cases where 'a trustee or other fiduciary in breach of trust disposes of trust property to a stranger'. In the latter case, that trustee 'comes under an immediate duty to make restitution';[35] 'the cause of action is constituted simply by the payment away of [the plaintiff's] moneys in breach of trust and the loss is quantified in the amount of those moneys, subject to [the plaintiff] giving credit for the realisation of the security it received'.[36] Summary judgment was therefore entered in favour of the

[30] Summary judgment was also sought unsuccessfully in respect of the claims for damages.

[31] Either to be brought into court or to be paid to the plaintiff if the latter provided a bank guarantee for its repayment in the event that the court subsequently so ordered.

[32] The plaintiff also contended that, had the solicitors not released the sums in question before obtaining the legal charges the funds would never have been released at all because the vendor would have withdrawn from the transaction—there was no obvious source of funds with which the purchase by the Jersey company could have been completed other than those so released. On appeal, the solicitors contended that in so far as Warner J had relied on this contention he had not been entitled to do so since the question whether the vendor would have withdrawn was a triable issue. This argument was accepted by the CA (n. 16 above, at 1104, *per* Peter Gibson LJ, with whom Hirst LJ agreed, and at 1100, *per* Ralph Gibson LJ—less specifically) and this conclusion was accepted by the plaintiff in the HL (see n. 12 above, at 358, *per* Lord Browne-Wilkinson).

[33] N. 16 above.

[34] Ralph Gibson LJ, *ibid.* 1100, dismissed the appeal on the ground that any arguable defence which the solicitors had was of such an uncertain nature that only conditional leave to defend should be given (he had to consider this point specifically since he also dismissed the cross-appeal); the majority, having allowed the cross-appeal and ordered summary judgment, necessarily had to dismiss the appeal.

[35] *Ibid.* 1104 citing *Alliance & Leicester Building Society* v. *Edgestop*, 18 Jan. 1991, unreported, and *Bishopsgate Investment Management* v. *Maxwell* [1993] BCLC 120.

[36] N. 16 above, at 1104.

plaintiff for the sum of £1,490,000[37] with interest thereon less the net proceeds of the sale of the properties. Ralph Gibson LJ dissented.[38] The solicitors appealed to the House of Lords, which restored the order of Warner J.[39]

Lord Browne-Wilkinson, with whose speech the other members of the House[40] agreed, emphasised that the breach of trust left the plaintiff

> in exactly the same position as it would have been if there had been no such breach; [the plaintiff] advanced the same amount of money, obtained the same security and received the same amount on the realisation of that security. In any ordinary use of words, the breach of trust by [the solicitors] cannot be said to have caused the actual loss ultimately suffered by [the plaintiff] unless it can be shown that, but for the breach of trust, the transaction would not have gone through,[41]

something which had to be assumed not to be the case.[42] Consequently, the decision of the Court of Appeal could only be maintained on the basis that 'even if there is no causal link between the breach of trust and the actual loss eventually suffered by [the plaintiff] (i.e. the sum advanced less the sum recovered) the trustee in breach is liable to bear (at least in part) the loss suffered by [the plaintiff]'.[43] His Lordship observed that '[i]f the law as stated by the Court of Appeal is correct, it applies to cases where the breach of trust involves no suspicion of fraud or negligence', giving as an example a transfer to the borrower one day before

[37] The aggregate of the two sums paid away (£1,250,000 and £240,000). The remaining £35,000 of the advance of £1,525,000 had been properly expended on stamp duty and fees.

[38] His lordship agreed with Warner J that the solicitors should have conditional leave to defend, stating at n. 16 above, 1099–1100 that '[i]n considering whether it is open to a defendant, who has committed a breach of trust by paying away without authority money held by him on trust, to contend that the loss caused by his loss would have happened if there had been no breach of trust, it is necessary for the court to examine the nature of the relationship between the plaintiff and the defendant out of which the fiduciary duty arises. If it appears just to the court, having regard to that relationship, and its purpose, and the obligations of the parties within it, and the way in which the parties would have behaved, for the court to regard the breach as having caused no loss to the plaintiff, because the loss would have happened if there had been no breach, then the court can and must so hold.'

[39] N. 11 above. Conditional, rather than unconditional, leave was given because of the high probability that at trial the plaintiff would succeed in its contention that, had the solicitors not released the funds before obtaining the legal charges, the vendors would have withdrawn from the transaction because of the lack of any other obvious funds with which the purchase by the Jersey company could have been completed; Lord Browne-Wilkinson said (at 366–7) that the suspicion that this was the case was not 'dissipated' by the letter from the solicitors untruthfully informing the plaintiff that the purchase and the charges had been completed.

[40] Lord Keith of Kinkel, Lord Ackner, Lord Jauncey of Tullichettle, and Lord Lloyd of Berwick.

[41] N. 11 above, at 358.

[42] Because it was common ground before the House that whether or not this was the case was a triable issue.

[43] N. 11 above, at 358.

the execution of the mortgage due to an honest and non-negligent error such as a computer failure, saying that '[t]o my mind in the case of an unimpeachable transaction this would be an unjust and surprising conclusion'.[44] To describe a hypothetical breach of trust as 'unimpeachable' when the issue before the House was whether or not it would give rise to any liability seems somewhat circular. Lord Browne-Wilkinson frankly admitted that he approached 'the consideration of the relevant rules of equity with a strong predisposition against' the conclusion reached by the Court of Appeal since this did not accord with the principle that 'a defendant is only liable for the consequences of the legal wrong he has done to the plaintiff and to make good the damage caused by such wrong. He is not responsible for damage not caused by his wrong or to pay by way of compensation more than the loss suffered from such wrong.'[45] Such a principle is contrary not only to the conclusion reached by the majority of the Court of Appeal but also to virtually all the authorities which govern fiduciaries' liability for breach of their duty of loyalty; however, given the context in which Lord Browne-Wilkinson was speaking, he presumably intended to apply this principle only to liability for making good breaches of trust which produce a loss for the beneficiaries and not to breaches of trust which produce only a profit for the trustees.

Lord Browne-Wilkinson then[46] isolated two separate lines of reasoning within the arguments in favour of the conclusion reached by the Court of Appeal: first, an argument that the plaintiff was 'now (i.e. at the date of judgment) entitled to have the "trust fund" restored by an order that [the solicitors] reconstitute the trust fund by paying back into client account the moneys paid away in breach of trust'; secondly,

> the argument accepted by the majority of the Court of Appeal that, because immediately after the moneys were paid away by [the solicitors] in breach of trust there was an immediate right to have the 'trust fund' reconstituted, there was then an immediate loss to the 'trust fund' for which loss [the solicitors] are now liable to compensate [the plaintiff] direct.

He commented[47] that it was necessary to establish the precise rights of the beneficiary in question before any question arose as to the extent and quantification of his compensation and emphasised that the right to have the trust reconstituted only arises automatically where, as in the

[44] N. 11 above, at 358–9.

[45] *Ibid.* 359. Lord Browne-Wilkinson had already observed that '[a]t common law there are two principles fundamental to the award of damages. First, that the defendant's wrongful act must cause the damage complained of. Second, that the plaintiff is to be put "in the same position as he would have been in if he had not sustained the wrong for which he is now getting his compensation or reparation" '. He added that 'those two principles are applicable as much in equity as at common law', even though 'in many ways equity approaches liability for making good a breach of trust from a different starting point'.

[46] *Ibid.* 359. [47] *Ibid.* 360.

case of a traditional trust for persons by way of succession, the trust is ongoing;[48] where, on the other hand, the beneficiary is or has become absolutely entitled, the court will normally order the payment of compensation directly to him rather than the reconstitution of the trust property.[49]

Given that the plaintiff had at all times been absolutely entitled to the funds in question under a bare trust, this conclusion would obviously have made the first argument, that the plaintiff was entitled as at the date of judgment to have the trust fund reconstituted, very doubtful even if the trust in question had been a traditional trust. However, Lord Browne-Wilkinson rejected the applicability of rules developed in the context of traditional trusts to a bare trust which had arisen as 'but one incident of a wider commercial transaction involving agency'. While funds held by solicitors on client account were undoubtedly trust funds and could be the subject matter of an order for restoration if wrongfully paid away prior to the completion of the underlying commercial transaction, 'to import into such a trust an obligation to restore the trust fund once the transaction had been completed would be entirely artificial'. He therefore held that 'once a conveyancing transaction has been completed the client has no right to have the solicitor's client account reconstituted as a "trust fund" '.[50]

In the course of so disposing of the first argument in favour of the conclusion reached by the Court of Appeal, Lord Browne-Wilkinson made the following important statement of general principle:[51]

> But in my judgment it is in any event wrong to lift wholesale the detailed rules developed in the context of traditional trusts and then seek to apply them to trusts of quite a different kind. In the modern world the trust has become a valuable device in commercial and financial dealings. The fundamental principles of equity apply as much to such trusts as they do to the traditional trusts in

[48] *Ibid.* His lordship held that in such circumstances 'a trustee in breach of trust must restore or pay to the trust estate either the assets which have been lost to the estate by reason of the breach or compensation for such loss' (citing *Nocton* v. *Lord Ashburton*, n. 17 above, *Caffrey* v. *Darby* (1801) 6 Ves. 488 and *Clough* v. *Bond* (1838) 3 M & C 490) and added that this was the case even where the immediate cause of the loss had been the dishonesty or failure of a third party provided that there was some causal connection between the breach of trust and the loss and that, but for the breach, the loss would not have occurred (citing Underhill and Hayton, *Law of Trusts & Trustees* (14th edn., 1987), 734–6 (see now 15th edn., 1995, 833–6); *In re Dawson, decd.*, n. 15 above (Sup. Ct. of NSW); *Bartlett* v. *Barclays Bank Trust Co. (Nos 1 and 2)*, n. 16 above; *In re Miller's Deed Trusts* (1978) 75 LSG 454; and *Nestlé* v. *National Westminster Bank*, n. 18 above). Virtually all these authorities had also been relied on by the majority of the CA.

[49] Thus in *Bartlett* v. *Barclays Bank Trust Co. (Nos 1 and 2)*, n. 16 above, the compensation payable for breach of trust, although quantified by reference to what the fund would have been but for the breach of trust, was payable directly to those beneficiaries who were by then absolutely entitled in possession.

[50] N. 11 above, at 362. [51] *Ibid.*

relation to which those principles were originally formulated. But in my judgment it is important, if the trust is not to be rendered commercially useless, to distinguish between the basic principles of trust law and those specialist rules developed in relation to traditional trusts which are applicable only to such trusts and the rationale of which has no application to trusts of quite a different kind.

These sentiments had been manifested in slightly earlier decisions in relation to specific fiduciary duties. Thus in *Kelly* v. *Cooper*[52] the Privy Council stated that, despite the fact that it is normally a breach of an agent's duty to act for competing principals, it is the business of estate agents to act for numerous principals and to acquire information which is confidential to each principal. The Board consequently held[53] that '[i]t cannot be sensibly suggested that an estate agent is contractually bound to disclose to any one of his principals information which is confidential to another of his principals'; therefore 'the scope of the fiduciary duties owed by the [estate agents] to [their principal] (and in particular the alleged duty not to put themselves in a position where their duty and their interest conflicted) are to be defined by the terms of the contract of agency'.[54] The Board added[55] that '[t]he position as to confidentiality is even clearer in the case of stockbrokers who cannot be contractually bound to disclose to their private clients inside information disclosed to the brokers in confidence by a company for which they also act' and so their fiduciary duties are equally to be defined by the terms of their contract. In the same sort of way in *Clark Boyce* v. *Mouat*[56] the Privy Council held that

When a client in full command of his faculties and apparently aware of what he is doing seeks the assistance of a solicitor in the carrying out of a particular

[52] [1993] AC 205, [1992] 3 WLR 936 (on appeal from the CA of Bermuda). The case concerned a purchase by the American billionaire and former Presidential Candidate Mr Ross Perot of two adjoining houses which had effective, if not exclusive, use of a common beach. Both had been marketed by the same estate agents and the plaintiff, the vendor of the second to be sold, claimed that the estate agents should have informed him of the fact that Mr Perot had already agreed to purchase the other house since this obviously made the second house much more valuable to him and so might have affected the course of the negotiations. The PC rejected the plaintiff's claim that the estate agents were not only not entitled to their commission but were also liable in damages to him for breach of contract and fiduciary duty.

[53] [1992] 3 WLR 936 at 941–2.

[54] *Ibid.* 942.

[55] *Ibid.*

[56] [1994] 1 AC 428, [1993] 3 WLR 1021 (on appeal from the CA of New Zealand). The plaintiff agreed to mortgage her house to secure a loan to her son, who subsequently defaulted. The son's own solicitor having declined to act in the matter, the defendant firm agreed to act for both mother and son; the nature of the transaction and the risk which she was running was fully explained to the mother who declined three invitations to take independent legal advice. The PC dismissed her subsequent claim for damages for breach of contract, negligence, and breach of fiduciary duty.

transaction, that solicitor is under no duty whether before or after accepting instructions to go beyond those instructions by proffering unsought advice on the wisdom of the transaction.

However, it has never before been stated as a general principle that the specialist rules developed in relation to traditional trusts are not applicable to trusts of a different kind; nor has such a principle, whether specific or general, been applied in order to limit the remedies available for an admitted breach of fiduciary duty rather than in order to decide whether or not there has been a breach of fiduciary duty in the first place. As will be shown later on,[57] the effect of the principle enunciated by Lord Browne-Wilkinson is capable of extending far outside the specific area which his lordship was actually considering and, in particular, may well have a considerable effect upon the remedies available against fiduciaries who have made a profit out of a breach of their duty of loyalty.

Lord Browne-Wilkinson then[58] turned his attention to the second argument in favour of the conclusion reached by the Court of Appeal, namely the argument actually accepted by the majority of that court that when the solicitors paid away the funds in breach of trust the plaintiff had an immediate right to have them replaced and so there was then an immediate loss for which the solicitors were still liable to compensate the plaintiff. As his lordship said,[59] 'in the view of the Court of Appeal one "stops the clock" at the date the moneys are paid away: events which occur between the date of breach and the date of trial are irrelevant in assessing the loss suffered by reason of the breach'. Indeed, if this argument is pushed to its logical conclusion, there seems no obvious reason why the Court of Appeal should have ordered the plaintiff to give credit for the net proceeds of sale of the properties; after all, the sale necessarily occurred between the date of breach and the date of trial. In this connection Peter Gibson LJ had merely said[60] that '[t]he elastic remedies of equity are sufficiently flexible to require a beneficiary who subsequent to the loss receives a benefit from the trustee's actions to give credit for that benefit' and Lord Browne-Wilkinson[61] merely repeated this observation without further comment. The fact that the Court of Appeal needed to have recourse to such an argument in order to prevent the principle which it was applying from producing a result which would have been patently absurd must in itself cast some doubt on the validity of the principle in question. Lord Browne-Wilkinson[62] criticised the distinction advocated by the Court of Appeal between cases in which a breach of trust consisted of some failure in the administration of the trust and cases where a trustee disposes of trust property to a stranger, holding:[63]

[57] Text to n. 101 ff. below.
[58] N. 11 above, at 359.
[59] *Ibid.* 363.
[60] N. 16 above, at 1104.
[61] N. 11 above, at 357–8.
[62] *Ibid.* 363.
[63] *Ibid.*

But the fact that there is an accrued cause of action as soon as the breach is committed does not in my judgment mean that the quantum of the compensation is ultimately fixed as at the date when the breach occurred. The quantum is fixed at the date of judgment at which date, according to the circumstances then pertaining, the compensation is assessed at the figure then necessary to put the trust estate or the beneficiary back into the position it would have been in had there been no breach. I can see no justification for 'stopping the clock' immediately in some cases but not in others: to do so may, as in this case, lead to compensating the trust estate or the beneficiary for a loss which, on the facts known at trial, it has never suffered.

He went on to hold[64] that the distinction advocated by the Court of Appeal was not consistent with the authorities: *In re Dawson, decd.*[65] establishes that equitable compensation for breach of trust has to be assessed as at the date of judgment and not at an earlier date whether this was, as in that case, favourable to the beneficiaries or, as in *Target Holdings* v. *Redferns*, favourable to the trustees; *Canson Enterprises* v. *Boughton & Co.*[66] establishes that '[e]quitable compensation for breach of trust is designed to achieve exactly what the word compensation suggests: to make good a loss in fact suffered by the beneficiaries and which, using hindsight and common sense, can be seen to have been caused by the breach'.[67] His Lordship[68] distinguished *Alliance & Leicester Building Society* v. *Edgestop*,[69] *Bishopsgate Investment Management* v. *Maxwell (No 2)*[70] (both of which had been relied on by the Court of

64 N. 11 above, at 363–5.

65 N. 15 above (Sup. Ct. of NSW). An Australian trustee had paid trust money from a New Zealand estate to a stranger. Street J held that his obligation to compensate the estate was to pay the amount of Australian pounds that the sum paid away was worth at the date of judgment and not the lesser amount that it had been worth at the date of the payment, the Australian currency having depreciated against the New Zealand currency in the meantime.

66 N. 18 above. The plaintiffs were advised in respect of a purchase of property by the defendant solicitor who, in breach of fiduciary duty, failed to inform them that the vendor was making an improper profit. The warehouse which the plaintiffs subsequently built on the property was defective due to the negligence of contractors. The Sup. Ct. held unanimously that, despite the fact that but for the defendant's breach of fiduciary duty the plaintiffs would not have bought the property and so would not have built the warehouse, the defendant was not liable to compensate the plaintiffs for the defective building (only McLachlin J (speaking for the minority) dealt with the rules applicable to equitable compensation for breach of trust since LaForest J (speaking for the majority) considered that damages for breach of fiduciary duty were instead governed by the common law rules of remoteness).

67 N. 11 above, at 365.

68 *Ibid.* 365–6.

69 N. 35 above. In another case of mortgage fraud the defendant solicitors had in breach of trust paid away funds paid to them by the plaintiff building society, which obtained orders for interim payment. However, Hoffmann J found as a fact that the building society would not have made the advance had it known the true facts, the contrary to what had to be assumed in *Target Holdings* v. *Redferns.*

70 [1994] 1 All ER 261. Summary judgment was ordered for damages to be assessed against a director of a company which was a trustee of a pension fund because he had

Appeal) and *Nant-y-Glo and Blaina Ironworks Co.* v. *Grave*[71] and held that *Jaffray* v. *Marshall*[72] had been wrongly decided. This last decision demonstrates convincingly the iniquities to which the distinction advocated by the Court of Appeal can lead. A house owned in undivided shares by a settlement and by its tenant for life was in breach of trust mortgaged to secure the borrowings of the tenant for life; it was eventually sold by the mortgagee who took the whole proceeds of sale and so the interest of the settlement therein was wholly lost. It was held[73] that the compensation payable by the trustees to the settlement was the appropriate proportion of the highest intermediate value of the property between the date of the breach of trust and the date of judgment, by which time its value had fallen considerably as a result of a general decline in land values. The settlement thus obtained significantly more than the value of its interest in the property would have been worth at the date of judgment.[74]

Having rejected both the arguments in favour of the conclusion reached by the Court of Appeal, Lord Browne-Wilkinson therefore concluded that, on the factual assumption which had to be made,[75] the plaintiff had not demonstrated that it was entitled to any compensation for breach of trust and so the solicitors were entitled to leave to defend. However, because of the high probability that at trial the plaintiff would succeed in its contention that had the solicitors not released the funds before obtaining the legal charges the vendors would have withdrawn

improperly transferred to a stranger shares held by the pension fund. The shares were irretrievably lost apart from the possibility of the plaintiff pursuing hazardous litigation against the stranger, something which it was not obliged to do in order to try to mitigate the liability of the director. Here it was clear that the breach of fiduciary duty had caused the loss of the trust property, the contrary to what had to be assumed in *Target Holdings* v. *Redferns*.

71 (1878) 12 Ch. D 738. This case concerned not a claim in respect of any loss suffered by a beneficiary but rather a claim for an account of the profits which had been made by a director from shares which he had improperly received in breach of fiduciary duty; such claims are dependant on the profit made by the fiduciary, not the loss suffered by the beneficiary.

72 [1993] 1 WLR 1285. Lord Browne-Wilkinson held (n. 11 above, at 366) that the principles applicable in an action for an account of profits were wrongly applied to a claim for compensation for breach of trust but the case would probably have been decided the same way if the principle advocated by the CA had been applied instead.

73 By Nicholas Stewart QC, sitting as a Deputy Judge of the High Ct.

74 It was clear that, but for the mortgage sale, the trust moneys would at all times have been invested in the provision of a residence for the tenant for life; however it was held that, given that the trustees had had the power to sell the property at any time, the theoretical possibility but practical impossibility that they might have sold at the top of the market had to be presumed against them. Lord Browne-Wilkinson held (n. 12 above, at 366) that the judge had been wrong to make this assumption when he had also found as a fact that no sale would have taken place even if there had been no breach of trust.

75 That the breach of trust by the solicitors could not be said to have caused the actual loss ultimately suffered by the plaintiff (see text to nn. 42–4 above).

from the transaction because of the lack of any other obvious funds with which the purchase by the Jersey company could have been completed, his lordship restored the order of Warner J giving only conditional leave to defend.

The decision of the House of Lords in *Target Holdings* v. *Redferns* is important for two reasons. First, in relation to the specific issue with which it was concerned, the measure of recovery of losses caused by breaches of trust, the decision has established that, no matter what the nature of the breach of trust, the trustees are only liable to compensate the beneficiaries for those losses which, looking at the matter as from the date of judgment, have actually been caused by the breach and not also for losses which the beneficiaries would in any event have suffered even if there had been no such breach. This decision seems instinctively right and, in that it has removed the harsh consequences of the decisions arrived at in *Jaffray* v. *Marshall* and in the Court of Appeal, is undoubtedly of a liberalising nature. Secondly, and perhaps potentially more significantly, the decision contains the enunciation of a most important general principle which, as will be shown later on,[76] may have an equally liberalising effect upon the remedies available against fiduciaries who have made a profit out of a merely technical breach of their duty of loyalty.

THE CLASSIFICATION OF COMMERCIAL RELATIONSHIPS AS FIDUCIARY

The courts have generally been reluctant to discover fiduciary obligations in commercial relationships entered into at arm's length and on an equal footing. This is fortunate because the effect of imposing fiduciary duties on the parties to a commercial relationship is to expose those parties to the proprietary remedies to which fiduciaries are potentially subject. Proceedings instituted in order to establish the existence of fiduciary obligations in a commercial relationship almost invariably have as their primary objective the imposition on one of the parties to that relationship of a constructive trust in favour of the other party in respect of the benefits which the former has obtained by entering into some transaction on his own behalf. Such a trust is obviously capable of stripping away a substantial proportion of the assets of the constructive trustee, particularly if the constructive trust is imposed in such a way as to deprive him of both the past and future profits of the transaction in question. These will be profits to which the fiduciary will have appeared to be entitled and whose disappearance is capable of reducing very considerably the assets available for his general creditors, who will necessarily not be before the court to defend their interests.

[76] See text to n. 101 ff. above.

Until the recent decision of the Privy Council in *In re Goldcorp Exchange*[77] the principal authorities were decisions of the High Court of Australia. In *Hospital Products International* v. *United States Surgical Corporation*[78] a distributor utilised its exclusive rights to distribute in Australia certain surgical products as the means of establishing itself as a manufacturer of similar products and then, having deferred fulfilment of orders for the manufacturer's products, terminated its relationship with the manufacturer and fulfilled the accumulated orders with its own products. Four of the five members of the High Court held that the express[79] terms of the contract did not impose any fiduciary obligations on the distributor because the arrangement between the parties was a commercial transaction entered into at arm's length and on an equal footing and because it had been clear from the start that the whole purpose of the transaction from the distributor's point of view had been to make a profit;[80] the manufacturer's claim that the distributor was not only liable in damages for breach of contract but also held its business on constructive trust for the manufacturer was therefore denied.[81] On the other hand in *United Dominions Corporation* v. *Brian*[82] the High Court unanimously imposed fiduciary obligations on three companies who were about to enter into a joint venture agreement on the ground that the arrangements between the future partners had passed the stage of mere negotiation; consequently, a mortgage of the joint venture land by one of the companies to another on terms which charged this land with sums advanced to the mortgagor company on any account was held to amount to a breach of the fiduciary duty owed to the third company by the mortgagee company, which was therefore unable to rely on these terms. Both decisions emphasise the enormous possibilities open to the courts of intervening in commercial dealings by the simple expedient of classifying the relationship between the parties as fiduciary. Sir Anthony Mason, the former Chief Justice of Australia, both in his dissent in *Hospital Products International* v. *United States Surgical Corporation* and in

[77] [1995] 1 AC 74.

[78] (1984) 156 CLR 41.

[79] The Court unanimously rejected certain terms which had been implied into the contract by the CA of NSW ([1983] 2 NSWLR 157).

[80] The fifth member of the Court, Mason J, however held that there was a limited fiduciary duty arising out of the exclusive responsibility of the defendant for marketing the plaintiff's products in Australia and the manner in which those products were to be promoted which placed the defendant under a duty not to make a profit by virtue of its fiduciary position.

[81] By three members of the Court. Mason J, having held that the distributor was under a limited fiduciary duty, obviously dissented and Deane J, who had agreed that the distributor was not subject to any fiduciary obligations, also dissented on the basis that it could nevertheless have been held liable as a constructive trustee on another ground (see n. 78 above, at 125).

[82] (1985) 157 CLR 1.

his extra-judicial observations, has manifested a greater preparedness than that of the majority in that case to discover fiduciary obligations in commercial relationships, describing the fiduciary relationship as 'the spearhead of equity's incursions into the area of commerce';[83] he has concluded[84] that

a fiduciary relationship will arise out of a commercial arrangement when one party undertakes to act in the interests of the other party rather than in his or her own interests in relation to a particular matter or aspect of their arrangement and that other party, being unable to look after his or her interests in that matter or aspect of the arrangement is basically dependent upon the first party acting in conformity with his or her undertaking.

Curiously enough, it is precisely the authority on which Sir Anthony Mason principally relied for the latter proposition, the decision of the Court of Appeal of New Zealand in *Liggett* v. *Kensington*[85] which has just been reversed by the Privy Council in *In re Goldcorp Exchange.*[86] The majority of the Court of Appeal of New Zealand[87] had imposed fiduciary obligations on a gold-dealer which had offered its purchasers the option of leaving their bullion in its custody on the purchasers' behalf as 'non-allocated bullion'. Purchasers who did so were issued with a certificate of ownership and were entitled to take physical possession of their bullion on seven days' notice. The gold-dealer subsequently became bankrupt and the question arose whether such purchasers were entitled to an equitable proprietary claim in priority to a debenture holder. The conclusion that the company was a fiduciary (and that the purchasers consequently had priority) was based on two propositions: first, that it was bound to protect the interests of the purchasers and, secondly, that it was, for all practical purposes, free from control and supervision by the purchasers. However, the Privy Council referred to the warnings given many decades ago by Lindley LJ in *Manchester Trust* v. *Furness*[88] and by Atkin LJ in *Re Wait*[89] of the dangers of applying equitable doctrines to commercial transactions. Lord Mustill heeded these warnings, saying:[90]

But what kind of fiduciary duties did the company owe to the customer? None have been suggested beyond those which the company assumed under the con-

[83] In (1994) 110 *LQR* 238 at 245.
[84] *Ibid.* 245–6.
[85] [1993] 1 NZLR 257.
[86] N. 12 above.
[87] Cooke P and Gault J (McKay J dissented).
[88] [1895] 2 QB 539 at 545.
[89] [1927] 1 Ch. 606 at 634 ff. A few weeks before the PC handed down its Opinion in *In re Goldcorp Exchange, Re Wait* was applied by Judge Paul Baker QC in *In re Stapylton Fletcher* [1994] 1 WLR 1181 at 1203 in order to hold that a company which was storing stocks of wine on behalf of its owners did not owe any fiduciary duties to the latter.
[90] N. 12 above, at 98.

tracts of sale read with the collateral promises; . . . No doubt the fact that one person is placed in a particular position vis-à-vis another through the medium of a contract does not necessarily mean that he does not also owe fiduciary duties to that other by virtue of being in that position. But the essence of a fiduciary relationship is that it creates obligations of a different character from those deriving from the contract itself. . . . Many commercial relationships involve just such a reliance by one party on the other, and to introduce the whole new dimension into such relationships which would flow from giving them a fiduciary character would (as it seems to their Lordships) have adverse consequences far exceeding those foreseen by Atkin L.J. in *In re Wait*. It is possible without misuse of language to say that the customers put faith in the company, and that their trust has not been repaid. But the vocabulary is misleading; high expectations do not necessarily lead to equitable remedies.

Despite the fact that these observations of Lord Mustill constitute the present law of New Zealand, they are clearly unlikely to find much favour with Sir Anthony Mason and may well not commend themselves to many or any of the four distinguished Speakers from Australia and New Zealand who have already spoken at this Conference in the Session on Fiduciary Duties and Liabilities. It might well be expected that a less critical view would be taken by a speaker from what may fairly be called a more traditional jurisdiction (although some may prefer to adopt the less flattering description utilised by a New Zealand commentator[91] who, when considering an observation by the President of the Court of Appeal of New Zealand that England, Canada, Australia, and New Zealand 'are all driving in the same direction',[92] concluded that 'England is in the slow lane'). English commentators can and should be encouraged to regard the attitude evinced by Lord Mustill as admirable, not merely acceptable; this is not just because his approach is likely to be followed here, quite irrespective of what happens elsewhere. The resulting preservation in this jurisdiction for at least the foreseeable future of the general reluctance to discover fiduciary relationships in commercial transactions is in fact highly desirable. Not only does it avoid the almost inevitable loss of priority of and consequential prejudice to the interests of the third-party creditors of the parties to such relationships; more significantly for present purposes, it also protects the parties themselves from the imposition of the proprietary remedies which are at present the virtually inevitable consequence of the existence of fiduciary obligations. For this reason the decision of the Privy Council in *In re Goldcorp Exchange* can justifiably be regarded as continuing the liberal tradition of the previous authorities and therefore as forming a significant part of the ongoing general liberalisation of the law governing remedies for breach of trust.

[91] N. S. Peart in (1989) 7 *Otago LR* 100 at 140.

[92] In *Pasi* v. *Kamana* (1986) 4 NZFLR 417 at 419.

THE LIABILITY OF FIDUCIARIES FOR BREACH OF A DUTY OF LOYALTY

The attitude of English law towards fiduciaries is, generally speaking, a harsh one. In *Aberdeen Railway Co.* v. *Blaikie Brothers*[93] Lord Cranworth LC, speaking of those having fiduciary duties, said: 'it is a rule of universal application, that no one, having such duties to discharge, shall be allowed to enter into engagements in which he has, or can have, a personal interest conflicting, or which possibly may conflict, with the interests of those whom he is bound to protect'. Admittedly in *Bray* v. *Ford*[94] Lord Herschell said that this 'inflexible rule of a court of equity' 'might be departed from in many cases, without any breach of morality, without any wrong being inflicted, and without any consciousness of wrongdoing'. However, it has always been clear, as Lindsay J recently held in *In re Drexel Burnham Lambert Pension Plan*,[95] that this passage is 'not a licence for the rule to be departed from when it can be seen that no breach of morality or wrongdoing would ensue'. Thus the decided cases provide innumerable examples of courts penalising fiduciaries (particularly trustees) totally irrespective of whether there was any serious conflict between their duty of loyalty and their self interest. Perhaps the best known example is the decision of the House of Lords in *Boardman* v. *Phipps*,[96] where the trust solicitor and one of the beneficiaries of a trust, who were not express trustees but had represented the trust at the meetings of a company of which the trust was a minority shareholder, were held accountable to the other beneficiaries as constructive trustees for the profit which they made by themselves acquiring a majority shareholding in the company, an operation which had first been suggested to and rejected by the trustees and which in any event proved highly beneficial to the trust in financial terms. Their representation of the trust had incontrovertibly enabled them to obtain information which would not have been made available to the general public and the House of Lords held unanimously (and indisputably) that they had placed themselves in a fiduciary relationship out of which they had obtained the opportunity to make a profit and the knowledge that a profit was there to be made. A bare majority of the House then went on to hold that the solicitor had placed himself in a position where his duty and interest might conflict if, for example, the trustees had sought his

[93] (1854) 1 Macq. 461 at 471.

[94] [1896] AC 44 at 51–2.

[95] [1995] 1 WLR 31 at 37. His lordship however held (at 41) that 'the rule does not apply with such force as to deny the court even the *jurisdiction* to give directions' where the trustees of a pension fund, all of whom were also beneficiaries and therefore had a conflict of interest and duty, sought approval of a scheme for the disposal of the actuarial surplus of a pension fund which had to be wound up following the liquidation of the employer.

[96] [1967] 2 AC 46.

advice as to the merits of the trust acquiring a majority holding in the company. Quite apart from the remoteness of the possibility of such a situation arising given that the trustees had already been offered and declined the opportunity to do exactly that, it has been observed,[97] most persuasively, that in this eventuality he could, like any other solicitor, have declined to advise the trustees or, if they insisted, he could have declared his interest. In the opinion of the majority, it was quite immaterial that the two defendants had acted honestly and openly in a manner highly beneficial to the trust in a situation in which the trust could not itself have utilised the information which they had received.[98] This is merely the most extreme of the many cases in which the courts have appeared to be more concerned to penalise a fiduciary for having taken up an opportunity of entering into a profitable transaction on his own behalf than to ascertain whether or not there has been any real conflict between his duty of loyalty to his principal and his own self-interest.

An authority which has been repeatedly cited and applied in cases of this type is *Keech* v. *Sandford*,[99] decided by Lord King LC as long ago as 1726, where a trustee who renewed for his own benefit a lease which the landlord was not prepared to renew to the trust was held to hold the benefit of the lease on constructive trust for the trust. This decision was wholly understandable at that time; not only was the trustee depriving the lease of a grant which it had a right to expect since many ecclesiastical, charitable and public bodies were by law restricted as to the length of leases which they were able to grant and leases were therefore renewed more or less as a matter of right; this was also a time of extravagant financial speculation and even more extravagant financial collapses. However, this decision has not only produced a line of authority concerning the extent to which a fiduciary may renew for his own benefit a lease held by his principal and the associated question of whether a fiduciary may purchase the freehold reversion of property of which his principal is lessee; it has also had a profound effect on the general question of what opportunities a fiduciary is entitled to utilise for his own benefit. Thus, in *Regal (Hastings)* v. *Gulliver*[100] the House of Lords held that company directors who had subscribed for shares in a subsidiary when the company lacked the funds to take them up itself were liable to the company (and so in effect to the subsequent purchasers of both

[97] By P. D. Finn, writing pre-judicially, in *Fiduciary Obligations* (1977), 244–6. See also Professor Gareth Jones: (1968) 84 LQR 472.

[98] The dissentients took the view that the remoteness of the possibility of any conflict of interest arising and the various factors referred to in the text which the majority had found irrelevant led inescapably to the conclusion that the defendants had not breached their duty of loyalty to the trust.

[99] (1726) Sel. Ch. Cas. 61.

[100] (1943) [1967] 2 AC 134 (Note).

company and subsidiary) as constructive trustees for the profit which they had made on the sale of these shares to them. Lord Russell of Killowen stated that it made no difference at all that the company could not itself have subscribed for the shares—the trust in *Keech* v. *Sandford* could not itself have obtained a new lease and that had made no difference there.

It is hard to think of a better example of the practice so eloquently condemned by Lord Browne-Wilkinson in *Target Holdings* v. *Redferns*[101] when he said that 'it is in any event wrong to lift wholesale the detailed rules developed in the context of traditional trusts and then seek to apply them to trusts of quite a different kind'. Why should a rule handed down in the eighteenth century in the context of a traditional trust to the effect that a trustee is not entitled to renew for his own benefit a lease which the landlord was not prepared to renew to the trust be automatically applied in the twentieth century to penalise company directors for purchasing shares of a subsidiary which the company lacked the funds to take up? Nothing in his speech suggests that Lord Browne-Wilkinson intended the principle which he was enunciating to be limited to the issue actually before the House of Lords, whether trustees are liable to compensate beneficiaries not only for losses caused by a breach of trust but also for losses which the beneficiary would, in any event, have suffered even if there had been no such breach. The question whether fiduciaries are obliged to pay over to their principals profits which those principals could never have made themselves is in many ways the converse situation. Is it therefore too much to hope that the approach advocated by Lord Browne-Wilkinson might also be applied to the liability of fiduciaries for breach of their duty of loyalty?

Some hope of, at the very least, a relaxation of the penal attitude displayed by the authorities which have already been discussed can be drawn from the recent decision of the High Court of Australia in *Warman International* v. *Dwyer*.[102] The plaintiffs held an agency terminable on three months' notice for the distribution of Italian gearboxes. At a time when the plaintiffs were reducing their activities in respect of this product, the manufacturer proposed to them a joint venture for the assembly of its products in Australia. The plaintiffs made it very clear that they were not interested. After unsuccessfully seeking other partners, the manufacturer finally gave the plaintiffs notice and formed a joint-venture company with the defendant, the employee of the plaintiffs most closely concerned with the distributorship, although he had neither been consulted about nor participated in the plaintiffs' decision to reject the manufacturer's proposal. The plaintiffs sought a declaration

[101] N. 11 above, at 362. [102] (1995) 128 ALR 201.

that the goodwill of the joint venture was held on trust for them and an account of profits to date.[103] It was predictably held that there had been a breach of fiduciary duty in that the conduct of the employee had probably caused the manufacturer to terminate its agency 'earlier than it otherwise would have done'.[104] However, the primary judge[105] refused to make a declaration of trust of the goodwill 'on the basis that it was undesirable to thrust the parties into a continuing business relationship when it was clear that there was no confidence or comity between them'.[106] No appeal was made against this decision, the defendant appealing only as to which of the two possible personal remedies the plaintiffs were entitled, an account of profits[107] or damages for their losses.[108] The High Court eventually held in favour of an account of the first two years' profits of the joint venture 'less an appropriate allowance for the expenses, skill, expertise, effort and resources contributed by [the joint venturers]'.[109] In relation to the possibility of the imposition of a constructive trust, the High Court said this:[110]

The outcome in cases of this kind will depend on a number of factors. They include the nature of the property, the relevant powers and obligations of the fiduciary and the relationship between the profit made and the powers and obligations of the fiduciary. Thus, according to the rule in *Keech* v. *Sandford*,[111] a trustee of a tenancy who obtains for himself the renewal of a lease holds the new lease as a constructive trustee even though the landlord is unwilling to grant it to the trust. But the rule 'depends partly on the nature of leasehold property' and partly on the position which the trustee occupies.[112] A similar approach will be adopted in a case in which a fiduciary acquires for himself a specific asset which falls within the scope and ambit of his fiduciary responsibilities, even if the asset is acquired by means of the skill and expertise of the fiduciary and

[103] The statement of claim had also sought a declaration that the defendant held his shares in the joint venture companies on trust but this claim does not seem to have been pursued at the hearing (see the joint judgment of the High Court, n. 102 above, at 213).

[104] *Ibid.* 205.

[105] Derrington J in the Sup. Ct. of Queensland.

[106] N. 102 above, at 206. See also Trial Transcript at 26–7.

[107] Derrington J awarded an account of the first four years' profits of the joint venture plus a further one year's profits by way of payment for goodwill less, in both cases, an allowance of 50% for the time, energy, skill, and capital brought into the business by the joint venturers (Transcript at 23–6). This conclusion was affirmed by McPherson JA (dissenting) in the CA of Queensland.

[108] The majority of the Queensland CA (Macrossan CJ and Pincus JA) held that the plaintiffs could recover only the loss which they had suffered due to the defendant's breaches of fiduciary duty (Transcript of their joint reasons at 27–8).

[109] N. 102 above, at 216. The High Ct. specifically held (at 208) that an account 'gives rise to a liability, even in a case of a fiduciary, which is personal'.

[110] *Ibid.* 211–2.

[111] N. 99 above.

[112] Citing *Griffith* v. *Owen* [1907] 1 Ch. 195 at 203–4, *Re Biss* [1903] 2 Ch. 40 at 57, and *Chan* v. *Zacharia* (1984) 154 CLR 178 at 181–2, 201.

would not otherwise have been available to the person to whom the fiduciary duty is owed.

But a distinction should be drawn between cases in which a specific asset is acquired and cases in which a business is acquired and operated . . .[113]

In the case of a business it may well be inappropriate and inequitable to compel the errant fiduciary to account for the whole of the profit of his conduct of the business or his exploitation of the principal's goodwill over an indefinite period of time. In such a case, it may be appropriate to allow the fiduciary a proportion of the profits, depending upon the particular circumstances. That may well be the case when it appears that a significant proportion of an increase in profits has been generated by the skill, efforts, property and resources of the fiduciary, the capital which he has introduced and the risks he has taken, so long as they are not risks to which the principal's property has been exposed. Then it may be said that the relevant proportion of the increased profits is not the product or consequence of the plaintiff's property but the product of the fiduciary's skill, efforts, property and resources. This is not to say that the liability of a fiduciary to account should be governed by the doctrine of unjust enrichment, though that doctrine may well have a useful part to play; it is simply to say that the stringent rule requiring a fiduciary to account for profits can be carried to extremes and that in cases outside the realm of specific assets, the liability of the fiduciary should not be transformed into a vehicle for the unjust enrichment of the plaintiff.

These enlightened remarks of the High Court of Australia may, if followed and applied in this jurisdiction, have a profound effect on the nature of the liability of fiduciaries who have made a profit as the result of a purely technical breach of fiduciary duty. That is not to say that the adoption of the approach advocated by the High Court would necessarily have altered the result of the decisions in *Regal (Hastings)* v. *Gulliver* and *Boardman* v. *Phipps*. The distinction drawn by the High Court is between cases in which a specific asset is acquired which falls within the scope and ambit of a fiduciary's responsibilities as such and cases in which a business is acquired and operated. *Regal (Hastings)* v. *Gulliver* and *Boardman* v. *Phipps* would only be decided differently if the shares acquired by the respective fiduciaries could be held not to fall within the scope and ambit of their fiduciary responsibilities. It seems somewhat improbable that such a conclusion would ever be reached on the facts in *Regal (Hastings)* v. *Gulliver*; on the other hand, it has already been suggested that this conclusion should have been reached in *Boardman* v. *Phipps*. Be that as it may, the adoption of the distinction advocated by the High Court would certainly have a profound effect on the liability of fiduciaries who acquire and operate businesses as a result of a purely technical breach of fiduciary duty. No longer would they be liable more

[113] Citing *Re Jarvis* [1958] 1 WLR 815 and *Clegg* v. *Edmondson* (1857) 8 De GM & G 787 at 814.

or less automatically to surrender the entire profits of such businesses but would have the possibility of being allowed to retain such proportion of those profits as seemed appropriate in the particular circumstances. This would be an admirable first step towards the much greater liberalisation which would occur if the remarks of Lord Browne-Wilkinson in *Target Holdings* v. *Redferns* were to be applied to this area of the law. Such an application and the consequential confining of precedents established in the context of traditional trusts to that context alone would indeed be likely to alter the result of the decisions in *Regal (Hastings)* v. *Gulliver* and *Boardman* v. *Phipps* (hopefully by no liability whatsoever being imposed in the former case and by liability in the latter case being limited to the value to the defendants of the information acquired out of their representation of the trust[114]). Such a larger step would really liberalise the liability of fiduciaries for breaches of fiduciary duty and would produce a much more general liberalisation of remedies for breach of trust. It is much to be hoped that sooner or later this step is taken.

'ACCESSORY LIABILITY'

Another remedy which may be available to beneficiaries who have been victims of a breach of trust is the imposition of what has in recent years generally been known as liability for 'knowing assistance'. This form of liability imposes the obligations of trusteeship[115] on anyone who, with the requisite level of knowledge, has assisted in bringing about a dishonest and fraudulent misapplication of property in breach of trust. Its

[114] Fiduciaries, like anyone else, may be held liable under the equitable obligation of confidence. In a number of cases where information obtained in confidence has been used without the consent of the person who originally communicated it, the courts have been content to consider the whole gamut of remedies open to them and award that remedy which is most appropriate to the situation. A leading case decided at about the same time as *Boardman* v. *Phipps* is *Seager* v. *Copydex* [1967] 1 WLR 923. This approach has been consistently adopted in cases involving a breach of confidence where there was no pre-existing fiduciary relationship between the parties and has been adopted in one case involving principal and agent (*North and South Trust* v. *Berkeley* [1971] 1 WLR 471). It is arguable that the utilisation of the equitable obligation of confidence in *Boardman* v. *Phipps* would have produced a more justifiable result. See generally Goff and Jones, *The Law of Restitution* (4th edn., 1993), 679–702; Finn, *Fiduciary Obligations* (1977), 130–68.

[115] The vast majority of the decided cases describe this liability as the imposition of a constructive trust. However, it is only ever necessary to impose this form of liability in respect of property which has not been received beneficially by the person held liable (a beneficial recipient will be caught by the probably more stringent liability for 'knowing receipt', discussed in the text to nn. 153–166 below) and it is questionable to what extent a person who has received no property can correctly be described as a constructive trustee. As Millett J confirmed in *Agip (Africa)* v. *Jackson* [1989] 3 WLR 1367 at 1388, it is in fact more appropriate to regard such cases as examples of equity imposing a quite distinct remedy—a personal liability to account in the same manner as a trustee.

elements were considered in *Baden* v. *Société Générale*,[116] where Peter Gibson J analysed the famous statement by Lord Selborne LC in *Barnes* v. *Addy*[117] that 'strangers are not to be made constructive trustees merely because they act as the agents of trustees in transactions within their legal powers . . . unless they assist with knowledge in a dishonest and fraudulent design on the part of the trustees'. Peter Gibson J isolated four distinct elements: the existence of a trust, the existence of a dishonest and fraudulent design on the part of the trustee of the trust; the assistance by the stranger in that design, and the knowledge of the stranger. The second and fourth of these requirements, which have always been both the most important and the most controversial, have been significantly changed in two important respects by the decision of the Privy Council on an appeal from Brunei Darussalam in *Royal Brunei Airlines* v. *Tan*.[118] The airline sought to impose this form of liability on the managing director and principal shareholder of an insolvent travel agency which had paid into its ordinary current account the ticket moneys which, according to IATA regulations, it held on trust for the airline. The Court of Appeal of Brunei Darussalam had rejected this claim on the grounds that, while the evidence revealed what Lord Nicholls described as 'a sorry tale of mismanagement and broken promises, . . . it was not established that [the travel agent] was guilty of fraud or dishonesty.'[119] This conclusion was based on the decision of the Court of Appeal in *Belmont Finance Corporation* v. *Williams Furniture*[120] that the requirement for a dishonest and fraudulent design signifies something more than mere misfeasance or breach of trust. In *Baden* v. *Société Générale*[121] Peter Gibson J applied these statements of the Court of Appeal and held, quoting *R.* v. *Sinclair*,[122] that what was required was 'the taking of a risk to the prejudice of another's rights, which risk is known to be one which there is no right to take'. This view was adopted in all the subsequent English decisions.[123] However, the Privy Council rejected it and reversed the decision of the Court of Appeal of Brunei Darussalam, concluding that

[116] (1983) [1993] 1 WLR 509 (Note) at 573. The full name of this case is *Baden* v. *Société Générale pour Favoriser le Développement du Commerce et de l' Industrie en France S.A.*

[117] (1874) 9 Ch. App. 244 at 251–2.

[118] N. 14 above.

[119] *Ibid.* 383.

[120] [1979] Ch. 250. The Court rejected the view enunciated by Ungoed-Thomas J in *Selangor United Rubber Estates* v. *Cradock (No 3)* [1968] 1 WLR 1555 at 1582, 1590 that the adjectives 'dishonest' and 'fraudulent' must be understood in accordance with equitable principles for equitable relief and consequently conduct which is morally reprehensible suffices.

[121] N. 116 above, at 574.

[122] [1968] 1 WLR 1246 at 1249.

[123] This view has also been adopted in New Zealand. The Australian courts have continued to adopt the view of Ungoed-Thomas J in *Selangor United Rubber Company* v. *Cradock (No 3)* which was rejected by the CA in *Belmont Finance Corporation* v. *Williams Furniture.* See generally Cope (ed.), *Equity Issues and Trusts* (1995) 62.

what matters is the state of mind of the third party sought to be made liable, not the state of mind of the trustee. . . . *his* state of mind is essentially irrelevant to the question whether the *third party* should be made liable to the beneficiaries for the breach of trust. If the liability of the third party is fault-based, what matters is the nature of his fault, not that of the trustee. In this regard dishonesty on the part of the third party would seem to be a sufficient basis for his liability, irrespective of the state of mind of the trustee who is in breach of trust'.[124]

This conclusion would in itself have been sufficient to dispose of the appeal; since it had been conceded that there had been a breach of trust in which the managing director had assisted with actual knowledge, he had necessarily been dishonest and was therefore inevitably liable for having assisted in bringing about the disposition of the ticket moneys in breach of trust. However, the Privy Council did not restrict its observations to this particular aspect of accessory liability, holding that it was 'necessary to take an overall look at the accessory liability principle. A conclusion cannot be reached on the nature of the breach of trust which may trigger accessory liability without at the same time considering the other ingredients including, in particular, the state of mind of the third party'.[125] Lord Nicholls considered and rejected the two extreme possibilities of imposing either no liability whatever or strict liability on a third party who assists a trustee to commit a breach of trust but does not himself receive any trust property. The former possibility was rejected on the ground that '[a]ffording the beneficiary a remedy against the third party serves the dual purpose of making good the beneficiary's loss should the trustee lack financial means and imposing a liability which will discourage others from behaving in a similar fashion';[126] the latter possibility was rejected on the ground that 'ordinary, everyday business would become impossible if third parties were to be held liable for *unknowingly* interfering in the due performance of such personal obligations' as 'the fiduciary obligations undertaken by the trustee'.[127] Having thus necessarily opted for the imposition of some form of fault-based liability, Lord Nicholls reviewed the existing authorities in England and in New Zealand and the opinions of the commentators and stated that 'in the context of the accessory liability principle acting dishonestly, or with a lack of probity, which is synonymous, means simply not acting as an honest person would in the circumstances. This is an objective standard'.[128] Following a review of some of the problem areas, he made this observation:

To enquire, in [cases where there is real doubt], whether a person dishonestly assisted in what is later held to be a breach of trust is to ask a meaningful

[124] [1995] 2 AC 378 at 385. [125] *Ibid.* 386. [126] *Ibid.* 387–8. [127] *Ibid.* 388.
[128] *Ibid.* 389.

question, which is capable of being given a meaningful answer. This is not always so if the question is posed in terms of 'knowingly' assisted. Framing the question in the latter form all too often leads one into tortuous convolutions about the 'sort' of knowledge required, when the truth is that 'knowingly' is inapt as a criterion when applied to the gradually darkening spectrum where the differences are of degree and not kind'.[129]

Then, in answer to the crucial question of 'whether an honest third party who receives no trust property should be liable if he procures or assists in a breach of trust of which he would have become aware had be exercised reasonable diligence',[130] he concluded that

dishonesty is an essential ingredient here. There may be cases where, in the light of the particular facts, a third party will owe a duty of care to the beneficiaries. As a general proposition, however, beneficiaries cannot reasonably expect that all the world dealing with their trustees should owe them a duty to take care lest the trustees are behaving dishonestly'.[131]

The conclusion of the Privy Council as to the law, set out in a paragraph headed 'The accessory liability principle' deserves to be reproduced in full.

Drawing the threads together, their Lordships' overall conclusion is that dishonesty is a necessary ingredient of accessory liability. It is also a sufficient ingredient. A liability in equity to make good resulting loss attaches to a person who dishonestly procures or assists in a breach of trust or fiduciary obligation. It is not necessary that, in addition, the trustee or fiduciary was acting dishonestly, although this will usually be so where the third party who is assisting him is acting dishonestly. 'Knowingly' is better avoided as a defining ingredient of the principle, and in the context of this principle the *Baden* scale of knowledge is best forgotten'.[132]

This decision, although technically constituting the law only of Brunei Darussalam, is in practice enormously significant for English law. It has given the Law Lords their first recent opportunity to review what must now presumably be referred to as 'accessory liability' rather than as liability for 'knowing assistance'. The Privy Council seems to have completely rejected the requirement for the existence of a dishonest and fraudulent design on the part of the trustee of the trust and has thus imposed a stricter rule than that of any other jurisdiction.[133] This conclu-

[129] [1995] 2 AC 378 at 391. [130] *Ibid.* [131] *Ibid.* 392. [132] *Ibid.*

[133] New Zealand has adopted and applied the decision of the CA in *Belmont Finance Corporation* v. *Williams Furniture*, n. 120 above (see *Westpac Banking Corporation* v. *Savin* [1985] 2 NZLR 41, *per* Sir Clifford Richmond at 70) so the decision of the PC is likely to be enormously significant there as well. Australia has adopted the more stringent view of Ungoed-Thomas J in *Selangor United Rubber Estates* v. *Cradock (No 3)*, n. 120 above at 1582, 1590, that the adjectives 'dishonest and fraudulent' must be understood in accordance with equitable principles for equitable relief and consequently conduct which is morally reprehensible suffices (see *Consul Development* v. *D.P.C. Estates* (1975) 132 CLR

sion does to a limited extent[134] increase the possibility of the imposition of liability on third parties who have assisted in a disposition of trust property in breach of trust but it is impossible to disagree with Lord Nicholls' observation[135] that 'it would make no sense' to excuse a dishonest third party from liability merely because the trustee did not act dishonestly. Further, the decision of the Privy Council has also resolved the problem of the status of the nineteenth century authorities prior to *Barnes* v. *Addy*, in particular the decision in *Eaves* v. *Hickson*[136] where a father who produced a forged marriage certificate to the trustees of a settlement in order to convince them that his children were legitimate[137] and so entitled to the trust property was held personally liable to account as a trustee to those otherwise entitled to the property to the extent that it could not be recovered from the children. Prior to the decision of the Privy Council, it was unclear whether this decision was an example of a quite distinct head of liability for 'knowing inducement' of a breach of trust[138] or whether it had simply been overtaken by *Barnes* v. *Addy* and would thereafter have had to have been decided differently;[139] the Privy Council has established that it is an unusual but straightforward example of 'accessory liability'. This important and welcome change in the law unquestionably forms part of the *ratio decidendi* of the Board.

On the other hand, because of the concession that the managing director had had actual knowledge of the breach of trust, it is technically possible to argue that the remaining observations of the Board as to the standard of conduct required for the imposition of 'accessory liability' are no more than dicta. However, in the light of the fact that the Board itself not only made no distinction of this kind but also referred to the necessity of taking 'an overall look at the accessory liability principle', these observations are likely to be equally influential. The five categories of knowledge identified by Peter Gibson J in *Baden* v. *Société Générale*[140]

373, *per* Gibbs J at 398 and McTiernan J at 386 (High Ct. of Australia) and *Equiticorp Finance* v. *Bank of New Zealand* (1993) 32 NSWLR 50, *per* Kirby P at 105). The PC has gone even further in that any breach of trust, whether morally reprehensible or not, now appears to suffice.

[134] Only to a limited extent because, as Lord Nicholls commented at 392, the trustee or fiduciary will usually be acting dishonestly when the third party who is assiting him is acting dishonestly.

[135] N. 124 above, at 389.

[136] (1861) 30 Beav. 136. Other authorities are *Fyler* v. *Fyler* (1841) 3 Beav. 550 and *A.G.* v. *Corporation of Leicester* (1844) 7 Beav. 176. See generally C. Harpum in Birks (ed.), *Frontiers of Liability* (1994), 9.

[137] He had married the mother of the children after their birth but at that time there was no doctrine of legitimation by subsequent marriage.

[138] This was advocated by C. Harpum, n. 136 above, 9.

[139] This was suggested by the author of this paper in Cope (ed.), n. 123 above, 62.

[140] N. 116 above, at 575–6. The five categories are '(i) actual knowledge; (ii) wilfully shutting one's eyes to the obvious; (iii) wilfully and recklessly failing to make such inquiries

have clearly been rejected in favour of the principle that liability should be imposed on third parties who have dishonestly, but not negligently, assisted in a disposition of trust property in breach of trust.[141] Although this principle is quite distinct in approach, the results of its application are in practice unlikely to be significantly different from those of the pre-existing law. Its great advantage is its simplicity and clarity in comparison with the difficulty of applying what have justifiably been described[142] as the 'unhelpful' and 'unrememberable' categories identified by Peter Gibson J. It remains to be seen whether the courts will adopt a wholly objective standard when considering whether or not any particular third party has been dishonest or also take into account more subjective factors applicable only to the specific third party so as to impose either a higher or a lower standard of behaviour on him. It has been persuasively suggested[143] that the burden of establishing any such higher or lower standard of behaviour should be on the party alleging its applicability.

The decision of the Privy Council was subsequently considered in the Chancery Division in *Brinks* v. *Abu-Saleh (No 3)*.[144] The theft of over £26,000,000 from the plaintiff's Heathrow warehouse had been facilitated by one of the plaintiff's employees, a security guard who had pro-

as an honest and reasonable man would make; (iv) knowledge of circumstances which would indicate the facts to an honest and reasonable man; (v) knowledge of circumstances which would put an honest and reasonable man on inquiry'. Prior to the decision of the PC it was generally accepted that liability would only be imposed on a third party who fell within the first three of these categories of knowledge (see particularly *Polly Peck International* v. *Nadir (No 2)* [1992] 4 All ER 769, *per* Scott LJ at 777 and the other authorities referred to therein). Nevertheless the conflicting line of authority begun by *Selangor United Rubber Company* v. *Cradock (No 3)*, n. 120 above, to the effect that liability would be imposed on a third party who fell within any of the five categories of knowledge had never actually been overruled.

[141] It has often been stated that the principal justification for only imposing liability on third parties who fall within the first three of these categories of knowledge was the pre-existing law as to the meaning of a dishonest and fraudulent design on the part of the trustee. As Millett J stated in *Agip (Africa)* v. *Jackson*, n. 115 above, at 1389, '[t]here is no sense in requiring dishonesty on the part of the principal while accepting negligence as sufficient for his assistant.' Perhaps the most interesting aspect of the decision of the PC is the fact that the adoption of a much stricter approach in relation to the conduct of the trustee has not brought with it a stricter approach in relation to the conduct of the third-party assister, something which is the case in Australia where the stricter interpretation of dishonest and fraudulent design has brought with it the imposition of liability on any party who falls within the first four of the categories of knowledge identified by Peter Gibson J (see *Consul Development* v. *D.P.C. Estates*, n. 133 above), *per* Gibbs J at 398 and Stephen J at 214 (High Ct. of Australia) and *Equiticorp Finance* v. *Bank of New Zealand*, n. 134 above, *per* Kirby P at 228 (CA of NSW).

[142] By Blanchard J in *Nimmo* v. *Westpac Banking Corporation* [1993] 3 NZLR 218 at 228 (High Ct. of New Zealand).

[143] By R. Nolan in [1995] *CLJ* 507.

[144] *The Times*, 23 Oct. 1995. The author has been provided with a full transcript of the judgment by the courtesy of The New Law Publishing Co., of Quality House, Quality Court, Chancery Lane, London WC2.

vided both a key to the premises and information about its security arrangements to the other persons involved in the robbery. The plaintiffs subsequently sought recovery of the stolen property or damages in respect of its loss from no fewer than fifty-seven defendants. In these particular proceedings,[145] the plaintiff was contending that, because the robbery had taken place as a result of the actions of a dishonest fiduciary (the security guard[146]), it 'had an equity to trace into [the proceeds of the robbery], which were in the nature of trust moneys'.[147] It therefore sought the imposition of 'accessory liability' upon one of the defendants who had accompanied her husband on various trips by car in the course of which he had transported to Zurich over £3,000,000 of the proceeds of the robbery for one of the convicted robbers, thereby enabling this sum to be laundered. Rimer J held[148] that both the defendant and her husband had believed that the money was derived from the robber's business empire and was the subject of a tax-evasion exercise. The plaintiff argued that it was only necessary to prove, first, that the defendant had rendered assistance in what, objectively assessed, was a dishonest transaction and, secondly, that the transaction had involved a breach of trust.[149] Rimer J actually held[150] that, since the defendant had gone on the trips merely in her spousal capacity, her presence did not constitute relevant 'assistance' in furtherance of the breach of trust complained of.

[145] Earlier proceedings (unconnected with any question of 'accessory liability') are reported *sub nom. Brinks* v. *Abu-Saleh* [1995] 1 WLR 1478 and *Brinks* v. *Abu-Saleh (No 2)* [1995] 1 WLR 1487.

[146] The classification of the security guard as a dishonest fiduciary was accepted by counsel for the defendant (see Transcript, 17) and so there was obviously no discussion of this point. A conclusion to this effect might be thought to have been inevitable in the light of the earlier decisions in *A.G.* v. *Goddard* [1948] 2 KB 268 and *Reading* v. *A.G.* [1951] AC 507 that a police officer and an RAMC Sergeant were fiduciaries in respect of bribes received respectively from brothel-keepers and smugglers. However, those cases concerned only the liability of the respective fiduciaries and it must be at least questionable whether their classification as fiduciaries would have been reached with the same ease if, as in *Brinks* v. *Abu-Saleh (No 3)*, its objective had been to bring about the imposition of consequential liabilities on third parties.

[147] Transcript, 2. Rimer J rejected a contention by counsel for the defendant that the security guard did not owe a fiduciary duty sufficient to impress the proceeds of the robbery with a trust. His lordship relied on a statement by Millett J in *Agip (Africa)* v. *Jackson*, n. 116 above, at 1387 that 'there is a receipt of trust property when . . . a company's funds are misapplied by any person whose fiduciary position gave him control of them or enabled him to misapply them' and held: '[The security guard] was not an officer or a directing mind of Brinks. But he was employed in an important position of trust by them and in such position he possessed valuable information relating to the security arrangements affecting property in Brinks's custody at the Heathrow premises. He owed a duty to Brinks not to divulge that information to anyone not entitled to it. In breach of that duty he disclosed material information to the robbers and so gave them vital assistance enabling them to commit the robbery. In my judgment that breach of fiduciary duty was sufficient to bring into play the equitable remedies on which Brinks rely.'

[148] Transcript, 15.

[149] *Ibid.* 16. [150] *Ibid.* 18–19.

This rather generous finding of fact was obviously enough to dispose of the case. However, his Lordship went on to state[151] that he did not consider that the Privy Council had 'intended to suggest that an accessory could be made liable regardless of whether he had any knowledge of the existence of the trust' in question. He said this:

In my view the judgment proceeds on the basis that a claim based on accessory liability can only be brought against someone who knows of the existence of the trust, or at least of the facts giving rise to the trust; and all that the judgment is directed at clarifying is what further is also needed to be shown in order to make the accessory liable. The only further ingredient is dishonesty on the part of the accessory, and that is a sufficient ingredient.

Consequently, even if the defendant had been guilty of assistance, 'accessory liability' would not have been imposed upon her because she had not been aware of the existence of any trust. This clearly suggests that knowledge of the existence of a trust or other fiduciary relationship is a prerequisite of the imposition of 'accessory liability'.

In the vast majority of reported cases, claims for the imposition of 'accessory liability' have been brought against persons who were at all times necessarily fully aware of the existence of a trust or other fiduciary relationship; prior to the decision in *Royal Brunei Airlines* v. *Tan* the crucial question was usually whether or not they knew or ought to have known of the misapplication of some property subject thereto. However, in what seems to be the only other reported case in which knowledge of the existence of such a relationship has been relevant, Millett J reached the opposite conclusion. In *Agip (Africa)* v. *Jackson*[152] he held that:

it is no answer for a man charged with having knowingly assisted in a fraudulent and dishonest scheme to say that he thought that it was 'only' a breach of exchange control or 'only' a case of tax evasion. It is not necessary that he should have been aware of the precise nature of the fraud or even of the identity of its victim. A man who consciously assists others by making arrangements which he knows are calculated to conceal what is happening from a third party, takes the risk that they are part of a fraud practised on that party.

The fact that *Royal Brunei Airlines* v. *Tan* has now substituted a requirement of dishonesty for the pre-existing requirement of knowledge that some property was being misapplied does not necessarily mean either that any pre-existing requirement for knowledge of the existence of a fiduciary relationship has also ceased to exist or that the knowledge in question should have to fall within any of the categories identified by Peter Gibson J in *Baden* v. *Société Générale* which were so firmly rejected by the Privy Council. However, not only does the possibility of the existence of such a requirement seem wholly contrary to the earlier state-

[151] Transcript, 21. [152] N. 115 above, at 1391.

ments of Millett J in the only other relevant authority; its continued existence would be extremely difficult to reconcile with the de-emphasis on the requirement of knowledge which formed such an important part of the advice of the Privy Council. It is therefore submitted that in this respect the judgment of Rimer J should not be followed. It is in any event certainly to be hoped that the decision of the Privy Council has not been in any way undermined so soon by a return to concepts which the Board so specifically rejected.

Whatever the true effect of the decision in *Brinks* v. *Abu-Saleh (No 3)*, the decision of the Privy Council in *Royal Brunei Airlines* v. *Tan* has certainly brought about a much needed and, in some respects, unexpected clarification of the law. Because it has permitted the imposition of personal liability upon third parties who have assisted in bringing about a disposition of property in breach of trust in circumstances where such a remedy was previously thought to be unavailable, it can hardly be said to have had a liberalising effect upon the position of such third-party accessories. However, its enunciation of principle can undoubtedly be seen as forming part of the general rethinking of the nature of remedies for breach of trust which has been taking place recently and so can fairly be said to have had a liberalising effect on the general development of this area of the law.

ANALOGOUS AREAS OF THE LAW WHICH REQUIRE RECONSIDERATION

Finally, brief consideration must be given to two analogous areas of the law which would benefit from a similar process of judicial reconsideration and possible liberalisation: the prerequisites of liability for 'knowing receipt' and the extent to which equitable proprietary claims are available to follow property into its product.

Liability for 'Knowing Receipt'

Liability for 'knowing receipt' can be imposed on anyone who, with the requisite level of knowledge, has received for his own benefit property which has been misapplied in breach of fiduciary duty. This form of liability is only one of a number of claims which may be available to the person from whom the property has been abstracted. If the property or its product is still identifiable in the hands of the recipient or of any third party to whom it has been subsequently transferred, he will also have the possibility of bringing a proprietary claim, either at law or in equity, to enable him to follow the property into the hands of its present holder. Additionally he may be able to bring a personal action at law for money had and received against the recipient, a personal action in equity against whoever was responsible for initiating the misapplication, and a claim for the imposition of the obligations of trusteeship against anyone who is caught by the 'accessory liability' principle.[153]

For present purposes, it is important only to distinguish between, on the one hand, the possibility of following the misapplied property into the hands of its recipient and, on the other hand, the possibility of the imposition of liability for 'knowing receipt'. Where property subject to a trust has been misapplied, the interests of the beneficiaries in that property are, in accordance with the basic principles of property law, enforceable against the whole world unless and until the property in question reaches the hands of someone who takes it free of their equitable proprietary interests therein. Any recipient of misapplied property who is liable to such an equitable tracing claim will, of course, be a trustee of such property as is in his hands—this is simply because the equitable interests of the beneficiaries therein must necessarily take effect behind a trust of the legal estate. However, the fact that it is thus possible to trace the property into its product does not necessarily mean that the obligations of trusteeship will be imposed on the recipient in respect of all the property originally transferred to him. Indeed, only in three situations will it be necessary to seek the imposition of liability for 'knowing receipt': first, where the recipient has dealt with the property in such a way that it can no longer be followed: secondly, where the property has depreciated in value while in the hands of the recipient; and, thirdly, where the recipient has obtained some incidental profit from the property. In these circumstances, the equitable tracing claim will only lead to the recovery of such property, if any, as remains in the hands of the recipient; the loss caused by any dealing with or reduction in value of the property and any incidental profit obtained will only be recoverable if the recipient is held to have been a constructive trustee of the whole of the property originally transferred to him. In the vast majority of the cases in which the imposition of liability for 'knowing receipt' has been

[153] In *Agip (Africa)* v. *Jackson*, *ibid.* (Millett J, CA), the plaintiff sought the following relief: at law, a proprietary claim to follow the funds into the hands of the defendants and a personal claim for money had and received; and, in equity, a proprietary claim to follow the funds into the hands of the defendants and the imposition of the obligations of trusteeship for 'knowing receipt' and under the 'accessory liability' principle. In *Lipkin Gorman* v. *Karpnale* [1987] 1 WLR 987 (Alliott J), [1989] 1 WLR 1340 (CA) [1991] 3 WLR 10 (HL), where a partner of a firm of solicitors had drawn from the firm's client accounts funds which he subsequently gambled away at a casino, the solicitors claimed that its bank was liable for conversion of cheques, for conversion of a draft, for breach of contract, and under the 'accessory liability' principle and that the casino was liable for money had and received, for negligence, for conversion of cheques, for conversion of a draft, and for 'knowing receipt' and, additionally, was liable in equity to both proprietary and personal claims as a result of its receipt of the solicitors' funds.

sought, the recipient has dealt with the property in such a way that it can no longer be followed.

Liability for 'knowing receipt' has never been dependent on the existence of any dishonest or fraudulent design on the part of the person who misapplied the property; all that the claimant has to establish is the fact of receipt[154] and the existence of the requisite level of knowledge; it is for him to prove these elements, not for the alleged recipient to disprove them.[155] The level of knowledge which will give rise to the imposition of this form of liability is still assessed by reference to the five categories of knowledge identified by Peter Gibson J in *Baden* v. *Société Générale*[156] which have of course recently been specifically rejected by the Privy Council in so far as 'accessory liability' is concerned.[157] These categories are '(i) actual knowledge; (ii) wilfully shutting one's eyes to the obvious; (iii) wilfully and recklessly failing to make such inquiries as an honest and reasonable man would make; (iv) knowledge of circumstances which would indicate the facts to an honest and reasonable man; (v) knowledge of circumstances which would put an honest and reasonable man on inquiry'.

It is at least clearly established that a recipient who does not fall within any of the five categories of knowledge identified by Peter Gibson J in *Baden* v. *Société Générale* will not be liable for 'knowing receipt'; this is the case whether or not he has given value.[158] However, it is wholly unclear precisely which of the five categories will suffice for the imposition of this form of liability because of the existence of two conflicting lines of authority. One line of authority[159] suggests that liability for

[154] This can sometimes be extremely difficult to establish; in such circumstances, it is determined by the application of the rules governing legal and equitable tracing claims. The judgment of Millett J in *El Ajou* v. *Dollar Land Holdings* [1993] BCLC 735, at 753–7 contains a good illustration of the difficulties which can arise and of the manner in which they can be resolved.

[155] All these points were emphasized by Scott LJ in *Polly Peck International* v. *Nadir (No 2)*, n. 140 above, at 777.

[156] N. 116 above.

[157] In *Royal Brunei Airlines* v. *Tan*, n. 14 above; text to nn. 115–144.

[158] In *Re Diplock* [1948] Ch. 465, volunteers who had no knowledge whatever of the breach of trust in question were held not liable for 'knowing receipt'. In *Cowan de Groot Properties* v. *Eagle Trust* [1992] 4 All ER 700 directors of a company which lacked liquid funds sold five properties at a gross undervalue in order to make an urgent payment needed to keep an important company project in existence. Subsequently the company repudiated the sale and claimed that the purchaser was liable for 'knowing receipt'. Knox J held that the purchaser did not fall within any of the five categories of knowledge identified by Peter Gibson J and so was consequently not liable for 'knowing receipt'. On the other hand, whether or not the recipient has given value will of course be highly relevant in relation to an equitable tracing claim, since only if he has will he be able to make out the defence of *bona fide* purchase for value without notice.

[159] *Nelson* v. *Larholt* [1948] 1 KB 339, as interpreted in dicta in *Belmont Finance Corporation* v. *Williams Furniture (No 2)* [1980] 1 All ER 393 at 405, *International Sales and Agencies* v. *Marcus* [1982] 3 All ER 551 at 558, and *Agip (Africa)* v. *Jackson*, n. 115 above, at 1388, was

'knowing receipt' will be imposed if the recipient has any of the five categories of knowledge identified by Peter Gibson J, while the other line of authority[160] suggests that only the first three of those five categories should give rise to such liability. To make matters still worse, two recent cases[161] have adopted a *media via*, suggesting that the question whether the fourth and fifth categories of knowledge suffice only arises in non-commercial transactions, since in commercial transactions only the first three categories can possibly suffice for the imposition of liability. These conflicting lines of authority urgently require a considered review[162] similar to that which the Privy Council has recently made of 'accessory liability' since any clearly expressed statement of the law would be preferable to the existing confusion.[163]

When the time comes for this review to be made, it is to be hoped that it will not be confined to a consideration of these conflicting lines of authority but will also consider the different proposals for reform which have been made, both inside and outside the courts.[164] These proposals

cited as authority for this proposition in *Cowan de Groot Properties* v. *Eagle Trust*, n. 159 above. This approach clearly constitutes the law of New Zealand—see *Westpac Banking Corporation* v. *Savin*, n. 133 above (CA of New Zealand); in Australia at least the first four categories of knowledge and possibly also the fifth suffice for the imposition of liability—see *Consul Development* v. *D.P.C. Estates*, n, 133 above, *per* Stephen J at 410 and McTiernan J at 378, 386 (High Ct. of Australia) and *Equiticorp Finance* v. *Bank of New Zealand*, n. 133 above, *per* Kirby P at 103 (CA of NSW).

[160] *Nelson* v. *Larholt*, n. 159 above, as interpreted in *Carl-Zeiss Stiftung* v. *Herbert Smith (No 2)* [1969] 2 Ch. 276, *Re Montagu's Settlement* [1987] Ch. 264, *Lipkin Gorman* v. *Karpnale*, n. 153 above, *Barclays Bank* v. *Quincecare* (1988) [1992] 4 All ER 363.

[161] *Eagle Trust* v. *S.B.C. Securities* [1993] 1 WLR 484, *Cowan de Groot Properties* v. *Eagle Trust*, n. 158 above.

[162] In *Polly Peck International* v. *Nadir (No 2)*, n. 140 above, at 777, Scott LJ did not consider an interlocutory appeal to be 'the right occasion for settling the issue'; however, he left the question open by accepting that the third category of knowledge would lead to liability for 'knowing receipt' while admitting to 'some doubts' whether the fifth category of knowledge would also do so.

[163] The author of this paper was for a long time of the opinion that only the first three of the five categories of knowledge identified by Peter Gibson J should give rise to liability for 'knowing receipt' (see *Constructive Trusts* (2nd edn., 1987) 103–10); however, the PC's recent specific rejection of these categories in respect of 'accessory liability' suggests that all the conflicting authorities listed above in the preceding footnotes may well be discarded in favour of one of the more radical suggested solutions mentioned below in the next n.

[164] P. D. Finn writing pre-judicially in Waters (ed.), *Equity, Fiduciaries and Trusts 1993* (1993), 195 argues for the abandonment of much, if not all, of the existing law and its replacement by the following three questions, all of which need to be answered in the affirmative before what he denominates 'participatory liability' can be imposed: (1) has a fiduciary committed a breach of fiduciary duty or breach of trust? (2) has the third party participated in the manner in which the breach has occurred? (3) in so doing, did that party know or have reason to know that a wrong was being committed by the fiduciary on his or her beneficiaries? This view was cited with approval by Kirby P in *Equiticorp Finance* v. *Bank of New Zealand*, n. 133 above, at 105. In England, Lord Hoffmann writing extra-judicially in *Frontiers of Liability*, n. 136 above, 1 has advocated that liability for 'knowing receipt' should arise, if at all, under the law of tort and in particular the torts of negligence

have addressed not only the unsatisfactory and uncertain state of the law governing 'knowing receipt' but have also considered whether so many different remedies should continue to be available for the same misapplication of property. The principal difficulty is the existence of what have been described as 'arbitrary and anomalous distinctions'[165] between the claims at law and the claims in equity. Personal actions at law for money had and received will succeed quite irrespective of the state of mind of the recipient of the money, whereas liability in equity for 'knowing receipt' depends entirely on the knowledge of the recipient. The most popular proposal for reform, which it is anticipated may well be adopted by the Law Commission in its forthcoming consultation paper on this subject, is for the introduction of strict liability for 'knowing receipt' subject to the defence of change of position recognized by the House of Lords in *Lipkin Gorman* v. *Karpnale*.[166] However, the adoption of this proposal by the courts would involve a very considerable change to the present law since this would involve the imposition of liability on a recipient who had no knowledge whatever of the misapplication of the property. So radical a change may well only be able to be made by the legislature. Nevertheless, any judicial review, even at Court of Appeal level and even if confined to the existing conflicting lines of authority, would be extremely welcome; it is to be hoped that such a review would continue the ongoing process of the liberalisation of remedies for breach of trust.

The Scope of Equitable Proprietary Claims

An equitable proprietary claim can obviously only be pursued if the claimant has an equitable proprietary interest in the property in question and it is generally said that he can only trace his equitable proprietary interest into its product if he can point to the existence of a fiduciary relationship. The requirement 'has been widely condemned and depends on authority rather than on principle'.[167] Historically there

and deceit and that all the forms of equitable liability should be abolished. Several commentators, including P. B. H. Birks in [1993] *LMCLQ* 218 and C. Harpum in *Frontiers of Liability*, n. 136 above, 9, have advocated strict liability for 'knowing receipt', subject to the defence of change of position established in England by the decision of the HL in *Lipkin Gorman* v. *Karpnale*, n. 153 above. This view has been echoed by Millett J in *El Ajou* v. *Dollar Land Holdings*, n. 154 above, at 759, where he said: 'I do not see how it would be possible to develop any logical and coherent system of restitution if there were different requirements in respect of knowledge for the common law claim for money had and received, the personal claim for an account in equity against a knowing recipient and the equitable proprietary claim.'

165 By Millett J in *El Ajou* v. *Dollar Land Holdings*, n. 154 above, at 757. Millett J contended that these distinctions should not be insisted upon.

166 N. 153 above.

167 *Per* Millett J in *Agip (Africa)* v. *Jackson*, n. 115 above, at 1386.

was no such requirement[168] but it is generally thought that in *Re Diplock*[169] the Court of Appeal interpreted the decision of the House of Lords in *Sinclair* v. *Brougham*[170] as establishing, in the words of Goulding J in *Chase Manhattan Bank* v. *Israel-British Bank (London)*[171] 'that an initial fiduciary relationship is a necessary foundation of the equitable right of tracing'. It is questionable both whether this was really the opinion of the Court of Appeal in *Re Diplock* and whether *Sinclair* v. *Brougham* imposed any such requirement. However, the courts have strained the concept of fiduciary relationship to its limits, if not well beyond them, in order to satisfy this requirement. Even so, an absolute legal and beneficial owner of property cannot possibly point to any fiduciary relationship and therefore, according to the present understanding of the law, is apparently not entitled to trace in equity. Consequently, if the property of such a person is stolen and its product is mixed with other money in a bank account, the victim of the theft will be entitled to trace neither at law (because of the mixing) nor in equity (because of the absence of a fiduciary relationship). This ridiculous anomaly could be rectified either by the abolition of the requirement for a fiduciary relationship[172] or by concluding that a thief holds the property which he has stolen on trust for his victim.[173]

These prerequisites of an equitable proprietary claim will inevitably be

[168] In *Re Hallett's Estate* (1880) 13 Ch. D 696, the defendant solicitor sold bonds belonging partly to his own marriage settlement and partly to a client and mixed the proceeds with his own funds in a bank account. The beneficiaries of the marriage settlement could clearly point to the existence of a fiduciary relationship, but the client was also permitted to trace in equity on the basis that she was the legal and beneficial owner of the property which she had deposited with the defendant. In *Banque Belge pour l'Etranger* v. *Hambrouck* [1921] 1 KB 321, the defendant had fraudulently obtained £6,000 by drawing cheques on his employers which he paid into his own account with another bank, an account into which no other substantial sums were ever paid. From this account, he drew out cash which he paid to his mistress, who in turn paid it into yet another account. The majority of the CA held that these funds could be traced at law but Scrutton LJ held that they could be traced only in equity and the majority stated that, had they not held the plaintiff able to trace at law, they also would have permitted an equitable tracing claim. None of the members of the court stated any requirement for the existence of a fiduciary relationship as a prerequisite to an equitable proprietary claim. There is, of course, no doubt whatever that a fiduciary relationship could have been found in both these cases had it been necessary since both the defaulting solicitor and the fraudulent employee could undoubtedly have been held to be constructive trustees of, respectively, the proceeds of the bonds and the proceeds of the cheques. The significant fact is that none of the judges felt it necessary to look for and find such a relationship.

[169] N. 158 above.

[170] [1914] AC 398.

[171] [1980] 2 WLR 202 at 209.

[172] Something which was done in New Zealand in *Elders Pastoral* v. *Bank of New Zealand* [1989] 2 NZLR 180.

[173] As was held in Australia by the High Ct. in *Black* v. *S. Freeman & Co.* (1910) 12 CLR 105, *per* O'Connor J at 110. This possibility appeared to commend itself to Lord Templeman in *Lipkin Gorman* v. *Karpnale*, n. 153 above.

satisfied when the claimant is the beneficiary under an express, a resulting or a constructive trust. The controversial question which is at present being considered by the House of Lords in *Westdeutsche Landesbank Girozentrale* v. *Islington London Borough Council*[174] is whether void, voidable, and mistaken transactions also satisfy these prerequisites. It has been held that the recipient of property under such a transaction holds that property on trust for the transferor, thus providing him with both of the existing prerequisites of an equitable proprietary claim, both an equitable proprietary interest and a fiduciary relationship.

Westdeutsche Landesbank Girozentrale v. *Islington London Borough Council* concerned a ten-year interest-rate swap agreement under which the bank had made an 'up-front payment' of £2,500,000 to the local authority which had subsequently made four interest payments totaling £1,354,474.07. At this point, such interest-rate swap agreements were held to be outside the powers of local authorities and therefore void *ab initio*[175] so no further payments of interest were made. At first instance and in the Court of Appeal, the bank was held to be entitled to recover the balance of its advance on two distinct grounds: first, at law as money had and received to the use of the bank by which the local authority had been unjustly enriched and, secondly, in equity on the basis of its continuing equitable proprietary interest in the money advanced. Although most of the attention of the lower courts was directed towards the claim at law (because the claim in equity was on all fours with the binding decision of the House of Lords in *Sinclair* v. *Brougham*[176]), the existence of the claim in equity was crucial to the availability of compound, rather than simple, interest. Consequently, it is inevitable that the controversial decision in *Sinclair* v. *Brougham* will be reviewed and, hopefully, reconsidered by the House of Lords.

Sinclair v. *Brougham*[177] arose out of the liquidation of the Birkbeck Permanent Benefit Building Society, in the course of which it became apparent that a banking business which the Society had been running was in fact *ultra vires.* A question of priorities therefore arose between the shareholders of the society and the depositors in the banking business (both had agreed that the outside creditors should be paid off first). The possibility of an equitable proprietary claim being available to the depositors was raised for the first time in the House of Lords as a result of a suggestion to counsel by Viscount Haldane LC. Four of the members

[174] [1994] 4 All ER 890 (QBD and CA). The decision of the CA was handed down as long ago as Dec. 1993; the HL heard the appeal in Trinity Term 1995 but has not yet delivered judgment. [The decision of HL is now reported at [1996] 2 W.L.R. 802]

[175] This was held by the HL in *Hazell* v. *Hammersmith and Fulham London Borough Council* [1992] AC 1 (the interest payments were actually stopped following the decision of the Div. Ct. of the QBD, later affirmed by the HL).

[176] N. 170 above.

[177] *Ibid.* [*Sinclair* v. *Brougham* was overruled by HL, N. 174 above].

of the House of Lords subsequently held that the depositors did indeed have an equitable proprietary interest arising under a trust.[178] It is, frankly, hard to justify the existence of such a trust;[179] the depositors had made their deposits with the intention of becoming general creditors of the building society, and there is no obvious reason why they should have been held to have an equitable proprietary interest and potential priority over its other general creditors.[180] Further, even if such an equitable interest could initially have been found, it is not obvious how this could have survived the mixing of the depositors' funds in the hands of the building society; the depositors must necessarily have intended the building society to have the right to mix their deposits with other funds—how else could the deposits have produced any interest for the depositors? Exactly the same is true of *Westdeutsche Landesbank Girozentrale* v. *Islington London Borough Council*; the bank had entered into the transaction with the intention of becoming a general creditor of the local authority and certainly intended the latter to have the right to mix the sums advanced with its other funds.

Both these decisions concerned transactions which were void *ab initio* and so this will clearly be the principal issue to be considered by the House of Lords. However, a similar conclusion was reached by Millett J in relation to a voidable transaction in *El Ajou* v. *Dollar Land Holdings*,[181] where persons induced to purchase shares by fraudulent misrepresentations were held to be 'entitled to rescind the transaction and revest the equitable title to the purchase money in themselves, at least to the extent necessary to support an equitable tracing claim'.[182] More controversial still was the much earlier decision by Goulding J in *Chase Manhattan Bank* v. *Israel-British Bank (London)*[183] to attribute the same consequences to a payment made as a result of a mistake.[184] This latter deci-

[178] Viscount Haldane LC and Lord Atkinson held that the trust in question was 'a resulting trust, not of an active character', while Lord Parker of Waddington held that it was a constructive trust; Lord Sumner did not indicate with which of these two views he agreed.

[179] A person who deposits money with a bank must necessarily make the bank absolute legal and beneficial owner thereof since otherwise the bank would be unable to utilize the funds other than in accordance with the rules governing trust investments and certainly would not be able to make unsecured loans.

[180] This equitable proprietary interest would have given the depositors priority over the outside creditors had it not already been agreed that they should be paid off first. It must be at least questionable whether any trust in their favour would or could have been found to exist if this agreement had not already been reached.

[181] N. 154 above, affirmed by the CA without discussion of this particular point at [1994] 1 BCLC 464.

[182] Unless the existence of fraud is in itself a ground for obtaining an equitable proprietary interest, there is no obvious justification for the priority given here either.

[183] [1980] 2 WLR 202. [This decision cannot survive the HL decision, N. 174 above)

[184] A New York bank as the result of a clerical error made twice rather than once a payment of $2,000,000 to another New York bank for the credit of a London bank, which subsequently became insolvent. The legal effects of the mistaken payment had to be determined in accordance with the law of the State of New York, where a payment under

sion was expressly applied by Cooke P in the Court of Appeal of New Zealand in *Liggett* v. *Kensington*[185] but when this case reached the Privy Council (*sub nom. In Re Goldcorp Exchange*[186]) Lord Mustill declined to express an opinion whether or not *Chase Manhattan Bank* v. *Israel-British Bank (London)* had been correctly decided.[187] This may encourage the House of Lords to include voidable and mistaken transactions in any review of the law which it may carry out in *Westdeutsche Landesbank Girozentrale* v. *Islington London Borough Council.* Such transactions are similar, in that each claimant entered into the transaction in question with the intention of becoming a general creditor and that every payment was made in order to discharge a supposed contractual debt; the difference is that no question of authorising any mixing could possibly have arisen because each payer thought that once-and-for-all payments were being made in discharge of the debt in question. Despite this difference, however, as a matter of principle neither void nor voidable nor mistaken transactions should, without more, be held to satisfy the prerequisites of an equitable proprietary claim.[188] It is therefore to be hoped that the House of Lords overrules at least *Sinclair* v. *Brougham*[189] and preferably also the decisions in which its effect has been extended to voidable and mistaken transactions; if *Sinclair* v. *Brougham* is indeed overruled, perhaps the anomalous and unjustifiable requirement for the existence of a fiduciary relationship as a prerequisite of an equitable proprietary claim will fall with it[190]. In the event that any of these reforms actually occurs, the unjustifiable priority which the transferors of property under void, voidable, and mistaken transactions at present enjoy over the general creditors of their transferees will be eradicated; in this event remedies for breach of trust will in this respect too have been considerably liberalised.

a mistake of fact of money which the payee cannot conscientiously withhold gives rise to the imposition of a constructive trust. Goulding J held, rather unexpectedly, at 208 that this was 'also in accord with the general principles of equity as applied in England'. This is highly questionable. It is not obvious how either an equitable proprietary interest or a fiduciary duty could conceivably have arisen as the result of a payment made through a third party bank intended to be in settlement of a commercial debt.

185 [1993] 1 NZLR 257

186 N. 12 above.

187 *Ibid.* 103.

188 This question, which has been the subject of considerable discussion by commentators in recent years, is discussed in more detail in [1995] CLJ 377, *passim* but particularly at 397–404 where the authorities and the different views of the commentators are analysed.

189 [*Sinclair* v. *Brougham* was indeed overruled by HL in *Westdeutsche Landesbank Girozentrale* v. *Islington London Borough Council* n. 174 above; *Chase Marhattan Bank* v. *Israel-British Bank London* n. 183 above also appears unlikely to have survived.

190 [HL left this requirement intact, n. 174 above, 836]

CONCLUSION

The four different aspects of remedies for breach of trust which have been the subject of recent judicial reconsideration all manifest, to a greater or lesser extent, the liberalising nature of such remedies. The decision of the House of Lords in *Target Holdings* v. *Redferns* is perhaps the most important, in relation to the specific issue with which it was concerned, the measure of recovery of losses caused by breaches of trust, and, perhaps potentially more significantly, because of the enunciation by the House of a general principle which may affect the liability of fiduciaries who have made a profit out of a breach of their duty of loyalty, an area of the law which has already been substantially liberalised by the decision of the High Court of Australia in *Warman International* v. *Dwyer*. The decision of the Privy Council in *In re Goldcorp Exchange* has continued and confirmed the reluctance of the courts to discover fiduciary relationships in commercial transactions and, while the decision of the same tribunal in *Royal Brunei Airlines* v. *Tan* can hardly be said to have had a liberalising effect on the position of third-party accessories to breaches of trust, its enunciation of general principle can undoubtedly be seen as forming part of the general rethinking of the nature of remedies for breach of trust. This ongoing liberalisation can and must be carried forward, first by the House of Lords in *Westdeutsche Landesbank Girozentrale* v. *Islington London Borough Council* in respect of the availability of equitable proprietary claims and, when an appropriate occasion arises, in respect of the elements of liability for 'knowing receipt'. If the present process continues, the English law governing remedies for breach of trust should shortly have thrown off the shackles of the nineteenth century authorities and be in a position to start the twenty-first century in good shape.

11

Trust Law for the Twenty-first Century

SIR WILLIAM GOODHART QC

Trusts have a long history in English law. The 'use', the ancestor of the trust, can be traced back at least to the reign of Henry III in the early thirteenth century.[1] By the end of the fourteenth century, the Chancellor was beginning to enforce uses in his Court of Chancery.[2] By the late seventeenth century, due in large part to the work of Lord Chancellor Nottingham, something recognizable to modern lawyers as the law of trusts had emerged.[3]

More than 300 years after Nottingham's death,[4] trusts are flourishing as never before. Enormous amounts of money are still held in private family settlements. Their purpose and nature has of course changed. The old Victorian and pre-Victorian strict settlement was designed to keep land in the family, to ensure that it passed from father to eldest son, and that successive owners could not sell or mortgage the land to put money into their own pockets. Thus was created a rigid and complex structure of life estates, estates in tail male and tail general, jointures for wives and widows, charges to secure portions for daughters and younger sons, and so on. Interest in this archaic aspect of the law has had a minor revival as the result of the BBC television serialization of 'Pride and Prejudice'. There has been an interesting correspondence in the press on the question why, if Mr Collins was the heir to the Longbourn estate, his surname was not Bennet.[5] By contrast, the modern trust, though still intended in part to keep money out of the hands of children unless and until they become capable of managing it, is mainly driven by the motive of tax avoidance and will frequently be set up and managed in an off-

[1] Pollock and Maitland, *History of English Law* (2nd edn.), 228 ff.

[2] Holdsworth, *A History of English Law*, iv, 419–20.

[3] *Ibid.*, vi, 641–4.

[4] Heneage Finch, first Earl of Nottingham, b. 1621, Lord Keeper 1673, Lord Chancellor 1674, d. 1682. Curiously, his entry in the *Dictionary of National Biography* contains no reference to his immense influence on equity law.

[5] A possible explanation is that the original owner was Mr Bennet's maternal grandfather, who (having no sons) settled Longbourn on trust for his elder daughter for life, with remainder to Mr Bennet for life, with remainder to Mr Bennet's sons successively in tail, with remainder (in default of any sons or younger brothers of Mr Bennet) to the settlor's younger daughter (who married a Mr Collins) for life, with remainder to her sons successively for life or in tail.

shore tax haven—usually an island where the banks outnumber the indigenous inhabitants.

But trusts are not limited to traditional trusts of family property. Charitable trusts have of course been with us for a very long time. For a time, in the eighteenth and early nineteenth centuries, trusts became an important mechanism for carrying on trade through the so-called deed of settlement companies.[6] These disappeared when the process of incorporation was simplified by the Joint Stock Companies Act 1844 and limited liability was extended to joint stock companies by the Limited Liability Act 1855.[7] But trusts still play an important part in commerce through unit trusts and debenture trust deeds. Unincorporated associations such as clubs, societies, political parties,[8] even the Inns of Court, which own land or investments do so through the medium of a trust. Above all, occupational pension trusts have grown to truly vast proportions. The assets of funded pension schemes were estimated at £500 *billion* in January 1992.[9] Over ten and a half million employees were members of pension schemes in 1991 and seven million pensions were being paid.[10] Private-sector self-administered pension schemes, which are responsible for a little more than half the total pension scheme membership[11] in 1991 received £10.7 billion in contributions and £16 billion in investment income and paid out £13½ billion in pensions and other benefits.

Nor is the role of the trust likely to diminish in the foreseeable future. Whatever the colour of the next government, it seems likely that enterprising or lucky individuals will continue to be able to accumulate large funds and will use trusts as the most favoured method of passing them on to their descendants. Occupational pension schemes, whose total membership has been in slight decline in recent years, may well expand again, particularly if current proposals that all employees should be required to have funded pensions are adopted.[12] The Goode Committee endorsed the view that 'trust law in itself is broadly satisfactory and should continue to provide the foundation for interests, rights and duties arising in relation to pension schemes'.[13] Finally, the trust in recent years has been attracting increasing interest from countries whose legal systems do not currently recognize trusts. The Hague Con-

[6] See Gower's *Principles of Modern Company Law* (5th edn.), 30–1. Several of the leading insurance companies trace their ancestry back to deed of settlement companies.

[7] *Ibid.*, 38–47.

[8] See Art. 8.3 of the Constitution of the Liberal Democrat Party.

[9] The Report of the Pension Law Review Committee (the Goode Committee), 1993, Cm 2342, para. 3.1.69.

[10] *Ibid.*, App. 4, Tables 1, 5.

[11] *Ibid.*, App. 4, Table 10.

[12] See Frank Field and Matthew Owen, 'Private Pensions for All', 1993.

[13] N. 9 above, para. 4.1.14 and Recommendation 2.

vention on the Law Applicable to Trusts and on their Recognition—incorporated into the law of the United Kingdom by the Recognition of Trusts Act 1987—provides a mechanism by which the concept of trust law can be exported. It is at least possible that the trust will in the twenty-first century join those other English inventions, such as football and the steam engine, which have swept the world.[14]

But the continued success and expansion of trusts makes it all the more surprising that the statutory framework governing trust law has not had a major overhaul for seventy years. It was seventy years ago that the 1925 property legislation came into force. That precedes the date of birth of most if not all of those contributing to this book. Those seventy years represent nearly a quarter of the period between us and Lord Nottingham and some two-fifths of the period that separates us from that other great equity Chancellor, Lord Eldon.[15] Yet the Trustee Act 1925, together with the Settled Land Act 1925 in relation to trusts of land and the Administration of Estates Act 1925 in relation to testamentary trusts, remain in most respects hardly altered.

The statutory powers given to trustees are unduly narrow and hedged about by out-of-date restrictions. The most notorious example is the power of investment. The power conferred by section 1 of the Trustee Act 1925 reads like something out of the 'Forsyte Saga'. By 1961, when it was replaced by the Trustee Investments Act, it had become a total absurdity. Let me give you a few examples of authorized investments under the 1925 Act:

'India 7, 5½, 4½, 3½, 3 and 2½ per cent stock, or any other capital stock which may at any time be issued by the Secretary of State in Council of India under the authority of any Act of Parliament and charged on the revenues of India'.[16]

'In the debenture or rentcharge or guaranteed or preference stock of any railway company in the United Kingdom incorporated by special Act of Parliament, and having during each of the ten years last past before the date of investment paid a dividend at the rate of not less than three per centum on its ordinary stock.'[17]

'In the B annuities of the Eastern Bengal, the East Indian, the Scinde Punjaub and Delhi, Great Indian Peninsula and Madras Railways.'[18]

'In nominal or inscribed stock issued or to be issued by any Commissioners incorporated by Act of Parliament for the purpose of supplying water, and having a compulsory power of levying rates over an area having according to the returns of the last census prior to the date of investment a population exceeding 50,000, provided that during each of the ten years last past before the date of

[14] So far, however, Italy is the only civil law country to have signed the Convention.

[15] John Scott, first Earl of Eldon, b. 1751, Lord Chancellor 1801–6, 1807–27, d.1838.

[16] Trustee Act 1925, s. 1(1)(d).

[17] *Ibid.*, s. 1(1)(g). [18] *Ibid.*, s. 1(1)(j).

investment the rates levied by such commissioners have not exceeded 80 per centum of the amount authorised by law to be levied.'[19]

What the Trustee Act 1925 did not confer was any power at all to invest in equities. Trustees, under the statutory powers, could invest in the B annuities of the Scinde Punjaub and Delhi Railways but not in the ordinary shares of ICI.

By 1961—fourteen years after Indian independence and the nationalization of the British railways—action was eventually taken. The Trustee Investments Act was enacted. It undoubtedly improved the situation but it did not go far enough in extending the power of investment while at the same time it imposed complex administrative rules on trustees. In particular, it notoriously required a 50–50 split of the trust fund before the power to invest in wider-range securities could be exercised. No competent investment manager would have advised in 1961 or at any time since that it was right to invest as much as half the trust fund in fixed-interest securities, even where the beneficiaries were the most helpless of widows and orphans. It has been estimated that if a fund had been initially split 50–50 in 1961 between a representative selection of narrower- and wider-range investments the narrower-range part would, by 1995, have represented only 5 per cent of the total fund.[20] In 1982, the Law Reform Committee described the Act as 'tiresome, cumbrous and expensive in operation'.[21]

Indeed it is my view—and that of a number of other practitioners in the field—that any professional person who drafts a trust instrument which leaves the powers of investment to be governed by the Trustee Investments Act would be guilty of professional negligence.

But it is not only in relation to powers of investment that the trustee legislation is unduly narrow. The power to borrow money in section 16 of the Trustee Act 1925 is very limited. While it is probably right that the trustees should not be given a statutory power which would enable them to gear the trust fund by borrowing to buy more investments,[22] trustees are, strictly speaking, not even authorized to run a short-term overdraft on their bank account. Under section 19 of the Act, trustees are authorized to insure trust property only against loss or damage by fire and only up to three quarters of its value. It seems clear that section 23 of the Act authorizes the delegation only of administrative acts and not of the exercise of a discretion such as the selection of investments. The power of delegation to an attorney under section 25 of the Act (as amended by the Powers of Attorney Act 1971) does extend to discretions but it was

[19] Trustee Act 1925, s. 1(1)(n).

[20] Submission of Fleming Private Asset Management Ltd. to the Treasury, June 1995.

[21] Report on the powers and duties of trustees, Cmnd. 8733, para. 3.17.

[22] See *Re Suenson-Taylor's Settlement Trusts* [1974] 1 WLR 1280.

intended to cover delegation by an individual trustee who for some reason would not be able to participate in a decision and it is doubtful whether the section can be used to authorize collective delegation of powers by the trustees through the execution of parallel powers of attorney.

Some of the powers in the Settled Land Act 1925 to deal with land are also unduly restrictive or archaic.[23] These powers, of course, are also given to trustees holding land on trust for sale.[24] I wonder when land was last sold in consideration of a perpetual rent—a power conferred by section 39 of the Act. There are detailed regulations about the permissible terms of leases which can be granted under the Act.[25] It is doubtful whether it is possible under the statutory powers to grant a lease including a rent review clause.[26] Is it really necessary to provide that:

'A sale of land may be made subject to a stipulation that all or any of the timber and other trees, pollards, tellers, underwood, saplings and plantations on the land sold or any articles attached to the land shall be taken by the purchaser at a valuation and the amount of the valuation shall form part of the price of the land, and shall be capital money accordingly'?[27]

The power to grant options requires the price payable on the exercise of the option to be fixed at the time of the grant, and limits the time for exercise of the option to ten years.[28] The requirement that the price should be fixed at the time of the grant of the option is particularly inconvenient in relation to options over potential development land, where the value of the land may be greatly affected by the nature of the planning permission to be obtained. There is an amazingly detailed list of improvements authorized by the Act.[29] These include such matters as:

'saw-mills, scutch-mills, and other mills, water-wheels, engine-houses and kilns',

'tramways, railways, canals, docks',

'Erection of buildings in substitution for buildings within an urban sanitary district taken by a local or other public authority, or for buildings taken under compulsory powers, but so that no more money be expended than the amount received for the buildings taken and the site thereof',

'Residential houses for land or mineral agents, managers, clerks, bailiffs, woodmen, gamekeepers and other persons employed on the settled land',

[23] See, e.g., *Re Rycroft's Settlement* [1962] Ch. 263.

[24] Law of Property Act 1925, s. 28(1).

[25] Settled Land Act 1925, ss. 41–8.

[26] The objections are that it may not be possible to grant a lease at an increasing rent (*Hallett to Martin* (1883) 24 Ch. D. 624) or to determine rent by arbitration.

[27] N. 25 above, s. 49(2).

[28] *Ibid.*, s. 51(1), (2).

[29] *Ibid.*, s. 83 and Sch. 3.

'Engine houses, engines, gasometers, dynamos, accumulators, cables, pipes, wiring, switchboards, plant and other works required for the installation of electric, gas or other artificial light in connexion with any principal mansion house or other house or buildings, but not electric lamps, gas fittings, or decorative fittings required in any such house or building'.

Nor are good works ignored. Thus a tenant for life may, for a nominal price or at a nominal rent, sell or let land:

'For the site of a place of religious worship, residence for a minister of religion, school house, town hall, market house, public library, public baths, museum, hospital, infirmary or other public building, literary or scientific institution, drill hall, working men's club, parish room, reading room or village institute'.[30]

There are no other Acts of Parliament, and few works of literature, which are as redolent as the Settled Land Act of a world which was already dying in 1925 and has long since disappeared—the world of the great landowner, mining his own coal, transporting it over his own tramways to his own docks, building his own gasometer to provide gas light for his principal mansion house, and providing small dwellings to which his grateful workers return at the end of the working day after their visit to the public baths to decide whether to spend the evening in the literary institute or the working men's club.

But perhaps even more important than the unreasonable restrictions imposed by the trustee legislation is the absence of statutory authority for many of the powers which any ordinary modern trust is likely to need. Thus the Trustee Act contains no power to pay professional trustees for their work. There is no statutory power to hold trustee investments in the names of nominees—an increasingly important power as the result of the reduction in the length of the Stock Exchange settlement period and the proposed introduction of the CREST system for dematerialized transfers.[31] There is no statutory power, except in the case of settled land, to buy a house as a residence for a beneficiary, even if the trust instrument allows the purchase of land as an investment.[32] Except in the case of personal representatives acting in the distribution of an estate,[33] there is no general power to appropriate trust assets to the shares of individual beneficiaries.

But if statutory trust law contains so much that is now archaic and inconvenient, and omits so much that is now a practical necessity, how

[30] N. 25 above, s. 55.

[31] It is possible, however, that if shareholding in nominee names became so widespread as to represent the usual course of business, it might become legitimate for trustees to adopt it: see *Speight* v. *Gaunt* (1883) 9 App. Cas. 1.

[32] *Re Power* [1947] Ch. 572.

[33] Administration of Estates Act 1925, s. 41.

has it survived for seventy years with so little change? The answer, of course, is that the statutory powers are not exhaustive. They can be enlarged and further powers can be conferred by the trust instrument. Almost all English trust instruments controlling trust funds of any size have, for many years past, included as a minimum wide powers of investment (including a power to buy property for occupation or use by a beneficiary); extended powers of lending and borrowing; wide powers of disposal and management of land held on trust; power to insure trust assets up to full replacement value; powers of appropriation; power to appoint trustees resident outside the United Kingdom; and clauses allowing trustees to claim payment for their services and to retain fees for acting as directors of companies in which the trust holds shares. More recent trust instruments commonly contain powers for trustees to employ nominees, to appoint investment advisers and delegate fund management to them, to give guarantees and indemnities and to change the forum of administration and the proper law of the trust. It is now usual to include a power for trustees to enter into transactions with one or more of themselves, contrary to the self-dealing rule, though this power is usually exercisable only on condition that there is at least one trustee who is not personally interested on the other side of the transaction. Finally, it is increasingly common to include a power for trustees to confer on themselves yet further administrative powers, to plug any gaps which become apparent in future years.[34]

But if it is so easy and so common for the trust instrument to confer all the administrative powers which trustees could reasonably require, why bother to change the law? There are, I believe, two answers to this question. First, not every trust instrument is drafted with competent professional advice. Home-made wills in particular can give rise to serious problems. Land may be left on trusts which bring it within the complex régime of the Settled Land Act rather than on the much simpler trust for sale. The trustees may be forced to rely on the Trustee Investments Act for their powers of investment. It may be impossible to get a professional adviser to act as a trustee because there is no trustee charging clause. Even trust instruments which were adequate when they were drafted twenty or thirty years ago may lack powers such as the employment of nominees or the delegation of fund management which are now regarded as necessary.

Secondly, I believe that it is undesirable for law and practice to become so far removed from each other. It is the duty of the law to provide a satisfactory infrastructure for the operation of trusts. At present this is not the case. I believe it would be helpful if the model of company law

[34] See Underwood, Bruce-Smith, Hallam, and Clark, 'Practical Trust Precedents', Sections A1 and H.

was adopted,[35] and a new Trustee Act provided an updated 'Table A' containing all the standard trustee powers which were appropriate for a small- to medium-sized trust. The new Table A would be sufficient to provide an adequate basic framework if no additional powers were conferred. It would save tedious repetition of standard clauses. It would of course, as at present,[36] be subject to restriction or extension if the settlor or testator so wished.

The need for reform has been obvious for many years. The Law Reform Committee published in 1982 an excellent *Report on the Powers and Duties of Trustees.*[37] The Report contained a list of fifty-six recommendations for changes in the law. Only five of those recommendations have been wholly or partly implemented. Two of the five are simply consequential on one of the others. The three substantive changes in the law that have been enacted are that personal representatives or trustees are allowed, with the leave of the court, to act on the advice of an appropriately qualified lawyer on a question of construction of a will or trust;[38] that personal representatives have, in effect, been given power to retire with the leave of the court;[39] and that personal representatives must act unanimously when disposing of land (but not other property) comprised in the deceased's estate.[40]

It is extremely depressing that there should have been such a meagre result from such an expert and detailed report. The skies are, however, at last beginning to brighten.

Following the publication of the Report of the Goode Committee,[41] many important reforms of the law governing pension trusts have been introduced by the Pensions Act 1995. Most of the reforms are highly specific to the field of pension trusts and therefore not appropriate for discussion in this paper. But some of the reforms have a potentially wider application and could form a model for use in other fields.

The main reforms in this category are the new statutory power of investment and delegation of fund management. Section 34 of the Act sweeps away all formal restrictions on types of investment and provides

[35] See the Companies (Tables A to F) Reg., SI 1985/805.

[36] Trustee Act 1925, s. 69.

[37] Cmnd. 8733.

[38] Administration of Justice Act 1985, s. 48. See Report, n. 37 above, 67, Recommendation 36.

[39] Administration of Justice Act 1985, s. 50 (which authorizes the court to appoint a substitute personal representative in place of an existing one, or to terminate an appointment if there will be one or more continuing personal representatives). See Report, n. 37 above, 67, Recommendation 43, and 68, Recommendations 47 and 49, which are consequential.

[40] Law of Property (Miscellaneous Provisions) Act 1994, s. 16. See Report, n. 37 above, 68, Recommendation 51.

[41] Report of the Pension Law Review Committee, n. 9 above.

baldly that: '[t]he trustees of a trust scheme have, subject to any restriction imposed by the scheme, the same power to make an investment of any kind as if they were absolutely entitled to the assets of the scheme.' The section also gives trustees power to delegate discretion on investment decisions to fund managers. However, trustees and fund managers must have regard to the need for diversification and the suitability of any proposed investment.[42] Trustees who have not delegated their powers must obtain proper advice on proposed new investments[43] and on their existing portfolio.[44] Trustees are relieved from liability for the default of a fund manager if they have taken all reasonable steps to satisfy themselves that the manager has appropriate knowledge and experience and is acting competently.[45] However, liability for negligence in performing investment functions can not be excluded or restricted by the scheme documents.[46]

In April 1995 the Government enlarged the powers of charity trustees to invest in equities by altering the balance between wider and narrower range investments from 50–50 to 75–25.[47] In November, the Government announced its intention to enlarge the powers of all trustees to the same extent by statutory instrument under section 13 of the Trustee Investments Act 1961. The Government is also considering the possibility of using its powers under the Deregulation and Contracting Out Act 1994 to carry out a wider liberalization of trustee investment powers, and will soon publish a discussion paper on that subject. The Government already has power under section 71 of the Charities Act 1993 to make regulations extending the investment powers of charity trustees in ways not authorized by the Trustee Investments Act.

Mr Charles Harpum has been appointed a Law Commissioner with a specific remit to review and overhaul trust law, rather as Prof. Julian Farrand and Mr Trevor Aldridge reviewed conveyancing and land law a few years ago. In carrying out his duties, Mr Harpum has been authorized to work in co-operation with the Trust Law Committee. This is an independent body, set up in 1994 largely on the initiative of Mr Michael Jacobs, who is now its Secretary. It is chaired by Sir John Vinelott. Prof. David Hayton is its Deputy Chairman, and I am one of its members.

There is now, therefore, a real climate of opportunity to reform the law on the powers and duties of trustees. By the end of the century we may have created a trust law fit for the twenty-first century, rather than the twentieth or even the nineteenth—given that much of the 1925 legislation merely re-enacted the provisions of Victorian statutes such as the

[42] Pensions Act 1995, s. 36(2). [43] *Ibid.*, s. 36(3).
[44] *Ibid.*, s. 36(4). [45] *Ibid.*, s. 34(4). [46] *Ibid.*, s. 31.
[47] Trustee Investments Act 1961, s. 13: Charities (Trustee Investments Act 1961) Order, SI 1995/1092.

Settled Land Act 1882 or the Trustee Act 1893. I therefore turn to the question of how we should try to reform the law.

As I have already suggested, I believe that the law should provide the framework of powers and duties which trustees will reasonably require for the conduct of a small- to medium-sized trust. In doing this, we should try to avoid as far as possible detailed and rigid lists of things which trustees can or cannot do. It has, of course, always been true that trustees are bound not only to consider whether they have formal power to do some proposed act but whether that act would be proper in all the circumstances. It is, however, not always easy to convince trustees that they might be committing a breach of trust by investing a large slice of the trust fund in Cosa Nostra plc if there is a list of authorized investments and Cosa Nostra plc falls within it. Flexibility should be retained as far as possible by minimizing the formal restrictions on the powers of trustees and concentrating on their duty to consider whether their proposed action is in all the circumstances in the interests of the trust as a whole and represents a proper balance between any conflicting interests of the various beneficiaries.

How would these principles transfer into detailed reforms of trust law? Let me imagine myself in the happy position of having single-handed authority to change trust law.

Action is at last being taken to get rid of the Settled Land Act by implementing the Law Commission's admirable 1989 Report on Trusts of Land.[48] At present, the Act performs two functions. First, it creates an elaborate structure by which the legal title to the land and most of the powers of dealing and management are vested in the tenant for life rather than in the trustees. Secondly, it contains the detailed powers of disposition and management which apply to all trusts of land, whether the land is settled land or held on trust for sale.[49] The first of these functions is now largely obsolete. Hardly any trust instruments in recent years have been deliberately drafted so as to invoke the Settled Land Act régime. This régime is complex. It is unnecessary, and it may result in the powers of management becoming vested in a person who is not competent to exercise them.[50] The provisions governing the second function are archaic and far too complex, as I have already indicated.

Instead, the Law Commission proposed a single category of trusts of land, based on the trust for sale régime but replacing the misleading and inaccurate description of such trusts as 'trusts for sale'. The present power to delegate powers of leasing and management to a person en-

[48] Law Commission Report No. 181.

[49] See s. 28(1) of the Law of Property Act 1925, which confers on trustees for sale 'all the powers of a tenant for life and the trustees of a settlement under the Settled Land Act 1925'.

[50] See *Hambro* v. *Duke of Marlborough* [1994] Ch. 158.

titled to an interest in possession[51] would be enlarged to permit delegation of any functions. The Settled Land Act régime would be abolished immediately for future trust instruments. The Law Commission proposed that trustees of land should be given all the powers of an absolute owner, subject to general equitable duties as to the exercise of those powers and subject to any restrictions imposed by the trust instrument.

These proposals have now been incorporated into the Trusts of Land and Appointment of Trustees Bill, which received its formal first reading in the House of Lords on 23 November 1995. Clause 2 of the Bill provides that no settlement for the purposes of the Settled Land Act can be made after the commencement of the new Act. Clause 4 incorporates into all trusts for sale of land—including existing trusts—a power to postpone sale of the land for an indefinite period. Clause 6 gives trustees of land all the powers of an absolute owner, subject to any direction to the contrary in the trust instrument. It also provides that land may be purchased for occupation by a beneficiary, but only where the trustees already hold other land and are therefore trustees of land as defined in the Bill or where the trust includes the proceeds of sale of other land.[52] Clause 6 applies to existing trusts for sale but not to existing Settled Land Act settlements. Clause 9 authorizes trustees to delegate revocably any of their functions relating to the land to a beneficiary entitled to an interest in possession, but the exercise of this power is likely to be seriously inhibited by sub-clause (7), which makes the trustees vicariously liable for any act or default of the beneficiary to whom the functions are delegated. Finally, Schedule 1 to the Bill prevents the future creation of entailed interests, thereby rendering obsolescent a great deal of learning on such arcane matters as protectors of the settlement, the creation of base fees, and the Fines and Recoveries Act 1833.

The Bill seems to me to be in most ways admirable. I have a few criticisms of it, however. First I would get rid of the Settled Land Act more quickly by making the new Bill apply to existing settled land on the termination of the interest of the person who now is the tenant for life or has the powers of a tenant for life under section 20 or 21 of the Settled Land Act. Secondly, I would remove the vicarious liability of trustees for acts or defaults of a beneficiary to whom they have delegated any function. Instead, I would make the trustees liable to the same extent as pension trustees who delegate investment powers to a fund manager—

[51] Law of Property Act 1925, s. 29.

[52] See the Trusts of Land and Appointment of Trustees Bill, cl. 17. Where a trust of personalty includes a power to purchase land as an investment but no power to purchase land as a residence, it seems that the trustees would have no power to purchase land as a residence so long as the trust fund remained wholly invested in personalty but could acquire that power if they first purchased other land as an investment, thereby converting themselves into trustees of land.

that is, they must have taken reasonable steps to satisfy themselves that the beneficiary has appropriate knowledge and experience to handle the delegated functions and is acting competently.[53] I would remove the provisions for automatic revocation of the delegation on the retirement of a trustee or the appointment of a new trustee. I would authorize Settled Land Act trustees to confer the new administrative powers on tenants for life by delegation immediately. Finally, I would extend the power to purchase land for occupation to any settlement which contains a power to invest in land, whether or not the trustees are or have been trustees of land as defined in the Bill.

Next, investment. The Government's forthcoming consultation paper is likely to say that sections 1 to 5 of the 1961 Act need to be replaced with a broad new power requiring no division of the trust fund into parts. Amen to that. But there are two approaches to reform. One is to create a broader and updated definition of authorized investments. This was the approach proposed by the Law Reform Committee in 1982.[54] The more radical approach is to scrap the concept of authorized investments altogether and to rely, instead, on trustees' duties to act with prudence, good faith, and reasonable skill in the exercise of their powers of management. This is the approach adopted by the Pensions Act and likely to be favoured by the Government's consultation paper. It is also the approach taken in the USA, where the Uniform Prudent Investor Act permits trustees to invest in any property or any type of investment (whether or not yielding income) so long as they comply with certain standards. The basic standards are:

(a) A trustee shall invest and manage trust assets as a prudent investor would, by considering the purposes, terms, distribution requirements and other circumstances of the trust. In satisfying this standard, the trustee shall exercise reasonable care, skill and caution.
(b) A trustee's investment and management decisions respecting individual assets must be evaluated not in isolation but in the context of the trust portfolio as a whole and as part of an overall investment strategy having risk and return objectives reasonably suited to the trust.

On this issue, I am firmly in favour of the radical approach.

Nomineeship need not take up much time. There is general agreement that in the modern financial world there should be a statutory power to vest trust assets in nominees, and it remains only to identify who should be eligible to become a nominee and what safeguards are to be provided.

[53] Pensions Act 1995, s. 34(4).

[54] Report, n. 21 above, paras. 3.1–3.25. Their proposal that there should be no statutory power to invest in foreign securities seems, with the passage of time, unduly restrictive and is contrary to the rules on freedom of movement of capital within the European Union.

Collective delegation of trustees powers and duties is a more complicated issue. The Trust Law Committee has already produced a lengthy draft paper. The Law Commission's Property Team is in course of producing its own consultation paper on this subject.[55]

The need for reform is not quite as pressing as in the case of investment powers. Small trusts cannot afford and do not need active fund management. It is better for them to put the money into a unit trust. Large trusts usually have the necessary express powers. Nevertheless, there is now a fairly broad consensus that reform is needed.

Here again, there are two possible approaches. One is to identify the fields where, in practice, delegation is useful and give authority for delegation in those fields. Portfolio management is the most obvious, but there are other categories such as estate management for landholding trusts. The other approach is to authorize the delegation of all managerial and administrative functions. In either case, trustees would not be authorized to delegate powers which directly affect beneficial interests, such as powers of advancement or appointment or the allocation of income of discretionary trusts. Trustees should not be liable for the misconduct of those exercising delegated powers, provided that (as is required in the case of delegation under the Pensions Act) they have taken all reasonable steps to satisfy themselves that the delegate has appropriate knowledge and experience and is acting competently.

I have already touched on some other statutory powers which need reform, such as the power of insurance, and new powers which are needed, such as powers of appropriation. I would certainly like to see a statutory power to pay reasonable remuneration to an individual acting as a trustee in the course of his profession or to a trust corporation. The old concept that a trustee acts voluntarily is wholly unrealistic except in relation to family members or to charity trustees, where trusteeship is a form of contribution to the work of the charity. The absence of a power to pay trustees is simply a handicap, in that it prevents the appointment of professional trustees.

There are some powers which are frequently found in trust instruments but which, for one reason or another, I do not think would be suitable for inclusion in the list of statutory powers. For example, I would not include a power to appoint non-resident trustees or to export the administration or proper law of the trust. It is not the function of a Trustee Act to assist tax avoidance.[56] Powers for trustees to carry on a

[55] The Law Commission recently produced a Report (No. 220) on delegation by individual trustees, but this covered a much narrower field, mainly to do with delegation under enduring powers of attorney.

[56] See *Re Weston's Settlements* [1969] 1 Ch. 223. It has to be said, however, that tax avoidance was the main purpose for which the Variation of Trusts Act 1958 has been used.

business should not, in my view, be included in the statutory list and should only be exercisable on the express direction of the settlor or testator.

Powers of self-dealing are more complicated. The basic rule that a trustee should not obtain a personal benefit from the trust and should not place himself in a position where his personal interest conflicts with his fiduciary duty is fundamental to the law of trusts. On the other hand, if this rule is pressed too far it can lead to inconvenient consequences. I have already mentioned one aspect of this rule which falls into this category, which is the absence of a right to payment for professional trustees. Another inconvenience is that the self-dealing rule inhibits transactions between trusts which have one or more common trustees, even if none of them has a personal interest in either trust. This seems pointless, and I would relax the self-dealing rule so that it only applies to transactions in which a trustee has a personal interest. I would not, however, go further than that. I would not relax the self-dealing rule in cases where a trustee has a personal interest conflicting with the trust, even on the footing that there must be an independent trustee who concurs in the transaction.

Finally, are there any ways in which trust law should become more restrictive rather than more permissive? There is certainly one. It is common for trust instruments to contain very wide exemption clauses, which exempt trustees from liability for anything except personal fraud or dishonesty. In two recent cases, in England[57] and Jersey[58], clauses giving exemption from gross negligence or even wilful and reckless breaches of trust were held to be valid as a matter of general law. I wrote an article some years ago suggesting that in some circumstances an exemption clause might be rendered void by the Unfair Contract Terms Act 1977.[59] I think this was probably wrong.[60] However, I believe the principle is correct and that paid professional trustees should not be permitted to be exempt from collective or personal liability for negligence, except in special circumstances. One such circumstance might be where the fund is so large that liability might exceed the professional negligence insurance cover which the trustee could reasonably be expected to obtain. Greater scope should be given to the exemption of unpaid trustees, but even there it is doubtful whether exemption from personal (as opposed to collective) negligence should be generally permitted.

[57] *Armitage* v *Nurse* (17 July 1995, Jacob J, unreported)

[58] *Midland Bank Trustee (Jersey) Ltd* v *Federated Pension Services Ltd* [1996] Pensions LR 179. However, it was held that liability for gross negligence could not be excluded because of Article 5 of the Trusts (Amendment) (Jersey) Law 1989.

[59] (1980) 44 *Conv.* 333.

[60] See *Duke of Norfolk's Settlement Trusts* [1982] Ch. 61.

But it is not simply a question of exemption clauses. The Trustee Act itself, as it has been interpreted by the courts,[61] is too generous in exempting trustees from liability. Section 30 of the Trustee Act 1925 should be amended to make it clear that the indemnity given by that section applies only to vicarious liability and does not exempt trustees from any liability for personal negligence, including a failure to exercise proper supervision over the conduct of agents.

I am conscious that, in this paper, I have concentrated almost entirely on the administrative and managerial functions of trustees. I have said nothing about the substantive law of trusts. This is mainly because the substantive law seems to me to be in much less need of reform. The rule against perpetuities, for example, which is the subject of a recent Law Commission Working Paper, has basically worked well since it was reformed in 1964,[62] though it has produced a few problems in relation to options and easements. About the need to reform the powers and duties of trustees however there can be no doubt. The absence of any serious reform since 1925, apart from the misconceived Trustee Investments Act, has left us with trust law which is seriously out of date. I hope that, over the next few years, we will be able to bring trust law up to date and make it fit for the twenty-first century.[63]

[61] *Re Vickery* [1931] 1 Ch. 572.

[62] Perpetuities and Accumulations Act 1964.

[63] Since this paper was written, amendments to the Trusts of Land and Appointment of Trustees Bill have met some of the criticisms of it made above. In particular, under cl. 9(8) of the Bill trustees be liable for default by a beneficiary in the exercise of delegated powers 'if, and only if, the trustees did not exercise reasonable care in deciding to delegate the function to the beneficiary.'

12

Equity's Reaction to Modern Domestic Relationships

ANTHONY J. H. MORRIS

INTRODUCTION

The evolution of equity, particularly over the last two centuries, has predictably responded to the social and economic circumstances which prevailed in England—and subsequently in other common law jurisdictions—for the greater part of that period. Of individual litigants, and particularly of those litigating in courts of equity, the great preponderance were persons of financial substance. Whatever may have been the situation amongst the less advantaged members of the community, traditional social orders were firmly rooted amongst the wealthy and privileged.

It would be a mistake to underestimate the strength of prevailing *mores*, both religious and social, for the greater part of that period. The traditional family unit, presided over by a husband and father, was not merely the norm; it was, in practical terms, the *only* accepted social unit. Irregular relationships, such as those involving unmarried heterosexual couples and homosexual couples, undoubtedly existed, as they have existed throughout history; but they were not recognized. Society may have tolerated *de facto* relationships amongst the lower orders; amongst the higher orders, society may have winked at a man's keeping a mistress, or even maintaining what was ostensibly a close friendship with another man; and, in the days before oral contraception, the birth of children out of wedlock was a frequent, if somewhat distasteful, fact of life. But a person of any substance in society—which invariably meant a man—was expected to have a dutiful and obedient wife, and loving and respectful children. That family unit was the only one which counted. Blackstone no doubt accurately expressed not only the law, but also the temperament of contemporary society, in his observation that[1] '[t]he *holiness* of the matrimonial state is left entirely to the ecclesiastical law:

[1] 1 Bl.Com. (1st edn., 1765–9), 421 (the spelling has been modernized, but italicization is original).

the temporal courts not having jurisdiction to consider unlawful marriages as a *sin*, but merely as a civil inconvenience.'

Within such a family unit, the master's role was one of privilege but, at the same time, of responsibility. Until the emancipation of married women's property rights—which commenced in 1857[2] but was not completed until 1882[3]—a woman was less than a servant or vassal of her husband; in the eyes of the common law, she had virtually no independent existence. To quote again from Blackstone:[4]

> By marriage, the husband and wife are one person in law: that is, the very being or legal existence of the woman is suspended during the marriage, or at least is incorporated and consolidated into that of the husband: under whose wing, protection, and *cover*, she performs every thing: and is therefore called in our law-french a *feme-covert*; is said to be *covert-baron*, or under the protection and influence of her husband, her *baron*, or lord; and her condition during her marriage is called her *coverture*. Upon this principle, of an union of person in husband and wife, depend almost all the legal rights, duties, and disabilities, that either of them acquire by marriage.

But even after married women were 'given full proprietory rights'[5] by the Act of 1882, the practical reality is that men remained the dominant property-owners in society. Estates—particularly landed estates, but often also the investment estates of the increasingly wealthy bourgeoisie—continued to pass from father to son and to grandson; and accumulated (as opposed to inherited) wealth was, until quite recent times, practically impossible for women—and especially married women—to achieve. Even after 1882, equity's continued development has occurred against a background of economic and social circumstances which largely excluded women from the acquisition and ownership of property. There is considerable force in the view that:[6]

> [The] principle of separation of property, which accords ownership to the person providing the purchase money [acts] unfairly in the context of a typical domestic economy. It is also out of step with partners' own views that marriage is a partnership involving a sharing of jointly-acquired and jointly-used property.

It must be said, however, that the law not only followed religious and social *mores*, and economic realities, in conferring privileges on a man as head of his family; it also imposed duties and responsibilities on him. According to Blackstone[7] a husband was bound to provide his wife with 'necessaries', and was obliged to pay debts contracted by the wife for

[2] Matrimonial Causes Act 1857; Married Women's Reversionary Interests Act 1857.
[3] Married Women's Property Act 1882.
[4] N. 1 above, 430.
[5] *Petitt* v. *Pettit* [1970] AC 777, *per* Lord Morris of Borth-y-Gest at 797.
[6] J. Dewar, *Law and the Family* (2nd edn., 1992).
[7] N. 1 above, 430.

such 'necessaries'; and, in the case of legitimate children,[8] the duties of the father were said to 'principally consist in three particulars; their maintenance, their protection, and their education'.

It is significant that equity—once the most flexible and dynamic branch of English law—largely became what it is today in the period down to the *Judicature Act* reforms in 1873. This is what the learned authors of Meagher, Gummow, and Lehane[9] describe as the 'period of systemisation', during which: 'equity developed positive rules and shed its *ex tempore* characteristics. Equity henceforth had principles, just as common law had rules. The whims of the Lord Chancellor were no longer sufficient.' Equity became, or at least achieved the appearance of having become, 'cut and dried'; the problem being that what is 'cut and dried' is, by definition, dead.

Meanwhile, society has moved on at an accelerating pace. Social commentators may be correct in ascribing change, and the increasing rate of change, to the upheavals of two World Wars and the effects of the Great Depression, as well as the consequences of industrialization and modern technologies. But, for present purposes, it is irrelevant to identify the causes of social change; or even to consider whether those changes are desirable: it is enough to note, as a fact, that change has occurred. A poignant example was offered by Peter Young J of the New South Wales Supreme Court in the 1993 case of *Parker* v. *Parker*:[10]

> The law and attitude of the community to persons living outside wedlock and having children has varied tremendously over the last few hundred years. Three hundred years ago the law would solve the present situation simply. The community would have shown its disapproval of the conception of children out of wedlock by having the plaintiff stripped to the waist and publicly whipped outside the parish church after morning prayer before being transported to America with her children. The defendant would have to pay to stop the children being a charge on the parish until transportation and would thereafter be left to carry on his life. Nowadays the plaintiff argues that she is entitled to $2 million from the defendant and to be supported by him in the lifestyle to which he made her accustomed.

Statute law has, by and large, kept pace with—if not, in some instances, exceeded the pace of—social change. As previously observed, the proprietary and contractual rights of married women have been legislatively assimilated to those of men; the adverse legal consequences of illegitimacy have been swept aside by statutory reform; all enlightened jurisdictions have emulated the English example, following the Wolfenden Report, of decriminalizing homosexual acts between consenting adults

[8] *Ibid.* 434.
[9] *Equity—Doctrines and Remedies* (2nd edn., 1984), para. 114, 7–8.
[10] (1993) 16 Fam. LR 863, at 869.

in private; discrimination on the basis of sex has been outlawed in most jurisdictions, and discrimination on the basis of sexual orientation or preference has been outlawed in many; and an increasing number of jurisdictions have enacted legislation to protect the rights of parties to *de facto* relationships.

It is apparent, however, that equity has not entirely kept pace with the community's changing social orders. The purpose of this paper is to examine those principles of equity which are inconsistent with modern social conceptions or inadequate to deal with contemporary social relationships; to explore current trends which suggest a willingness on the part of the courts to reform those principles in light of changing social conditions; and to suggest areas in which further development of equitable principles may be anticipated.

PROPRIETARY RIGHTS

As a separate branch of the law, equity owes much of its earlier development—and perhaps its genesis—to the conception that a court exercising equitable jurisdiction, acting *in personam*, can recognize and enforce proprietary rights which are not recognized or enforceable at common law, through the imposition of trusts or proprietary estoppels.

For present purposes, express trusts are not of immediate concern, since the existence of an express trust does not depend upon the existence of any prior relationship between the parties. But, in relation to resulting and constructive trusts, and proprietary estoppels, equity has traditionally attached particular significance to the nature of the parties' antecedent relationships. The question which arises for consideration is whether equity will be prepared to extend principles which have been developed in the context of marital and familial relationships, and which are largely premised on concepts of primogeniture and the dominant role of the father and husband within a traditional family unit, to cases which involve domestic relationships of a very different kind.

Resulting Trusts

Perhaps the greatest anachronism in modern equity is to be found in the fixed and arbitrary rules which have been developed in circumstances where the court must determine the beneficial ownership of a property which a person purchases and pays for, but places in the name of another. Save in those cases where a presumption of advancement arises, the purchaser is presumed (in the absence of proof to the contrary) to have intended to retain beneficial ownership; but in those categories of cases where the presumption of advancement applies, the opposite result obtains. It is therefore critical, in such cases, to ascertain which of two possible presumptions is operative: whether it is a case in which a presumption operates in favour of the person who provided the purchase price; or a case in which a presumption operates in favour of the legal owner. Under established principles of equity, the determination of that question depends entirely upon the nature of the parties' antecedent relationship. This gives rise to the following anomalies:

(1) There is a presumption of advancement where a man places property in the name of his wife, but not where a woman places property in the name of her husband. The traditional rule in respect of transfers between wife and husband was summarized by Street CJ in Equity (with whom Cullen CJ and Gordon J concurred) in *Moore* v. *Whyte (No 2)*,[11] in these terms:

> The . . . question for consideration . . . is whether the circumstances show that Mrs. Moore intended to make a gift to her husband of the moneys in question or whether there is a presumption of a resulting trust in her favour. The question is entirely one of intention. 'In every case,' said *Romer*, L.J., in *Mercier* v. *Mercier*[12] 'where money of the wife comes to the husband, whether from capital or income, the question is whether a gift was intended or not.' The fact that a husband is found in possession of his wife's separate estate, even with her assent, is not *per se* sufficient evidence of a gift to him for his own use, and in the absence of evidence to the contrary he will be taken to be a trustee for her. Each case, however, must depend upon its own circumstances and in each case the whole of the circumstances must be considered for the purpose of ascertaining whether there is a presumption of a resulting trust, or whether the proper inference to be drawn from the facts is that a gift was intended: see *e.g. Re Curtis.*[13] Unless the evidence showing an intention to make a gift is sufficient to rebut the presumption of a resulting trust that presumption will prevail, and in that sense it may be true to say that the burden of proof lies upon those who assert a gift.

(2) Similarly, there is a presumption of advancement where a man places property in the name of his child, but not where a woman places property in the name of her child. This inconsistency has been the cause of much perplexity amongst equity judges for over a century. In the 1868 case of *Sayer* v. *Hughes*[14] the Vice-Chancellor, Sir John Stuart, remarked:

> It has been argued that a mother is not a person bound to make an advancement to her child, and that a widowed mother is not a person standing in such a relation to her child as to raise a presumption that in a transaction of this kind a benefit was intended for the child. But the case of a stranger who stands *in loco parentis* seems not so strong as that of a mother. In the case of *Re De Visme*[15] it

[11] (1922) 22 SR (NSW) 570, at 579–80. [12] [1903] 2 Ch. 98, at 101.
[13] (1885) 52 LT 244. [14] (1868) LR 5 Eq. 376, at 381.
[15] (1863) 2 DeGJ & S 17, 46 ER 280.

was said that a mother does not stand in such a relationship to a child as to raise a presumption of benefit for the child. . . . But maternal affection, as a motive of bounty, is, perhaps, the strongest of all, although the duty is not so strong as in the case of a father, inasmuch as it is the duty of a father to advance his child. That, however, is a moral obligation, and not a legal one.

His Lordship, having referred to the decision of Eyre CB in *Dyer* v. *Dyer*[16] continued: 'The word "father" does not occur in Lord Chief Baron *Eyre's* judgment, and it is not easy to understand why a mother should be presumed to be less disposed to benefit her child in a transaction of this kind than a father.'

In the 1879 case of *Bennet* v. *Bennet*[17] the Master of the Rolls (Sir George Jessel) demonstrated both an anxiety to preserve what his Lordship regarded as the established principle, and a measure of embarrassment that the established principle was difficult to justify rationally. His Lordship observed:[18]

The first question is, what is the law upon the subject; for I must say that I am very much embarrassed by the authority.

The doctrine of equity as regards presumption of gifts is this, that where one person stands in such a relation to another that there is an obligation on that person to make a provision for the other, and we find either a purchase or investment in the name of the other, or in the joint names of the person and the other, of an amount which would constitute a provision for the other, the presumption arises of an intention on the part of the person to discharge the obligation to the other; and therefore, in the absence of evidence to the contrary, that purchase or investment is held to be in itself evidence of a gift.

In other words, the presumption of gift arises from the moral obligation to give.

. . .

So that a person *in loco parentis* means a person taking upon himself the duty of a father of a child to make a provision for that child. It is clear that in that case the presumption can only arise from the obligation, and therefore in that case the doctrine can only have reference to the obligation of a father to provide for his child, and nothing else.

But the father is under that obligation from the mere fact of his being the father, and therefore no evidence is necessary to shew the obligation to provide for his child, because that is part of his duty. In the case of a father, you have only to prove the fact that he is the father, and when you have done that the obligation at once arises; but in the case of a person *in loco parentis* you must prove that he took upon himself the obligation.

But in our law there is no moral legal obligation—I do not know how to express it more shortly—no obligation according to the rules of equity—on a mother to provide for her child: there is no such obligation as a Court of Equity recognises as such.

[16] (1788) 2 Cox 92, at 93, 30 ER 42, at 43.

[17] (1879) LR 10 Ch. D 474.

[18] *Ibid.* 476–8.

From *Holt* v. *Frederick*[19] downwards it has been held that no such obligation exists on the part of a mother; and therefore, when a mother makes an advancement to her child, that is not of itself sufficient to afford the presumption in law that it is a gift, because equity does not presume an obligation which does not exist.

Dealing with *Sayer* v. *Hughes*,[20] Jessel MR remarked:[21] 'I may say I should have had no hesitation in deciding *Sayer* v. *Hughes* in the same way as the Vice-Chancellor did, having regard to the evidence; though I should not have arrived at the same conclusion irrespective of the evidence.' But, as I have said, his Lordship sought to ameliorate this anomaly; he did so by the suggestion that, whilst no presumption of advancement arises as between mother and child, nonetheless:[22] 'in the case of a mother—this is the case of a widowed mother—it is easier to prove a gift than in the case of a stranger: in the case of a mother very little evidence beyond the relationship is wanted, there being very little additional motive required to induce a mother to make a gift to her child.'

The question has twice arisen in the High Court of Australia, the first occasion being the 1917 case of *Scott* v. *Pauly*.[23] Two members of the Court—Gavan Duffy J[24] and Rich J[25]—regarded the case as one turning upon the evidence, in which it was unnecessary to consider the equitable doctrine of presumption of advancement, or the onus of establishing or rebutting the existence of a resulting trust. But the presiding member of the Court, Sir Isaac Isaacs, offered these observations:[26]

The appellants start their case by showing that Rebecca Shade bought and paid for the land, and that the respondent Pauly, into whose name it was transferred . . . , gave no consideration for it. This, on well established principles, raises *prima facie* a resulting trust for Rebecca Shade, and, if nothing more appeared, that would have to be so determined (see *In Re Scottish Equitable Life Assurance Society*[27]). But something more does appear: Rebecca Shade was her mother, and the doctrine of presumed advancement is invoked in her behalf. On the balance of authority as it at present stands, that single circumstance is not sufficient to rebut the presumption of resulting trust. No doubt, when all the circumstances are before the Court, the intention of the purchaser to make or not to make the holder of the title trustee is to be determined as a question of fact. But the burden of proof . . . may also seriously affect the conclusion, and the burden of proof may shift. Therefore, it is necessary to consider the steps. The case of a father having an obligation in conscience to provide for a child, either unadvanced or treated as unadvanced, is different from the case of a mother dealing with a daughter, and particularly where the daughter is married and in fairly good circumstances (*Bennet* v. *Bennet*[28]). In the first case the facts are in themselves sufficient to rebut the presumption of resulting trust; in the second, according to

[19] (1726) 2 P Wms. 357, 24 ER 763. [20] N. 14 above. [21] N. 17 above, at 479.
[22] *Ibid.* 479–80. [23] (1917) 24 CLR 274. [24] *Ibid.* 285. [25] *Ibid.* 287.
[26] *Ibid.* 281–2. [27] [1902] 1 Ch. 282. [28] N. 17 above.

Bennet v. *Bennet*, they are not. That case, drawing a distinction between father and mother, has not, so far as I am aware, been judicially doubted (see *Re Orme*; *Evans* v. *Maxwell*,[29] and *Preston* v. *Greene*[30]). Some text-writers doubt it, while others do not. It is unnecessary now to consider its correctness, and I assume it is right. If it ever comes to be questioned, it may be that the solution will be found in the circumstance that the 'presumption' there spoken of is an *inference* which the Courts of equity in practice drew from the mere fact of the purchaser being the father, and the head of the family, under the primary moral obligation to provide for the children of the marriage, and in that respect differing from the mother. In case of his death the inference called a presumption as to the mother might well be different from that where the father was still alive.

A more conservative view emerges from the judgment of Dixon J, sitting at first instance in the exercise of the High Court's original jurisdiction, in the 1933 case of *Stewart Dawson and Co. (Victoria) Pty. Limited* v. *Federal Commissioner of Taxation*.[31] His Honour considered that the suggestion of Isaacs J, to the effect that the so-called 'presumption' of advancement is but 'an inference which the Courts of equity in practice drew from the mere fact of the purchaser being the father' was 'not altogether in conformity with'[32] the English authorities. Sir Owen Dixon cited the judgment of Cussen J in *Davies* v. *National Trustees Executors and Agency Co. of Australasia Ltd*[33] as containing 'what is, perhaps, the best modern statement of the whole doctrine', in the following terms:[34]

Where a husband or father (as the case may be) purchases property in the name of his wife or child, and is proved to have paid the purchase-money in the character of a purchaser, a prima facie but rebuttable presumption arises that the wife or child takes by way of advancement—that is to say, takes beneficially. Evidence may be given to rebut this presumption and to show that the husband or father did not intend the wife or child to take by way of advancement, and on the other hand evidence may, where necessary, be given to support the presumption. If on the whole of the evidence the Court is satisfied that the husband or father did not intend at the time of the purchase that his wife or child should take by way of advancement, the rule of law is that there is a resulting trust for the husband or father.

More recently, two decisions in the Supreme Court of New South Wales, whilst acknowledging the entrenched rule, argued for its revision. In *Dullow* v. *Dullow*,[35] the leading judgment was delivered by Hope JA. Significantly, however, it was concurred in by two judges—Kirby P, and McHugh JA—who have since been advanced to the High Court of Australia. Hope JA remarked:[36]

[29] (1883) 50 LT 51. [30] (1909) 1 IR 172. [31] (1933) 48 CLR 683.
[32] *Ibid.* 690. [33] [1912] VLR 397, at 401. [34] N. 31 above, at 690.
[35] (1985) 3 NSWLR 531. [36] *Ibid.* 541.

it is not necessary for me to consider what the correct principle is as to any presumption of advancement when a mother places property in the name of a child. I should say however that, as at present advised, I think that if the law is to be left constrained by presumptions, the same presumption should apply to gifts to children by both mother and father.

Most recently, in *Brown* v. *Brown*,[37] each member of the New South Wales Court of Appeal expressed *dicta* to the same effect. Gleeson CJ (with whom Cripps JA concurred) said:[38]

We are here dealing with a transaction that occurred in 1958. In the social and economic conditions which apply at the present time the drawing of a rigid distinction between male and female parents, for the purposes of the application of the presumptions of equity with which we are concerned, may be accepted to be inappropriate. I would be prepared, although with rather less conviction, to say the same about conditions in 1958. I would, therefore, not decide this case upon the basis that, Mrs. Brown being a mother rather than a father, the presumption of advancement did not apply.

Kirby P went rather further, citing both Canadian[39] and New Zealand[40] authority in support of the following conclusion:[41]

The reasons of legal authority, principle and policy therefore combine to support the proposition, advanced for the appellants in this Court, that they were entitled [at first instance] to have the benefit of the presumption of advancement to assist the decision in their case. . . . To so determine involves no rejection of binding authority. It is simply the application of the law as to presumptions in the circumstances of Australian society at the relevant times for which those presumptions are invoked. The hesitations which may restrain judges in the development, modification or expansion of rules of substantive law do not apply when a judge is invited to develop, modify or expand (in accordance with legal authority, principle and policy) a procedural rule or a principle of evidence defining the content of a presumption which assists in judicial reasoning.

(3) Whilst the presumption of advancement applies where a man places property in the name of his wife, and perhaps where a man places property in the name of his fiancée prior to their marriage,[42] it is now well-settled—at least in Australia—that no such presumption applies as between parties to a *de facto* relationship. From the last century, there is authority in the Supreme Court of Victoria to the contrary: see *Murdock* v. *Aherne*,[43] although the result in that case may have been influenced by the fact that the male partner (who had been transported to Hobart

[37] (1993) 31 NSWLR 582. [38] *Ibid.* 591.

[39] *Re Dagle; Dagle* v. *Dagle Estate* (1990) 70 DLR (4d) 201.

[40] *Pickens* v. *Metcalf and Marr* [1932] NZLR 1278 and *Re Lloyd* [1960] NZLR 947.

[41] N. 37 above, at 599.

[42] See, e.g., *Moate* v. *Moate* [1948] 2 All ER 486; *Wirth* v. *Wirth* (1956) 98 CLR 228.

[43] (1878) 4 VLR (Eq.) 244.

Town, leaving a wife in England) contracted a bigamous marriage with the woman by representing himself to her as a widower. Molesworth J said:[44]

When a woman discovers that a man to whom she has been married has a former wife she, if she pleases, is discharged from the connexion. If she continues to live apparently as his wife, his liabilities, to the world without, are as if she were so. As between themselves, they may make any bargain they like. As to rights of property, in the absence of distinct evidence, I think they should be taken to be, as near as may be, those of married people. . . . [The case involves] invested property, land purchased in her name, of which she has now the legal estate, and upon which buildings have been erected with his knowledge, in a great degree with money produced by business which he allowed her to carry on, and savings which she made. As to these, if she was his wife, I would take the investments to be a gift to her; and that the right should not now be shaken, by the proof of something of conjugal fraud, to which Murdock submitted.

As recently as 1980, at least one member of the High Court of Australia was prepared to regard it as an 'open question' whether a presumption of advancement could arise in the case of *de facto* partners. In *Napier* v. *Public Trustee (Western Australia)*,[45] Gibbs J said:

It was not suggested on behalf of the respondent in the present case that there is a presumption of advancement when a man purchases property in the name of a woman to whom he is not married but with whom he is living in a permanent *de facto* relationship as man and wife. The authorities support the view that no presumption of advancement arises in those circumstances, although there are some cases that may appear to provide support for a submission to the contrary: see *Murdock* v. *Aherne*,[46] which is cited in *Wirth* v. *Wirth*,[47] and see also the discussion in *Carkeek* v. *Tate-Jones*.[48] It is not necessary for present purposes to consider whether it would be right, having regard to the changed attitudes of society, which are so different from those which prevailed in the nineteenth century when *Rider* v. *Kidder*[49] and *Soar* v. *Foster*[50] were decided, to make a presumption of advancement in such a case, and if so whether the law is sufficiently flexible to permit that to be done. I would treat those questions as open ones.

But those open questions were resolutely closed by a majority of the High Court four years later, in *Calverley* v. *Green*.[51] Only one member of the Court—Sir Harry Gibbs, who had by that time been elevated to the Chief Justiceship—would have concluded that such a presumption is available. His Honour's remarks, although dissenting from the majority, are instructive:[52]

[44] (1878) 4 VLR (eq.), 249.
[45] (1981) 55 ALJR 1 at 2.
[46] N. 43 above, at 249.
[47] N. 42 above, at 238.
[48] [1971] VR 691, 695–6.
[49] (1805) 10 Ves. Jun. 360, 32 ER 884.
[50] (1858) 4 K & J 152, 70 ER 64.
[51] (1984) 155 CLR 242.
[52] *Ibid.* 250–1.

The question is whether the relationship which exists between two persons living in a *de facto* relationship makes it more probable than not that a gift was intended when property was purchased by one in the name of the other. The answer that will be given to that question will not necessarily be the same as that which would be given if the question were asked concerning a man and his mistress who were not living in such a relationship. The relationship in question is one which has proved itself to have an apparent permanence, and in which the parties live together, and represent themselves to others, as man and wife. It is true that in some cases a person may maintain a *de facto* relationship for the very purpose of preventing the other party to the relationship from obtaining any right or claim to property, but the question now asked arises only when the party has taken the deliberate step of purchasing property in the name of the other. Once one rejects the test applied in *Soar* v. *Foster*[53] as too narrow, and rejects any notion of moral disapproval, such as is suggested in *Ryder* v. *Kidder*,[54] as inappropriate to the resolution of disputes as to property in the twentieth century, it seems natural to conclude that a man who puts property in the name of a woman with whom he is living in a *de facto* relationship does so because he intends her to have a beneficial interest, and that a presumption of advancement is raised. Cases such as *Soar* v. *Foster*,[55] where the relationship was based on an invalid marriage ceremony, or *Murdock* v. *Aherne*,[56] where the relationship was founded on a bigamous marriage, would be a fortiori. For these reasons I consider that there was a presumption of advancement in the present case.

In a joint judgment, two subsequent Chief Justices—Sir Anthony Mason and Sir Gerard Brennan—emphatically adopted a contrary stance, saying:[57]

Such an inference is appropriate only as between parties to a lifetime relationship (like the presumption of advancement of a wife: *Carkeek* v. *Tate-Jones*[58]). The exclusive union for life which is undertaken by both spouses to a valid marriage, though defeasible and oftentimes defeated, remains the foundation of the legal institution of marriage (*Hyde* v. *Hyde and Woodmansee*;[59] *Kahan* v. *Kahan*[60]) though it is no necessary element of the relationship of *de facto* husband and wife. The term '*de facto* husband and wife' embraces a wide variety of heterosexual relationships; it is a term obfuscatory of any legal principle except in distinguishing the relationship from that of husband and wife. It would be wrong to apply . . . the presumption of advancement . . . to a relationship devoid of the legal characteristic which warrants a special rule affecting the beneficial ownership of property by the parties to a marriage.

In a separate concurring judgment, Sir William Deane agreed, making these remarks:[61]

[53] N. 50 above. [54] N. 49 above. [55] N. 50 above.
[56] N. 43 above. [57] N. 51 above, at 259–60.
[58] N. 48 above. [59] (1866) LR 1 P & D 130, at 133.
[60] [1963] VR 203, at 204. [61] N. 51 above, 268–9.

The exceptional cases in which equity assumes an intention of 'advancement' and thereby precludes a presumption of a resulting trust are defined by reference to recognized categories of relationships rather than by the actual presence of love or affection. Originally, those relationships were the ones which equity saw as involving obligations of support owed by the person providing the consideration to the person who would otherwise be presumed to hold upon implied resulting trust: a man to his child or other person to whom he stood in loco parentis; a husband to his wife. Those categories of relationships are not, however, finally settled or closed, at least in this Court: see, e.g., *Wirth* v. *Wirth*[62] where an intention of advancement of an 'intended wife' was presumed. . . . It is arguable that they should be adjusted to reflect modern concepts of the equality in status and obligations of a wife vis-a-vis a husband (see *Moore* v. *Whyte (No 2)*[63] and *Robinson* v. *Robinson*[64]) and of a mother vis-a-vis a father: see *Scott* v. *Pauly*.[65] Any adjustment of those relationships must however, be made by reference to logical necessity and analogy and not by reference to idiosyncratic notions of what is fair and appropriate. In their judgment in the present case, Mason and Brennan JJ. advance what seem to me to be convincing reasons for denying that either logic or analogy warrant the extension of those categories of relationships to encompass the relationship which existed between Mr. Calverley and Miss Green at the time of the purchase of the Baulkham Hills property. It is, however, unnecessary that I form a concluded view in that regard since the question has, as I see the matter, been resolved by the recent decision of this Court. In *Napier* v. *Public Trustee (W.A.)*,[66] it was held by Aickin J., in a judgment with which Mason, Murphy and Wilson JJ. expressed general agreement, that 'no presumption of advancement arises in favour of a de facto wife' to preclude the ordinary implication of resulting trust.

The fifth member of the Court, Murphy J, adopted an entirely different approach, arguing for the abandonment of presumptions as a basis, either for the imposition or for the exclusion, of a resulting trust.[67]

(4) The courts' refusal to recognize a presumption of advancement as between parties to a heterosexual *de facto* relationship renders it extremely unlikely that the courts will do so even in the case of the most stable relationships between persons of the same sex. The fact that Mason and Brennan JJ, in *Calverley* v. *Green*,[68] referred to the term '*de facto* husband and wife' as embracing 'a wide variety of *heterosexual* relationships' could not reasonably be understood as meaning that their Honours intended to leave open the possibility that a different result might be reached in the case of unmarried partners in a homosexual union.

It might be observed, however, that there is at least one arguable reason for contending that courts of equity should find it easier to con-

[62] N. 42 above, at 238, 241, 248. [63] N. 11 above. [64] [1961] WAR 56.
[65] N. 23 above, at 281–2, 285. [66] N. 45 above, at 3.
[67] N. 51 above, at 264–5. [68] *Ibid.* 260.

clude that a presumption of advancement exists as between homosexual couples, than in the case of *de facto* heterosexual couples. The fact is that heterosexual couples, if they wish to enter into what Mason and Brennan JJ described as an 'exclusive union for life',[69] at least have the opportunity and legal right to do so (unless prevented from doing so because, for example, one party is still married to another person). Where a party to a heterosexual relationship chooses not to marry, there may be some force in the suggestion of Gibbs CJ, that that may be 'for the very purpose of preventing the other party to the relationship from obtaining any right or claim to property';[70] no such suggestion can be made in the case of homosexual couples.

Nonetheless, the reasoning which underlies the majority views in *Calverley* v. *Green* applies with equal force in respect of homosexual partners, as it does in respect of heterosexual *de facto* couples. The difficulty, in each instance, is to draw the line at an appropriate point in the continuum between two extremes: on the one hand, relationships which involve a mutual commitment for life—arrangements which constitute a marriage in everything except legal form and ceremony; and, on the other hand, relationships of the most brief and tenuous kind. It is reasonable to assume that, at least in the short term, the courts will adopt the same approach in respect of homosexual relationships as the courts have adopted in respect of *de facto* heterosexual relationships: the approach of assuming that a relationship, which is not sanctified by legal marriage, cannot be assumed to be of sufficient permanence as to justify equity's presuming that a voluntary transfer of property from one party to the other is intended to advance the recipient.

It is inconsistent with equity's genius that such anomalies should be allowed to continue unresolved. It is suggested that three avenues of resolution are open.

First, there is the extreme approach suggested by Murphy J in *Calverley* v. *Green*[71]—and at least hinted at by Hope JA (with the concurrence of Kirby P and McHugh JA) in *Dullow* v. *Dullow*[72]—of dispensing altogether with presumptions as a means of resolving disputes as to the beneficial ownership of property. Whilst that approach has some attractions, it is unlikely to be achieved in the foreseeable future. As Deane J—himself one of the more 'progressive' or 'innovative' members of the High Court bench in recent years—observed in *Calverley* v. *Green*:[73]

> The relevant presumptions are, however, too well entrenched as 'land-marks' in the law of property (per Eyre L.C.B., *Dyer* v. *Dyer*[74]) to be simply discarded by judicial decision. Indeed, the law embodying them has been said in this Court to

[69] *Ibid.* 259. [70] *Ibid.* 250. [71] *Ibid.* 264–5. [72] N. 35 above, at 541.
[73] N. 51 above, at 266. [74] N. 16 above, at 92 (Cox), 43 (ER).

be so clear that it 'can . . . no longer be the subject of argument': per Dixon C.J., McTiernan, Williams, Fullagar and Taylor JJ., *Charles Marshall Pty. Ltd.* v. *Grimsley.*[75] If they are to be modified to avoid prima facie assumptions that a person intends the opposite to that which he does, it must be by legislative intervention which will not disturb past transactions which may conceivably have been structured by reference to them.

The second possibility is a reform of the existing law by way of piecemeal or *ad hoc* revision of established principles in the light of modern social conditions. The possibility of that happening would seem to be recognized in Deane J's observation that the 'categories of relationships are not . . . finally settled or closed';[76] and the judgments in *Brown* v. *Brown*[77] suggest—albeit by way of *obiter dicta*—that the process is already under way. The essential problem, however, is that such a 'piecemeal' or *ad hoc* approach addresses only the symptoms, rather than the underlying problem; and even then, may only be expected to address the symptoms in gradual progression, commencing with the most egregious. No doubt, in a short space of time, it will be possible to say with confidence that the same presumption applies between mother and child as has traditionally applied between father and child; and one may even feel some degree of optimism that, in the not too distant future, a wife's presumed intentions as regards her husband will be assimilated with a husband's presumed intentions as regards his wife. But it will be a very long time before any such process of revision gathers sufficient momentum to justify a reconsideration of *Calverley* v. *Green,*[78] so that *de facto* heterosexual and homosexual couples may enjoy the same legal protections as married couples.

It is submitted that there is a third option, for which there is respectable authoritative support, and which has the merits of being capable of logical justification. It will be recalled that, in *Scott* v. *Pauly,*[79] Sir Isaac Isaacs suggested that:

> If it ever comes to be questioned, it may be that the solution will be found in the circumstance that the 'presumption' . . . is an *inference* which the Courts of equity in practice drew from the mere fact of the purchaser being the father, and the head of the family, under the primary moral obligation to provide for the children of the marriage, and in that respect differing from the mother. In case of his death the inference called a presumption as to the mother might well be different from that where the father was still alive.

The notion of regarding what has traditionally been characterized as a 'presumption' as being, in fact, an 'inference', is not, on analysis, very different from what Sir George Jessel said in *Bennet* v. *Bennet,*[80] where his

[75] (1956) 95 CLR 353, at 364. [76] N. 51 above, at 268. [77] N. 37 above.
[78] N. 51 above. [79] N. 23 above, at 282.
[80] N. 17 above, at 476–7.

Lordship suggested that 'the presumption of gift arises from the moral obligation to give'. However, I would respectfully put the proposition in a slightly different way: an intention to advance may be inferred from the existence of a personal, social or domestic relationship which is of such a nature as to provide a rational foundation for the drawing of that inference.

The attraction of approaching the problem in terms of 'inferences' rather than 'presumptions' is that presumptions are absolute; inferences are infinitely variable in their degree. The traditional rule requires that the same presumption be applied in the case of (for example) a property purchased by a man in his wife's name, even where they have been separated for many years and each of them has entered into relationships with new partners; but such a presumption may never arise in the case of *de facto* partners, even if they have lived as husband and wife for many years.

There is no logical or rational reason why an intention to advance may not be inferred in the case of any personal, social, or domestic relationship, involving features such as mutual love and affection, cohabitation, or personal intimacy; and that is so, whether the relationship is one of blood or marriage, or is merely consensual. Nor is there any logical or rational reason why the parties' property rights, as adjudged by a court of equity, should depend upon essentially irrelevant considerations, such as whether the parties have undertaken a religious or civil ceremony of marriage; or whether any such marriage was legally valid; or the respective sexes of the purchaser and transferee.

'Presumptions', according to an American Judge, 'may be looked on as the bats of the law, flitting in the twilight but disappearing in the sunshine of actual facts'.[81] Where a presumption requires the court to assume—one should add, as the presumption is rebuttable, until the contrary is proved—that all men intend to advance their wives and children, but that women never intend to advance their husbands and children, and that partners in unmarried relationships (whether of the same or different sexes) never intend to advance their co-partners, then presumption becomes a mere fiction; and the rule should be *fictio cedit veritati: fictio juris non est ubi veritas* ('fiction yields to truth; where there is truth, fiction of law does not exist').[82]

If it is too much to hope that the pernicious influence of fixed and arbitrary presumptions will not disappear altogether from the law relating to resulting trusts, it is to be hoped—at the very least—that courts exercising equitable jurisdiction will follow the approach adopted by

[81] Lamm J, *Mocowik* v. *Kansas City, St. Joseph and Council Bluffs Railroad* (1906) 196 No 550, 551, 94 SW 256.

[82] 11 Co. Rep. 51; *Broom's Legal Maxims* (10th edn., 1939), 78–82.

McInerney J in *Carkeek* v. *Tate-Jones*,[83] of regarding such presumptions as readily rebuttable. As his Honour said:

> If . . . the real inquiry is as to the intention with which the transfer and payments were made . . . it is obvious that an intention of conferring a beneficial interest might be shown to exist notwithstanding that the parties were not married: *Murdock* v. *Aherne*[84]. . .
>
> In the present case, I have had evidence from both the plaintiff and the defendant as to [the] relationship existing between them at all relevant times. The presumption of a resulting trust must take its place with the rest of the evidence. For, as *Thayer*[85] observes, presumptions are 'merely prima facie precepts; and they presuppose only certain specific and expressed facts. The addition of other facts, if they be such as to have evidential bearing, may make the presumption inapplicable. All is then turned into an ordinary question of evidence, and the two or three general facts presupposed in the rule of presumption take their place with the rest, and operate with their own natural force, as a part of the total mass of probative matter . . .'.
>
> In other words, the question is what conclusion should I draw from the totality of the facts established in the evidence, including the matters giving rise to the presumption of a resulting trust. At the stage when it becomes my task to draw those conclusions, the operation of the presumption is exhausted.

Constructive Trusts and Proprietary Estoppels

As contrasted with equitable principles relating to resulting trusts, those applying to constructive trusts and proprietory estoppels have, in the last quarter-century, developed substantially in the direction of recognizing modern domestic relationships. This trend may conveniently be examined as involving three separate phases.

The first phase involved the recognition that a beneficial interest by way of constructive trust may arise through a person's contribution towards the acquisition or improvement of property, otherwise than by way of direct monetary payment. In relation to married couples, that had been accepted by the House of Lords in the 1971 case of *Gissing* v. *Gissing*;[86] but the earlier Court of Appeal decision in *Diwell* v. *Farnes*[87] limited a *de facto* partner to the recovery of his or her actual contributions to the purchase price. It was not until the 1972 case of *Cooke* v. *Head*[88] that a *de facto* partner (described in the judgments as a 'mistress') was accorded rights commensurable with those of a married spouse in similar circumstances. Lord Denning MR said:[89]

[83] N. 48 above, at 696. [84] N. 43 above.
[85] *A Preliminary Treatise on Evidence at the Common Law* (1898), at 346.
[86] [1971] AC 886.
[87] [1959] 1 WLR 624.
[88] [1972] 1 WLR 518.
[89] *Ibid.* 521.

In the light of recent developments, I do not think it is right to approach this case by looking at the monetary contributions of each and dividing up the beneficial interest according to those contributions. The matter should be looked at more broadly, just as we do in husband and wife cases. We look to see what the equity is worth at the time when the parties separate. We assess the shares as at that time. If the property has been sold, we look at the amount which it has realized, and say how it is to be divided between them. Lord Diplock in *Gissing* v. *Gissing*[90] intimated that it is quite legitimate to infer that:

> 'the wife should be entitled to a share which was not to be quantified immediately upon the acquisition of the home but should be left to be determined when the mortgage was repaid or the property disposed of.'

Likewise with a mistress.

Karminski LJ, in a separate concurring judgment, said:[91]

I desire to express my entire agreement with what Lord Denning MR has said about the principles of law in a case of this kind between a man and his mistress when they intend to set up a home together and intend also to marry when they are free. It is in no way different from the principles applicable in the cases of husband and wife who have built up a home together. The duty of the court in deciding the correct proportions is to be found in the opinion of Lord Diplock in *Gissing* v. *Gissing*,[92] where he said:

> 'on the basis of what would be fair having regard to the total contributions, direct or indirect, which each spouse has made by that date. Where this was the most likely inference from their conduct it would be for the court to give effect to that common intention of the parties by determining what in all the circumstances was a fair share.'

In this case, as very often happens, the major contribution in cash was made by the man, who in this case was earning a good deal more than the woman. She was a young secretary employed locally in a dairy. What is important and difficult to ascertain here is the value of what they each put physically into the building of the house. The plaintiff says that she worked very hard with her hands, did heavy work, including the use of a sledge hammer and a wheelbarrow loaded with heavy materials. . . . The real difficulty I also have found is how the figure of one-twelfth in all the circumstances of this case was arrived at. In my view I too think that one-twelfth was far below the real value of what she contributed towards this home in cash and by way of labour; and I agree that one-third is the proper estimate of the share of the nett proceeds.

The second phase commences with the case of *Ogilvie* v. *Ryan*,[93] which recognized that a constructive trust could arise even though the constructive beneficiary had not contributed to the acquisition or improvement of the property in money or money's worth. As Holland J concluded:[94]

[90] N. 86 above, at 909.
[91] N. 88 above, at 522.
[92] N. 86 above, at 909.
[93] [1976] 2 NSWLR 504.
[94] *Ibid.* 518.

an appropriate constructive trust will be declared in equity to defeat a species of fraud, namely, that in which a defendant seeks to make an unconscionable use of his legal title by asserting it to defeat a beneficial interest in the property which he . . . has agreed to or promised; or which it was the common intention of the parties that the plaintiff should have, in return for benefits to be provided by, and in fact obtained from, the plaintiff in connection with their joint use or occupation of the property.

Such an approach received appellate approval in the 1977 case of *Allen* v. *Snyder*.[95] Glass JA (with whom Samuels JA concurred) commenced his judgment with these remarks:[96]

Where the parties have not been married . . . the courts may only declare rights, however difficult it may be to unravel the tangled skein of human association, and apply to it considerations of legal principle. This is such a case, and it requires an examination of relevant principles of property and equity law which have been recently agitated in relation to contemporary innovations in the patterns of domestic life. It will be seen that the law does not countenance, in this respect, different rules for the married and the unmarried. Nor should it be overlooked that the rules, however they come to be formulated, ought to apply indifferently to all property relationships arising out of cohabitation in a home legally owned by one member of the household, whether that cohabitation be heterosexual, homosexual, dual or multiple in nature.

The velocity of social change affecting, not only the financial balance in the relationship of husband and wife, but also producing new forms of association outside marriage has, indeed, produced a flurry of litigious activities. New situations have, it appears, produced some new legal rules. It is inevitable that judge made law will alter to meet the changing conditions of society. That is the way it has always evolved. But it is essential that new rules should be related to fundamental doctrine. If the foundations of accepted doctrine be submerged under new principles, without regard to the interaction between the two, there will be high uncertainty as to the state of the law, both old and new. So it seems to me that a construction of the new rules which can accommodate them within the old structure is to be preferred to one which does not.

The members of the Court of Appeal were at pains to stress that a constructive trust enforces the parties' actual intentions, whether expressed in an oral agreement, or inferred from their conduct; not an imputed intention which the parties did not have, even if they might have formed such an intention had they applied their minds to the question.[97] But, at the same time, it was recognized that the existence of a marital or analogous relationship was relevant in determining the parties' actual intentions, either as a matter of construing the words used by them, or as a matter of inferring their intentions from their conduct. As Mahoney JA said:[98]

[95] [1977] 2 NSWLR 685. [96] *Ibid.* 689.
[97] *Ibid.* 690 (*per* Glass JA), 701 (*per* Samuels JA), 706 (*per* Mahoney JA).
[98] *Ibid.* 705–6.

It is settled law in Australia that the proprietory interests of persons in such relationships are to be determined by the application of the ordinary principles of law. . . . But this does not mean that, in determining whether the factual situation warrants the imposition of a trust, the relationship between the parties is to be ignored. It may be significant in a number of ways. The fact that the parties are in such a relationship may be relevant in deciding whether they intended the things which they said and did in relation to the property to have legal results. . . .

The relationship will be relevant also in determining what is the meaning and significance to be given to what the parties have said and done. Assuming that what is said and done is intended to have legal results, things which are intended to indicate an attitude to proprietory rights as between strangers, and what would be expected between strangers, if proprietory rights were intended to be created, will often be very different from what takes place between, e.g., husband and wife. . . . When the court is concerned to determine, e.g., whether a payment of money was intended to lead to the creation of a proprietory right in the matrimonial house, statements of less formal kinds may, in such circumstances, be given a meaning beyond that which, between strangers, they would bear.

But, having determined what is the meaning and significance of what the parties said and did, it still remains to determine whether the factual situation so emerging warrants or requires the imposition of a trust.

Allen v. *Snyder*[99] was followed in the Supreme Court of Victoria by O'Bryan J in *Hohal* v. *Hohal*,[100] and by the Full Court (Young CJ, Starke and Fullagar JJ) in *Thwaites* v. *Ryan*.[101] The principle applied in the former, and approved in the latter, was:[102]

the essential elements of the trust are, first, that the parties formed a common intention as to the ownership of the beneficial interest. This will usually be formed at the time of the transaction and may be inferred as a matter of fact from the words or conduct of the parties. Secondly, that the party claiming a beneficial interest must show that he, or she, has acted to his, or her, detriment. Thirdly, that it would be a fraud on the claimant for the other party to assert that the claimant had no beneficial interest in the property.

Before moving to the third and most significant phase in the development of equitable principles imposing constructive trusts in respect of property jointly enjoyed by the parties to a marital or analogous relationship, it is important to observe that the first and second phases are of continuing relevance; it would be a mistake to imagine that they have been entirely superseded by the principles laid down in the cases of *Muschinski* v. *Dodds*[103] and *Baumgartner* v. *Baumgartner*,[104] to which reference will shortly be made. The decision of the New South Wales Court of Appeal in the 1989 case of *Green* v. *Green*[105]—which came after the decisions in both *Muschinski* v. *Dodds* and *Baumgartner* v. *Baumgartner*—demonstrates that there is continuing scope for the im-

[99] N. 95 above. [100] [1981] VR 221. [101] [1984] VR 65.
[102] N. 100 above, at 225. [103] (1985) 160 CLR 583. [104] (1987) 164 CLR 137.
[105] (1989) 17 NSWLR 343.

position of constructive trusts either as a reflection of the value of one party's contributions to the acquisition or improvement of a property held by the other party (whether those contributions are made in money or money's worth),[106] or to give effect to the parties' common intentions as evidenced by express agreement or inferred from the parties' conduct.[107]

The third phase was comprised of the landmark decisions in *Muschinski* v. *Dodds*[108] and *Baumgartner* v. *Baumgartner*.[109] It is not proposed on this occasion to deal with either case in detail, as both decisions are well-known. The significance of both cases is that the High Court of Australia recognized that a constructive trust may be imposed by a court exercising equitable jurisdiction, where it would be unconscionable for the legal owner to assert exclusive proprietary rights, without evidence necessarily demonstrating either an express agreement to share the property, or conduct from which the existence of such an agreement can be inferred. The gravamen of both cases may be summarized in two passages from the majority judgment (Mason CJ, Wilson and Deane JJ) in *Baumgartner v Baumgartner*:[110]

> the foundation for the imposition of a constructive trust in situations of the kind mentioned is that a refusal to recognise the existence of the equitable interest amounts to unconscionable conduct and that the trust is imposed as a remedy to circumvent that unconscionable conduct.
>
> The case is accordingly one in which the parties have pooled their earnings for the purposes of their joint relationship, one of the purposes of that relationship being to secure accommodation for themselves and their child. Their contributions, financial and otherwise, to the acquisition of the land, the building of the house, the purchase of the furniture and the making of their home, were on the basis of, and for the purposes of, that joint relationship. In this situation the appellant's assertion, after the relationship had failed, that the . . . property, which was financed in part through the pooled funds, is his sole property, is his property beneficially to the exclusion of any interest at all on the part of the respondent, amounts to unconscionable conduct which attracts the intervention of equity and the imposition of a constructive trust at the suit of the respondent.

The principle adumbrated in *Muschinski* v. *Dodds* and *Baumgartner* is open to the following criticisms:

1. There is some substance in the view that it is pure judicial legislation, without a foundation in established equitable doctrine, as is demonstrated by the powerful dissent of Brennan J (now Brennan CJ) in *Muschinski* v. *Dodds*,[111] with which Dawson J concurred.[112] Purists will no doubt continue to cavil with the use of the expression 'construc-

[106] (1989) 17 NSWLR, *per* Gleeson CJ at 353–4. [107] *Ibid.*, *per* Gleeson CJ at 355.
[108] N. 103 above. [109] N. 104 above.
[110] N. 104 above, at 147, 149. [111] N. 103 above, esp. at 608–9. [112] *Ibid.* 624–5.

tive trust' to describe an obligation imposed on the parties by the court, rather than one which is found by the court to exist in their common intentions. But, accepting that the principle involves a new and significant departure from the antecedent jurisprudence of equity, whether or not that is objectionable depends upon one's personal attitude to the phenomenon of 'judicial activism'. The force of Sir Gerard Brennan's dissent is to be considered in the context of his Honour's own candid acknowledgment, in *O'Toole* v. *Charles David Pty. Ltd.*,[113] that:

> Nowadays nobody accepts that judges simply declare the law; everybody knows that, within their area of competence and subject to the legislature, judges make law. Within the proper limits, judges seek to make the law an effective instrument of doing justice according to contemporary standards in contemporary conditions. And so the law is changed by judicial decision, especially by decision of the higher appellate courts. Thereafter, the law is taken to be and to have been in accordance with the principle which informs the new decision: the ratio decidendi. The ratio, which is expressed in or necessarily implied by reasons for judgment to which a majority of the participating judges assent, is the law. It is not merely a judicial opinion as to what the law is; it is a source of law.

2. There is, it may be argued, an element of *petitio principii*—or circular reasoning—in the imposition of an equitable interest, under the name of a constructive trust, on the ground that a party has acted unconscionably in refusing to recognize the existence of an equitable interest. To use a common law analogy, it is something like arguing that a defendant's conduct can be characterized as being negligent on the ground that the defendant negligently failed to recognize that committing such conduct would be negligent. If an equitable interest exists prior to a party's denial of the existence of that interest, then the pre-existing interest—rather than the unconscionable denial of it—should be the foundation of the trust which the court imposes; and if no equitable interest existed at the time of the defendant's refusal to recognize its existence, it is difficult to understand how a party's refusal to recognize the existence of that which does not presently exist can be characterized as unconscionable. In substance, the majority formulation of the principle in *Baumgartner* amounts to a recognition that a trust, described as a constructive trust, may be imposed by a court of equity if, in all of the circumstances of the case, the court is of the view that fairness and justice require the imposition of such a trust. The pretext which is adopted for the imposition of such a trust, namely to characterize as unconscionable the defendant's refusal to

[113] (1991) 171 CLR 232, at 267.

recognize the existence of an equitable interest, serves only to obfuscate the reality that the trust is one imposed by the court by reference to judicial conceptions of what is fair and just in the circumstances of the case.

3. That approach, of characterizing a defendant's refusal to recognize the existence of an equitable interest as unconscionable conduct, introduces an element of 'moral turpitude' into the process of legal ratiocination, which is both legally and socially undesirable, for a number of reasons:
   (a) The need for a plaintiff to allege and prove unconscionable conduct on the part of a defendant is unlikely to be conducive towards either reconciliation or a negotiated resolution in cases which will, almost invariably, already involve a degree of animosity between the parties. If one accepts the view of Lord Simon of Glaisdale that, although 'as a means of resolution of civil contention litigation is certainly preferable to personal violence', 'it is not intrinsically a desirable activity',[114] it might respectfully be suggested that the need to plead and prove unconscionable conduct as an element in the establishment of a case for a constructive trust is unlikely to conduce towards the socially desirable aim of reducing litigation between persons who had previously enjoyed some degree of mutual affection as partners in a marital or analogous relationship.
   (b) There may be cases (perhaps many cases) in which it is difficult to characterize a defendant's conduct as unconscionable, despite the fact that a court ultimately concludes that the plaintiff is entitled to a greater interest in the subject property than the defendant has been prepared to concede. Take the case where a defendant—for example, a person who had previously been in a *de facto* relationship with the plaintiff—is willing to acknowledge that the plaintiff has a legitimate claim in respect of the property in which the parties previously cohabited. Let it be assumed that the plaintiff is claiming a 50 per cent interest, and the defendant—whilst conceding that the plaintiff is entitled to some interest—is not prepared to accept that the plaintiff's interest amounts to 50 per cent. If a court ultimately concludes that equity and good conscience require the recognition of a one-quarter or one-third interest on the part of the plaintiff, can the defendant's conduct in refusing to accept the plaintiff's excessive demand be characterized as being unconscionable ? Should the defendant be stigmatized by having a court find that his conduct was unconscionable, when he has done no more than resist an excessive

[114] *Ampthill Peerage Case* [1977] AC 547, at 575.

claim by the plaintiff? But, on the other hand, should the plaintiff be denied the declaration of an appropriate constructive trust, merely because the plaintiff has made an over-reaching claim which the defendant has reasonably resisted?

(c) The difficulty in assessing an appropriate apportionment of the parties' interests—as to which I will make some further comments below—creates an air of artificiality in the notion that a defendant's conduct should be characterized as unconscionable because the defendant (or, more probably, the defendant's legal advisers) under-estimated the apportionment upon which a court ultimately fixes. A good example is afforded by the case of *Cooke* v. *Head*,[115] in which the judge at first instance (Plowman J) concluded that the plaintiff was entitled to a one-twelfth interest in the subject property, whereas the Court of Appeal concluded—without any real attempt at mathematical precision, as contrasted with an intuitive assessment of what was reasonable in all of the circumstances—that the plaintiff was entitled to one-third. Had the defendant in that case made an open offer prior to trial, to transfer to the plaintiff a share in the property which exceeded the share determined by the trial judge but which was less than the share determined by the Court of Appeal, could it really have been suggested that the defendant was acting unconscionably because he (or, more accurately, his lawyers) were guilty of nothing more than an error of judgement which, in the circumstances of that case, was not so 'wide of the mark' as the trial judge's?

(d) Arguably, the need for the plaintiff to plead and prove—and for the court to find—that the defendant's conduct was unconscionable places an unduly heavy burden on plaintiffs. Although I am unaware that the question has been agitated, it seems to me strongly arguable that a determination whether a defendant's conduct has been unconscionable involves a finding of such a grave moral character as to require what is commonly described as the '*Briginshaw* standard of proof'.[116] As the High Court of Australia (comprising Barwick CJ, Kitto, Taylor, Menzies and Windeyer JJ.) observed in *Rejfek* v. *McElroy*:[117]

> The 'clarity' of the proof required, where so serious a matter as fraud is to be found, is an acknowledgment that the degree of satisfaction for which the civil standard of proof calls may vary according to the gravity of the fact to be proved: see *Briginshaw* v. *Briginshaw*;[118] *Helton* v. *Allen*;[119] *Smith Bros.* v. *Madden*.'[120]

[115] N. 88 above.
[116] See *Briginshaw* v. *Briginshaw* (1938) 60 CLR 336.
[117] (1965) 112 CLR 517, at 521.
[118] N. 116 above, at 362, *per* Dixon J.
[119] (1940) 63 CLR 691, at 701, *per* Starke J.
[120] [1945] QWN 39, at 42, *per* Dixon J.

Is it appropriate that, in order to recover a reasonable share of jointly enjoyed property, the plaintiff must face the hurdle of proving unconscionability on the part of the defendant to that standard ? But, at the same time, is it appropriate that a defendant should be subjected to a finding of unconscionable conduct, unless that standard of proof has been satisfied?

4. Neither *Muschinski* v. *Dodds*[121] nor *Baumgartner*[122] offers a significant measure of guidance as to the way in which the respective parties' interests in property are to be apportioned. The nearest that the High Court comes to articulating a principle of general application is the following passage in the majority judgment in *Baumgartner*:[123]

> Equity favours equality and, in circumstances where the parties have lived together for years and have pooled their resources and their efforts to create a joint home, there is much to be said for the view that they should share the beneficial ownership equally as tenants in common, subject to adjustment to avoid any injustice which would result if account were not taken of the disparity between the worth of their individual contributions either financially or in kind. The question which has caused us particular difficulty is whether any such adjustment is necessary in the circumstances of the present case to avoid any injustice which would otherwise result by reason of disparity between individual financial contributions. The conclusion to which we have come is that some such adjustment is necessary.

That principle—if it can be described as a principle—arguably raises more questions than it answers. Reference is made to circumstances where 'the parties have lived together for years': recognizing that the expression 'for years' offers no specific guidance as to the period of cohabitation which is necessary to give rise to a *prima facie* entitlement to an equal share, is it to be assumed that shorter periods of cohabitation may justify a discounting in the plaintiff's share of the beneficial ownership ? And, to the extent that it is relevant that the parties have 'pooled their resources and their efforts to create a joint home', is it appropriate that the court take into account that either party—plaintiff or defendant—has 'pooled' only a moiety of that party's 'resources and . . . efforts', such as where one party continues to make contributions (in money or in kind) to a former spouse or the children of a former marriage? What considerations are inferior courts to apply in determining the question which caused the majority in *Baumgartner* 'particular difficulty', namely whether adjustment is necessary 'to avoid any injustice which would result if account were not take of the disparity between the worth of [the parties'] individual contributions either financially or in kind'? And where such an adjust-

[121] N. 103 above. [122] N. 104 above.
[123] *Ibid.* 149–50, *per* Mason CJ, Wilson and Deane JJ.

ment is warranted, how is to be quantified? If the disparity relates to the worth of the parties' individual financial contributions, is it to be a purely arithmetical exercise of reconciling (to the extent that the evidence permits) the total amount of the plaintiff's and defendant's respective contributions? Or is it more a matter of determining whether each party has contributed to the full extent of that party's financial capacity? What is meant by a 'disparity' between the 'worth' of the parties' individual contributions in kind: does the court examine the 'worth' of those contributions having regard to their commercial value, so that a female partner's contributions in the form of home-making are accorded a 'worth' commensurable with the market cost of domestic services? Or is the expression 'worth' intended to raise for consideration an assessment of the moral or social worthiness of a party's individual contributions ? And if a 'disparity' is found to exist, either in terms of the parties' individual financial contributions or in terms of the 'worth' of their individual contributions in kind, what mechanism is to be used to quantify the adjustment to the parties' entitlements to 'avoid any injustice which would result if account were not taken' of that disparity ?

5. The lack of any specific guidance as to the way in which the parties' entitlements are to be quantified—the absence, to borrow Lord Coke's colourful phrase, of any 'golden met-wand and measure to try the causes of the subjects'[124]—creates a number of practical problems:
   (a) As already observed, in a case where the defendant acknowledges an entitlement on the part of the plaintiff, but the parties are in dispute as to the extent of that entitlement, it is difficult to see how the defendant's refusal to acknowledge what is ultimately determined to be the full extent of the plaintiff's entitlement can be characterized as unconscionable conduct, especially where there is legitimate scope for disagreement—even as between lower and appellate courts, or between different members of an appellate bench—as to the proper measure of the plaintiff's entitlement.
   (b) The possibility that different views may legitimately be taken as to the scope of a plaintiff's entitlement is conducive to litigation, rather than reconciliation and negotiated resolution.
   (c) The opacity of the principles to be applied inevitably commits the parties to complex litigation, which necessarily involves both delay and expense in the case of those parties who can afford such litigation, and the unavailability of access to a judicial determination of their rights in the case of ordinary citizens who cannot

[124] *Prohibitions Del Roy* (1608) 12 Co. Rep. 63, at 65, 77 ER 1342, at 1343.

afford such litigation.[125] The reality, as the Tribunal observed in *Re Hope and the Secretary, Department of Society Security,*[126] is that 'most of the people who get divorced do not have the money to afford the luxury of divorce'; so, most of the people who have been parties to failed domestic relationships cannot afford the luxury of the kind of complex litigation which the decisions in *Muschinski* v. *Dodds* and *Baumgartner* require.

6. There is, finally, some force in the argument that the ordinary courts of general jurisdiction are ill-equipped to make 'value-judgements' of the kind required in such cases. Social policy has recognized, in most common law jurisdictions, that the issues involved in matrimonial proceedings are more satisfactorily resolved by specialist courts—such as the Family Division in England, and the Family Court of Australia—which, ideally, provide to the parties the prospect of a swifter and less expensive resolution of their differences; a reduced level of formality; a judiciary which is attuned to and sympathetic with the personal considerations which play a significant role in any litigation arising out of a break-down in domestic relationships; and institutional facilities offering support to the parties by way of counselling and mediation. By the same token, ordinary courts of general jurisdiction often lack the judicial and other resources necessary to deal with growing numbers of such claims. There is much to be said for the model, now adopted in some Australian jurisdictions, of specific legislation conferring on specialist tribunals the function of determining and adjusting the rights of parties to failed domestic relationships.

For the reasons stated, it is submitted that the recent trend of developments in equity, concerning the imposition of constructive trusts or proprietary estoppels as a means of resolving property disputes arising out of failed domestic relationships, is unlikely to prove, over time, to be a successful means of meeting the underlying social-policy objective, which is to resolve such disputes in a way which is fair and just. The experiment has been tried; and if it has not yet failed, all indications suggest that it is doomed to ultimate failure. Equity has been taken as far as it can in providing a resolution to the problems arising in such cases; the time has arrived for legislative intervention—along the lines already adopted in jurisdictions such as New South Wales, Victoria, the Northern Territory of Australia, and the Australian Capital Territory—to furnish an efficient and satisfactory mechanism for the resolution of such disputes.

[125] See R. Bailey-Harris, 'Property Disputes in De-facto Relationships: Can Equity Still Play a Role?', in M. Cope (ed.), *Equity—Issues and Trends* (1995), 193–4.

[126] (1990) 21 ALD 523, at 524 (Commonwealth Administrative Appeals Tribunal).

UNFAIR DEALINGS

Under the rubrics of 'undue influence' and 'unconscionable conduct', courts of equity exercise a jurisdiction to relieve parties from the consequences of unfair transactions. Those principles take on a particular relevance in the context of domestic relationships, either because the very existence of the relationship is a relevant factor in determining whether the transaction may be avoided in equity, or because the relationship furnishes the background and context against which the fairness of the transaction is required to be assessed.

Undue Influence

We are not particularly concerned, for present purposes, with those cases in which the onus is on the party seeking to avoid a transaction to prove *actual* undue influence. Where the evidence suffices, equity poses no obstacle to a husband's proving that he was subject to undue influence by his wife, or a partner in a *de facto* heterosexual or homosexual relationship showing that undue influence was exerted by the other party to that relationship.

But in those cases where undue influence is *presumed*, the presumption rests upon the very nature of the parties' relationship. Leaving aside those relationships, giving rise to a presumption of influence, which are not of a purely personal or domestic character—such as relationships between solicitor and client, physician and patient, or confessor and penitent—anomalies become apparent when one examines the circumstances in which equity presumes the exertion of undue influence by reason of the existence of particular domestic relationships.

(1) It is said that no such presumption arises in respect of a transaction by which a wife transfers property to her husband. But if there is no presumption of undue influence, there is authority for the application of special considerations in respect of such a transfer, due to the strong possibility that undue influence may have been exerted.

Thus, in *Yerkey* v. *Jones*,[127] Latham CJ said:

> there is no general rule of universal application that the rule of equity as to confidential relationships necessarily applies to the relation of husband and wife so as to throw on the husband or on the person who is suing the wife the onus of disproving an allegation of undue influence. For a definite statement of this proposition by the highest judicial authority, see *Bank of Montreal* v. *Stuart*.[128] It is true that undue influence may be more easily proved in the

[127] (1939) 63 CLR 649, at 658–9.
[128] [1911] AC 120, at 137.

case of husband and wife than in cases where no special relationship exists between the parties, but there is no presumption of such influence from the marital relationship.

Dixon J. concurred, expressing the principle in these terms:[129] '[t]hough the court was more ready to believe that a disposition in favour of the husband had been improperly procured, yet the burden of showing it by evidence rested upon her as in other cases.' His Honour also cited *Story*,[130] as authority for the proposition that:[131]

The doctrine is now firmly established in equity that she [a wife] may bestow her separate property, by appointment or otherwise, upon her husband as well as upon a stranger. But at the same time, courts of equity examine every such transaction between husband and wife with an anxious watchfulness and caution, and dread of undue influence.

'In substance', says Dixon J,[132] 'this position has been maintained until the present day.'

(2) But whilst there is no presumption of influence between a man and his wife, such a presumption may operate between a man and a woman whom he is engaged to marry. This appears first to have been decided in *Page* v. *Horne*,[133] in which Lord Langdale MR said:

It is true that no influence is proved to have been used; but no one can say what may be the extent of the influence of a man over a woman, whose consent to marriage he has obtained. Here the husband having mortgaged the property, we are told, by the report of the Master, that no undue influence had been used. The Court, however, will look with great vigilance at the circumstances and situation of the parties in such cases as the present, and will not only consider the influence which the intended husband, either by soothing or violence, may have used, but requires satisfactory evidence that it has not been used.

The continuing application of this principle in relatively modern times was recognized in the 1961 case of *Zamet* v. *Hyman*.[134] But the Court was reluctant to accept the proposition that such a presumption arose between all engaged couples. Lord Evershed MR said:[135]

I do not, of course, forget that this is 1961 and what might have been said of the position, independence, and the like, of women in 1848 would have to be seriously qualified to-day. It may well be in some cases that the court would rightly draw the inference of a fiduciary relationship not existing in the man towards the woman but in the woman towards the man. But taking, I hope, a sensible view of the position of women in modern society, I cannot be

[129] N. 127 above, at 671.
[130] *Equity Jurisprudence* (1835), sec. 1395.
[131] N. 127 above, at 674.
[132] *Ibid.*
[133] (1848) 11 Beav. 227, at 235–6, 50 ER 804, at 807.
[134] [1961] 1 WLR 1442.
[135] *Ibid.* 1446.

persuaded that this court ought now to say that these principles, illustrated in the cases I have mentioned, have ceased altogether to be part of our law. I say only that in modern conditions, at any rate, one should not necessarily assume the existence of such influence in every case. I would put it somewhat thus: that in any transaction of the kind of a deed or arrangement or settlement (and I make that qualification bearing in mind . . . the case of a young man who may be persuaded to give an extravagant engagement ring to his fiancee) made between an engaged couple which upon its face appears much more favourable to one party than the other, then in the circumstances of the case the court may find a fiduciary relationship of the nature I have mentioned so as to cast an onus on the party benefited of proving that the transaction was completed by the other party only after full, free and informed thought about it.

The decisions of the House of Lords in *Barclays Bank PLC* v. *O'Brien*[136] and *CIBC Mortgages PLC* v. *Pitt*[137] constitute the first systematic attempt in modern times to articulate and rationalize the law relating to undue influence. It is significant that Lord Browne-Wilkinson, whose leading speech in each case attracted unanimous concurrence, commenced his consideration of the relevant principles in the former case with a passage dealing with 'policy considerations',[138] observing:

The large number of cases of this type coming before the courts in recent years reflects the rapid changes in social attitudes and the distribution of wealth which have recently occurred. Wealth is now more widely spread. Moreover a high proportion of privately owned wealth is invested in the matrimonial home. Because of the recognition by society of the equality of the sexes, the majority of matrimonial homes are now in the joint names of both spouses. Therefore in order to raise finance for the business enterprise of one or other of the spouses, the jointly owned home has become a main source of security. The provision of such security requires the consent of both spouses.

In parallel with these financial developments, society's recognition of the equality of the sexes has led to a rejection of the concept that the wife is subservient to the husband in the management of the family's finances. A number of the authorities reflect an unwillingness in the court to perpetuate law based on this outmoded concept. Yet . . . although the concept of the ignorant wife leaving all financial decisions to the husband is outmoded, the practice does not yet coincide with the ideal. In a substantial proportion of marriages, it is still the husband who has the business experience and the wife is willing to follow his advice without bringing a truly independent mind and will to bear on financial decisions. The number of recent cases in this field shows that in practice many wives are still subjected to, and yield to, undue influence by their husbands. Such wives can reasonably look to the law for some protection when their husbands have abused the trust and confidence reposed in them.

On the other hand, it is important to keep a sense of balance in approaching these cases. It is easy to allow sympathy for the wife who is threatened with the loss of her home at the suit of a rich bank to obscure an important public interest

[136] [1994] 1 AC 180. [137] [1994] 1 AC 200. [138] N. 136 above, at 188.

viz., the need to ensure that the wealth currently tied up in the matrimonial home does not become economically sterile. If the rights secured to wives by the law renders vulnerable loans granted on the security of matrimonial homes, institutions will be unwilling to accept such security, thereby reducing the flow of loan capital to business enterprises. It is therefore essential that a law designed to protect the vulnerable does not render the matrimonial home unacceptable as security to financial institutions.

Lord Browne-Wilkinson's speech adopted the classification of 'undue influence' cases suggested by the Court of Appeal in *Bank of Credit and Commerce International S.A.* v. *Aboody*[139] as follows:[140]

Class 1: *Actual undue influence*

In these cases it is necessary for the claimant to prove affirmatively that the wrongdoer exerted undue influence on the complainant to enter into the particular transaction which is impugned.

Class 2: *Presumed undue influence*

In these cases the complainant only has to show, in the first instance, that there was a relationship of trust and confidence between the complainant and the wrongdoer of such a nature that it is fair to presume that the wrongdoer abused that relationship in procuring the complainant to enter into the impugned transaction. In Class 2 cases therefore there is no need to produce evidence that actual undue influence was exerted in relation to the particular transaction impugned: once a confidential relationship has been proved, the burden shifts to the wrongdoer to prove that the complainant entered into the impugned transaction freely, for example by showing that the complainant had independent advice. Such a confidential relationship can be established in two ways, viz.,

Class 2(A)

Certain relationships (for example solicitor and client, medical adviser and patient) as a matter of law raise the presumption that undue influence has been exercised.

Class 2(B)

Even if there is no relationship falling within Class 2(A), if the complainant proves the de facto existence of a relationship under which the complainant generally reposed trust and confidence in the wrongdoer, the existence of such relationship raises the presumption of undue influence. In a Class 2(B) case therefore, in the absence of evidence disproving undue influence, the complainant will succeed in setting aside the impugned transaction merely by proof that the complainant reposed trust and confidence in the wrongdoer without having to prove that the wrongdoer exerted actual undue influence or otherwise abused such trust and confidence in relation to the particular transaction impugned.

His Lordship's speeches in the two cases further stand as authority for these propositions:

[139] [1990] 1 QB 923, at 953. [140] N. 136 above, at 189–90.

- The relationship between husband and wife does not give rise to a Class 2(A) presumption, although in any particular case a wife may well be able to demonstrate that she did leave decisions on financial affairs to her husband thereby bringing herself within Class 2(B).[141]
- There is a 'special tenderness of treatment afforded to wives by the courts' on the basis that 'the risk of undue influence affecting a voluntary disposition by a wife in favour of a husband is greater than in the ordinary run of cases where no sexual or emotional ties affect the free exercise of the individual's will'.[142]
- In a case where undue influence is presumed—that is to say, a class 2(A) or (B) case—the decision of the House of Lords in *National Westminster Bank PLC* v. *Morgan*[143] stands as authority for the proposition that 'the claimant must show that the impugned transaction was disadvantageous to him in order to raise the presumption of undue influence',[144] although 'the exact limits of the decision in *Morgan* may have to be considered in the future'.[145]
- However, there is no requirement for a complainant to show manifest disadvantage where actual undue influence has been exercised and proved.[146]

Whether Australian courts will adopt Lord Browne-Wilkinson's approach in its entirety is yet to be seen. Significantly, however, at least one judge at first instance—Kelly SPJ, of the Supreme Court of Queensland—anticipated the decision in *Pitt* four years earlier, in *Baburin* v. *Baburin*.[147] Quite apart from the great advantages of being simple and logically consistent, it is well-adapted to dealing with the wide range of personal, social, and domestic relationships which exist in contemporary society.

It may be anticipated that equity will continue its 'tender treatment' of married women, at least so long as it remains the case (in the words of Lord Browne-Wilkinson[148]) that 'even today, many wives repose confidence and trust in their husbands in relation to their financial affairs'. But that 'tender treatment' should not be confined to women who are parties to lawful marriages; the *ratio* of *O'Brien* and *Pitt* would allow the same 'tender treatment' to be extended to the female party in a *de facto* relationship. And, by the same token, where it is shown that the male party in a heterosexual relationship (whether married or *de facto*) reposes confidence and trust in the female party[149] in relation to their

141 *Ibid.* 190. 142 *Ibid.* 190–1. 143 [1985] AC 686.
144 *Pitt* n. 137 above, at 207. 145 *Ibid.* 209. 146 *Ibid.*
147 [1990] 2 Qd. R 101. 148 *O'Brien* n. 136 above, at 196.
149 cf. *Brooks* v. *Alker,* (1975) 60 DLR (3d) 577 at 591, where it was found that the woman was the dominant partner in a marital relationship.

financial affairs, or where it is shown that such confidence and trust is reposed in one party to a homosexual relationship by the other, it may be anticipated that the same 'tender treatment' will apply.

The Principle in *Yerkey* v. *Jones*

The judgment of Sir Owen Dixon in *Yerkey* v. *Jones*[150] has, for more than half a century, been relied upon in Australia as authority for the proposition that a special rule exists where a wife guarantees or furnishes other security for her husband's indebtedness. The supposed 'special rule' is stated in the head-note to the report in the Commonwealth Law Reports in these terms:[151]

> if a husband procures his wife to become surety for his debt and it appears that circumstances existed which, if they alone had been the parties to the transaction, would make it liable to be set aside as against the husband, then the guarantee or security may be invalidated also against the creditor if he relied upon the husband to obtain it from his wife and had no independent ground for reasonably believing that she fully comprehended the transaction and freely entered into it.

The existence of such a 'special rule' in England was specifically repudiated by the House of Lords in *O'Brien*,[152] where Lord Browne-Wilkinson (with the concurrence of Lords Templeman, Lowry, Slynn of Hadley and Woolf) proposed that the applicable principle be re-stated in these terms:

> Where one cohabitee [sic.; the *Oxford English Dictionary* prefers 'cohabitant'] has entered into an obligation to stand as surety for the debts of the other cohabitee and the creditor is aware that they are cohabitees: (1) the surety obligation will be valid and enforceable by the creditor unless the suretyship was procured by the undue influence, misrepresentation or other legal wrong of the principal debtor; (2) if there has been undue influence, misrepresentation or other legal wrong by the principal debtor, unless the creditor has taken reasonable steps to satisfy himself that the surety entered into the obligation freely and in knowledge of the true facts, the creditor will be unable to enforce the surety obligation because he will be fixed with constructive notice of the surety's right to set aside the transaction; (3) unless there are special exceptional circumstances, a creditor will have taken such reasonable steps to avoid being fixed with constructive notice if the creditor warns the surety (at a meeting not attended by the principal debtor) of the amount of her potential liability and of the risks involved and advises the surety to take independent legal advice.
>
> I should make it clear that in referring to the husband's debts I include the debts of a company in which the husband (but not with the wife) has a direct financial interest.

[150] N. 127 above. [151] *Ibid.*, 649. [152] N. 136 above, at 198–99.

It is to be noted, in particular, that notwithstanding the use of the feminine possessive pronoun in the first paragraph of that excerpt, and the references to 'husband' and 'wife' in the second paragraph, the principle as laid down by the House of Lords is not confined to 'cohabitees' who are married; nor is it confined to circumstances where the cohabitee who becomes the surety is female. As Lord Browne-Wilkinson observed:[153]

> in my judgment the same principles are applicable to all other cases where there is an emotional relationship between cohabitees. The 'tenderness' shown by the law to married women is not based on the marriage ceremony but reflects the underlying risk of one cohabitee exploiting the emotional involvement and trust of the other. Now that unmarried cohabitation, whether heterosexual or homosexual, is widespread in our society, the law should recognise this. Legal wives are not the only group which are now exposed to the emotional pressure of cohabitation. Therefore if, but only if, the creditor is aware that the surety is cohabiting with the principal debtor, in my judgment the same principles should apply to them as apply to husband and wife.
>
> In addition to the cases of cohabitees, the decision of the Court of Appeal in *Avon Finance Co. Ltd.* v. *Bridger*[154] shows (rightly in my view) that other relationships can give rise to a similar result. In that case a son, by means of misrepresentation, persuaded his elderly parents to stand surety for his debts. The surety obligation was held to be unenforceable by the creditor inter alia because to the bank's knowledge the parents trusted the son in their financial dealings. In my judgment that case was rightly decided: in a case where the creditor is aware that the surety reposes trust and confidence in the principal debtor in relation to his financial affairs, the creditor is put on enquiry in just the same way as it is in relation to husband and wife.

In Australia, however, the status of *Yerkey* v. *Jones* is less clear. It was applied, albeit reluctantly, in a series of New South Wales cases between 1985 and 1993: *European Asian of Australia Ltd* v. *Kurland*;[155] *Bawn* v. *Trade Credits*;[156] *Warburton* v. *Whiteley*;[157] *Carrington Confirmers Pty. Ltd* v. *Atkins*;[158] *Peters* v. *Commonwealth Bank of Australia*;[159] and *Garcia* v. *National Australia Bank Ltd.*[160] The Court's reluctance to follow *Yerkey* v. *Jones* is demonstrated by the decision of the Court of Appeal in *Warburton* v. *Whiteley*,[161] where Kirby P remarked that:

> The mere knowledge by the creditors that one guarantor is the wife of the other should not, without more, be sufficient in Australian society today to establish

[153] *Ibid.* 198. [154] [1985] 2 All ER 281.
[155] (1985) 8 NSWLR 192 (Rogers J).
[156] [1986] NSW Conv.R ¶55–290 (Needham J).
[157] [1989] NSW Conv.R 58,283 (CA).
[158] Unreported decision, No 50582 of 1989, delivered 23 Apr. 1991 (Giles J).
[159] [1992] NSW Conv.R ¶55–629 (Brownie J).
[160] (1993) 5 BPR 11,996 (Young J). [161] N. 157 above, at 58,287.

> that the wife was under a special disability as to her own interests in relation to the transaction. To hold otherwise would be to hold wives in a permanent subordinate and inferior position for no reason other than that they are wives.

but concluded that: '[i]t is possible that the High Court, with a fresh opportunity to review *Yerkey*, would refine the principle there stated. . . . But until the High Court, or the legislature, does so I do not believe that this Court is free to act as the creditors urge.' Similar remarks fell from Clarke JA,[162] with whom McHugh relevantly concurred:

> The respondents' counsel has, in this case, submitted that the rule first arose when the position of a married woman was vastly different than it is today. He submitted that in contemporary society the rule is an affront to women and should be treated as having fallen into disfavour. In cases in which a married woman seeks equitable relief against unconscionable dealing, her rights should fall to be determined in the same manner as are the rights of any other person. . . .
>
> Notwithstanding that it may be no longer appropriate to regard married women as being under a special disability it is, I think, proper to point out that the invalidating presumptions of which Dixon J. spoke reflect a response to the fact that there have been many cases in which wives have been overborne by their husbands and thus have been shown to be in need of some special protection. No doubt the powers of the court to grant relief in cases of the exercise of undue influence have provided an adequate remedy in some of these cases. None the less there have been cases in which undue influence could not be shown but in which the dominance of the husband places his wife at a disadvantage.
>
> While it may be true to say that the need to recognise the disadvantaged position of a wife would appear less frequently today there are still to be found women in the community who are overbourne by their husbands. The need for protection of those women is as great as ever. . . .
>
> On the other hand, it may be that the principles applied in *Amadio*,[163] which clearly extend to guarantees, provide sufficient protection and there is now no case for retaining the separate doctrine under discussion. However, that doctrine has been applied by the High Court and until that court indicates that it no longer is good law I consider that I should continue to apply it.

Other State courts have adopted a similar attitude of reluctantly applying *Yerkey* v. *Jones*, whilst recognizing that it is open to criticism as being based on an outdated stereotypical perception of wives: see, for example, the decision of Cox J in the Supreme Court of Tasmania in *Australia & New Zealand Banking Group Ltd* v. *McGee*.[164]

But on 5 August 1994, the New South Wales Court of Appeal broke ranks in the case of *Akins* v. *National Australia Bank*.[165] The majority—

[162] N. 157 above, 58,290–1.

[163] *The Commercial Bank of Australia Ltd* v. *Amadio* (1983) 151 CLR 447.

[164] [1994] ASC ¶56–278.

[165] (1994) 34 NSWLR 155.

Clarke JA, with whom Sheller JA concurred—were of the view that the disapproval of *Yerkey* v. *Jones* by the House of Lords in *O'Brien*[166] constituted a sufficient ground for reconsideration of the Court's own decision in *Warburton* v. *Whiteley*[167] that *Yerkey* v. *Jones* should continue to be applied in the Supreme Court of New South Wales. And, upon such reconsideration, their Honours were of the view that any continuing scope for the application of the special rule in *Yerkey* v. *Jones* have been superseded by the High Court's adopting, in *Amadio*,[168] a principle of unconscionability which is of general application. Accordingly, their Honours held that:[169] 'the special rule should no longer be applied and . . . the principles discussed in *Commercial Bank of Australia Ltd.* v. *Amadio* should be applied to the resolution of a case such as the present.'

The third member of the Court, Powell JA, took a different tack. His Honour was of the view that *Yerkey* v. *Jones* did not, in truth, establish any 'special rule'.[170] But his Honour added this:[171] '[i]f, however, what Dixon J. said in his judgment is to be taken as meaning something more than what I have earlier written then, I can but say that, on this occasion, Homer nodded: Horace, *Ars Poetica* 323.' An annotation to the report in the New South Wales Law Reports[172] indicates that '[a]n application for special leave to appeal to the High Court has been filed'; but it does not appear that the application was proceeded with. Perhaps the respondent—being one of Australia's four largest trading banks—was sufficiently satisfied to have had the New South Wales Court of Appeal give *Yerkey* v. *Jones* its quietus, at least for that State, and then reached a settlement with the appellant.

But that is not the end of the story. Thirteen days after judgment was delivered in *Akins*, Hunter J (in the Commercial Division of the Supreme Court of New South Wales) gave judgment in *Teachers Health Investments Pty. Ltd* v. *Wynne*.[173] Showing remarkable strength of character, Hunter J added an addendum to his Reasons for Judgment, which included the following remarks:

> Since preparing these reasons, the decision of the Court of Appeal in *Akins* v. *National Australia Bank* has come to my attention. In that case, the appellant, appearing in person, sought relief under the principle in *Yerkey*. Somewhat surprisingly, in the light of the decision of the Court of Appeal in *Warburton* of which Clarke J.A. was a member, the Court of Appeal in *Akins* decided that the principles of *Yerkey* have not survived *Amadio*. This same question was considered by *Warburton* which came to a contrary conclusion on the basis that it was not for the Court of Appeal but for the High Court to decide whether *Yerkey* was to survive alongside *Amadio*. . . .

166 N. 136 above. 167 N. 157 above. 168 N. 163 above.
169 N. 165 above, at 173. 170 *Ibid.* 176. 171 *Ibid.* 178. 172 *Ibid.* 155.
173 (1994) 68 ALJ 837 (note), 6 BPR 13,499.

I note that in *Akins* it was not necessary to the decision that the *Yerkey* principle be reconsidered and that the Court did not have the benefit of argument of counsel for the appellant. So until such time as the High Court has resolved the question, I regard myself as bound by the decision of *Yerkey* and of *Warburton*.

As the editor of the *Australian Law Journal*, Peter Young J of the Supreme Court of New South Wales, remarked in a note published in that journal,[174] 'It will be interesting to see what develops.'

Unconscionability

The point has now been reached in Australia that equity recognizes a general principle pursuant to which transactions may be set aside on the ground of a party's unconscionable conduct: *Blomley* v. *Ryan*;[175] *Amadio*;[176] *Louth* v. *Diprose*.[177]

In *Blomley* v. *Ryan*, Fullagar J identified 'sex' along with 'poverty or need of any kind, sickness, age, . . . infirmity of body or mind, drunkenness, illiteracy or lack of education, lack of assistance or explanation where assistance or explanation is necessary' as 'circumstances adversely affecting a party, which may induce a court of equity either to refuse its aid or to set a transaction aside'.[178] In the context, 'sex', as a circumstance 'adversely affecting a party', can only have been intended to mean that being female is one such circumstance, which has 'the effect of placing one party at a serious disadvantage *vis-a-vis* the other'. Viewed through contemporary eyes, it may be thought to be more than mildly offensive to suggest that being female is, *per se*, a circumstance 'adversely affecting a party'; let alone to catalogue that 'circumstance' along with other 'disadvantages' such as poverty, sickness, infirmity of body or mind, drunkenness, and illiteracy or lack of education. It is notable that Kitto J offered a similar catalogue which did not, however, include 'sex' amongst those circumstances which affect a person's 'ability to conserve his own interests'.[179]

In *Amadio*, the High Court focused on expressing the general principle, rather than illustrating it with examples of the kinds of circumstances in which it may be invoked. Thus Mason J observed that the situations mentioned by Fullagar J and Kitto J in *Blomley* v. *Ryan* are:[180]

> no more than particular exemplifications of an underlying general principle which may be invoked whenever one party by reason of some condition or circumstance is placed at a special disadvantage vis-a-vis another and unfair or

[174] (1994) 68 (ALJ) 838. [175] (1956) 99 CLR 362. [176] N. 163 above.
[177] (1992) 175 CLR 621. [178] N. 175 above, at 405. [179] *Ibid.* 415.
[180] *Amadio* n. 163 above, at 462.

unconscientious advantage is then taken of the opportunity thereby created. I qualify the word 'disadvantage' by the adjective 'special' in order to disavow any suggestion that the principle applies whenever there is some difference in the bargaining power of the parties and in order to emphasise that the disabling condition or circumstance is one which seriously affects the ability of the innocent party to make a judgment as to his own best interests, when the other party knows or ought to know of the existence of that condition or circumstance and of its effect on the innocent party.

Any remaining scope for the notion that sex, *per se*, may be characterized as such a 'disabling condition' was rejected in *European Asian of Australia Ltd* v. *Kurland*,[181] in which Rogers J said:

In more recent times, it has been acknowledged that the concept appealed to, in relation to a married woman, is at best a survivor from the days when a married woman was almost incapable in law. I feel compelled to say that in the year 1985 it seems anachronistic to be told that being a female and a wife is, by itself, a sufficient qualification to enrol in the class of persons suffering a special disadvantage. However, counsel for Mrs. Kurland submitted that the iron grip of precedent requires me to submit to such a finding. Were this to be correct, it would affix a badge of shame to this branch of the law. In my opinion, stated in the extreme form embraced by counsel, the proposition is not correct but, nonetheless, it has sufficient claim to accuracy to require a review of this branch of the law so as to bring it into conformity with current thinking and standards. That being a female spouse should place a person shoulder to shoulder with the sick, the ignorant and the impaired is not to be tolerated.

The better view, it is suggested, is that the circumstances which give rise to a 'special disadvantage' of the kind referred to by Mason J in *Amadio* include those circumstances where a person—regardless of that person's sex or marital status—is seriously affected in that person's ability to make a judgement as to that person's best interests, by reason of that person's reposing trust and confidence in the other contracting party. If that sounds like a restatement of the circumstances in which a party may be entitled to seek to have a transaction set aside on the ground of undue influence, I make no apology for that. In *Louth* v. *Diprose*, Brennan J opined that the 'similarity between the two jurisdictions'—that is to say, the similarity between the jurisdiction to set aside a gift obtained by unconscientious exploitation of a donor's special disadvantage, and the jurisdiction to set aside a gift obtained by undue influence—'gives to cases arising in the exercise of one jurisdiction an analogous character in considering cases involving the same points in the other jurisdiction'.[182] In substance, the same point was made by Deane J, in his observing that:[183]

181 N. 155 above, at 200. 182 N. 177 above, at 628. 183 *Ibid.* 638.

On [the trial Judge's] findings, the case was not simply one in which the respondent had, under the influence of his love for, or infatuation with, the appellant, made an imprudent gift in her favour. The case was one in which the appellant deliberately used that love or infatuation and her own deceit to create a situation in which she could unconscientiously manipulate the respondent to part with a large proportion of his property. The intervention of equity is not merely to relieve the plaintiff from the consequences of his own foolishness. It is to prevent his victimisation.

Louth v. *Diprose* shows that the *Amadio* principle has a particular application in relation to domestic relationships. The very nature of such a relationship may by itself, or in combination with other circumstances, constitute the 'special disadvantage' which is the first element necessary to found the court's jurisdiction. And, unlike other cases where a party is subject to a 'special disadvantage', it will seldom be possible for the other party to deny knowledge of the circumstances giving rise to the 'special disadvantage'. The only remaining question, in any such case, is whether unfair or unconscientious advantage was taken of the 'special disadvantage' constituted (wholly or partly) by the nature and circumstances of the parties' relationship.

CONCLUSIONS

It follows from the foregoing analysis that equity has, in the last two decades, made great advances in the protection which it affords to the parties to modern domestic relationships.

Of the applicable doctrines of equity, that which is in most urgent need of reconsideration and reform is the so-called 'presumption of advancement' which may be raised to rebut the existence of a resulting trust. There are indications, already, that the anachronistic differentiation between male and female parents as regards the presumption which is made concerning their intentions to advance their children is unlikely to survive. But, for the time being at least, there seems little prospect of judicial reconsideration of the anomaly by which a presumption of advancement is made in favour of wives, but not in favour of husbands or parties to *de facto* heterosexual or homosexual relationships. It is submitted that scope for review of the existing doctrines may be found in the suggestion of Sir Isaac Isaacs in *Scott* v. *Pauly*[184] that the so-called 'presumption' is merely an inference, so as to admit of the possibility that similar inferences—although, perhaps, similar inferences carrying reduced persuasive force—may be available as between

[184] N. 23 above, at 282.

wife and husband, or as between parties to other domestic relationships regardless of sex.

By contrast, recent developments of the equitable doctrine relating to constructive trusts, especially in the decisions of the High Court of Australia in *Muschinski* v. *Dodds*[185] and *Baumgartner* v. *Baumgartner*,[186] have gone a substantial way towards recognizing and protecting the rights of parties in non-traditional domestic relationships. The principal difficulties with the approach articulated in those decisions are pragmatic rather than conceptual. It is socially undesirable, and procedurally unattractive, that the recognition of the rights of *de facto* partners should depend upon the plaintiff's pleading and proving, and the court's finding, that the defendant's conduct is unconscionable; and the absence of any clear guidance as to the methodology by which the parties' equitable interests in property are to be apportioned between the parties creates significant practical problems. It is suggested that these decisions of the High Court of Australia take equity as far as it can reasonably be taken as a means of recognizing and protecting the property rights of parties in domestic relationships: any further reform in this branch of the law must come from legislatures.

The present uncertain state of the law in Australia concerning the equitable doctrine of undue influence is to be contrasted with the position obtaining in England following the decisions of the House of Lords in *Barclays Bank PLC* v. *O'Brien*[187] and *CIBC Mortgages PLC* v. *Pitt*.[188] The propositions adumbrated in those cases possess a number of attractive features: they are simple and therefore readily capable of application in a wide variety of cases; they are intellectually satisfying; and they strike a happy balance between the social-policy objective of protecting victims of undue influence, and the need to ensure that alleged perpetrators of undue influence are not unnecessarily exposed to the hardship or injustice of proving their innocence. It is to be hoped that, when the High Court of Australia next has occasion to reconsider this branch of equity, the decisions of the House of Lords will be accorded the persuasive respect which they command.

The supposed rule in *Yerkey* v. *Jones*[189] has been defenestrated for England by the decision of the House of Lords in *Barclays Bank PLC* v. *O'Brien*,[190] and the indications suggest that it is soon to meet its quietus in the Australian courts. It will not be sadly missed, especially in the circumstance that recent Australian development of the doctrine of unconscionable conduct affords a far more satisfactory resolution to cases of the kind in which the supposed rule had previously been invoked.

Of the doctrines of equity which have a peculiar relevance to modern

185 N. 103 above. 186 N. 104 above. 187 N. 136 above.
188 N. 137 above. 189 N. 127 above. 190 N. 136 above.

domestic relationships, that which has sustained the most progressive development in recent years is that relating to the jurisdiction to set aside transactions which are the result of unconscionable conduct. The decision of the High Court of Australia in *The Commercial Bank of Australia Limited* v. *Amadio*,[191] especially when read in the light of the High Court's subsequent decision in *Louth* v. *Diprose*,[192] sets this branch of equity on a firm footing to relieve the parties to every form of domestic relationship from the consequences where unfair or unconscientious advantage is taken of a special disadvantage arising from the existence and circumstances of the relationship.

The developments of the last quarter-century show that equity has recovered some semblance of the dynamism and flexibility which were its original *raison d'être*. Although considerable scope remains for equity's doctrines to be accommodated to the social-policy demands of modern domestic relationships, substantial progress has already been made. It is anticipated that equity's inherent genius and vitality will continue to meet the social realities of an evolving society.

Ultimately, it is suggested that this will be achieved by a recognition that personal and domestic relationships—relationships characterized by features such as cohabitation, mutual dependence and support, and personal intimacy—involve one unifying feature, whether the relationship is a legal marriage, the *de facto* relationship of a heterosexual couple, or a similar relationship between persons of the same sex. The unifying feature is the mutual trust and confidence which the parties repose in one another. It is unsuprising that Lord Browne-Wilkinson, in *Barclays Bank PLC* v. *O'Brien*,[193] identified 'trust and confidence' as the circumstance which must be proved to exist in order that a presumption of undue influence may be made in those cases falling outside the specific relationships which automatically give rise to such a presumption. What is perhaps surprising is that it has not yet been fully recognized that one party's reposing of trust and confidence in the other party is the essential ingredient which attracts equity's intervention in virtually all cases involving domestic relationships, whether under the rubric of a constructive trust, relief against undue influence, or relief against unconscionable conduct.

In other branches of equity, the words 'mutual trust and confidence' are the ritual incantation invoked to create duties of a fiduciary nature, such as between business partners and joint venturers.[194] A domestic relationship, whether sanctified by a legal marriage, and whether heterosexual or homosexual, undoubtedly involves 'mutual trust and

[191] N. 163 above. [192] N. 177 above. [193] N. 136 above, at 189.

[194] See, e.g., *United Dominions Corporation Ltd* v. *Brian Pty. Ltd* (1985) 156 CLR 1, at 8 (*per* Gibbs CJ), 12 (*per* Mason, Brennan, and Deane JJ), and 16 (*per* Dawson J).

confidence' in a degree no less than, and in many instances far exceeding, that which exists between parties to a business or commercial relationship. The recognition of that fact—and of the necessary concomitant that such domestic relationships are essentially fiduciary in character—will bring rational unity to the various disparate mechanisms by which equity presently offers a measure of protection to the parties to such relationships. The acknowledgment of fiduciary obligations flowing from the parties' mutual trust and confidence will, at one and the same time, furnish the beneficial interest which permits equity to impose constructive trusts in respect of property which has been utilized in the course of the parties' relationship; give rise to the relationship of influence which enables equity to set aside transactions which result from that influence; and provide the circumstance of special disadvantage which enables equity to set aside transactions procured by the unfair or unconscientious exploitation of that disadvantage.

13

Taxing the Constructive Trustee: Should a Revenue Statute Address itself to Fictions?

JOHN GLOVER

In revenue, as in private law, there is a marked difference between common law jurisdictions concerning the constructive trust. The United States and Canada take a functional approach—which may be dictated by fiscal imperatives as well as by remedial theories of the device. Revenue law in the United Kingdom and Australia still acknowledges fictions of the equitable sort. Amenability of revenue systems to the constructive trust will be evaluated here, as well as the hold which the equitable property idea has in Anglo-Australian law. Our point of departure will be the position in Australia, described neatly by the decisions in *MacFarlane* v. *FCT*[1] and *Zobory* v. *FCT*.[2]

MacFarlane operated a petrol station with his wife. He and his wife agreed that the business would be owned by them in equal shares, although the station site was leased to a company which MacFarlane controlled. He was also a small-time tax evader. Profits were understated in the business tax returns over several years. 'Black petrol' was sold in undisclosed cash transactions. Deductions were claimed for fictitious employees. Eventually the Federal Commissioner of Taxation ('the Commissioner') caught up with MacFarlane and served on him amended tax assessments for several previous years. By way of defence, MacFarlane alleged that at all material times his wife had been beneficially entitled to one-half of the income. As equity would decree a resulting or constructive trust in her favour, he argued, the wife was the party liable for tax on a one half share. The claim was rejected by Enderby J at first instance.[3] The reason he gave was that the wife's constructive trust entitlement was fiscally inefficacious until relief was actually granted. MacFarlane appealed to the Federal Court. Beaumont J disagreed with Enderby J and said (for the Court):[4] 'since equity will

[1] (1986) 13 FCR 356 (Fed. Ct. FC).
[2] (1995) 129 ALR 484 (Fed. Ct. Burchett J).
[3] *Masterman* v. *FCT, MacFarlane* v. *FCT* (1985) 85 ATC 4015 (NSW SC).
[4] (1986) 13 FCR 356, 368 (Fisher and Burchett JJ agreeing).

regard as done that which ought to be done, the existence of equitable interests does not depend on the making of a curial order granting equitable relief, even in the case of a constructive trust: see *Muschinski* v. *Dodds* (1985) 60 ALJR 52, *per* Deane J at 65.' The Commissioner must 'pick up' and assess the parties according to their positions at general law, he said. The conclusion followed that the amended assessments were erroneous. Income of the business had been derived equally by MacFarlane and his wife.

Mr Zobory was a thief. He stole more than $1 million from his employer and invested it in interest-bearing accounts in his name or under his control. For two years Zobory filed tax returns which showed interest earned on the money taken from his employer as part of his own income. Then he was found out. Zobory was convicted of theft and consented to judgment in a civil suit brought by his employer to recover the $1 million. The sum and the interest it had earned whilst he possessed it was duly repaid. Zobory then objected to previously being assessed to tax on the interest earned—contending that the money taken from his employer was held by him on constructive trust. This was said to have the effect of diverting tax liability to the employer beneficially entitled when the income was derived. Section 96 of the Income Tax Assessment Act 1936 (Cth) ('the Act') was cited. It provides that: 'except as provided in this Act, a trustee shall not be liable as trustee to pay tax upon the income of a trust estate'. The Act makes no provision for taxing constructive trustees. Interest income derived in a trustee's name either forms part of a trust estate, or belongs to the trustee personally, Burchett J reasoned, before determining that the relevant assessments should be overturned.[5] Pursuant to the 'rule' that a constructive trust takes effect from the time at which the conduct which gives rise to its imposition occurs, the interest earned was a gain which belonged to the employer. For the purpose, 'a constructive trust, as well as an express trust or resulting trust, would be fully effective to divert the liability to income tax to the beneficiary'.[6] Zobory was accordingly held not liable to the tax on the income product of the stolen sum.

By contrast, courts in the United States ignore constructive trusts in determining whether income has been derived. Outstanding repayment obligations are disregarded and constructive trustees are taxed simply on what they receive. The leading case is *James* v. *United States*.[7] Like Zobory, James misappropriated money from his employer. After James was caught, the Internal Revenue prosecuted him for the federal crime of

[5] *Ibid.*, 487; see below.

[6] (1995) 129 ALR 484, at 486–7, Burchett J. The Commissioner has appealed to the Full Fed. C. against this decision.

[7] 366 US 213 (1961), reversing *CIR* v. *Wilcox*, 327 US 404 (1946).

failing to include the moneys misappropriated in his income tax returns for the relevant years. Warren CJ gave the majority judgment. James, he said, had such 'control' over the embezzled money and derived from it such 'readily realisable economic value' that it was the equivalent of income.[8] Federal tax liabilities could not be determined by such 'attenuated formalities' as whether the embezzler lacked title to what he appropriated. What if he did lack title to the gains he enjoyed? To free him from tax would involve the 'incongruity of having the gains of the honest labourer taxed and the gains of the dishonest labourer immune'.[9] Zobory contrasts with the earlier US case of *Kurrle* v. *Helvering*.[10] The eighth circuit Court of Appeals there said that 'income from any source' within the meaning of the Code includes profits from the investment of misappropriated funds.[11] Even if a defrauded bank had an action to make an embezzler a constructive trustee, the embezzler's profit from investing the misappropriated sum was still his income receipt.[11]

Canada follows the United States. It did so even in the years when courts used the more traditional constructive trust theory of the United Kingdom. In *R.* v. *Poynton*[12] the taxpayer was a director and the office manager of a company in the building trade. He obtained secret commissions (or 'kickbacks') from the company's suppliers, which he failed to declare in his income tax returns. He was later discovered and paid over to the company the commissions he received. The taxpayer was then prosecuted for tax evasion in the years that the commissions were not declared as income. The Ontario Court of Appeal found that the misappropriated money was of an income nature despite the taxpayer's obligation to repay. The fact that the money received was 'subject to trusts' was not critical beside 'the manner of receipt, the control over it, the liabilities and restrictions attaching to it, the use made of it by the holder [and] the person to whom the benefits accrue'.[13]

THE REVENUE STATUTE

Revenue statutes in Australia, Canada, and the United States have an important feature in common. Liability to income tax is based on a 'global' concept of income, though the statutes do not thoroughly define the 'income' word. Courts are left to elaborate the concept.[14] A 'global' concept of income was described by the United States Supreme Court in

[8] *Ibid.* 216, citing *CIR* v. *Glenshaw Glass Co.* 348 US 426, at 431 (1955).
[9] *Ibid.* 218. [10] 126 F 2d 723 (1942). [11] *Ibid.* 725, Reeves DJ.
[12] (1972) 72 DTC 6329 (Ont CA). [13] *Ibid.* 6335, Evans JA.
[14] See AUST Income Tax Assessment Act 1936 (Com), US Internal Revenue Code of 1986, CAN *Income* Tax Act 1970–71–72, c. 63 and R Parsons, *Income Taxation in Australia* (1985), 8–12.

CIR v. *Glenshaw Glass Co.*[15] as 'undeniable accessions to wealth, clearly realised, and over which the taxpayers have complete dominion'. The idea contrasts with the 'schedular' system of income tax liability in the United Kingdom. Income in the schedular system is taxable according to its source. Profits made and gains derived in the United Kingdom only become liable to tax when they come within the terms of enumerated 'schedules'.[16] The significance for constructive trustees is this. Under the schedular system, the constructive trustee is only assessable to the extent to which his or her gains in that capacity are seen to derive from a taxable source. Under the 'global' system, a constructive trustee's gains are prima facie assessable just as the gains of any other taxpayer.

None of the revenue statutes in Australia, Canada, and the United States makes any specific provision for constructive trusts. Only in Australia has there been an attempt to fit the liability of constructive trustees within that part of the revenue statute which deals with 'trusts'.[17] This will be examined under a later heading. Revenue authorities in the United States treat constructive trustees like any other taxpayer and reserve the trusts provisions in the Code for 'express trusts and genuine trust transactions'.[18] Revenue Canada acts similarly. It has published an interpretive bulletin which maintains that the wrongful gains of a person engaged in fraudulent activities are taxable in his or her hands.[19] Many constructive trustees make fraudulent gains. Is there any general aspect of the global 'income' concept which yet precludes the wrongful gains of constructive trustees from being assessable?

Illegality

Occasional illegality of constructive trustees' gains cannot prevent them from being assessable. Australia, Canada, the United States, and the United Kingdom all assesses illegal income gains.[20] It is not seen as degrading for the revenue 'to become a silent partner in an unlawful

[15] 348 US 426, at 413, Warren CJ (judgment of the court).

[16] See UK Income and Corporations Taxes Act 1988, ss. 18 and 19.

[17] e.g., *Zobory* v. *FCT* (1995) 129 ALR 484, at 486–7, Burchett J.

[18] See B.I. Bittker, *Federal Taxation of Income Estates and Gifts* (1981), iii, 82, quoting a passage from *Stoddart* v. *Eaton*, 22 F 2d 184, at 186–7, which continues 'A revenue statute does not address itself to fictions.'

[19] IT 256R (27 Aug. 1979): non-fraudulent constructive trustees will be considered below in connection with the 'claim of right' doctrine.

[20] US: *Commissioner of Inland Revenue* v. *Wilcox*, 327 US 404 (1946), at 408–9, Murphy J; M. Chirelstein, *Federal Income Taxation* (5th edn., (1988), 51. UK: *Minister of Finance* v. *Smith* [1927] AC 193; *IRC* v. *Aken* [1990] STC 197 (CA), at 505, Parker LJ; P. Whiteman *et al.* (eds.) *Whiteman on Income Tax* (3rd edn., 1988), 152–3; K. Day, 'The Tax Consequences of Illegal Trading' [1971] *BTR* 104, at 108–9. CAN: *R* v. *Poynton* (1972) 72 DTC 6329 (Ont. CA), Bulletin IT 256R. AUST: TR 93/25, also R. Parsons, *Income Taxation in Australia* (1985), 32. But cf EIRE: *Hayes* v. *Duggan* [1929] IR 406.

business' by taxing its profits.[21] Authorities on the United Kingdom's schedular system have come to the same conclusion, yet in a way which seems to deny the assessability of money misappropriated and liable to be repaid. Gains made by 'housebreaking' and 'burglary' are said not to be subject to tax in the United Kingdom. That much is clear.[22] There is no 'trade' of housebreaking or burglary which the law will acknowledge.[23] However, an activity which is incidentally illegal can still amount to a taxable 'trade' within the UK revenue statute.[24] The *Zobory* type of constructive trustee could scarcely be pursuing a taxable 'trade' by doing as he did and would therefore seem immune from UK income tax, whether or not the misappropriations were repaid. The conclusion may be dictated by the UK system of income taxation by source. It need not apply to Australia. Yet Australian Taxation Ruling 93/25 reached a similar conclusion after reasoning from the source of gains, rather than from their nature. The ruling concluded that only the proceeds of certain 'systematic' criminal activities were assessable. Several 'schedular' authorities from the United Kingdom were cited without qualification. Taxability of the proceeds was treated as though the matter depended on their having a source in criminal activities amounting to a 'trade'.

Beneficial Entitlement

One version of the law of constructive trusts provides that constructive trustees are deprived of title to the trust property as and from the time of their delinquency. Another maintains that entitlement is removed only upon the making of the decree. We will deal with this later. Tax relevance of beneficial entitlement at any stage is in question now. Burchett J in *Zobory*[25] cited the 'fundamental principle' that the *Income Tax Assessment Act* 1936 was 'directed to income to which a taxpayer is beneficially entitled'. Various other Australian taxes on land, succession, and gifts often expressly base liability on 'beneficial entitlement'. Law reports are replete with references to the idea.[26] Being for a long time a familiar term in revenue cases, it is not surprising that 'beneficial entitlement' was

[21] B. Bittker, n. 18 above, iii, 6–57.

[22] *Southern* v. *AB Ltd* (1933) 18 TC 43, Finlay J; *F. A. Lindsay, A. E. Woodward and W. Hiscox* v. *CIR* (1932) 18 TC 43, at 56, *ser* Lord Sands, 58, Lord Morison (Ct of Sess).

[23] *F. A. Lindsay, A. E. Woodward and W. Hiscox* v. *CIR, ser*, 56, *ser* Lord Sands, 58, *ser* Lord Morison.

[24] Now see Income and Corporation Taxes Act 1988 (UK), s. 18 (Sched. D Cases I and II): *Partridge* v. *Mallandaine* (1886) 2 TC 179; *Mann* v. *Nash* [1932] 1 KB 752; *F. A. Lindsay, A. E. Woodward and W. Hiscox* v. *CIR*, n. 22 above.

[25] (1995) 129 ALR 484, at 486.

[26] eg, *Commissioner of Stamp Duties* v. *Livingstone* (1964) 112 CLR 12 (PC)—succession and probate duty; *Hollingworth* v. *Commissioner of Land Tax* (1968) 118 CLR 45, at 51, *ser* Barwick, Kitto, and Menzies JJ—land tax.

used indifferently for income tax liability as well.[27] In *Income Taxation in Australia*[28] R. Parsons advances fifteen 'propositions' on the nature of income. One is to the effect that 'the character of income' must involve a gain by the taxpayer'. Another is that 'there is no gain unless an item is derived by the taxpayer beneficially'. Parsons cites surprisingly little authority for the latter proposition. He relies mainly on section 96 of the Act and the Federal Court decision in *FCT* v. *Everett*.[29] Section 96 provides that 'a trustee shall not be liable as trustee to pay income tax upon the income of a trust estate.' The provision has stood since the Act was introduced in 1936 and may be part of a functional conception for the taxation of 'trusts and estates', inspired by contemporary revenue provisions in the United States.[30] If the Parsons proposition were correct, it is hard to see whatever could have been its use. What need could there be for section 96 if a 'gain' of nature implied beneficial entitlement? *Everett's Case* concerned whether a taxpayer's equitable income assignment avoided his derivation of income assigned. Bowen CJ found for the taxpayer, in an analysis confined to the application of division 6, the 'trusts' part of the Act. It was never observed that the assignor's tax liability was deflected by the transfer of beneficial entitlement.[31] Deane J was explicit in dissent. Contrary to Parsons, he treated beneficial entitlement as bearing no necessary relation to the derivation of income. Taxpayers should rather be assessed on profits and gains they actually make.[32] The matter was not considered in judgments delivered in the High Court appeal.[33]

'Beneficial entitlement' to income evokes a relation between taxation and property rights. 'Taxes are public duties', said Learned Hand J, 'attached to the ownership of property'.[34] Such a view is questioned in this paper. Consider the Canadian decision in *Sura* v. *Minister of National Revenue*.[35] A husband and wife lived under a regime in Quebec which provided, as between themselves, for a 'community' of property acquired during the course of a marriage. The husband was legally entitled to administer the property and to dispose of it with unrestricted enjoyment during the marriage's continuance. Mr Sura argued that he should only be liable to tax on one half of his salary and rentals income during

[27] Defensive denial of tax liability by alleging a constructive trust entitlement is not uncommon in tax litigation: see *Case 36/93*, 93 ATC 402 and *Case 50/94*, 94 ATC 440.

[28] N.14 above, propositions 4 and 5, 36–8.

[29] (1978) 38 FLR 27 (FC).

[30] The odd and undefined expression 'trust *estate*' is used: see s. 219 of the US *Revenue Act of 1919*.

[31] N.29 above, at 34–5. Fisher J wrote a separate judgment agreeing with Bowen CJ.

[32] *Ibid.*, 54–5, being the view adopted in *Hadlee* v. *CIR* [1993] AC 524 (PC).

[33] (1980) 143 CLR 440.

[34] *National City Bank of New York* v. *Helvering*, 98 F 2d 93, 96 (1938).

[35] (1962) 62 DTC 1005 (SC of Can).

a particular tax year. The wife was said to be liable to tax on the other half. The Supreme Court denied the claim. Taschereau J said that 'the Income Tax' is imposed on 'the person and not the property':[36] 'the Act does not address itself to capital or ownership of property. It addresses itself to the person and the amount of tax is determined by the benefits the person receives'.[37]

The significance of title to assessable income was also discussed in two of the dissenting judgments in *James* v. *United States*.[38] Black J reasoned that an 'embezzlement' could not be a 'gain' or 'income' to the embezzler if the fund embezzled still belonged to the rightful owner. Embezzled funds, he thought, were no more taxable than borrowed funds. No gain is realized by borrowing 'because of the offsetting obligation'.[39] Whittaker J also dissented on the ground of entitlement. As he expressed the matter: 'an embezzler, like a common thief, acquires not a semblance of right, or interest in his plunder, and whether he spends it or not, he is indebted to his victim in the full amount as surely as if he had left a promissory note at the scene of the crime'.[40] This is interesting. Whittaker J distinguishes embezzlement from other illegal activities that produce assessable income because the law recognizes a debtor–creditor relationship in embezzlement, but not the other activities. Restitutionary rights do not arise in the other transactions because they are void *ab initio*. A void transaction's gain is wholly taxable in the wrongdoer's hands. By contrast, the embezzler's or extortionist's gain is legally recoverable by the victim. The transaction can be reversed by this party, whose right of recovery antedates the wrongdoer's obligation to pay tax.

In its own terms, the force in the *James* minority reasoning is undeniable. A plunderer, of course, is not beneficially entitled to his plunder. The difference with the majority view may be more in the revenue-raising conception. Title considerations are not employed in measuring the gains realized by taxpayers and the enjoyment over which they have control.[41] Realization of a gain and enjoyment of it are undiminished where the taxpayer has no right to do as he did. If railroad collects excessive fares, the excess is income, despite the passengers having theoretical rights to restitution.[42]

[36] *Ibid.*, 1006 (for the Court), quoting *McLeod* v. *Minister of Customs and Excise* (1926) 1 DTC 85 (SC of Can), Mignault J.

[37] *Ibid.*, 1009. [38] 366 US 213 (1961).

[39] *Ibid.*, 227, quoting Sibley J in *McKnight* v. *CIR*, 127 F 2d 572, at 573 (1942).

[40] *Ibid.*, 251.

[41] See *Eisner* v. *Morcomber*, 252 US 189 (1920), at 270 and *CIR* v. *Glenshaw Glass Co.* 348 US 426 (1955), at 431 (1946).

[42] *Chicago R I & P R Co.* v. *CIR*, 47 F 2d 990, quoted by Burton J (diss) in *CIR* v. *Wilcox*, n. 7 above, at 415.

The 'Claim of Right'

In the years before *James* was decided, courts in the United States insisted that taxpayers had a 'claim of right' to moneys they received as a pre-condition to tax liability.[43] Saying that a constructive trustee has a 'claim of right' is comparable to saying that he or she is 'beneficially entitled'. Embezzlers and many constructive trustees could claim no right to what they received and were held immune from tax thereon, though gains derived from an illicit trade in liquor were still taxable.[44] The majority in *James* suggested that if the taxpayer did make restitution, he or she would be entitled to a deduction in the year of repayment.[45] The harsh effect of taxing wrongdoers on gains they restore is reduced. Shortly before the *James* decision, section 1341 was inserted in the *Internal Revenue Code*. It also mitigates the effect of tax on sums refunded. The section is conditional on taxpayers having repaid a sum of money, having previously had a 'claim of right' to and being taxed on the amount. It provides that in addition to a deduction for the amount in the year of repayment, taxpayers are given the option of receiving a tax credit equal to the amount of the extra tax they paid in the year of receipt. Section 1341 avoids an unfairness in an annual accounting system. A subsequent deduction may not offset the effect of high marginal rates applicable to what may be an exceptional receipt.[46] Relief is given only to non-fraudulent constructive trustees.[47] Zobory would be ineligible. Section 1341 is probably inapplicable to MacFarlane, too. It assumes that he will have previously accounted to his wife for her income share.

Treating the Constructive Trust as a 'Trust' for Revenue Purposes

Most tax consequences under the US Internal Revenue Code follow transfers of value. The structure of the Code suggests that it is a category mistake to confuse the constructive trust remedy with provisions for

[43] See *Healy* v. *CIR*, 345 US 278 (1953); *CIR* v. *Wilcox*, n.7 above; *McKnight* v. *CIR*, 127 F 2d 572 (1942); *North American Oil Consolidated* v. *Burnet*, 286 US 417 (1932); Annot. 95 L Ed. 563.

[44] *United States* v. *Sullivan*, 274 US 259 (1927).

[45] N.38 above, at 220: see R. Manicke, 'A Tax Deduction for Restitutionary Payments? Solving the Dilemma of the Thwarted Embezler' [1992] *U Ill. L R* 593.

[46] Explained in *US* v. *Skelly Oil Company*, 394 US 678 (1969), at 681–2, *ser* Marshall J; see also *Zadoff* v. *US*, 638 F Supp. 1240, at 1243, *ser* Sprizzo J; and *Webb* v. *IRS* 15 F 3d 203 (1994).

[47] *Hankins* v. *US* 403 F Supp. 257 (1975); *McKinney* v. *US* 574 F 2d 1240 (1978)—embezzlers who repaid their victims ineligible; *Perez* v. *US*, 553 F Supp. 558 (1982); *Zadoff* v. *US* n. 26 above,—bribes not within s. 1341; *Van Cleave* v. *US*, 718 F 2d 193 (1983)—repayment cannot be voluntary.

'trusts' or 'trust estates'.[48] Income distributed by trusts is taxed to the beneficiaries. Accumulated income is taxed to the trust. Fiduciaries, agents, and 'grantor trusts'[49] are treated as transparent formalities, in effect, which do not affect persons' tax liabilities under the Code. There is no room for the taxation of constructive trustees as such.[50] In Canada, the *prima facie* position is much the same. The Canadian Income Tax Act provides that trusts are conduits to beneficiaries and are taxed only on retained income.[51] Ambiguity surrounding the income of a constructive trust would disturb this structure. However a discordant strain of authority has emerged. The Court in *Fletcher* v. *MNR*[52] found that a constructive trust was a 'trust' for the purpose of allocating capital losses under s.115(1)(b) of the Canadian Act. Commentators have been struck by the possibilities of this.[53] Revenue Canada seems, surprisingly, to have endorsed the decision.[54] Constructive trusts are sometimes used defensively, to deflect liabilities in tax litigation.[55] However the revenue position with regard to the *Zobory* type of constructive trust was made plain, as we saw, in Interpretive Bulletin IT–256 of 1979. Proceeds of criminal fraud are taxable in the hands of the recipient. Fraudulent embezzlers are required to report all money and the 'fair cash value' of any property misappropriated, or face penalties under section 163(2) of the Canadian Act.[56] No reported case records the attempt of the UK IRC to tax a constructive trustee on gains made in that capacity comparably to the proceeds of illegal activities. Schedular liability is problematic.[57]

[48] Internal Revenue Code of 1986, s. 1(e), imposing tax on 'every estate' and 'every trust'. Under s. 7701(a)(6), 'Fiduciary means a guardian, trustee . . . or any person acting in any fiduciary capacity for any person'; see B. I. Bittker, n. 18 above, iii, 2–25.

[49] Ch. 1 Subch. J, Subp. E of the Internal Revenue Code of 1986 'Grantors and other treated as substantial owners' (see § 677): persons will be taxed with the income of trusts which they can control or revoke.

[50] Confirmed by J. Moore and R. Sorlien in 'Homeless Income' (1953) 8 *Tax Law Review* 425, at 429.

[51] Sec. 104(2), (6); see V. Krishna, *Fundamentals of Canadian Income Tax* (4th edn., 1993), 215–221.

[52] (1987) 87 DTC 624, at 627–9, Sarchuk TCJ (Tax Ct of Can, 1st instance).

[53] See M. C. Cullity, 'General concepts and Types of Trusts for Tax Purposes' in *Report of Proceedings of the 40th Tax Conference* (Canadian Tax Foundation, 1988), 36.1, 36.3; S. Bowman, 'Constructive Trusts—Whether Recognised for Tax Purposes' (1987) 35 *Canadian Tax Journal* 1464, at 1466.

[54] 'Revenue Canada Round Table', n. 53 above, 53.1.

[55] See *Savoie* 93 DTC 50,607 and *Holizki*, 93 DTC 50,635.

[56] See n. 19, above.

[57] Such income may be liable to tax as the profits of a 'trade' under Case I or of a 'profession or vocation' under Case II of Sched D: see (17th edn., *Pinson on Revenue Law* B. Pinson and R. Thomas, (1986), 25; K. Day 'The Tax Consequences of Illegal Trading Operations' [1971] *BTR* 104, 108.

Constructive Trusts

The constructive trust which might apply in the *MacFarlane* and *Zobory* situations could take several forms. The phenomenon is an equitable device with a confusing name.[58] Claimants who assert the breach of legal or equitable obligations are enabled to obtain specific property as a remedy. A significant feature of constructive trusts is their retrospective effect. According to the current law of most common law countries, the defendant is obliged to 'hold' disputed property for the claimant together with any product of that property from the time that the claimant's entitlement to the remedy arose. Thus the effect of a constructive trust will often precede the time of the claimant's application to court—a phenomenon which engages the fiction of 'equitable property'.

The Commissioner was a third party to constructive trusts that MacFarlane and Zobory invoked. It was not alleged that this official had behaved unconscionably, or had been unjustly enriched. Indeed, in each case the Commissioner's intervention in the parties' affairs was an event which occurred after the conduct which occasioned the remedy. It would appear that none of the policies behind or 'aims' of the constructive trust isolated by Gbolahan Elias could apply.[59] 'Perfection' of some dispositive choice implicating the Commissioner was certainly not in question. There is no choice about paying the taxes. Nor could it be said that there was any unjust enrichment of the Commissioner to enliven the 'restitution' aim, or loss caused to attract the 'reparation' rationale. The Commissioner had no *inter partes* right to be heard on the decision to grant or withhold constructive trust relief, if ever that decision were taken. At the same time, displacing the effect of tax assessments years after they were made and satisfied is highly inconvenient to the Commissioner. It threatens the integrity of a system of taxation

[58] 'Constructive trust' is an oxymoron, of sorts. Courts may infer the existence of a constructive trust where the beneficiary actively distrusts the trustee, or is not aware of the trustee's existence. *Scott 's Law of Trusts* says that 'the word 'constructive' derives etymologically from the verb 'construe', not from the verb 'construct'' ' (4th edn.), v, 462.4. The *New Shorter Oxford English Dictionary* (1993) records (and Scott acknowledges) that the verbs 'construct' and 'construe' both derive from the word: *constuere,* as "CON + *struere* lay, pile, build'. 'Construct' is the 'pa. ppl stem of *construere* and 'construe' is built on the verb's infinitive form. Dictionary meanings of each word correspond. 'Construe' denotes the 'interpretation or understanding of (an action, thing or person)'. 'Construct' denotes 'fitting parts together; build, erect [a mental conception]'. It follows that the proper objects of the 'constructive' activity, implied by the term 'constructive trust', must be something which the court fashions. An object, on the other hand, that one 'construes' rather than 'constructs', is logically anterior. It is a pre-existing thing, or *state of title.*

[59] G. Elias, *Explaining Constructive Trusts* (1990), 9–33.

based on annual gains.[60] The positions of the Commissioner and trustees of a bankrupt estate are comparable. Both officials must take the estates of debtors[61] and taxpayers[62] as they find them. Neither is a *bona fide* purchaser for value without notice for the purposes of a title claim.[63]

Consider the Australian tax assessment of a rogue who is the trusted employee of a corporation which owns a small business. For several years, undetected, the rogue takes cash out of the till. Eventually the business fails and the rogue's dealings are exposed by the corporation's liquidator. The rogue is prosecuted criminally and also civilly, so as to be declared a constructive trustee of what has been taken. The Commissioner wishes to bring the misappropriated sum to tax. If the Commissioner were to proceed against the corporation, there is a four year period from the time of the misappropriation to amend the corporation's previous tax assessments.[64] This is the time when the corporation's right to the income arose. When the undisclosed amounts are reassessed in the relevant years, the corporation may claim a countervailing deduction in those years for 'loss incurred through embezzlement, larceny defalcation or misappropriation'.[65] The effect is to negate the assessments. If the Commissioner chooses instead to assess the rogue, then the sort of argument which availed Mr Zobory may be used. The rogue is under no tax liability if he or she has no beneficial right to the income at the relevant time.[66]

[60] See *Missouri Pacific Railroad Company* v. *US*, 423 F 2d 727 (1970), at 734, *per* Skelton J; and S. Bowman, 'Constructive Trusts-Whether Recognized for Tax Purposes' (1985) *Canadian Tax Journal* 1464, at 1466.

[61] *Daly* v. *Sydney Stock Exchange* (1986) 160 CLR 371, at 379, *ser* Brennan J; *Re Goode* (1974) 24 FLR 61, at 68, *ser* White J and J. Glover, 'Bankruptcy and Constructive Trusts' (1991) 19 *ABLR* 97, at 98. In the US, a similar distinction has been drawn to that between 'equities' and 'equitable interests' in *Latec Investments Ltd* v. *Hotel Terrigal Pty. Ltd* (1965) 113 CLR 265, at 286–91, *ser* Menzies J. *US* v. *Brimberry*, 779 F 2d 1339, at 1348 held that a charge of bankruptcy fraud adverse to property claimed under a constructive trust could not be sustained. Prior to the court order, the victim had no interest in specific property.

[62] Often stated, e.g. see *Zobory* v. *FCT*, n. 2 above, at 486–7.

[63] See discussion in the American Law Institute, *Restatement of Restitution* (1937), para. 173, comment j.

[64] N. 14 above, 170(2)(b) of the Act (after 17 Jan., 1990).

[65] *Ibid.*, s. 71.

[66] Consider also what would have been the revenue consequence if the orders of the NSW CA had stood in *United States Surgical Corporation* v. *Hospital Products International Pty. Ltd* [1983] 2 NSWLR 157: HPI may have been entitled to relief in respect of tax paid in the 1978 and 1979 years. However, assuming that USSC had made a 'full and true disclosure' in its tax returns for the relevant years, the time in which to amend assessments for this taxpayer would have lapsed.

'Title Analysis'

This looks at the analytical basis of the equitable property entitlement. All forms of the constructive trust employ comparable equitable property analysis, excepting the version preferred by the minority of the Canadian Supreme Court in *Rawluk* v. *Rawluk*.[67] We will look at a typical Australian formulation. Mason CJ, Wilson and Deane JJ in *Baumgartner* v. *Baumgartner*,[68] having discussed behaviour which is 'unconscionable' and 'contrary to justice and good conscience', said: 'the foundation for the imposition of a constructive trust in situations of the kind mentioned is that a refusal to recognise the existence of the equitable interest amounts to unconscionable conduct and that the trust is imposed as a remedy to circumvent that unconscionable conduct.' The reasoning amounts to this. Constructive trusts are imposed because of the refusal of the defendant to recognise an interest which *ex hypothesi* already exists.[69] The foundation of the pre-existing interest is the constructive trust itself. Circularity is evident. The distinction between grounds for the remedy and the equitable interest which justifies it is elided. At stake in the case was the question whether a woman in a *de facto* relationship had an interest in a domestic home purchased with the pooled resources of herself and her *de facto* partner. Surely an appeal to the justice of the claim should have supplied the reason why it was upheld.

Circular reasoning of the *Baumgartner* type might be defensible, were it only a judicial blind to conceal the exercise of discretions in areas fraught with pain and embarrassment. The difficulty is that most other forms of 'equitable property' are constructed similarly. '[P]roperty status' is linked 'incestuously with proprietary consequence', as Kevin Gray remarks, providing a 'conceptual mirage' for persons affected.[70]

The error in this mode of reasoning may run deeper. Equity is sometimes unkindly referred to as 'mediaeval jurisprudence'. A case has been made that errors of the mediaeval schoolmen stamp the ways in which the constructive trust and its incidents are applied.[71] Equity courts may be guilty of 'essentialism' when they 'discover' pre-existing property as one of the formal attributes of the constructive trust.[72] The process is

[67] (1990) 65 DLR (4th) 161: further discussed below.

[68] (1987) 164 CLR 137, at 147.

[69] I am indebted on this and related points to P. O'Connor, 'Unadjudicated Claims to Equitable Interests under constructive Trusts: Their Status as Property under the Pension Assets Test' unpublished LL M thesis (1995).

[70] K. Gray, 'Property in Thin Air' (1991) 50 *CLJ* 252, 301, 305, analysing, *inter alia, Lac Minerals Ltd* v. *International Corona Resources Ltd* (1989) 61 DLR (4th) 14 and *Hospital Products Ltd* v. *United States Surgical Corporation* (1984) 156 CLR 41.

[71] M. Stone, 'The Reification of Legal Concepts: *Mushinski* v. *Dodds*' (1986) 9 UNSWLJ 63, 68. We must exempt from this criticism the version of the remedy preferred by the *Rawluk* minority.

[72] *Ibid.*

contrary to the canons of modern thought, structuralist and post-structuralist alike, where the existence of every entity's attributes is subordinate to the analyst's purpose in hand.[73] Equity's reasoning also contrasts strongly with the instrumentalism of courts enforcing the US Internal *Revenue Code.*

It is hard to generalize about the constructive trust as it applies in revenue situations. Constructive trusts used to deflect taxation liabilities are remedial in varying degrees in different jurisdictions. The Australian constructive trust, for example, whilst oftentimes described as remedial, may be remedial only in a limited and quasi-institutional sense.[74] UK courts seem yet to properly recognize the remedial constructive trust. Attention will be directed to the North American jurisdictions. These have been influenced by a purely remedial conception in the American Law Institute's *Restatement of Restitution* (1937).

Could the Remedial Constructive Trust be Adjusted to the Needs of Revenue Statutes?

Remedial status for the constructive trust concerns us for the discretion it implies. That discretion might extend to such features of the constructive trust as the equitable property device. In this connection it has been said that the constructive trust has one 'universally accepted'[75] characteristic. The claimant's property interest under a constructive trust becomes effective at the time that the remedy is raised from an unjust enrichment, instance of unconscionability, or other generative circumstance. By fiction, as it were, the beneficial entitlement is conferred on the claimant retrospectively. The view of this promulgated in § 160 of the American Law Institute's 1937 *Restatement of Restitution* was that the constructive trust property interest arises at the same time as the right to obtain a remedy for unjust enrichment. The idea is also identified with *Scott on Trusts.*[76] George Bogert supplies another 'theory of creation',

[73] See C. S. Pierce, 'How to Make our Ideas Clear' (1878) inJ. Hoopes (ed.), *Pierce on Signs* (1991), 160, at 175 'we may define the real as that whose characters are independent of what anyone may think them to be'; F. de Saussure, *Course in General Linguistics* (trans. W. Baskin 1959, 109: 'entities are not abstract since we cannot conceive of a street or train outside its material realisation'; M. Foucault, *The Birth of the Clinic* trans. A. Smith 1975, 118–9, 'The clinical gaze effects a nominalist reduction on the essence of the disease . . . 'pleurisy' has no more being than the word itself.'

[74] See below and *Mushinski* v. *Dodds* (1985) 160 CLR 583, at 614–7, *ser* Deane J, affd. *Baumgartner* v. *Baumgartner* (1987) 162 CLR 33; *Arthurs* v. *Public Trustee* (1988) 90 FLR 203; *Kintominas* v. *Secretary DSS* (1991) 23 ALD 572.

[75] A.J. Oakley, 'The Precise Effect of the Imposition of a Constructive Trust' in *Equity and Contemporary Legal Developments* 427, at 433.

[76] See *The Law of Trusts* 4th edn. by A. W. Scott and W. F. Fratcher, 1989), v, §462.4.

which, whilst emphasising the remedial nature of the constructive trust more, is similar to the *Restatement* in effect.[77] Bogert says that the underlying facts of a case give the claimant an election to seek a constructive trust, or some other remedy in equity or at law. If the constructive trust is the remedy chosen, the court decreeing it will establish the defendant as constructive trustee 'as of the date of his wrongful acquisition'. No further remedial discretion is allowed.

In the United Kingdom, a 'traditional' orthodoxy may still obtain. The constructive trust on this view, though occasionally described as 'remedial', is really a type of institution and not a remedy at all.[78] It is an obligation requiring one to hold property for the benefit of another imposed in circumstances defined by law. Fiduciaries and unconscionable conduct are usually involved. In the 1994 Privy Council decision in *Re Goldcorp*,[79] Lord Musthill reserved his opinion about the 'remedial constructive trust'. He said that it involved a restitutionary proprietary interest which did not arise from the transaction between the parties—or, at least, not directly. Relief was described as something imposed as 'a measure of justice after the event'. As the relevant law was said to be 'in a state of development', it was not 'necessary or appropriate' to consider the new form of remedy in that case.[80] A more appropriate set of facts has not yet come before the House.

Characteristics of a roving remedy are also eschewed in Australia. As Deane J put the matter:[81]

> [A]s an equitable remedy, [the constructive trust] is available only when warranted by established principles or by the legitimate processes of legal reasoning, by analogy, induction and deduction, from the starting point of a proper understanding of the conceptual foundation of such principles. . . . Viewed as a remedy, the function of a constructive trust is not to render superfluous, but to reflect and enforce, the principles of the law of equity.

Deane J's judgment cites and follows *Scott* on the point concerning when the equitable property interest arises.[82] However he suggested that courts should have a discretion to move the operative date of a constructive trust to meet the circumstances of the case.[83] This implies the analysis of Bogert rather than *Scott*. A claimant's equitable proprietary right

[77] *The Law of Trusts and Trustees* (revised 2nd edn. by G. G. Begert and G. T. Bogerr, 1978), 472, at 30–1.

[78] D. Waters, 'The Constructive Trust in Evolution: Substantive *and* Remedial" (1991) 10 *Estates and Trusts LJ* 334, at 339–40.

[79] [1994] 2 All ER 806, 822, 832 (PC).

[80] *Ibid.*, 832.

[81] *Mushinski* v. *Dodds* (n. 74 above, at 615, affd. *Baumgartner* v. *Baumgartner* n. 74 above.

[82] N. 74 above, at 614, referring to *Scott on Trusts* (3rd edn., 1967), §462.4.

[83] *Mushinski* v. *Dodds* n. 74 above, 615, discussed in D. Waters, n.74 above, 341.

may not automatically arise at the time of the conduct which occasioned the remedy. Purely prospective operation for the remedy could be decreed if third party rights intrude between the time of trial and when the claimant's rights originated. The qualification is significant. It has potential to eliminate many constructive trust problems in revenue contexts. Constructive trusts could be moulded so as not to interfere with tax assessments which have issued before a trust-declaring decree. Purely prospective operation for constructive trusts would make them the equivalent of sales, in revenue terms. The Commissioner would have to take account of the disposition of beneficial interests as though the parties had made a consensual transfer. Deane J, to this degree, endorses an instrumental constructive trust. Its status as a remedy controlled by the courts is emphasized.[84] One commentator has noted that Deane J's notion of a movable commencement date is 'out of character' with an otherwise institutional view of the constructive trust.[85] If Deane believes that the constructive trust, like any other trust, confers substantive property rights in defined circumstances, it is difficult to see the basis of a discretion to alter the time at which those rights become effective. The author is not aware of an Australian authority on constructive trusts where the commencement date discretion was exercised.

Canadian developments are more promising. Since the 1973 dissenting judgement of Laskin J in *Murdock* v. *Murdock*,[86] Justices of the Canadian Supreme Court have described the constructive trust as a remedy for unjust enrichment. Remedial theory of the American *Restatement* has been followed. In *Pettkus* v. *Becker*,[87] a majority of the Canadian Supreme Court adopted the view that the principle of unjust enrichment 'lies at the heart of the constructive trust' and would be enlivened when there was an enrichment, a corresponding deprivation and an absence of any jurisdic reason for the enrichment.[88] Trust-like simulacra used to infer constructive trusts in the House of Lords decisions in Pettitt v *Pettitt*[89] and *Gissing* v. *Gissing*[90] were given their Canadian quietus. Each of these Canadian and UK cases was concerned with matrimonial facts. Equities to be balanced arose in two-party configurations. Then in 1989 the Canadian Supreme Court handed down its decision in *Hunter Engineering Co. Ltd* v. *Syncrude Canada Ltd*.[91] Amenability of the unjust enrichment formula to a three-party commercial dispute came into

84 See M. Stone, n. 71 above, 75.
85 D. Waters, n. 74 above, 41.
86 (1973) 41 DLR (3d) 507.
87 (1980) 117 DLR (3d) 257, at 273, *ser* Dickson J.
88 *Ibid.*, referring to the judgment of Dickson J in *Rathwell* v. *Rathwell* [1978] 2 SCR 436.
89 [1970] AC 777.
90 [1971] AC 886.
91 [1989] 1 SCR 426, noted J. Glover (1990) 64 *ALJ* 297.

question. In the majority judgment, constructive trust relief was denied for the reason that there was a prior contractual entitlement to the fund in dispute.[92] The British Columbia Court of Appeal below had applied the *Pettkus* formula and discovered an enrichment of Syncrude at the expense of Hunter Engineering.[93] Dickson CJC for the Supreme Court majority turned this reasoning on its head. Whilst denying constructive trust relief in the presence of a contractual entitlement, he said that insistence by Hunter Engineering that Syncrude was unjustly enriched entailed Hunter Engineering itself being unjustly enriched. To impose a constructive trust in this case, 'carried the decision in the *Pettkus* case beyond the breaking point'.[94] Perhaps one can conclude from this that rights of third parties (like the Commissioner) are difficult to accommodate within the terms of the unjust enrichment formula.

The minority opinion in the Canadian Supreme Court case of *Rawluk* v. *Rawluk*[95] is more promising. Rawluk involved an unjust enrichment argued to have occurred in circumstances comparable to the intervention of a third party.[96] A marriage was dissolved and property had to be divided. The statutory 'valuation date' for the division was a time two years prior to trial. From that date the wife sought a constructive trust over her share in the property. This was so that she would become entitled to an accretion in the property's value which had occurred between the valuation date and trial. Like the rights of a third party, it was something which came into existence between the dates of the trial and the claim arising. The majority held that the wife was entitled to her order. Retrospective entitlement was held to be dictated by the nature of the device. Property interests under constructive trusts were seen to come into existence when the unjust enrichment occurs, in conformity with Scott and the *Restatement*.[97] Rights to any interim profit or accretion follow automatically. McLaughlin J, however, entered a strong minority judgment, supported by three out of seven justices.[98] In her opinion, the constructive trust was displaced by the Province's matrimonial laws. In the event, though, that the constructive trust had been applicable, she maintained that the fiction of 'equitable property' should not be allowed to dictate the case's result. Property interests which 'automatically' arise are alien to the nature of a discretionary remedy. Their imposition 'may interfere with the operation of other doctrines and the exercise by

[92] N. 91 above, 474, Dickson CJC.

[93] (1985) 68 BCLR 367, at 382, *see* Anderson JA, judgment for the Court.

[94] N. 91 above, 477.

[95] N. 67 above.

[96] Suggested in D. Waters, n. 78 above, 361.

[97] N. 67 above, 176–7, *ser* Cory J, quoting *Scott's Law of Trusts* (4th edn.) v. at 323–4.

[98] N. 67 above, 183–5.

others, including third parties, of the rights attendant on their interest in the property made subject to the trust.'[99] The minority view in *Rawluk*, if sensitively applied, has potential to reconcile the law of income tax with constructive trust entitlements. It is a more principled statement of Deane J's 'movable commencement date' in *Mushinski* v. *Dodds*[100] and, for that reason, likelier to become an enduring attribute of the remedy.

However, as the discussion in the first part of this paper may indicate, constructive trusts and the fiction of 'equitable property' are only superficially inconsistent with revenue statutes. Taxing authorities need not await equity's reformation. The better view may be that the constructive trust, however reformed, is *irrelevant* to revenue gathering.

[99] *Ibid.* 188. [100] *Ibid.*

[100] N. 74 above, at 615.

Selected Bibliography

Aitken, L. 'Developments in Equitable Compensation: Opportunity or Danger?' (1993) 76 *Aust. L.J.* 596

American Law Institute. *Restatement of Restitution: Quasi Contracts and Constructive Trusts.* St Paul, M.N.: American Law Institute Publishers, 1937.

Ames, J.B. 'The Failure of the Tilden Trust', (1892) 5 *Harv. L.R.* 389.

Baker, J.H. *An Introduction to English Legal History.* 3d ed. London: Butterworth & Co. (Publishers) Ltd., 1990.

Beatson, J. and Friedman, Daniel. *Good Faith and Fault in Contract Law.* Oxford: Clarendon Press, 1995.

Bell, George Joseph. *Commentaries on the Law of Scotland and on the Principles of Mercantile Jurisprudence.* 7th ed., [by John McLaren]. Edinburgh: Law Society of Scotland, Butterworth's, 1990.

Berryman, J., ed. *Remedies—Issues and Perspectives.* 1991.

Biedermann, K. *The Trust in Liechtenstein Law.* 2d ed. Bern: Stämpfli, 1984.

Birks, P.B.H. *An Introduction to the Law of Restitution.* Oxford: Clarendon Press, 1985.

——. *Civil Wrongs: A New World*; the *Butterworth Lectures*, 1990–1991 London: Butterworth & Co. (Publishers) Ltd., 1991.

——. *The Frontiers of Liability.* Oxford: Oxford University Press, 1994.

——. 'Persistent Problems in Misdirected Money: A Quintet', [1993] *L.M.C.L.Q.* 218.

Bittker, B.I. *Federal Taxation of Income Estates and Gifts.* Little, Brown U.K. Ltd., 1981.

Blackstone, Sir William. *Commentaries on the Laws of England.* 4 vols. Oxford: Clarendon Press, 1765–69.

Bogert, G.G. and Bogert, G.T., eds. *The Law of Trusts and Trustees.* Rev. 2d ed. St. Paul, M.N., 1978.

Bowman, S. 'Constructive Trusts: Whether Recognised for Tax Purposes', (1987) 35 *Canadian Tax Journal* 1464.

Bryant, M.J. 'Crown-Aboriginal Relationships in Canada: The Phantom of Fiduciary Law', (1993) 27 *U.B.C.L.R.* 19.

Buckland, W.W *A Textbook of Roman Law.* 3d ed., [revised by Peter Stein]. Cambridge: Cambridge University Press, 1963.

Burns, Fiona. 'The "Fusion Fallacy" Revisited', (1993) 5 *Bond L.R.* 152.

Campbell, D.L. 'Record-Keepers or Whistle-Blowers? A Look at the Role of Pension Fund Custodians', (1995) *Estates & Trusts J.* 26.

Canadian Tax Foundation. *Report of the Proceedings of the 40th Tax Conference.* Toronto: 1988.

Chirelstein, M. *Federal Income Taxation.* 5th ed.: Foundation Press, 1988.

Conder, A.J. 'The Office of the Protector', (1995) 4 *Trusts & Trustees* 12.

Cope, Malcolm. *Equity: Issues and Trends.* Sydney: The Federation Press Pty., 1995.

Corbin, Arthur Linton. *Corbin on Contracts: A Comprehensive Treatise on the Working Rules of Contract Law.* St Paul, MN.: West Publishing, 1963.

Crampin and Thomas. *Interntional Trust Laws.* Edited by John Glasson. London: Chancery Law Publishings, 1992.

Cullity, Maurice C., Q.C. 'The Role and Control of Protectors'. Paper delivered to a Law Society of Upper Canada seminar, Effective Estate Planning. Toronto, Ont., 7th July 1995. Forthcoming.

Davidson, O.E. 'The Equitable Remedy of Compensation', (1982) 13 *M.U.L.R.* 349.

Davies, J.D. 'Trusts', [1968] *A.S.C.L.* 437.

Day, I.C. 'The Consequences of Illegal Trading', [1971] *B.T.R.* 104.

DeMott, D.A. 'Fiduciary Obligations under Intellectual Siege: Contemporary Challenges to the Duty to be Loyal', (1992) *Osgoode Hall L.J.* 472.

Dewar, John with Stephen Parker. *Law and the Family.* 2d ed. London: Butterworth & Co. (Publishers) Ltd., 1992.

Duckworth, Antony. 'Protectors—Fish or Fowl?' Paper delivered to the 9th I.B.C. Annual Transcontinental Trusts Conference, The World in Perilous Transition. Geneva, 29th-30th June 1995. Unpublished.

Dyson, H. 'The Proposed New Law of Trusts in France', (1992) *Conv.* 407.

Elias, Gbolahan. *Explaining Constructive Trusts.* Oxford: Clarendon Press, 1990.

Evans, J.M. 'Purpose Trusts—Further Refinements', (1969) 32 *M.L.R.* 96.

Field, F. and Owen, M. *Private Pensions for All: Squaring the Circle.* London: The Fabian Society, 1993.

Finn, P.D. *Essays in Damages.* Sydney: The Law Book Co. Ltd., 1992.

——. 'Unconsionable Contract' (1994) 8 *J. Contract L.* 37.

——., ed. *Equity and Commercial Relationships.* Sydney: The Law Book Co. Ltd., 1987.

——., ed. *Essays in Equity.* Sydney: The Law Book Co. Ltd., 1985.

——., ed. *Essays on Law and Government.* Sydney: The Law Book Co. Ltd., 1995.

——., ed. *Fiduciary Obligations.* Sydney: The Law Book Co. Ltd., 1977.

Flannigan, R. 'Fiduciary Obligation in the Supreme Court', (1990) 54 *Sask. L.R.* 45.

——. 'The Fiduciary Obligation', (1989) 9 *O.J.L.S.* 285.

Ford, H.A.J. and Austin, R.P. *Ford and Austin's Principles of Corporations Law.* 7th ed. Sydney: Butterworth's, 1995.

——. and Lee, W.A. *Principles of the Law of Trusts.* 2d ed. Sydney: The Law Book Co. Ltd., 1990.

Gardner, S. *An Introduction to the Law of Trusts.* Oxford: Clarendon Press, 1990.

——. 'New Angles on Unincorporated Associations', (1992) *Conv.* 41.

Gillese, Eileen E. 'Contribution Holidays', (1995) *Estates & Trusts J.* 136.

Glover, J. 'Bankruptcy and Constructive Trusts', (1991) 19 *A.B.L.R.* 97.

——. 'Trusts and Trustees—Whether in a commercial case the circumstances give use to a constructive trust. Applicability of doctrine of unjust enrichment', (1990) 64 *A.L.J.* 297.

Goff, R.L.A., Lord and Jones, G.H. *The Law of Restitution.* 4th ed., [edited by G.H.

Jones]. London: Sweet & Maxwell Ltd., 1993.
Goldstein, Stephen, ed. *Equity and Contemporary Legal Developments.* Jerusalem: The Hebrew University of Jerusalem, 1992.
Goodhart, W. 'Trustee Exemption Clauses and the Unfair Contract Terms Act 1977', (1980) 44 *Conv.* 333.
Gower, L.C.B. *Gower's Principles of Modern Company Law.* 5th ed. London: Sweet & Maxwell Ltd., 1992.
Gravells, Nigel P. 'Public Purpose Trusts', (1977) *M.L.R.* 397.
Gray, John Chapman. 'Gifts for a Non-Charitable Purpose', 15 *Harv. L.R.* 509.
Gray, Kevin. 'Property in Thin Air', (1991) 50 *C.L.J.* 252.
Green, 'Universal Tankships— "The Trust Point" ', (1982) 45 *M.L.R.* 564.
Green, B. ' "Love's Labours Lost:" A Note on *Re* Grant's Will Trusts', (1980) 43 *M.L.R.* 459.
Grundy, M. *Grundy's Tax Havens; Offshore Business Centres: A World Survey.* 6th ed. London: Sweet & Maxwell Ltd., 1993.
Hackney, J. *Understanding Equity and Trusts.* London: Fontana Press, 1987.
Hanbury, H.G. and Maudsley, R.H. *Hanbury and Martin Modern Equity.* 14th ed., [by Jill E. Martin]. London: Sweet & Maxwell Ltd., 1993.
Harris, Nigel & Partners. *The Use of Offshore Jurisdictions.* Edited by St J. A Robillard. London: Longman Law, Tax and Finance, 1991.
Hart, William O. 'Some Reflections on the Case of *Re* Chardon', (1937) *L.Q.R.* 24.
Hayton, D.J. 'The Hague Convention on the Law Applicable to Trusts and their Recognition', (1987) 36 *I.C.L.Q.* 260.
—— and Marshall, O.R. *Cases and Commentary on the Law of Trusts.* 9th ed., [by D.J. Hayton]. London: Sweet & Maxwell Ltd./Stevens & Sons Ltd., 1991.
Heydon, J.D. 'The Negligant Fiduciary', (1995) 111 *L.Q.R.* 1.
Hindle, G.W. 'Purchase of Trust Property by a Trustee with the Approval of the Court', (1961) 3 *M.U.L.R.* 15.
Holdsworth, Sir William. *A History of English Law.* 16 vols. London: Methuen & Co. and Sweet & Maxwell, 1969.
Honoré, T. and Cameron, E. *Honoré's South African Law of Trusts.* 4th ed. Capetown, S.A.: Juta & Co. Ltd., 1992.
Huband, J.A. 'Remedies and Resolution for Breach of Fiduciary Duties'. Paper delivered at the Isaac Pitblade Lectures, 1993. Unpublished.
Hughes, C. 'The Fiduciary Obligations of the Crown to Aborigines', (1993) 16 *U.N.S.W.L.J.* 70.
Ingram, M. and Maxton, J.K. 'Equitable Remedies'. Paper delivered to a New Zealand Law Society seminar, 1994. Unpublished.
International Trident Trust Group. *The Trident Practical Guide to Offshore Trusts.* 2d ed. London: Eurostudy, 1991.
Jacobs, K.S. *Jacobs' Law of Trusts in Australia.* 5th ed., [by W.P. Meagher and W.M.C. Gummow]. Sydney: Butterworth's, 1986.
Jones, G.H. 'Unjust Enrichment and the Fiduciary's Duty of Loyalty', (1968) 84 *L.Q.R.* 472.
——. *History of the Law of Charity 1532–1837.* Cambridge: Cambridge University Press, 1969.
Keane, Ronan. *Equity and the Law of Trusts in the Republic of Ireland.* London:

Butterworth & Co. (Publishers) Ltd., 1988.

Keeton, G.W. and Sheridan, L.A. *The Law of Trusts.* 12th ed., [by Lionel Astor Sheridan]. Chichester: Barry Rose, 1993.

Kessler, J. *Drafting Trusts and Will Trusts.* 2d ed. London: Sweet & Maxwell Ltd., 1992.

Kiralfy, A.K.R. 'Purpose Trusts: Powers and Conditions', (1950) 14 *Conv.* 374.

Krishna, V. *Fundamentals of Canadian Income Tax.* 4th ed. 1993.

Langbein, J. 'The Contractual Basis of the Law of Trusts', (1995) 109 *Yale L.J.* 625.

Lawrence, R.C. 'The Role of the Protector—An Insulator for Corporate Beneficiaries?' [1993] *J. Int. P.* 88.

Lewin, Thomas. *Lewin on Trusts.* 16th ed., [by W.J. Mowbray]. London: Sweet & Maxwell Ltd., 1964.

Lovell, P.A. 'Non-charitable Purpose Trusts—Further Reflections', (1970) 34 *Conv.* 77.

Maitland, F.W. *Equity, Selected Essays.* 2d ed., [edited by H.D. Hazeltine, G. Lapsley, P.H. Winfield]. Cambridge: Cambridge University Press, 1936.

Manicke, R. 'A Tax Deduction for Restitutionary Payments? Solving the Dilemma of the Thwarted Embezzler', [1992] *U. Ill. L.R.* 593.

Martin, J. 'Fusion, Fallacy and Confusion; a Comparative Study', (1994) 47 *Conv.* 13

Mason, Keith and Carter, J.W. *Restitution Law in Australia.* 1995.

Mason, The Hon. Sir Anthony. 'The Place of Equity and Equitable Remedies in the Contemporary Common Law World', (1994) 110 *L.Q.R.* 238.

Matthews, Paul. 'Trusts to Maintain Animals', [1983] *L.S. Gaz.* 2451.

——. 'Gifts to Unincorporated Associations', (1995) *Conv.* 302.

——. 'A Heresy and a Half in a Certainty of Objects', [1984] *Conv.* 22.

——. 'Protectors: Two Cases, Twenty Questions' (1995) 9 *T.L.I.* 108.

——. 'The Asset Protection Trust: Holy Grail or Wholly Useless?' (1995) *The King's College L.R.* 62.

—— and Lunney, Mark. 'A Tortfeasor's Lot is Not a Happy One?' (1995) 58 *M.L.R.* 395.

—— and Malik, Hodge M. *Discovery.* London: Sweet & Maxwell Ltd., 1992.

Maudsley, R.H. *The Modern Law of Perpetuities.* London: Butterworth & Co. (Publishers) Ltd., 1979.

McCamus, J.D. 'Equitable Compensation and Restitutionary Remedies: Recent Developments'. Paper delivered at Special Lectures of the Law Society of Upper Canada, 1995. Forthcoming.

McKay, L. 'Trusts for Purposes—Another View', (1973) 37 *Conv.* 420.

McKendrick, E., ed. *Commercial Aspects of Trusts and Fiduciary Obligations.* Oxford: Clarendon Press, 1992.

McNair, David R. 'Cook Islands International Trusts Act, 1995–Amendments'. Paper delivered to a Canadian Institute conference, International Estate Planning. Toronto, Ont. 4th-5th December 1995. Unpublished.

Meagher, R.P., Gummow, W.M.C., and Lehane, J.R.F. *Equity, Doctrine and Remedies.* 3d ed. Sydney: Butterworth's, 1992.

Megarry, The Rt. Hon. R.E., Q.C. and Wade, H.W.R. *Megarry's Manual of the Law of Real Property.* 7th ed. London: Sweet & Maxwell Ltd./Stevens & Sons Ltd.,

1993.
Millett, P.J., Q.C. 'Equity—The Road Ahead', [1995] *The King's College L.J.* 1.
——. 'The Quistclose Trust: Who can enforce it?' (1985) 101 *L.Q.R.* 269.
Moffat, G. *Trusts Law: Text and Materials.* 2d ed. London: Butterworth & Co. (Publishers) Ltd., 1994.
Moore, J. and Sorlien, R. 'Homeless Income', (1953) 8 *Tax Law Review* 425.
Morris, J.H.C. and Leach, W. Barton. *The Rule Against Perpetuities.* 2d ed. London: Stevens & Sons, 1964.
Nathan, Joseph Arnold. *Equity through the Cases and Judicial Exposition.* London: Stevens & Sons Ltd., 1939.
Neuhoff and Pavel. *Trust and Foundations in Europe.* 1991.
Nicholas, Barry. *The French Law of Contract.* 2d ed. Oxford: Clarendon Press, 1992.
Nolan, R. 'Conflicts of Duty and the Morals of the Market Place', [1994] *C.L.J.* 34.
——. 'From Knowing Assistance to Dishonest Facilitation', [1995] *C.L.J.* 505.
O'Connor, P. 'Unadjudicated Claims to Equitable Interests under Constructive Trusts: Their Status as Property under the Pension-Assets Tests'. Unpublished LL.M. thesis, 1995.
Oakley, A.J. 'Has the Constructive Trust Become a General Equitable Remedy?' in *Current Legal Problems 1973.* Vol. 26, [edited by Lord Lloyd of Hampstead and Ernest H. Scamell]. London: Stevens & Sons Ltd., 1973.
Parker, D.B. and Mellows, A.R. *The Modern Law of Trusts.* 6th ed., [edited by A.J. Oakley]. London: Sweet & Maxwell Ltd., 1994.
Peart, N.S. 'A Comparative View of Property Rights in *de facto* Relationships: Are We All Driving in the Same Direction?' (1989) *Otago L.R.* 100.
Penney, Andrew. 'Rights and Powers of Trust Protectors: Rahman Revisited', [1995] *J. Int. P.* 31.
Pennington, R.R. *Pennington's Company Law.* 6th ed. London: Stevens & Sons Ltd., 1990.
Pettit, P.H. *Equity and the Law of Trusts.* 7th ed. London: Butterworth & Co. (Publishers) Ltd., 1993.
Pinson, B. and Thomas, R., eds. *Pinson on Revenue Law.* 17th ed. London: Sweet & Maxwell Ltd., 1986.
Pollock, J. and Maitland, F.W. *The History of English Law.* 2 vols. 2d ed. Cambridge: Cambridge University Press, 1968.
Potter, D.C. 'Trusts for Non-Charitable Purposes', (1949) 13 *Conv.* 418.
Rickett, C.E.F. 'Different Views on the Scope of the *Quistclose* Analysis: English and Antipodean Insights', (1991) 107 *L.Q.R.* 608.
——. 'Unincorporated Associations and their Dissolution', (1980) 39 *C.L.J.* 88.
——. and Gardner, T. 'Compensating for Loss in Equity: The Evolution of a Remedy', (1994) 24 *Vict. U. Well. L.R.* 19.
Saunders on Uses and Trusts. 4th ed. 1841.
Scott, A.W. *Scott on Trusts.* 4th ed., [by W.F. Fratcher]. Boston: Little, Brown & Co., 1990.
Sealy, L.S. 'The Director as Trustee', [1967] *C.L.J.* 83.
——. 'Fiduciary Obligations—Forty Years On', (1995) 9 *J.C.L.* 37.
——. 'Fiduciary Relationships', [1962] *C.L.J.* 69.

——. 'Some Principles of Fiduciary Obligation', [1963] *C.L.J.* 119.
Shepherd, J.C. *The Law of Fiduciaries.* Toronto: The Carswell Co. Ltd., 1981.
——. 'Towards a Unified Concept of Fiduciary Relations', (1981) 97 *L.Q.R.* 51.
Sheridan, Lionel Astor. 'Trusts for Non-Charitable Purposes', (1953) 17 *Conv.* 46.
Smart, P. St J. 'Holding Property for Non-Charitable Purposes: Mandates, Conditions and Estoppels', (1987) *Conv.* 415.
Snell, E.H.T. *Snell's Principles of Equity.* 29th ed., [edited by P.V. Baker and P.St J. Langen]. London: Sweet & Maxwell Ltd., 1990.
Spearing, Fiona. 'Discretionary Trust and Power: Distinction Without a Difference?' (1990) 4 *Trust Law & Practice* 117.
Stone, M. 'The Reification of Legal Concepts: Muschinski *v.* Dodds', (1986) 9 *U.N.S.W.L.J.* 63.
Story, J. *Commentaries on Equity Jurisprudence.* 2d ed. Boston: Little, Brown & Co., 1839.
Sweet, Charles. 'Restraints on Alienation', (1917) 33 *L.Q.R.* 342.
Thayer, James Bradley. *A Preliminary Treatise on Evidence at the Common Law.* S. Hackensack, N.J.: Rothman Reprints, 1969.
Thomas, J.A.C. *Textbook of Roman Law.* Amsterdam: Northern-Holland Publishing Co., 1976.
Trebilcock, M.J. 'The Liability of Company Directors for Negligence', (1969) 32 *M.L.R.* 499.
Underhill, A. and Hayton, D.J. *Law Relating to Trusts and Trustees.* 15th ed., [by D.J. Hayton]. London: Butterworth & Co. (Publishers) Ltd., 1995.
Underwood, Richard *et al. Practical Trust Precedents.* London: Longman Law, Tax and Finance, 1986.
Warburton, Jean. 'The Holding of Property by Unincorporated Associations', (1985) *Conv.* 318.
——. *Unincorporated Associations: Law and Practice.* London: Sweet & Maxwell Ltd., 1986.
Waters, D.W.M. 'The Constructive Trust in Evolution: Substantive and Remedial', (1991) 10 *Estates & Trust L.J.* 334.
——. *Law of Trusts in Canada.* 2d ed. Toronto: The Carswell Co. Ltd., 1984.
——., ed. *Equity, Fiducuaries and Trustees.* Toronto: The Carswell Co. Ltd., 1993.
White & Tudor's Leading Cases in Equity. 2 vols. 7th ed., [by Thomas Snow]. London: Sweet & Maxwell Ltd., 1897.
Whiteman, Peter G., ed. *Whiteman and Wheatcroft on Income Tax.* 3d ed. London: Sweet & Maxwell Ltd., 1988.
Williams, Glanville L. *Joint Obligations.* London: Butterworth & Co. (Publishers) Ltd., 1949.
Wilson and Duncan. *Trusts, Trustees and Executors.* 3d ed. 1995.
Youdan, T.G., ed. *Equity, Fiduciaries and Trusts.* Toronto: The Carswell Co. Ltd., 1989.

Index